Nixon's Comrades

Nixon's Comrades

A KREMLIN NOTE TAKER REMEMBERS

Andrey Vavilov

To my parents for the love that helped me stay the course.

Table of Contents

Preface

ON A MAY MORNING IN 1972, I sat across the table from President Richard Nixon who was speaking to General Secretary Leonid Brezhnev. I was taking notes at the first ever US-Soviet summit conference in the Kremlin.

Interpreting and writing up confidential memoranda of conversations - "memcons" - was my special assignment at high-level encounters. It started by chance with Leonid Brezhnev in 1960 in India. It concluded at his end game meeting with Jimmy Carter in 1979 in Vienna.

Some time ago, a friend asked me to speak to her Manhattan College students in New York. "US-Soviet summitry of the 1970s," she said. "Tell them about Brezhnev, Nixon and Kissinger - you knew them." I agreed, expecting a dozen bored youngsters corralled to listen to old history that might have happened on a distant planet.

The room was packed.

I said I will discuss Richard Nixon as a Human Being, Leonid Brezhnev as a Benevolent Leader, and Henry Kissinger as the Terminator (there were smiles), but the audience should expect a more complex picture.

The students were keen listeners, although my story did not fit their history books. Their image of the era was a mosaic with pieces missing. For them, Nixon meant Watergate, and Brezhnev – Communist totalitarianism. The questions started with "What sort of a man was he?"

After drinks, I walked in the dusk along the tree-lined streets of Riverdale. The talk triggered memories of a period in world history defined by some extraordinary - and baffling - individuals.

Soon after, Pam sent me a batch of reviews by her students - they were unexpectedly kind to the characters I portrayed. One wrote, "In a sense, they saved a generation from total war and served as a model for others." Another suggested "the world was a safer place during the Nixon era," and yet another student referred to "dangers confronting a lone super power." The poignant observations of young Americans born after the two leaders passed away and who only heard of a Russia governed by Gorbachev, Yeltsin and Putin, were a signal: interest in Richard Nixon's Soviet summits had not abated.

The story of the two men continues to fascinate. Neither survived the rigors of high office; public scorn and obscurity were the prediction. Both made a surprising comeback: Nixon in his late years as elder statesman, and Brezhnev posthumously in Russian opinion polls.

I decided to revisit the tidal point of the so-called "Soviet-American détente," when my career in the Russian diplomatic service crossed with Leonid Brezhnev. Rather than attempting another dissection of tortuous negotiations, I offer a basic picture of salient points. Researchers, chiefly in the US, have been skillfully processing the massive body of declassified material of the détente years. However, they are at a disadvantage: they were not physically present. No memcon, no document could do full justice to conference ambiance. My purpose was to bring into relief the times and the personalities of the main actors, including "Nixon's comrades," the men the US President faced.

A small group was involved in private talks with Richard Nixon and Henry Kissinger: Brezhnev, Foreign Minister Gromyko and three or four aides. After Nixon's resignation, they stayed on to negotiate with Gerald Ford and Jimmy Carter. We accompanied them - two principal Russian interpreters/note takers. Our mandate was to translate confidential conversations and provide a written record. There was a twist to our job: for reasons of their own Nixon and Kissinger placed trust in Soviet interpreters rather than in American ones, whom they barred from sensitive discussions. A closer look at the role of a top interpreter and note taker will shed light on some memorable episodes witnessed in my diplomatic life.

My vantage point was unique. It was not unlike passing through a looking glass into a privileged circle where one saw political leaders closer than most diplomats could in a lifetime. After several years and some two hundred hours in Nixon's and Kissinger's company, many more with Brezhnev and Gromyko, observing them across the green baize table in the Kremlin or in Nixon's cozy den in San Clemente - one formed riveting impressions.

Nixon and Brezhnev were intrigued by each other and attracted like opposite poles of a magnet: the ultimate Capitalist and the definitive Communist, commanding mammoth military machines poised to obliterate each other's homelands in hours. They met at annual summit meetings. They engaged through their aides, National Security Adviser (later Secretary of State) Henry Kissinger and Foreign Minister Andrei Gromyko. Never did a Soviet leader spend so much time negotiating with an American emissary. Never did a US President confer with a Russian Minister so often. They were the *alter egos* of the leaders, negotiating the fine details of all agreements. They were vital for maintaining the super power relationship during the Nixon Presidency and beyond. They enjoyed the support of the best teams of diplomatic experts I ever saw.

The two leaders were pursued by serious troubles - of politics and health. Brezhnev was aware of Watergate. Nixon saw he negotiated with a person whose physical capacity was impaired. Yet, neither took advantage of the other's weakness. So dissimilar in personality and manner, in the end, like two battle-scarred comrades, they clung in a strange embrace from which they drew strength and rationale for continuing in office. Both were on the path to self-destruction - in different ways. While Nixon fought, Brezhnev drifted. It did not work out for Nixon: cornered, he resigned. Almost simultaneously, Brezhnev's grasp on affairs of State slumped. He plodded on, precariously. Against hope, he longed to see in Gerald Ford and Jimmy Carter a revivification of his détente comrade. The brief post-Nixon summits were a downturn paralleled by Brezhnev's helpless slide into finality.

In the turbulent years that followed, the ship of the Soviet State listed. A bystander now, Nixon watched his comrade's spasmodic attempts to save détente - it was in tatters. In less than a decade after Brezhnev's death in 1982, the USSR disappeared in a traumatic collapse. The old balance of power unraveled. The political commitments negotiated by Nixon and Brezhnev became largely inoperative. Many of the closely guarded secrets were no longer important.

Private citizen Richard Nixon appraised Brezhnev and his successors with a revisionist's eye. My Foreign Service colleagues saw things differently. Nixon outlived Brezhnev by twelve years, but we had the luxury of looking back at the end of the Millennium, hopefully with more detachment.

Did public revelations about the personalities portrayed here influence my writing? Not really. They emerge as I saw them at the time, no better and no worse. As Kissinger reminded us in Zavidovo, "Truth is in the eyes of the beholder." Apart from human interest, my story is a tribute to the men and women – negotiators, brief writers, advance men, interpreters, secretaries – that helped their leaders shape history.

This story is mostly based on my recollections and private sources. Comparing my notes with declassified US memcons, I came to the conclusion that almost all of the latter were transcribed from tape recordings made before and after the shutdown of the White House taping system - without the knowledge of Soviet leaders. However, this last vestige of wiretapping proved fortunate for diplomatic history, which continuously faces its worst enemy, secrecy.

A long time ago, I learnt of two dangers facing a diplomat: the loss of national identity and of his sense of humor. A childhood in the United States did not make me an American, but it helped appreciate the American psyche, Nixon's homilies included. As to humor, my friends on both sides of the great divide were an inexhaustible source.

CHAPTER 1

Nixon Goes to the USSR, 1972

The Journey Begins

ON A MILD AND SUNNY Monday in May, I was at my desk at 13 Kensington Palace Gardens, the Soviet Embassy in London, writing a report about recent British thinking on the German question. The intercom rang: "Andrey, he wants to see you." It was Tolya, the Ambassador's private secretary. "Not the report, just come."

I put on my jacket and scurried up the creaky dark oak stairs. The double-glazed windows in the large study overlooking the quiet private road were shut. There was a barely audible whirring sound - the anti-bugging system was switched on. "Nutcracker Suite" we called it, though Embassy technicians claimed it was perfectly safe.

Ambassador Mikhail Smirnovsky gestured to a chair. Slender and stooping, ever polite, he gave me his usual shy look as if asking for forgiveness. Taking a thin pink paper slip he read out, "Urgently dispatch A. M. Vavilov to Moscow for a two-week assignment at the Center. Gromyko." Looking at the cable upside down, I could make out its classification: "Secret/Urgent."

"Andrey Mikhailovitch, I'll send a response to this. Administration is booking your ticket for the earliest flight. It appears you're in for some summit work." The Ambassador smiled sadly. The Embassy was still reeling from the expulsion of half of its diplomatic contingent in September, ostensibly for spying. The workload increased - every man counted. Nevertheless, His

Excellency must have felt secret pride that he could loan his staff directly to the Soviet leadership. This was not the first time his Second Secretary (Political) was plucked by Moscow Center to do other jobs. The previous year, I went on three missions as interpreter to the Four-Power talks on the status of West Berlin.

We suspected something was brewing in Moscow, judging by a spate of requests for position papers on US-British relations. In fact, I was drafting a cable on the two Germanys' – the FRG and the GDR – prospective admission to the United Nations.

Next morning I boarded an Aeroflot flight from Heathrow. Looking at the rolling clouds below, I thought about the task ahead. My knowledge of the impending US-Soviet summit was zero. My consolation was that the Ambassador, I suspected, knew little more.

Four hours later, I took the shuttle bus from Sheremetyevo Airport and soon unlocked the door of my apartment. I opened the windows wide to let the fresh air in, and called the office.

Surfacing from Smolenskaya Metro station, I looked up at the cream-colored Stalinist skyscraper with the huge coat of arms of the Soviet Union on the top three floors. The MFA - Ministry of Foreign Affairs - was ablaze with lights. I showed my diplomatic passport to the security guard at the entrance, and to a second one inside.

I took the elevator to the 14th floor to see an old friend, Victor Sukhodrev. He told me about the logistical effort in Moscow. Minister Gromyko asked him to assemble the best team of interpreters available, commandeering any person he saw fit from any government agency, including the vast array of Soviet Embassies abroad. "You were my first choice," Victor said. "You know the others." The first line of the list read, "Highest-level interpreters – V.M. Sukhodrev and A.M. Vavilov." This meant we two would cover private meetings between the leaders.

Victor briefed me on Henry Kissinger's trip to Moscow in April: the twenty hours he spent in talks with Brezhnev and Gromyko laid the foundation for the May summit. Secrecy was so total that Ambassador Jacob Beam was unaware of Kissinger's presence until the last moment. He suspected an important US visitor was in Moscow from radio signals intercepted by CIA receivers in the American Embassy. It was not the last time he would be sidelined.

"Two urgent matters," said Victor. "First, what do we call Brezhnev' post in English?"

I was perplexed: "Why, Secretary-General of the Central Committee of the Communist Party of the Soviet Union. Right?"

"Wrong. There is the UN Secretary-General, Secretaries-General of political parties... Some Foreign Ministry delegations have an administrative officer, the delegation secretary-general. We need to make a fitting distinction. I discussed this with Brezhnev's aide Alexandrov, and he agreed to my suggestion. We tried it out in April. The man will be called "General Secretary," no hyphen."

I said it sounded awesome.

"Second," Victor said, "is Nixon's TV address. This is Draft 9 sent over by the US Embassy. Our guys did a Russian translation; let's see if we can refine it."

The address was a Presidential first: Nixon will speak live to the Soviet population. The US Embassy hoped the rendition in Russian would convey the force of Nixon's personality, in particular his "sincerity." (The drafter, Bill Safire, caught a style that would appeal to Russian listeners.) After two hours, we had a decent product. Victor read a few passages aloud; he would be the US President's "Russian voice." I said it sounded stirring. Richard Nixon could rest assured: his message will reach the hearts of the Soviet people.

We attended to a sheaf of English translations of speeches and dinner toasts. The Communist Party Politburo has already approved all, and no major changes were expected. The MFA Translations Bureau did a first-rate job, but we brought the texts closer to American English.

Next was studying the summit brief, a thick loose-leafed volume containing background notes, draft agreements and talking points. It covered the history of Russian-American relations, from the first Russian trading outposts in Alaska in the 18th century, to disarmament, trade and space exploration.

Preparing the briefing book was quite a feat. This was before computers, in the times of the mechanical typewriter. They typed the first copy of each document on special yellow quality Verge paper, for the Politburo. The other five copies were for government departments and for filing. If there was a misprint, the whole page had to be retyped. No erasures or corrections were permitted. (Interestingly, US memos for the summit were typed in six copies as well.)

I held a mirror set of the brief the Soviet leaders will use. Well, not quite: excluded were confidential fallback positions and intelligence-related material. Some sensitive documents were withheld from interpreters for the time being, in particular, on strategic arms limitation talks – SALT. This was unfortunate, because we would be translating negotiations on this issue from the first day.

The interpreter and note taker has to know the subject matter. The summit agenda called for another requirement: mastery of the terminology of strategic nuclear arms, including launchers, throw-weight, silo dimensions, bomber aircraft, nuclear submarines and cruise missiles, both US and Soviet. There was a compounding difficulty: hardware designations used for the same weapons were different. In the atmosphere of pervasive secrecy, we were not aware of the precise names of our own systems. In the view of the Soviet military-industrial complex, Foreign Ministry negotiators "had no need to know." Therefore, the latter tacitly used American-given names, some peculiar. Thus, for a long time negotiations stalled on a sophisticated medium-range bomber which Nixon insisted was a long-range one. Both sides employed its US designation - "Backfire" - before the Soviets revealed the aircraft was Tupolev-22M.

The descriptions of intercontinental ballistic missiles (ICBM) and submarine-launched ballistic missiles (SLBM) were more confusing, because the US military used different names for the same Soviet weapon system. The name for the world's heaviest ICBM was, appropriately, "Satan," or SS-9. In reality, it was R-36. The Pentagon named its successor SS-18; it was known as R-36M in the USSR. The SS-11 was RS-10 in real life; the SS-N-6 was RSM-25, and so on. To add to the mystification, the missiles had Russian factory names that differed from the "official" military ones. Sometimes Brezhnev would mention, to blank stares on the American side, an "URS-100" or

"URS-200." Soviet defense experts at the talks knew the real designations, but kept mum. Lest confusion be total, MFA negotiators decided at an early stage to use American terminology: it brought consistency, if not clarity.

The summit brief elucidated the US position on every issue and explained our differences. There were no mutually exclusive options for negotiation strategy and tactics - the agencies concerned had discussed and resolved them beforehand. I was now reading the final product, the straightforward negotiating instructions - the "Politburo directives."

Comparing the briefs of the Soviet and US delegations is an interesting experience. Whereas US instructions - in the form of memos for the President - dealt mostly with tactics, the Russian directives were heavy on strategy. The text usually read, "Proceed from such and such decisions of the Politburo, the General Secretary's latest statements, etc." Then it went into detail. Each section had a short background note and talking points. If necessary, there was a fallback position, which began with words, "If the American side suggests..."

Soviet directives had leeway for creativity for negotiators on the ground - Foreign Minister Gromyko and Ambassadors Kornienko and Dobrynin - with the exception of sensitive arms control issues, which were the prerogative of the Ministry of Defense. The directives were businesslike and avoided moralizations: no allusions to ideology or Marxist terminology. There were no psychological portraits or personalized advice similar to what Kissinger gave in his memos to Nixon and later to Gerald Ford, in an imperative tone: "You should stress...You must...Your position is..." Soviet briefs contained personal portraits, but they emphasized career and political views of US leaders.

I continued with the Politburo directives. A curious item: President Nixon's middle name "Milhous" (derived from an ancestral German name on his mother's side), despite the Russian penchant for using full names, will not be used. (In 1979, we will have a hard time convincing Russian protocol that "Jimmy Carter" was how the American President wished to be called, rather than "James Earl Carter, Jr.")

According to the short biographies, Nixon's aides are mostly about my age, thirtyish. I reflected on the age difference of the chief negotiators: Nixon is 59, and Kissinger 49. Brezhnev is 65; Premier Kosygin and nominal President

Podgorny are even older. Gromyko is 63. I would not put their age against them. They are formidable negotiators backed by a solid support team, led by Ambassadors Anatoly Dobrynin and Georgy Kornienko.

Dobrynin's role was seminal. A former aircraft engineer drafted into the Foreign Service in 1944, he quickly rose through the ranks. His was a record posting of twenty-four years in the US, including as Soviet Ambassador to six US presidents. Working with him was a stimulating experience. He negotiated single handedly - a one-man show. According to Bill Safire, Kissinger did not need intelligent staff, just "smart robots." Not Dobrynin: he was receptive to ideas from staff. Still, he was an envoy in the 19th century tradition: he would have managed with a secretary, a code clerk and a good chef. He delegated day-to-day responsibilities to his aides.

Tall, gregarious and fast-talking, he dispensed with interpreters and note takers. With a quick mind and limitless memory capacity, he could quote verbatim what the White House told him in a hand-written "High Priority" cable to the Center. He never took notes at his rendezvous with Nixon or Kissinger. On return to the Embassy, he would dictate a conversation that went for an hour or more. Operating alone had reasons: the discussions were so frank and sensitive that the fewer people knew about them, the better. Besides, Dobrynin suspected that Kissinger occasionally tinkered with the record of a conversation, so he made sure to send detailed telegrams to Moscow. He was fastidiously reliable in his reporting, often blunt.

As a politician, Brezhnev was sometimes biased. Gromyko was cautious. Dobrynin was a functionary who suggested policy to the Center and implemented it. He had a direct telephone line to the White House and ready access to Nixon. His relations with Kissinger were unique – the latter spoke to him almost daily. Anatoly and Henry were as close to a genuine friendship as was possible at the time between a communist and a capitalist (Kissinger's almost exact words). They realized the confines in which they operated, and were not averse to a dose of cynicism, considering the overarching political goals of détente.

Dobrynin had an ability to make people feel at ease; he would have made a perfect "good cop" interrogator. Even a reticent foreign diplomat, after a few minutes of the Soviet envoy's gentle prodding, would feel the urge to talk. (This happened later with President Reagan: he was drawn to Dobrynin against the advice of conservative aides who wanted to expunge the vestiges of Nixon's foreign policy and keep relations with the Soviet Union in deep-freeze.)

Dobrynin had an equal in Georgy Kornienko, the Foreign Ministry's Head of the USA Department. Both were determined defenders of Russia's national interests. Their careers mirrored each other: with Anatoly in Washington, Kornienko looked after American affairs at the Center, in Moscow. He was the opposite of Dobrynin: smallish, an introvert who spoke little and mostly listened. He was deceptively timid, but was quick to demonstrate a tough core and strong diagnostic abilities (his background was intelligence analyst at the KGB). Coupled with total recall this made him an effective controller of negotiations. His memos were superlative diplomatic prose: concise, to the point, not a word devoid of meaning. He expected the same from staff. On one occasion, he returned a shoddy memo addressed to him: he redrafted it in his fine hand in black permanent ink. He never balked from facts and told the truth at the risk of his political masters' displeasure. He had an unobtrusive sense of humor. In 1973, he explained to Kissinger that while the three Soviet leaders were invited by Nixon to visit the US, "all have accepted but not all may come." Kissinger surmised it meant only Brezhnev, and could not resist a joke: "It would have been a little complex if the whole Politburo came at once!" Kornienko was a favorite with staff for forgiving professional lapses (this happened to me once). He went on to become First Deputy Foreign Minister, respected by both Gromyko and Brezhnev.

My indoctrination was almost complete.

The rapprochement/détente/opening between the United States and the USSR was based on objective need felt by both super powers. The Soviets found satisfaction in the prediction of Karl Marx, "The task emerges only when the material conditions for its solution exist, or at least are in the process of establishment." It also fitted his other maxim, "An idea whose time had come." Détente was destined to happen no sooner and no later than 1972.

All the pieces were in place, though they intertwined in a complex knot. The most important (and new) factor was parity in nuclear weapons, but it needed fine-tuning. Vietnam was an appalling problem for the US. The Soviet Union felt threatened by China. The US saw China as a "card," a lever, in dealing with the Russians - to help disentangle from Vietnam and to obtain an acceptable SALT agreement. Fortunately, tensions in Europe were lessening. The 1971 four-power agreement brought eased travel for West Berliners. Normalization was proceeding between the two Germanys; Willy Brandt's *Ostpolitik* was bearing fruit.

The summit was not a foregone event. There were unexpected hurdles. Just months before Nixon's trip to Moscow, the British expelled 105 Russian staff and family members including *bona fide* MFA diplomats. The White House considered the British action a slap in the face. Kissinger was furious upon hearing the news – it may endanger the summit. Détente overrode everything, and he castigated the CIA for failing to let him know about the sudden move by the British "cousins." He had a point. Before his death in 1972, J. Edgar Hoover called on Richard Nixon in Florida and asked him how he liked the FBI reports from Oleg Lyalin, a Soviet defector, on Russian spying in Britain. Nixon said he never received them. It appeared that James Jesus Angleton, the paranoid CIA counterintelligence chief, kept them locked in his safe in the belief they were part of a KGB disinformation campaign.[1] The scale of the expulsions and the timing remained a mystery; perhaps the British were jealous about détente. The move did not make a dent in summit preparations.

What could make or break the summit was Vietnam. The White House was bogged down militarily and under political siege at home. In a desperate gamble to reverse the situation on the ground and make the North Vietnamese amenable at the secret talks in Paris, Nixon ordered the mining of Haiphong and other harbors and the resumption of massive bombing. The escalation was risky. Nixon and Kissinger held their breath for the Soviet reaction. The gamble paid off: the White House rightly judged that in their obsession with China the Soviets would acquiesce. Nixon's trip to Beijing in February clinched the Moscow summit.

When Ambassador Dobrynin called on Kissinger to deliver Moscow's response on summit prospects, the latter suggested a bet, a case of champagne. He wrote out his expected version of the reply and handed it to Dobrynin: the summit will be postponed. The Ambassador showed him the letter: the summit will be held as planned. (He later said the champagne was never delivered.)

There were other reasons for the Kremlin's accommodating attitude. Brezhnev and his comrades were certain that the US war tactic was doomed – no amount of bombing (short of nuclear attack) could deflect North Vietnam and the Viet Cong from a winning strategy. Moscow was also exasperated with Hanoi. Soviet military aid was running at $5 million a day. The Soviet idea of solidarity with a Socialist country did not mean that Ho Chi Min should enjoy a veto over Moscow's relations with Washington.

Brezhnev was edgy and did not push his luck. He insisted that the Politburo take a collective decision. Several members favored a summit postponement. Kosygin, Gromyko, Andropov and, strangely, Suslov - "guardian of Communist ideology" – lent support to Brezhnev. The balance tilted in favor of the original plan. The stakes were too great: SALT, which embraced an interim agreement on offensive nuclear arms and the anti-ballistic missile (ABM) treaty, expanded trade, especially grain imports, US investments in developing Siberian gas deposits, Brezhnev's pet project - the European Security Conference - and a *modus vivendi* in most of the world's trouble spots. All would be breakthroughs. New agreements were ready for signing, including on cooperation in environment, health and space.

The Kremlin reasoned that the summit should come at a price: Nixon's anti-Communism should finally give way to recognizing the USSR as an equal partner in a super power duumvirate. Nixon was receptive: he was worried about a bigger threat than Communist ideological expansion – the mounting Soviet nuclear force. The USSR had a marked advantage: its defense expenditures encountered no political opposition. On the contrary, the public took pride in the massive buildup of sophisticated silent submarines and giant missiles.

A radically new situation drove the two super powers into each other's arms: for the first time in modern history, the world faced a non-ideological threat, a saturated arsenal of doomsday weapons. Nixon and Kissinger, as well as Brezhnev and Gromyko were prepared to go beyond "peaceful coexistence" agreed by Nikita Khrushchev and John F. Kennedy. They saw the Moscow summit as a winning game for all.

I wondered what sort of a man was Richard Nixon today. The negotiating brief dwelt on his political history and recent extraordinary transformation, including the opening to China - quite a *volte-face*. During the Korean War, he called for invading the Chinese Communist mainland from Formosa, where Chiang Kai-shek escaped with remnants of his army. I wondered if my ingrained view of the man would be refuted. The course I took of US contemporary history at the Moscow Institute of International Relations covered the times of Joe McCarthy, when the young Congressman from California was the Communist-baiting star of the House Un-American Activities Committee, the Nemesis of the blacklisted "Hollywood Ten" and Alger Hiss. I would have loved to ask Nixon what he thought of the 1950s today.

I will find the answers in a few days when I sit down in the Kremlin conference room to write down the US President's words. But enough for politics: my immediate concern is professional. I never translated for Nixon. I watched him on television and read his speeches. To know a political leader's speaking style is essential for the interpreter because he "translates history" (an expression coined by a friend, Igor Korchilov, who interpreted for Gorbachev and Reagan in the 1980s). Is Nixon a fast speaker or a slow one, is he coherent and logical in making a point, or tends to ramble, switching back and forth and sideways? Does he read from prepared notes or speak *ex tempore*? Does he like long passages ignoring the interpreter, or a clipped way that requires almost simultaneous interpretation? The other unknown for me was Henry Kissinger.

Victor translated for Nixon before. He said I would find no problem rendering him into Russian, including his prepared one-liners. I spent my childhood in the US, and 1940s American vernacular should come easy. The President is about the age of my parents - I can connect to his generation.

We settled on the work format: Victor will be up-front interpreting, and I will take notes. Whenever he needs to be relieved, I'll take over. We will service the top leaders exclusively – none can requisition our tandem except Brezhnev. Our interpreter colleagues will work below that level, including with Kissinger and Gromyko. I felt on safe ground with the Russian leaders; I knew them professionally, and what's more important, they knew me.

The US delegation will be the charge of two excellent translators - Alex Akalovsky and Bill Krimer.

I leafed through my copy of the glossy white 27-page protocol booklet with the USSR coat of arms on the cover - the Earth emblazoned with the hammer and sickle and encircled with sheaths of wheat. It contained names, assigned residences, telephones and car numbers of the Presidential party. The First Family will be ensconced in the Kremlin in a seven-room suite used by the Russian Tsars. "Kremlin" means "fortress" in Russian; they will be under the protection of the world's most efficient security service. The Kremlin address was also assigned to Major John V. Brennan (Room 1 - closer than anybody to the President). H.R. Haldeman, Assistant to the President, will stay in Room 6. Rose Mary Woods, Executive Assistant to the President, will be in Room 8, and Dwight Chapin, Deputy Assistant to the President, in 11. Ron Walker, Director of the White House Office of Presidential Advance, is further down in 12. Henry Kissinger and senior National Security Council staff also received quarters in the maze of Kremlin corridors.

It is Monday, 22 May 1972, a warm spring afternoon at Vnukovo-2, the government airport twenty miles south-west of Moscow. The white and blue Boeing 707, tail number 27000, touched down a few minutes before 4:00 p.m. (The copycat backup plane - number 26000 - is the one John F. Kennedy flew to Dallas on the fateful day in 1963; it carried his body back to Washington).

The *"Spirit of '76"* taxies to the welcoming area. Richard Nixon emerges into a slight drizzle, smiling broadly. He waves. In his dark blue suit, white shirt and blue tie, he looks tanned, lean and vigorous - not a day older than his official photo published this morning in *Pravda* and *Izvestia*.

Nikolai Podgorny, Chairman of the Presidium of the Supreme Soviet, greets Nixon at the bottom of the ramp. Prime Minister Alexei Kosygin and Foreign Minister Andrei Gromyko are in the welcoming party. My place is in the back, ready to rush forward to help with translation. I watch Henry Kissinger and his staff, briefcases bulging, scramble down the steps.

Standing in the VIP bay, we are aware of an invisible participant, Comrade Leonid Ilyich Brezhnev, General Secretary of the Central Committee of the Communist Party of the Soviet Union. While he does not hold any government position and there is no mention of his post in the Constitution, he is the senior person in the country. At this moment, he is sitting alone in an armchair in his study, smoking a cigarette, watching the welcoming ceremony on a large TV screen. Nixon's official schedule for the first day in Moscow contains a mysterious item, a "Reserved Time" window at 6:15 p.m. That's when he meets the USSR's emerging "Number One." This encounter will confirm Brezhnev's ascendancy to the unofficial Soviet throne.

Nixon and Podgorny stand on a square red carpet. The commanding officer of the guard of honor, a fierce looking giant, barks out a report and performs brief calisthenics with a long gleaming sword. I would not have liked to be his enemy. The Army brass band plays the *Star Spangled Banner* and the Soviet national anthem, *Soyuz nerushimiy respublik svobodnykh* ("Indestructible Union of Free Republics"). The Army, Navy and Air Force contingents march past to the strains of an ancient Russian battle song. They carry the three Armed Services flags: red with the gold hammer and sickle, white with a blue naval band, and a sky-blue one with yellow rays of the rising sun.

Leonid Kolokolov, Russian Chief of Protocol, introduces Nixon to the welcoming party: Politburo members, government Ministers and US Embassy officials. From behind a barrier, a small crowd of mildly enthusiastic Muscovites, handpicked and bussed from town, wave tiny American paper flags. The press enclosure is bursting. There are no speeches. The ceremony takes fifteen minutes.

In a group of protocol and security officers, I watch Nixon at close range: he looks strangely frail. I take out my miniature still camera, but a plain-clothes security man makes a warning gesture. The reason is unclear; I'm wearing a tiny colored badge in my lapel, an "all areas" pass. Copyright rules? I put the camera away; this is not the moment to argue. In time, the KGB will get used to my hobby. They never bothered me again, though competition was tough: Ollie Atkins, the White House photographer, and Vladimir Musaelyan, his Kremlin counterpart. Bob Haldeman was making amateur 8-mm movies, Larry Higby and Dwight Chapin as well. So did I.

Victor Sukhodrev, Interpreter Number One (I am Number Two), will ride in the main limousine, an armored black ZIL-114, with Nixon, Podgorny and Kosygin. Henry Kissinger (not Secretary of State William Rogers - hmm...) joins Gromyko in his limousine. I hop into one of the security cars. The other passenger is a US Secret Service agent on the front seat next to the driver. He is excited; it's his first trip to the Soviet Union. He points to an earphone plug and a miniature mike concealed in his jacket lapel: "I'm going to call Washington." I whistle: Soviet communications technology is a step behind - our officers carry walkie-talkies. The agent, in turn, says he likes the clean tree-lined boulevards of Moscow, the tall beige and rose-colored buildings, and no billboards. We pass an oversized coat of arms of the USSR and a huge portrait of Lenin.

The wide avenues of the most densely populated city in the USSR are almost deserted. It looks unnatural. I drove along this route a dozen times, among cheering crowds that broke police barriers from the sidewalks. That was the time of Jawaharlal Nehru, Indira Gandhi, and of Cosmonaut Yuri Gagarin's triumphant motorcade. Clearly, the authorities want to make a point to Nixon. Police keep the crowds at a distance: I can see throngs pressing against metal barriers in side streets. Stray pedestrians stare with polite curiosity at the black ZIL with an American and a Soviet ensign flying, escorted by motorcycle police in dazzling-white uniform. Some wave. There is a distinct chill in the air.

The motorcade approaches the Borovitski Tower at the southwest corner of the Kremlin and enters the ramp. We pass the massive oak and iron gates; the brick walls are at least fifteen feet thick. At this very point Brezhnev escaped an assassination attempt three years before - but I am not telling my American passenger. The Stars and Stripes is fluttering high against the azure sky atop the private quarters of the Russian Imperial family. The ZIL turns left into Emperor's Place, a trim courtyard next to the State Armory. The first American President to spend a night in the Kremlin emerges from his car, squinting in the sun. Kosygin, Podgorny and Gromyko escort the First Family to their third floor suite. Kissinger and his National Security Council aides hold a quick conference in the lobby, before trotting to their rooms.

Brezhnev sent word to Nixon: he could bring an interpreter to their private meeting. Nixon said he would come alone; he was comfortable with Victor whom he knew well. In the circumstances, it was improper for me to attend to take notes: two Russians accompanying Brezhnev were too many. I sympathized with Victor; he will have to translate for both leaders and prepare a memcon afterwards. Dispensing with other aides was a deliberate signal from the two leaders: they were in no need of advice. They had the fate of the world under control.

Shortly before 6:00 p.m., Nixon walked across the cobblestoned Kremlin compound to the Council of Ministers building. An Army officer took him up in an antique elevator to the third floor. Brezhnev was the gracious but reserved host. There were no opening jokes - they would become a ritual later on. After enquiring politely if the President was tired from jet lag (Nixon was not - he spent a restful night in Salzburg), Brezhnev set a businesslike tone.

He focused on the critical issues. He spoke of the need for "mutual frankness," warned Nixon about the opponents of US-Soviet cooperation, implying they existed on both sides, and skirted over Vietnam. He proposed non-use of nuclear weapons against each other, an idea tested informally on a skeptical Kissinger earlier. Brezhnev called this proposal "a peaceful bomb." Nixon's reaction was cautious - he did not wish to start the summit by rejecting something out of hand. He said he would study the matter "quietly."

Brezhnev will return to his idea at subsequent meetings; he would give Nixon no respite. He argued that a "normal person" could never contemplate nuclear strikes - it would mean the end of both countries, with "the Earth being ruled not by man, but by someone else." Brezhnev evoked "the American game of chicken" - of two cars hurtling towards each other until one veers first from a head-on collision. He thought it a dramatic comparison to the US-Soviet nuclear arms race. Brezhnev went further by suggesting that Nixon inform the US public about his "peaceful bomb" during the election campaign. The President must have considered this a grave risk to candidate Nixon, but said he followed the reasoning and that nuclear weapons "will not be used by the US."

This sweeping statement (I am sure Nixon regretted it later) strengthened Brezhnev's resolve to pursue his idea. He would try to sell it in different packaging at all his summits with Nixon, including as a non-aggression pact directed against the Chinese. He insisted it would raise the prestige of the two nations: "Both leaders will go down in history; the others would not dare use nuclear weapons if we do not." The initiative met with polite but stiffening resistance and never got off the ground. It was tantamount to the US renouncing its nuclear option and America's commitment to defend NATO allies against a Soviet ground attack in Europe. (In late 1972, Brezhnev admitted to Kissinger that Britain, France, China and others "may not like it," but he continued promoting it nevertheless.)

Brezhnev divulged another Soviet proposal, a set of basic principles of the two countries relations. Nixon raised no objection, probably because he hoped it would offset the need to promise the non-use of nuclear weapons.

Brezhnev made sure Nixon appreciated his newly won pre-eminence in the Soviet hierarchy. He was not too dexterous in snubbing his colleagues. "If the President should wish to meet separately with Podgorny or Kosygin," he said, "such meetings can be arranged." Nixon was quick to promise to follow his advice, and stressed that SALT and Vietnam be better discussed "between the two of us." Brezhnev confessed that it would be awkward for him to discuss the suggested basic principles of relations without Kosygin and Podgorny present, but he was glad that critical items will be reserved to him and the President exclusively. Nixon, for his part, intimated that Secretary of State William Rogers was not privy to some issues put up for the summit. Brezhnev knew this from Dobrynin's dispatches and did not comment. The smaller the group, the better.

The most important outcome of this one-on-one conversation was an official photograph published next morning in all Soviet newspapers: two statesmen contemplating each other unsmilingly across a bare conference table. Brezhnev's photographer captured the aura of assurance, strength and sense of responsibility of the two men embodied. The picture put an end to doubts as to who represented the USSR. Two or three years before, as the two sides broached the format of a future SALT arrangement, Lyndon Johnson, and later Nixon, corresponded with Premier Kosygin. This was to stop. Dobrynin and Kornienko specifically warned the White House about the new pecking order in the Kremlin.

Brezhnev was exhilarated with the first encounter with Nixon. He told Victor to prepare a memcon for immediate circulation to the Politburo members: he was eager to let them see his handling of the first round. This meant I would take Victor's place at the main table at the evening banquet in the Kremlin, while he toiled at the Central Committee offices a mile away.

Meanwhile, Kissinger called Dobrynin. He sounded shell-shocked: he wished to see the transcript. Yes, he was asking for the English version of the Soviet memcon, and he needed it before 8:00 a.m. the following morning. The request was highly irregular, though his predicament was understandable. It appeared Nixon failed to brief him in sufficient detail, and did not dictate a memo. It would not be the last occasion. We suspected that the President wished to keep certain things to himself, and to ration them out to his National Security Adviser. After all, information is power.

Kissinger had no idea of the restricted circulation of Soviet summit memcons: they were prepared exclusively for members and alternate members of the Politburo and Secretaries of the Party Central Committee - fewer than thirty addressees. Private assistants saw them as well. Some memcons trickled down to senior Ministers. A small group of officials had unrestricted access to the memcons - the top summit interpreters and note takers. The reason was practical: we had to maintain the style and logic of issues discussed so that the narrative flowed naturally from one encounter to the next. This ensured a common format and in the end saved editing time (that is if Brezhnev's aides wished to edit - they almost never did.)

Victor was holed up for the good part of the night. He told me he quickly obtained permission from Brezhnev's foreign policy aide Andrei Alexandrov to forward the memcon translation to Kissinger. He dictated the 15-page text to Julie Pineau, an attractive staffer with the National Security Council, in the romantic setting of the Kremlin. Kissinger showed up to check on the job's progress, and looking at the handsome Russian he wondered aloud whether he could leave them alone together.

The episode was a portent of things to come: too often, the American team overlooked the need to have their own memcon. The number of Kissinger and Nixon's unrecorded conversations with Soviet leaders must have run into several dozen. Most probably, they were irretrievably lost for White House files. For example, no American record was found of a crucial conversation between Kissinger and Vice Premier L. Smirnov on silo and missile dimensions during the 1972 summit.[2] This added to the confusion of the US team on the issue. Admittedly, some private exchanges are not fit for paper, such as derogatory remarks about high officials or references to information sources that could not be compromised. This case, however, meant disregard of basic diplomatic rules. The simple explanation was Kissinger's supercilious attitude to the written record. He found a way around it later.

The first official encounter of the leaders and their spouses occurred on June 22 at a dinner for 150 guests in the Kremlin's ancient Granovitaya Palata (Chamber of Facets), a spacious vaulted room with narrow windows, paintings of Russian saints on the walls and a huge chandelier with a hundred miniature bulbs.

It was a full turnout: Politburo members, Central Committee Secretaries and senior Ministers. I sat next to the host, Chairman Podgorny. The General Secretary and Mrs. Brezhnev had seats farther down: this time he yielded to his comrades. Podgorny and Kosygin made small talk with Nixon and the First Lady. The Kremlin wives looked overweight against Pat Nixon. Kosygin's graceful daughter Lyudmila (his wife died of cancer five years before) conversed in excellent English. The other Russian hosts remained mostly silent. Mikhail Suslov barely touched his plate - he suffered from ulcers. KGB Chief Yuri Andropov was uncommunicative. Across the table sat Alexander Shelepin, Chairman of the Trade Union Federation and an ambitious Party boss who had just ceded several important posts (Brezhnev suspected he was after his job). He wanted to know how my brain functioned when translating. I had no ready answer.

The US party was present in full. I saw Bob Haldeman in the back. During the summit, he was barely visible. A silent figure, he was not involved in negotiations - at dinners he sat quietly at the far corner of the banquet room, most probably to avoid squandering time in pointless conversation. He kept in the shadows and did not mingle with the locals. He did the tourist circuit: he liked the spires and battlements of the Kremlin. The redbrick walls were high and impregnable to strangers and the press. Here, there was no need for any "Berlin Wall" methods of shielding the President. He often huddled with Nixon.

The speeches resounded in the ancient room. Nixon said, "In a nuclear age, when there is no such thing as security in a preponderance of strength, great powers have learnt this fact of life: agreements based on exploiting the presumed weakness of one party only cause it to redouble its efforts to catch up, but agreements based on mutual respect and reciprocity have a far greater chance of enduring."

Podgorny used remarkably similar wording. Both toasts sounded as drafted by the same Kremlin speechwriter. After the toasts and clinks of the champagne glasses, the atmosphere felt less tense. Podgorny was a client of mine. I knew the stories he loved to tell. He described the history of the Granovitaya Palata to Nixon, with a punch line: "The Saints on the walls were Christ's Politburo." There was polite laughter - Podgorny glowed. This was the fifth time I translated the joke; it seemed to figure in the talking points of Politburo members from the days of Khrushchev.

The dinner ended a minute before midnight. Nixon and Kissinger drove home in the President's Lincoln. Victor, Tatyana Ovchinnikova (she assisted the First Lady) and I caught up with them in the brightly lit lobby of the residence. Mrs. Nixon went upstairs, but the President lingered. He was in high spirits. He wished to know our names. Good: we made sure he recognized our faces. In the coming days, we will hover closer to him and Pat than any KGB or Secret Service agent.

Victor introduced me: as a kid back in 1945, I lived in California where my father was Soviet Consul. Nixon asked what school I went to. Los Feliz, I said, an elementary off Hollywood Boulevard in LA. Nixon jabbed a finger in my chest and turned to Victor: "He's a good interpreter. Have you ever met Vernon Walters?" I did not. He told us about the Lieutenant General and CIA Deputy Director, a remarkable Army interpreter with a command of French, Spanish, German, and passable Russian. "When I met de Gaulle," Nixon said, "Walters didn't make a single note and reproduced the conversation in full. He also translated for Mr. Kissinger at his talks with the Vietnamese in Paris - same photographic memory." Nixon informed us he was a Quaker (we were unsure how to react).

We bade the President goodnight; the handshake was firm but his hand was unexpectedly thin and bony. The elevator doors slid shut.

Tomorrow will be a hard day: three sessions to cover most of the summit agenda. I took the Kremlin pool car home. I wondered about Nixon's story about Vernon Walters dispensing with taking notes. Even the best interpreter's memory is often arbitrary, and may play tricks. I found this after looking at my old transcripts. Some seemed written by another person: they differed from my recollections of substance discussed, probably tinged by evolving perceptions. Surely, I thought, Walters followed the work rule: always make a written memo of a conversation, the sooner the better. You never know what the ramifications might be; a note taker's memo may play no less a role than a wiretapping transcript.

Later events confirmed my supposition. The burglary of the Democratic National Committee in the Watergate Hotel in Washington occurred on June 17, less than three weeks after the Moscow summit. A few days after the break-in, Walters wrote a memo about a White House meeting with CIA's Richard Helms and Nixon aides Haldeman and Ehrlichman. The June 23 conversation was the "smoking gun" in the Watergate scandal. Walter's prolific memory and attention to detail shattered Nixon's claim of "national security."[3] The President's attempt to put pressure on the CIA to thwart the FBI investigation of the "plumbers" money connections did not work: there was no mention of any national security issue in Walters' memcon.

The first summit plenary session opened in the morning of Tuesday, 23 May, in St. Catherine Hall of the Kremlin. The former Throne Room boasts four picture windows, walls decorated in gold, white and blue, gilded chandeliers and huge porcelain floor vases. The splendor reminds the visitor that this is the heart of the Russian Empire. (TV viewers observe it as the tall bronze doors swing open and President Putin enters with his guest to sit down at the large white conference table.)

I led White House spokesman Ron Ziegler and Presidential Assistant Steve Bull, who bedecked himself with an assortment of Soviet badges, on a guided tour of the hall and adjoining rooms. I told them about a secret door that led to underground passages used to smuggle young officers in and out of Empress Catherine II boudoir. Most were since sealed for security reasons. My new comrades were awed. "Nothing like this in the White House," smiled Ziegler.

Just before the session, Nixon sprung a surprise: American interpreters will be barred from confidential meetings, though they could attend full-delegation plenary sessions. After initial interpreting and note taking in plenaries, Akalovsky and Krimer were shunted away. This was irregular. We wondered about the reasons. Poorly written memcons? Kissinger's dislike of Secretary Rogers? Fear of leaks? As it turned out, neither Nixon nor Kissinger wanted "State Department types snooping around." Nixon's suspicions trickled down to official interpreters, who, he feared, would be the source of leaks. Kissinger ruefully referred to the US bureaucracy's "culture of unrestrained leaking." This was the real reason for banning American interpreters from confidential conversations, although in his memoirs Nixon gave a different explanation: he felt Brezhnev would speak more freely if only the Soviet interpreter was present.

Nixon must have thought, "If Brezhnev trusts his Soviet Foreign Ministry interpreters, so will I." From the first summit onwards, he showed us utmost consideration, almost treating us as members of his staff. The bad news was a double workload. Under normal circumstances, the interpreter translates into his native language only, but these were not normal circumstances. We will have to translate both ways: for the Russian leaders into Russian and for Nixon and Kissinger into English.

The novel White House rules put the American side at a disadvantage. Gerard Smith, US SALT negotiator, made a biting comment: "Negotiations at times were conducted partially through the agency of Soviet interpreters. The American negotiator could only assume that what the Soviet negotiator had said in Russian was being accurately rendered into English - and what he said in English was being accurately conveyed in Russian. Traditional diplomatic practice is to avoid any such dependence on an agent of the other side. Any American who does not speak and understand Russian like a native should use an American interpreter in all Soviet-American arms control negotiations involving the use of Russian."[4] Prudent advice, but never followed in the Nixon White House.

Smith was not entirely correct. His experience was SALT. At the summit talks, there was another, technical, rather than political, reason for overreliance on Russian interpreters: they were better qualified than Americans in the subject matter.

I wondered who would take notes for Nixon and Kissinger. This came as another surprise.

The three men confronting Nixon in St. Catherine Hall looked and behaved differently. To an American reporter, President Podgorny appeared to be "gentle, almost grandfatherly," Premier Kosygin "tough and unsmiling," and Brezhnev "relaxed and self-assured."[5] Nixon was closer to the mark, when he described Podgorny as "a Midwestern senator," Kosygin a Communist "aristocrat," and Brezhnev "a big Irish labor boss," or [Chicago] "Mayor Daley."[6]

The personalities behind the facade differed from the descriptions. In reality, Podgorny was the boorish ideological hawk, Kosygin the pragmatic realist and a shy person in real life, and Brezhnev… Shrewd, polite and confident.

Nixon sat ten feet away from me across the table. He was well groomed and neatly dressed. While the two dozen photo reporters were in the room, he assumed studied poses. He had a measured logical way of putting his views across. He was courteous. He spoke with emphasis and force without being rude. He did not avert his eyes; he looked directly at the speaker opposite. I sat just behind Brezhnev, and had the impression he was looking squarely into my eye over the General Secretary's shoulder. He would scribble something on a writing pad. A little show: he was receptive to what his Soviet partner was saying. He addressed Brezhnev in the third person: "The General Secretary was right in saying… I agree with the General Secretary…" He nodded often, and laughed readily at Brezhnev's jokes. Small talk was the Russian's forte; he was a master storyteller and never rehearsed.

Occasionally, Nixon would turn to Kissinger, expecting substantiation of a point he was making. He referred to "Mr. Kissinger" rather than "Dr. Kissinger," as they addressed him in Russia. Probably there was a reason. We heard Kissinger's views on the way he wished to be addressed: "I don't stand on protocol; "Your Excellency" would be fine…"

Nixon's talking speed was medium. He spoke in short passages. He understood our job: he spoke, stopped, turned to the interpreter and listened to the sound of Russian, nodding, as if he was satisfied with the quality of translation. He expected to hear the same voice inflections: no mumbling interpreter for him.

Nixon did not look the "offspring of hell" that Nikita Khrushchev saw in 1960 and prayed for "angel" John F. Kennedy's victory in the election. He looked - I searched for an appropriate word – "suave?" I found hard to imagine the same man lambasting witnesses before the Un-American Activities Committee.

The first full-delegation session lasted for two hours. It started and ended on a high note. The leaders tried to infuse as much friendliness as possible. Nixon said that among his Soviet friends he may have an undeserved reputation as a hard-line anticommunist ("You do," Kosygin interjected), but he respected them for believing in their system. This was the farthest he would go in describing ideological differences; there will be no futile theoretical debates.

Brezhnev was at his best: he sailed through his talking points, argued positions, joked and seemed at ease with the brief. A good omen for the summit: the top Russian negotiator came well prepared. He seemed better versed in details than Nixon was; after all, he coordinated the Soviet defense industry. He used fine phrases: "To lead is not to observe, but to predict," and "We must see through the fog."

He leaned back to listen to his comrades - the arrangement was they would participate in the discussion. He did not interrupt Kosygin. When Podgorny praised the quality of Russian vodka, Brezhnev suggested he join Kissinger in opening a vodka business in the US, but Nixon quashed the plan: "Kissinger is making enough money as it is." They decided that Gromyko and Kissinger will address, if need be, the technicalities of SALT; they will negotiate in parallel to the leaders.

We met in two sessions that evening. In my notes, I underlined a point Nixon made several times: the two States should not be dragged into conflicts in peripheral areas that do not make an impact on the fate of the world (for some reason he mentioned Bolivia). What would make a difference are our relations, he stressed. This was music to Brezhnev's ears. He agreed that relations with the US were not on the same plane as with Finland, Norway, or for that matter, Bolivia. Guinea, Luxemburg, Albania and Poland were also mentioned as countries that need not matter (Nixon nodded in agreement). Brezhnev said he was fascinated by the fact that Luxemburg had only 90 police officers, and repeated this several times. Looking at his talking points, he corrected the figure to 78. "Even fewer," he said, with a twinkle. Apprehensions about "small countries" meddling in the privileged super-power relationship were to run through all Nixon-Brezhnev summits.

They spoke about the future. Casually, Nixon made a prediction: in 20 to 25 years, China and Japan might pose a military threat. Brezhnev nodded vigorously. Nixon spoke more of security, and Brezhnev stressed trade.

However, economic issues were clearly overshadowed by SALT and the document on principles of the two countries' relations. The agenda of the summit was long, but these two items became the focus and the dramatic outcome of the leaders' first encounter.

Inspecting my notes, I noticed that no mention was made of human rights. This issue had since become a key ingredient of high-level meetings. Whether the reason was a different era, or the imperial nature of both leadership structures, the issue was ignored. Well, almost, if one discounts the problem of Jewish emigration from the USSR.

TAKING NOTES FOR THE GENERAL SECRETARY

Despite the daunting task ahead, I felt calm: my background in interpreting and note taking at high levels of government spanned a dozen years. By 1972, I had translated for Premiers Nikita Khrushchev and Alexei Kosygin at their meetings with Jawaharlal Nehru, his daughter Indira Gandhi, Pakistan's President Ayub Khan, Emperor Haile Selassie, Prime Minister Harold Wilson, Lyndon B. Johnson, plus an assortment of Foreign Ministers and celebrities, including unforgettable Cosmonaut Yuri Gagarin. Back in the early 1960s, I translated for a relatively unknown Chairman of the Presidium of the Supreme Soviet, Leonid Ilyich Brezhnev.

Taking notes in Brezhnev's Kremlin office. (Vladimir Musaelyan)

My preference in the MFA translation service was taking notes. With my note pad, I usually occupied the last chair on the Soviet side of the negotiating table, or sat right behind the General Secretary. I dare say I possessed, using the phrase of Bill Henkel, Nixon's advance man, "a passion for anonymity."

I owed my romance with interpreting and note taking to my mentor and friend, Victor Sukhodrev. In the early 1960s, during my first diplomatic posting in our Delhi Embassy as *dragoman* (Oriental languages expert), Victor accompanied Khrushchev and other Soviet VIPs on visits to India. He noted my willingness to assist at official dinners, on sightseeing trips to the Taj Mahal in Agra and the "Whispering Palace" of Jaipur. He appreciated my discretion and, I liked to believe, genuine modesty, a reluctance to squeeze into the front row at photo opportunities, a certain fluency in translating, and knowledge of India and the United States. He saw me as a potential stand-in English translator and spoke to MFA Personnel. This promoted a vocation I never expected. I was 24 and eager to see the wheels of government in motion.

The start of my new career at the MFA Translations Bureau was an embarrassing flop. I saw an ad for a screen test at Mosfilm Studios for the part of Stalin's interpreter in a World War II blockbuster. The prototype was Vladimir Pavlov, who worked opposite Charles Bohlen (for FDR) and A. H. Biers (for Winston Churchill). I was the same slim build, wore glasses, and was the embodiment of official discretion. I was sure I would get the part. I also needed the money. I asked for permission from the Translations Bureau Chief. He said my request was unusual; I had better apply to Personnel. I loitered on the MFA's 15th floor where it weaved its elaborate strategy of postings, replacements and promotions. A friend from that department bumped into me by the elevator. He said, "You want my advice? Just go for it. Don't tell anybody."

I went to the Studios next day, to be rejected by a middle-aged lady from Casting: "The audience won't believe that the Soviet leader had such an unimposing translator." My allusions to the original interpreter - Pavlov - could not move her; nor did references to my current job.

I told a colleague about the vacancy. Oleg Aleinikov, a gregarious office clown, looked so distinguished in his double breasted pin-striped suit that he could easily pass for a British Ambassador of the old school. They snapped him up for an even better part, of Roosevelt's interpreter. His acting was flawless. He lost the battle of authenticity, though. Despite his claim that interpreters sat next to leaders at the conference table, the Mosfilm woman was adamant: they would please translate standing. Despite other incongruities in the final cut, the movie was realistic and showed allied wartime solidarity at its best.

Unfortunately, the Ministry fired Oleg after he insulted an African envoy during a sightseeing tour for the Diplomatic Corps. Unfairly, he said, but in all truth, he had a drinking problem. His slide was rapid. We tried to help: gave money that he squandered, bought food that he sold to buy liquor. He was rude to shop assistants and got into brawls with strangers. Eventually, charged with aggressive behavior and destruction of property, he landed in a labor camp. Unexpectedly, he achieved great popularity when the movie became part of the prisoners' re-education program. Each time it was screened, FDR's debonair interpreter received a standing ovation, the guards included. Oleg's performance stirred the parole board, which agreed to early release. He died soon after of delirium tremens. Once he confided to me that drinking was a tough vocation; he thought Ray Milland captured the agonies well in *The Lost Weekend*.

I never volunteered for movie roles again, and turned to serious training in interpretation and note taking.

My rapport with Victor Sukhodrev was based on mutual reliance and comparative advantage. Whenever there was a choice - to interpret or to take notes - I opted for the second. Victor was reassured to see me at the negotiating table. It gave him time for recuperation. If he translated for five hours nonstop, it would take him another five hours to write down the conversation. He was expected to do it quickly, because other members of the leadership, ministers, General Staff, whoever, were waiting to read the memcon in order to prepare for the next negotiating round. The conversation resumes after lunch, and he continues translating. The work piles up, and the only available time to dictate the memcon is night. Therefore, a reliable note taker is a godsend for the interpreter. Victor's expectation that I would produce a quality memcon was never shaken.

Victor had just replaced Oleg Troyanovsky, our best English interpreter, a warm and friendly personality, who proceeded to serve as assistant to several Russian leaders, and later Ambassador to Japan, China and the UN. As diplomatic interpreter, Victor was even better. He had no equals in the English-speaking world. A linguist, extrovert, life of the party, he presented a public image of Soviet leaders that outshone the original. He was a factor behind perceptions of "Brezhnev the Negotiator" in the West. By 1972, he was a Foreign Ministry Director responsible for the British desk, and remained Brezhnev's favorite interpreter. The General Secretary liked the sound of his spoken English so much that he used American acronyms instead of Russian ones. Thus, he said "MIRV" instead of "RGCh," the Russian abbreviation for "multiple independently targetable reentry vehicle."

The initial impression when mingling with political leaders is not unlike newspaper photographs coming to life. I remember my first experience at a large international gathering in Moscow. I gaped at Nicolae Ceausescu, Joseph Broz Tito, Walter Ulbricht and Brezhnev as they walked towards me along the corridor. They expected people to jump out of the way - I was almost trampled down by Ulbricht. You must stay close but remain inconspicuous. You have to be deferential without groveling.

The responsibility a top-level interpreter carries is tremendous. The job is exacting. Imagine sitting next to two most powerful men on Earth and translating their conversation. Suppose you forget or miss an important word? Or misjudge the message? Worse, have a mind block? It happened to me once, as I translated Major Yuri Gagarin's speech at a million-strong public rally in Bombay. Blinded by searchlights piercing the pitch-black Indian night, my mind suddenly went blank. I was speechless. The crowd waited. Yuri patiently repeated his last phrase twice, before I came to and continued with the translation. There are moments of frustration and panic, but also of exhilaration.

A top-level interpreter is the national leader's mouthpiece; he projects the man's thinking and elucidates the thinking of the negotiating partner. It is his final word that is heard and later read, as a memcon, by government departments. A great deal depends on the meticulous rendition of messages passing along this vital conduit; any inference may affect decision-making on both sides. The interpreter is not an automaton, but a key participant in nego-tiations. He has to know the foreign language equivalent of all issues under discussion, including technical nuances. Institutional memory is no less im-portant than the dictionary; you have to be in constant touch with the issue experts. Since negotiations are an intercultural exchange, the interpreter/note taker must know about young Colonel Brezhnev at the Belorussian front in World War II and about Nixon's childhood in Whittier, California.

The interpreter and note taker's functions are interchangeable; he is usu-ally the same person. If there is no note taker present, it falls to the interpreter, after a meeting ends, to dictate a memcon from his notes. Doing both is a chillingly hard task for even the best language expert. It takes twice the men-tal effort.

Translating prepared speeches is never a problem – one sees the text in advance. Negotiations and ad-lib public statements are a different category. Both sides of the Iron Curtain had their fill of stories when interpreters as-suaged the emotions of their political masters, and even censored them. To do so, the interpreter has to know them intimately and be prepared to take risks.

In 1960, Supreme Soviet Chairman Kliment Voroshilov paid a visit to Agra. He was unwell after an official dinner of spicy curry and tandoori chicken. An Indian reporter asked about his impression of the Taj Mahal. "Nothing spectacular," said Voroshilov. "The Great Moguls should have do-nated construction money to the people." Without batting an eyelid, Yuri Vinogradov, his interpreter, translated, "I bow my head in front of this jewel of Mogul architecture!" The Indian reporters applauded. Yuri turned to me and Aleksei Nikiforov, the Embassy's top Hindi interpreter, "Guys, now you know about political correctness."

Lord Powell, Margaret Thatcher's Private Secretary, recounted a tense meeting she had in the mid-1980s with the visiting President of the former French Congo, a Marxist. She leant across and said, "I hate Communists." The French interpreter, shattered by this introduction, said, "The Prime Minister says she was never wholly supportive of the ideas of Karl Marx."

Paul Schmidt, Hitler's interpreter, always tempered strong language re-served for foreign dignitaries. If the Fuehrer said, "I demand," Schmidt said, "the Reich Chancellor emphasizes." He rightly considered the interpreter's mission as "interpreting" his master's ideas, rather than merely "translating" his words. Fortunately, Hitler did not bring Schmidt to his senses in his usual way.

The interpreter must be ready to sacrifice his good name for a higher cause. At the Paris peace conference in 1946, the Allies negotiated peace treaties with Germany's former partners. When the new Italian Foreign Minister tried to bargain a better deal on a border issue with France, Soviet delegate Vishinsky, never known for niceties, ridiculed him, recalling that "Italian soldiers ran like rabbits." The Minister rose to storm out of the room. Vishinsky said the interpreter "misrepresented" his remarks. The latter readily admitted his "guilt." That same evening Vishinsky presented him with a Swiss gold watch - "For the rabbits," he said.

Years later, Brezhnev met with Americans who pleaded with him to reconsider boycotting the 1984 Olympics in Los Angeles (the US boycotted the 1980 Moscow Olympics in retaliation for the Soviet intervention in Afghanistan). Brezhnev suddenly agreed. Foreign Minister Gromyko winced. The interpreter saw that Brezhnev was drifting and said, "Reconsidering is out of the question." Gromyko relaxed. The same day he called the Chief of the MFA Translation Bureau, Vsevolod Pastoyev, and asked him to commend the interpreter. The Chief (of 1946 "rabbit" fame) presented the old Swiss watch to the interpreter – for intuition and courage. Leading Russian interpreter Vladimir Faekov now waits for a new act of bravery or sacrifice to pass on the trophy.

There is the problem of "eating on the job." It has been a long-standing Soviet tradition that the interpreter sits next to the top person at State lunches and dinners and is served the same fare. At the first dinner hosted by Richard Nixon in Moscow, US protocol tried to seat us behind the leaders. Victor Sukhodrev flatly refused, thus guaranteeing us a permanent seat (and food) at all future American-hosted functions. To eat and translate at the same time is a formidable task, though there are no known cases of choking to death. Translator Valentin Berezhkov experienced an unpleasant episode at the Big Three conference in Teheran in 1943. He missed lunch and had to interpret again at dinner. Taking advantage of a pause in the conversation, he mouthed a piece of juicy steak. Churchill said something. Berezhkov chewed frantically, trying to swallow the meat. Stalin hissed in his ear, "You found the right time to dine." There were no nasty repercussions, thus showing that, unlike functionaries, interpreters are indispensable.

Missing calories is a constant irritant for the interpreter. For this reason, during foreign trips, Victor and I availed ourselves of Soviet Embassy interpreters - they helped out at receptions, where there is minimal substantive conversation. Sometimes it led to comic results. Back in 1968, at a State dinner in Rawalpindi, Pakistan, I asked Embassy attaché Vladimir Pavlinov to help Kosygin converse with President Ayub Khan. I warned him that Kosygin was deaf in his right ear. I sat in the back of the room talking with the strikingly beautiful wife of the Chief of Police. Suddenly, I heard shouting from the main table. I strained to see, but it died down quickly.

Vladimir explained what happened. When Ayub Khan started with a pleasantry, Vladimir shouted the translation in Kosygin's good ear. Kosygin almost fell off his chair: he thought the interpreter had a hearing problem. Years later, Vladimir, now Ambassador to Cyprus, told me about the two leaders' great fallacies of memory. At the fateful dinner, Kosygin enquired about a painting of a snowy mountain range. He said it looked familiar - was it Pakistan? "Azad Kashmir," said Ayub Khan, with a sigh of sadness over the divided province. Vladimir knew (but decided not to say so) that the picture - of the Hindukush range in the Soviet republic of Tajikistan - was a present from the Premier to Pakistan's President the previous year in Moscow.

The interpreter, if no special note taker is present, must prepare a memcon. Once, Brezhnev showed Kissinger a report from Ambassador Dobrynin describing their recent conversation at the White House. Kissinger confirmed it was a precise account. When Dobrynin learnt about this, he said if he skewed the conversation, he would have lost credibility with Henry. Of course, a memcon's accuracy is not the household sense of the word. An experienced note taker will be liberal; he is not required to write down any odd remark at a cocktail party. Small talk and jokes will not change the course of history, though some are worth saving for posterity. The note taker relies on his judgment. Some leaders have pet phrases and stories they are hell-bent on seeing in the memcon. You just have to know, there is no other way.

Writing a lucid memcon is not easy, because political leaders are not always lucid. You must master the brief, and be responsible for "checking against delivery." Did your political master accidentally misrepresent the actual government position and thus confused his foreign partner? This was known to happen with Brezhnev - in such cases I took the liberty of correcting his spoken words in the transcript.

After years of serving on the Kremlin interpretation team one became adept and, what is more important, confident in reconstructing convoluted negotiations. Most conversations were editable; a few had to be written down almost word for word because of policy implications. The phrases of your boss, long-winded at times, must be arranged in a logical sequence. Invariably one has to pluck sentences from the end of the conversation to fit with the topic discussed in the beginning. This requires an overview of the conversation's progress - which may have lasted for hours - and audacity in editing. The final product has to be concise, if possible, logical and clear: no double meanings, no hazy allusions. Yours is the ultimate judgment, period.

Personal courage is necessary. Once, I showed, on Gromyko's instructions, a transcript of a conversation between Chairman Nikolai Podgorny and Emperor Haile Selassie of Ethiopia to the Head of the MFA African Department. He failed to understand a point made by Podgorny. He was right; I saw the difficulty and edited the phrase. The man went white: "How can you do that? These were Podgorny's words!" "They were," I said. "But now they are clearer - that's what he had in mind." This episode shows the dual role of the Kremlin interpreter. His job is service; he is also the keeper of the words of the leader. Therefore, he assumes some of his authority. In Russian practice, the interpreter/note taker is a highly respected individual. Quite often, officials regard him as a conduit to the boss - such approaches are to be discouraged.

In confidential diplomatic negotiations, there are cases when your political master says that something is "not for the record"; the note taker must lay down his pen. Another situation is a private exchange, often humorous, which carries no political import. In both cases, the note taker has to memorize because he might have to reproduce the missing portion. He would decide later on whether to include it in the memcon; this depends on its relevance. Russian note takers would rather drop private remarks than include them. I did this when I thought they would show my man in an unfavorable light.

The American way is to record everything spoken. The most striking example of this passion (which admittedly had reasons) was the White House taping system. A strong bent on a verbatim record can play havoc with politicians.

In my long career, I never left out anything of substance from a memcon. The multitude of jokes I cut left history untouched. The esteem in which the leadership, Soviet and American, held our small group of interpreters and note takers helped. Instances when someone dared edit our memcons were exceptional. In my memory, Brezhnev's aide Alexandrov did this once, of the SALT discussion on the first day of the 1972 summit: the brief was so secret that Victor and I were not shown in advance.

Preparing a record allows no procrastination: much of the dictation is done at night. You must work fast. No memcon is too insignificant to be left for the following day. The work quickly piles up, and after a day or two of negotiations, the meaning of scribbles and signs in your writing pad eludes you. Stress and constricted time-space are a curse. The divorce rate in the interpreters' community is akin to flight controllers; nervous breakdowns are not unheard of. I lost count of sleepless nights during summit conferences.

In the end, all these qualifications boil down to one: quiet professionalism.

The format of note taking for the higher Soviet echelons evolved over decades. It started with brief notes for the file during Lenin's time - he was fluent in English and German. It was perfected at Joseph Stalin's meetings with Churchill and Roosevelt during World War II. It turned into almost verbatim reports under Khrushchev, whose chitchat was considered official history.

I was 27 when assigned to translate for Khrushchev. No better training could be desired. His oratory concealed an embarrassing fact: he was practically illiterate. A compulsive talker, he could be quite amusing. He dictated outlines of foreign policy speeches and briefs, which he sent over to Foreign

Ministry experts for refinement. The texts ran into dozens of pages: long-winded expositions of often-bizarre ideas embroidered with homilies and historical references. He added guidance for speechwriters at the end.

Khrushchev drafts made interesting reading. His memory was phenomenal; he recalled facts and names of officials, drivers and cooks he met decades ago. A dictated draft message to a foreign leader included a point he raised earlier with British Prime Minister Harold Wilson and former US Senator William Benton, publisher of Encyclopedia Britannica. I read it at the MFA with some amazement: "Vavilov recorded the conversations; I have not seen the memcons, but here is what I want to see in the message…" So like Khrushchev; he was too impatient. His super-charged mind raced on producing new dazzling ideas.

In my first assignments for the Kremlin, I felt keenly the psychological pressure that comes with the job. As Victor Sukhodrev taught us, at the highest levels nothing can be lost in translation. A miss is as good as a mile; one mistake and you are through. Though not necessarily. Speaking in the Kremlin's St. George Hall, Khrushchev said, "Imperialism is spreading its tentacles over the world." The interpreter said "testicles" - to a roar of laughter from the diplomatic corps. To Khrushchev's credit, he thought the slip hilarious. In 1956, Khrushchev uttered the famed *"Mi vas pohoronim,"* a phrase that Victor correctly translated, as "We will bury you." Khrushchev meant Communism would outlive capitalism, i.e., "We will attend your funeral," but it is easy to edit with hindsight.

To be on the safe side with Khrushchev, we wrote lengthy memcons; no joke or proverb was too paltry to omit. One of the exotic was "We don't kill flies with our nostrils" (meaning "We are sufficiently competent"). He made this remark to Vice President Nixon during the "kitchen debate" at the American exhibition in Moscow in 1959. The interpreters - Yuri Lipanov and Alexander Akalovsky - struggled valiantly with Khrushchev's rich vernacular.

After Khrushchev's ouster in 1964, in the short interregnum of Prime Minister Kosygin, note taking became terse and focused on substance. Kosygin's views on translating and recording conversations came as a release. His snappish manner of speaking and editing were flawless: not a word out of context, not a phrase without meaning. Early on, he decided that memcons should not exceed five pages and must focus on the "dry residue," i.e., specific points discussed, resolved, or left pending. His engineer's mind demanded clarity and specifics. He viewed the memcon as material for government follow-up, rather than a historical record. The new mode made taking notes easier, but much of the color was lost.

Under Brezhnev, note taking again expanded to almost verbatim lengths. Brezhnev was a talker. He rarely read the finished transcript. We put a standard footnote at the bottom of the first page: "Memcon not reviewed by L.I. Brezhnev." Stalin went over his memcons with the note taker to check their veracity. Brezhnev never had the time, unless there was something too personal to ignore, in which case he read the transcript and the footnote was struck. Sometimes a Brezhnev foreign policy aide - Alexandrov or Blatov - added his name next to the note taker, to show he checked the text.

Brezhnev was not difficult to translate. He usually relied on talking points. If he deviated - this occurred often as his status rose - he did it in an easy, off-hand way. Never in a hurry: he had all the time in the world. As his illness progressed, he would revert to reading prepared notes.

Nixon wrote some of his speeches and worked on drafts submitted by speechwriters. Not Brezhnev: he sometimes suggested an outline he wanted the drafters to follow. He relied on experts. I participated in a speechwriters' group preparing a long statement by the General Secretary ("long" meant very long: it took from one to two hours to read aloud). My charge was the arms control section. In a secluded dacha in a Moscow suburb, I experienced the drudgery of committee drafting. The speech was circulated to Politburo members who made small edits. The General Secretary dutifully read it out. Audience applause and favorable press reaction were predictable.

"Make your threat!"

On May 24, we piled into cars and set off at break-neck speed to Novo Ogarevo, a sprawling forested compound on the Moskva River, for a small informal dinner. Brezhnev maneuvered Nixon into his limousine and drove away before the main American party located their transport. The other two members of the ruling troika headed in the same direction in their own cars. Brezhnev wanted private time with the President: he was steadily monopolizing him.

I never liked dinners at government dachas; they tend to turn into never ending table talk, toasting, drinking and overeating. This time I looked forward to drama. The Soviet leadership planned some hard talk on Vietnam. Nixon probably expected it.

When Kissinger arrived a few minutes later, Nixon took him for a walk; they conversed in low tones. Brezhnev and the rest followed at a discreet distance. We approached a high riverbank. The view was magnificent - Novo Ogarevo is a 19th century guesthouse amid a vast English-style garden. (Occasionally used by the Imperial family, it is now Vladimir Putin's country residence.)

The hushed conversation over, Brezhnev invited Nixon for a cruise in a speedboat. I found a free seat in the second one, next to Kissinger and Kosygin. The captains must have commanded torpedo boats: they swished up and down the river sending cold sprays at each sharp turn. Thankfully, it was too early in the season for bathers. We held to the sides - not a good occasion for talking, just nervous laughter. The security details stranded on land were pleased to see us back. Nixon appeared shaken.

The dinner party was not to be your neighborly barbeque. It started with a negotiating session in a bare wood-paneled conference room on the ground floor. Nixon and Kissinger sat down at one side of the green felt-topped table, facing Brezhnev, Kosygin and Podgorny. Victor sat next to Brezhnev; I found a small table in the corner of the room and opened my pad. All of a sudden, Kissinger jumped up and left the room: his aides were missing. He did not wish to rely on the Soviet record of the bashing he was expecting. Nixon lowered his eyes; he refrained from small talk. He stooped. Nobody spoke.

Minutes ticked by. The mood was somber, as if two armies were mustering troops before battle.

At last, Kissinger led in his soldiers - red faced Winston Lord and John Negroponte. Their driver missed the turn to the dacha. They sat down and took out the notepads. The session commenced. Brezhnev peered into his talking points and launched into a twenty-minute lecture over Vietnam. He appealed to Nixon's reason; the useless war had to be terminated.

Nixon's face was stony; he listened in silence.

Kosygin took over, intense and aggressive. He referred to South Vietnamese President Nguen Van Thieu as "that carcass in Saigon."

Nixon looked up: "Who elected the President of North Vietnam?"

"The whole nation," retorted Kosygin. "Even the South Vietnamese regard Ho Chi Min as their President."

Nixon let the remark pass by. There was no love lost between him and Thieu, who was becoming a major obstacle for an agreement with the North Vietnamese in Paris.

I never saw Kosygin so angry. He lashed Nixon for bombing Haiphong harbor where US planes hit a stranded Soviet merchant ship. Staring coldly into Nixon's eyes he warned: "As yet, other Socialist countries have not entered the war though the Chinese said they'd be ready to send troops..."

Nixon clenched his teeth, straightened and growled, "We're not afraid of your threat, go ahead and make it." This sounded ominous, coming from a man who rarely vented his anger in public. I made sure I recorded the exact words he used; wars have started on a lesser pretext.

Nixon's outburst incensed Kosygin: "Why on earth do you regard our words as a threat, and what you're actually doing - not a threat? Your bombs exploded 150 meters from our ships in Haiphong harbor; our sailors were killed. Your pilots simulate dive-bombing at Soviet ships!"

Nixon tried to explain this was counter to his strict instructions - he will investigate. He sounded defensive. (He later admitted in his *Memoirs* that four Soviet ships were hit.)

Podgorny joined in: "You are murderers of old people, women and children! When are you going to stop this senseless war?"

The Soviet troika had a point: bombing was getting the US nowhere. The spirit of defiance the Vietnamese demonstrated could not be broken. No one in Moscow seriously believed rumors that Kissinger was considering the "final solution," dropping a nuclear bomb on North Vietnam. Probably, the White House wanted to frighten Ho Chi Min into submission, a useless exercise.

In their memoirs, Nixon and Kissinger thought the angry lecturing was "a show." This was partly true. The Soviet troika expressed their true feelings; they were not acting (especially Kosygin and Podgorny). The anger was genuine; it was also born of frustration. Although the Soviet Union sent military supplies and MiG-21 fighter pilots in disguise to engage American F-4 Phantoms, Moscow would never join the hostilities overtly. It chose political means to help both sides conclude the war, but the secret talks in Paris were going nowhere.

The discussion went on for three hours non-stop, with a sullen Nixon listening to bitter accusations. At last, carefully choosing his words, he said, "I don't like diplomatic sentimentalities. We agreed to an unconditional cease-fire, we did everything short of surrender…"

The Russian troika seemed relieved. They believed Nixon: he wished to go down in history as the President who ended the war. They nodded: yes, a cease-fire, resumption of talks in Paris, get rid of Thieu, establish a tripartite government… "Peace will bring you glory, Mr. President," said Brezhnev. "And next year…"

"Next year I may be swimming in the Pacific," Nixon said, wistfully.

"But we do expect your reelection," Brezhnev protested.

It was almost 11:00 p.m. The distasteful portion of the Moscow summit was over. We stood and trailed after Brezhnev to the second floor dining room, to a lavishly laid out table. This eyeball-to-eyeball clash was the only one Brezhnev and Nixon had during their three summits.

The dinner was boisterous; it went well into the night, with drinking toasts and countless jokes, mostly told by the host. Sample: "In the event of nuclear war, everyone should slowly crawl to the cemetery. Why crawl? To prevent panic!" His other story was about a dog participating in a race. It promised the owner it would win. With every lap, the dog fell farther behind, but it kept shouting to the owner not to worry. The dog lost the race and he demanded an explanation. The dog said meekly, "Well, it just didn't work out." The message, Brezhnev explained, was simple: for the two super powers, failure was not an option. This was a rare case of a humorous story relevant to the discussion. Most of them did not relate to the agenda - just fun.

For Nixon, this was the first taste of Brezhnev's sense of humor. He felt at ease, he laughed. Kissinger never showed he heard the stories before; he was not one to keep track of his own funny stories. Brezhnev first tried his humor on Kissinger during the latter's secret trip to Moscow in April. They hit it off. Brezhnev's "anecdotes" were no less amusing than Kissinger's repartees, and helped to tackle complicated issues. To break the tension, Brezhnev would say, "This reminds me of a joke," and tell a story. The one he loved was about a man buying two television sets. When the sales clerk queried why two, he said his mother-in-law promised to give her life for a TV set.

Victor and I ate to our heart's content, translating the stories in turn. I took no more notes. I wondered why Gromyko did not show up at the dinner. True, he was not yet member of the Politburo; perhaps Brezhnev thought that four was a crowd.

We reached town after 1:00 a.m. A sympathetic Alexandrov suggested I get some sleep and do dictation in the morning; another interpreter would take notes.

In the event, they cancelled the morning session due to exhaustion of the participants, most certainly Brezhnev. A lull is always good news for the note taker. I went to the Central Committee offices in the morning, and dictated a 29-page record of the previous day. I delivered the transcript to Alexandrov.

In 2007, a joint publication was released of US and Soviet records of the Moscow summit.[7] I saw that some of the harsher exchanges, which I kept in my memcon (on Thieu, killed Soviet sailors and murdered Vietnamese children), were expunged - by both sides. Perhaps the editors thought that in the original versions the Soviets sounded too aggressive, while Nixon appeared too timid. Thirty-five years after the event tempers did not run as high.

Victor and I bid good-bye to summit colleagues, all top MFA interpreters - Gventsadze, Krokhalev, Zaitsev, Bratchikov and others. They will continue to interpret and take notes at plenary sessions, at experts' meetings and the parallel Kissinger-Gromyko breakout talks. Our job was exclusive Nixon-Brezhnev confidential conversations. Most occurred in Brezhnev's office on the third floor of the Kremlin. A private meeting was scheduled for four o'clock in the afternoon, and another one in the evening. We entered Brezhnev's study a few minutes before the appointed hour. In a good mood before battle, Brezhnev paced the floor, rubbed his hands, and spoke of negotiating tactics.

The battleground, a large rectangular oak table with ten chairs on each side, was almost bare: squat blue vases of cut crystal held an assortment of black, red and blue pencils. Microphones were scattered along the green baize top, to make even low voices audible. In front of each chair were two bottles of *Borjomi*, a Georgian mineral water, one bottle of *Sayani*, a Russian fizzy soft drink, two packs of *Laika* cigarettes, named in honor of the first space-dog launched in 1957, and two matchboxes. A large map of the world occupied half of the wall opposite the four large windows. Two sections of the map had curtains drawn over them (ICBM sites? The Americans never asked, but once Brezhnev told Kissinger it was the "attack plan" against the US).

A tall book cabinet stood against the far wall, but no books were visible - there were green curtains behind the glass. The cabinet was phony: as in a Gothic mystery movie, it swung inwards to reveal a passage to a rest area. A door to the right of the book cabinet led to Brezhnev's private bathroom. Karl Marx and Vladimir Lenin gazed down skeptically from large black and white portraits high on the wall. No interior decorator worked on the room: it was as it appeared to visitors during World War II and earlier at the time of the Russian Tsars, except for the cream-colored wall fabric that now covered the dark wood panels installed in the 1930s.

The heavy door swung open and Nixon and his party entered to smiles and warm handshakes. There were no American interpreters. Victor took his place at the butt of the conference table, and I sat at a miniature square table by the window right behind Brezhnev. It held a black telephone, a flip calendar, a writing set of brown polished granite, a box of paper clips, and very sharp scissors. There was an oversized green bell button of uncertain purpose and a stopwatch. I only needed a referee's whistle to break and resume proceedings at will. Smoke from Brezhnev's cigarette drifted over my head towards the high windows.

This was to be the setting for many private meetings. Apart from Nixon and Brezhnev, the usual participants were Kissinger, Gromyko, Alexandrov, Victor and I. Kornienko and Dobrynin often attended.

Kissinger tried to emulate me taking notes, but could not bear the strain of listening, speaking and writing simultaneously - making a full record was beyond his impressive abilities. At subsequent sessions, he brought in Helmut Sonnenfeldt to prepare the memcon. Later, Peter Rodman took over the job.

The atmosphere was different from plenary sessions. No Politburo colleagues were looking over Brezhnev's shoulder. He was excited: he fingered a cigarette lighter, shifted in his seat and looked around. He reminded me of a racehorse ready to charge down the track at the clang of the bell. As the conversation progressed, he relaxed. Several times he turned to Gromyko on his left for confirmation of a point he was making. He addressed him "Andrei" - they were on first name terms. Three members of our team were "Andrey" (or "Andrei" - spelt the same in Russian): Gromyko, Alexandrov and I. Every time Brezhnev uttered the name, all three looked at him in unison.

Nixon was composed, smiling slightly or looking serious, as appropriate. He was in agreement with much of what Brezhnev was telling him: he nodded slowly. He wished to be seen as a strategist, not concerned with petty details. He said that Brezhnev surely discovered that he did not nitpick. He wanted to project himself as a pragmatist, and repeatedly mentioned his desire to achieve a lasting change in Soviet-American relations.

Brezhnev went for the moral approach. After reading from his talking points, he put them aside and embarked on a lengthy elucidation of "our personal responsibility" and "wishes of the people." He evoked his father, who, he said, dreamed of the day Hitler and other warmongers "were hanged on Mount Everest" for the world to see. "This is the moment for the leaders of both countries," Brezhnev suggested, "to go down in history - the world will be grateful for what they had done." He described his vision of US-Soviet relations; it was optimistic. He reverted to the war theme often.

Nixon nodded. He knew the Great Patriotic War was a sacred theme for the Soviets. He said, "As long as we are around, I have no fear." But madmen like Hitler do come to power; therefore, our agreements have to be as balanced as possible. He accepted that Brezhnev had to sell the results to the Russian military, and he had Congress to deal with. This argument - the specter of hawks back home - was to run through all the US-Soviet summit conferences of the 1970s. On balance, it was more real for Nixon; but Brezhnev was not an entirely free agent: he had to obtain Politburo approval.

We settled into the usual routine. I dictated my notes to a stenographer or typist, made edits to the typed text, had it retyped, proofread and put my signature on the last page. This act was like a personal stamp of quality. The girl secretaries were superb: fast, efficient, almost no typos. This was important. Making corrections on a typewriter took much precious time. I usually did dictation on the seventh floor of the Foreign Ministry, in the Minister's typing pool, or at the Communist Party Central Committee offices in Staraya Ploshad (Old Square). I preferred the latter because they provided free cheese and ham sandwiches and steaming hot tea with sugar and lemon, served in a tall crystal glass in a silver holder. More importantly, there was less bureaucracy in handling documents. Classifying the memcon was the responsibility of the note taker. I usually chose "Secret," which was a notch higher than "For Internal Use," but lower than "Top Secret." The finished memcon was dispatched by the KGB messenger service to the person I served, Leonid Ilyich Brezhnev. (The service still retains its ancient German name – Feldjäger.)

Actually, the negotiation transcripts were delivered to Brezhnev's principal foreign policy assistant, the formidable Andrei Mikhailovitch Alexandrov-Agentov. His double-barreled name was cumbersome, and he dropped the second part. He read the memcons quickly and circulated them to Politburo members and appropriate agencies.

Alexandrov was drafted into the Central Committee apparatus from the Foreign Ministry. During World War II, he was a young attaché at the Soviet Embassy in Stockholm. His diplomatic credentials, powerful brain, propensity for hard work and unobtrusiveness telescoped him into a key position with the General Secretary, equaled only by Minister Gromyko. I went to see him in his wood-paneled office on the sixth floor of the Central Committee building, where we went through Brezhnev's memcons. He asked sharp questions and made small revisions. The buzzer sounded every ten or fifteen minutes, and Alexandrov dived at the green telephone, Brezhnev's direct line. He wrote little notes and dialed other cream-colored secure phones from a battery next to his desk to transmit Brezhnev's instructions to various Ministers, to Gromyko and his deputies.

Alexandrov was an accomplished writer and did the fastest dictation and editing I ever saw. His grasp of intricate foreign policy issues and closeness to the General Secretary ensured for him an unparalleled degree of influence on Soviet foreign policy, guiding it through the minefields of suspicions and ideological obstacles erected by conservatives. Small of stature and agile, he resembled a ferret or a humming-bird. Both polite and brusque with staff, he expected total efficiency. Able to scan complex documents in split seconds, he hated sloppy work - he let loose his biting sense of humor - but was exuberant when seeing a thoughtful and concise memo.

He rarely criticized. I was not involved in the technical experts' discussions, but had a good idea of the main issues. On the second day of the summit, Alexandrov called me about a transcript of a SALT session. He said he was unhappy about lack of precision in missile terminology. Although his tone was mild, I expected him to blow his top. My lame excuse was that we were not shown the secret brief on the subject. He said, "You should have insisted with the military." "What do you mean, insisted?" I said. "They'd say my clearance wasn't high enough." He gave me a hard look. "Never mind, let's correct this" - which he proceeded to do. He told me next time to please check terminology with the Chief of the General Staff or his deputies, whoever was present at Brezhnev's conversations.

If Alexandrov trusted somebody, it was complete trust. One late night, after finishing dictation, I went up to his office to check some passages. He was switching off the lights. He had already sealed his private safe and deposited the keys with security. "Why don't you take the papers along and come back tomorrow morning?" he suggested. I had an unfinished memcon in my briefcase, several classified papers and my notes. The elevator doors opened; we went down. A KGB lieutenant saluted.

I said I'd better drive to Smolenskaya Square to deposit everything with Gromyko's all-night duty officer. Alexandrov gestured in exasperation, "Come, you need some sleep. It's three in the morning. Don't worry, go straight home. Tell the driver to fetch you tomorrow. Just be here at nine." He pointed to one of the two black Volgas with official license plates parked by the curb.

I rode along the deserted streets clutching my briefcase; there was no other record of today's round of Nixon-Brezhnev negotiations. No American interpreter was present, and Kissinger did not take notes. I thought about getting killed in a traffic accident.

The temperamental swings of comrade Alexandrov and his sense of guilt for any personal slight he inflicted were very Russian. For us, he was "Kissinger with a Human Face." His influence extended beyond foreign policy; one might describe him as a hybrid of Henry Kissinger and Bob Haldeman. Kissinger was slow in appreciating the aide's exact role, and mistook his modesty for lack of authority - in his view, a sin of the first order. Alexandrov repaid him by nurturing suspicions in Brezhnev's mind, especially given the intelligence reports reaching the Kremlin of Kissinger's duplicity in conversations with the Chinese.

Hauteur seemed to be Kissinger's first reaction to a new face: it took him the better part of a year before he shook my hand (Brezhnev made a point of shaking hands with everybody in the room). It was odd, since I was one of five or six Russians sitting across from Nixon at the negotiating table. I do not hold a grudge against him for omitting my name in several US-version memcons.

On the second day of the summit, Nixon and Brezhnev addressed SALT. Both realized that clinching a deal would ensure the summit's success, and did their best to negotiate rapidly. Several issues had to be resolved before they could sign the two agreements: an interim freeze of offensive nuclear systems and a permanent treaty renouncing ballistic missile defense of national territories.

For years, the two super powers struggled to get at a workable numerical balance of the countries' strategic nuclear "triad," i.e., nuclear weapons on ICBMs, submarines and heavy bombers. For historical and geographical reasons they were asymmetric. Most of the Russian arsenal was land-based. The US relied on its submarine fleet and long-range bomber aircraft. There were substantial differences in numbers: the US had more warheads, but the throw-weight of Soviet missiles was greater. A nuclear strike from a submarine was less accurate than from a reinforced ICBM silo; communication with a submarine was less reliable. Each side had the capability to deal a deadly nuclear blow, but bringing this capacity to a common denominator was tricky. Missile technology was rapidly developing on both sides, and the asymmetries and numerical imbalances had to be quickly reconciled.

To compound the problem, perceptions of security were different - they stemmed from decades of distrust. How far was one side ahead in ICBMs, subs or bombers? How fast the other side was catching up? How one should deal with technological advance that is tilting the balance? How to set off constraints on offensive arms against defense capabilities? What about verification? Is equilibrium at all possible? Trade-offs had to be fair, preventing any side from gaining unilateral advantage.

For the Russians, there was the "Eastern factor" - China, perceived as a real military threat. The US faced no comparable threat in the Western hemisphere. Besides, it possessed forward-based nuclear weapon systems in Europe which threatened the USSR.

It was a strange sight: two leaders going into technical intricacies without the aid of experts from their SALT delegations, which had been fighting over the issues for years and at that very moment were negotiating the small print a thousand miles away in Helsinki.

Preparations for the Moscow summit were served by a secret "back channel," as it was later called, established between Henry Kissinger and Ambassador Dobrynin. It became the main communication link. The reporting lines extended directly to Nixon and Brezhnev. Designed to aid formal negotiations in Helsinki, the back channel often superseded them. Brezhnev liked the arrangement: it gave him a sense of being secretly in charge. When a complicated item had to be resolved, he would thump a fist against his palm, and tell Gromyko or Dobrynin, "Dump this into the channel." He pronounced it *kanal,* as in "Suez Canal." He expected magic; in many cases, he got it.

The "channel" meant different things to the two sides: it was a secret conduit for the White House, but not so much for the Kremlin. The arrangement put the US decision-making process at a disadvantage. Nixon and Kissinger's foreign policy had a life of its own, circumventing the "bureaucrats," the State Department and other agencies. Both men believed they possessed a singular quality in abundance - diplomatic skills. They did, but skills without professional backup are sterile. Serious preparations require pooling expertise, interagency coordination and boring paperwork. The inability of the White House to strike a proper balance between political decisions and expert backup was a weak spot of the Nixon Presidency in dealings with the USSR. Too often decisions were tailored to White House political requirements.

The Soviet end of the back channel was more democratic. It fed into a network of government departments, in particular, foreign affairs, the military, the intelligence branches and the omnipresent VPK, or Military-Industrial Commission. The latter oversaw a vast sector of the Soviet economy, employing millions of skilled workers, scientists and managers. In many ways, this interagency body had more influence than other ministries combined. All strands joined at the apex, the Communist Party Politburo, which made the final ruling on details of SALT. Throughout the Nixon-Brezhnev summits, the Politburo convened almost daily, with dozens of military and diplomatic experts on hand to explain the American proposals and suggest Soviet responses.

At the time described, arms control negotiations were my charge. As a summit note taker, I followed some exchanges through the channel. I knew from a SALT delegation member (we shared an office on the Ministry's tenth floor) that information from the Brezhnev-Nixon-Kissinger talks regularly reached Soviet negotiators in Helsinki. This gave them a tactical advantage over the US team, which remained in the dark and had to toe a constantly changing party line. It was doubly embarrassing when Ambassador Semyonov spoke to Gerard Smith, a negotiator of great skill and erudition, of certain things the latter was supposed to know from Kissinger, but did not. No wonder Smith was angry with the "Moscow White House party" - Kissinger and three or four aides - who debated SALT behind the Kremlin walls. The Soviet Helsinki team sympathized with Smith, but was unable to help.

The Brezhnev/Nixon discussion of offensive nuclear systems and ABM quickly descended into technicalities difficult to grasp by the uninitiated. An irate Smith said the Moscow summit phase was "somewhat murky...a case of negotiations being too important to be left to the negotiators."[8] The bulk of the American national security leadership was never consulted, though it was usually informed after the fact. The image of an American President discussing the fine differences between ICBM silo volume and missile volume permitted expansion, the arcane definitions of a heavy missile ("heavier than the heaviest of the lightest ones"), was "peculiar, if not dangerous." As a professional, Smith wanted to study the interpreter's notes of Kissinger's Moscow conversations, but there were none. "A Soviet interpreter had been used. I asked if there were memoranda of the conversations. Kissinger said that "eventually" there would be. I never saw them..." I can imagine the fury that the off-hand response provoked in the man charged with the responsibility to reach a nuclear balance with the archenemy.

The charade of discussing the President's reply to Brezhnev's message at a NSC meeting for the benefit of Smith, when the draft reply had been already intimated to Dobrynin, would have made any negotiator apoplectic. In the absence of an American record of US-Soviet exchanges, Smith took it upon himself to write a memo for the file on the discussion at the meeting. It served a historical purpose, and absolved Smith, but it hardly influenced the erratic course of the Nixon-Kissinger heavy-laden tanker traversing the ocean waters without lights. At one session with the Soviets, Kissinger said that Smith was "crying bitterly" but will do what he is told. He turned down Gromyko's suggestion to invite Smith to the Moscow summit. When he agreed to bring the Soviet delegation in the US plane (to save time, not airfares), he suggested leaving Smith behind "if the plane was not big enough." Perhaps he was joking.

In May 1973, Kissinger requested that Semyonov not discuss with Alexis Johnson, the new US negotiator in Geneva, any discrepancies between what the latter said and what Kissinger was telling Moscow. The prospective Secretary of State was conspiring with the Soviets to keep his own negotiator misinformed.

Smith must have felt vindicated when Kissinger found himself at the receiving end. In December 1973, Henry sent an angry telegram to General Alexander Haig, demanding the full report of Nixon's hour-long meeting with Dobrynin. Egyptian President Anwar Sadat, with whom Kissinger was conferring in Cairo, knew about the meeting from the Soviets, but Kissinger "was flying blind without it." Haig responded that Nixon simply urged continuous cooperation in a Middle East settlement and using Soviet influence with Syria regarding Israeli POWs. No memcon was found.[9]

Failure to make a written record was unthinkable in the Soviet foreign policy apparatus. Writing down a conversation was akin to brushing your teeth or putting on a clean shirt in the morning. This rule was never bent; lack of time was no excuse.

Disconnect between the back channel and US negotiators on the ground led to confusion over a number of issues. One was the meaning of "modernization" of ballistic missiles and launchers, permitted under the interim agreement. Both sides tried to block technological advance of the opponent while leaving own options open. The US was in the lead, but the USSR was steadily catching up. The issue of ICBM "silo dimensions" was an example of complexity that strained the technical knowledge of Nixon and Brezhnev, and even of Kissinger.

Since the number of fixed underground ballistic missile launchers was to be frozen, the US strove to prevent the Soviet Union from building larger missiles that might fit in existing silos. It felt particular concern about the mammoth SS-9 "Satan", a heavy missile of great destructive power. With a range of 10,000 miles and a throw weight of almost nine tons, it surpassed anything the US possessed at the time. Its accuracy made any plans to harden American ICBM silos a meaningless enterprise. The advanced model, SS-18, would be even deadlier. This was enough reason for the US wishing to prevent replacement of light ICBMs by heavy ones in the silos. This called for a clear dividing line between light and significantly bigger missiles.

The understanding reached meant that modernization should not be significant. Understandably, Kissinger insisted on specifying the meaning of "significant." A 10 to 15 percent increase of silo dimensions looked all right to him: he took it to mean diameter. Possibly, at an early stage in the SALT delegation talks in Helsinki and Vienna, the Russian term was erroneously translated as "dimensions" rather than "volume." Kissinger was perhaps unaware that increasing the silo's diameter by 15 percent might produce a 32 percent increase in its volume, thus permitting the Soviets to fit in a much larger missile. Besides, a silo could be deepened for a longer missile. While spy satellites could measure silo diameter, they are unable to check silo depth. Kissinger was worried lest the Soviets were building a thin long missile to reach deep down. He joked with Gromyko, "What if you strike oil down there?"

The diameter/depth/volume problem was thoroughly (and confusingly) debated for several years after the 1972 summit. Neither Kissinger nor Gromyko were military experts or mathematicians. All the same, they waded bravely into correlations between diameter and volume, depth and volume, and whether "Pi r squared" was applicable. Kornienko, with his background in natural sciences, tried to steer the discussion into geometrical bounds.

Translating was difficult; writing it down was even more. I called on my reserve of high school math to produce sensible language (I remembered the first few digits of Pi - 3.1415926..., but that did not help). The declassified US memcon is a lengthy and precise record of the discussion.[10] My version was laconic: "After prolonged discussion of the permissible increase of an ICBM silo dimensions, H. Kissinger and A.A. Gromyko arrived at a common understanding that the silo diameter or depth could not be increased by more than 15 percent, so that the new silo volume would not exceed 32 percent of the original volume." (In January 1976, Brezhnev and President Ford finalized the understanding.)

In Moscow in 1972, the confusing discussion took hours, including the definition of a heavy missile and the numbers of advanced submarines the parties were permitted to have.

Brezhnev was visibly tired. He showed his annoyance; he doodled and drew pictures of silos. When Kissinger interjected, trying to be helpful, he raised his voice: "Be quiet!" To relax, he launched into emotional life stories. He would recount his recent trip across Siberia, or muse on harvest prospects in the Ukraine or Kazakhstan. He would tell a joke in Ukrainian. Victor confessed he did not understand all the words, so Brezhnev translated it into Russian.

Nixon would patiently listen, nod, and then gently steer the General Secretary back to the issues (Kissinger did this with less success). Time was becoming a problem. Details of SALT required night discussions. Nixon and Brezhnev delegated them to aides. Supported by Helmut Sonnenfeldt and Bill Hyland, Kissinger faced Smirnov, Gromyko and Dobrynin. For all his erudition in weapon systems, Kissinger was no equal to Leonid Vasilievitch Smirnov, the custodian of the Soviet military industry. The Chairman of the Military-Industrial Commission did not laugh at Kissinger's jokes; this upset Henry and made him jumpy. Smirnov's authority was considerable. When Kissinger, in support of his understanding of the silo/missile and dimension/volume conundrum evoked Brezhnev's casual agreement with Nixon, Smirnov was brusque. He said there was no agreement to change the Soviet position, period; he spoke to comrade Brezhnev. This meant he overruled the General Secretary. Kissinger was so mad that he kept interrupting Smirnov and all but accusing him of tampering with the Brezhnev/Nixon understanding. Smirnov did not blink.

Kissinger felt aversion to Smirnov – here was the principal foe. Smirnov and the thousands of scientists and engineers perfected the Soviet war machine to such a degree that the United States renounced the idea of military superiority and accepted parity. In the final count, they played a central role in negotiations. But Kissinger found a way to take revenge. He quoted secret characteristics of Soviet weapon systems. This made Smirnov uncomfortable: he was not used to hearing this from a foreigner.

One sympathized with Kissinger: he battled on several fronts. In a befuddling night discussion, he overturned the position of the US SALT delegation in Helsinki, and even of General Haig in Washington (he explained that Haig was not familiar with all the details). The Soviets were better organized - they stuck to one consolidated position. It was past midnight, when an ironic Smirnov wished Kissinger "sweet dreams" after attending *Swan Lake* at the Bolshoi - dreams of swans, not evil forces, he added. To Kissinger's chagrin, he had to miss the ballet performance.

The negotiators in Helsinki, continuously instructed by the leaders sitting in Moscow, managed to resolve the fine print just in time for the signing ceremony in the Kremlin. The three aircraft that transported the US and Soviet delegations from Helsinki saw scenes of wracked nerves from typing the agreements on special paper and unbridled merriment.

The interim freeze set numerical limits. Nixon accepted a larger number of Russian ICBM launchers (1,618 against 1,054). Not publicly admitted, this was compensation for American forward-based nuclear systems in Europe in proximity to Soviet borders. The sides undertook to refrain from deliberately concealing the silos from spy satellites. The deal set ceilings for modern nuclear submarines: 710 launchers on 44 Trident subs for the US, and 950 launchers for the USSR on 62 Typhoon class subs. The numbers for heavy bombers (525 for the US and 140 for the USSR) were to be renegotiated later. The agreement was to run for five years, with talks continuing towards more complete measures.

All issues were resolved, but it was debatable to whose satisfaction. The US had no plans of building more launchers anyway. Brezhnev accepted the US lead in the number of warheads. He had reason to expect (without articulating this) that the superior throw-weight of Soviet missiles and development of MIRVs would rectify this imbalance in the future. The US superiority in strategic bombers was offset by the time they took to deliver nuclear bombs to the target - it takes about thirty minutes for an ICBM. In essence, the treaty ratified the actual state of the strategic arsenals of both countries.

They did not publish the Protocol to the Interim Agreement (with the figures) in the Soviet Union. The culture of secrecy was hard to shed. Probably the leadership did not wish to scare the population by publicizing the American arsenal.

The second SALT agreement, on anti-ballistic missiles, restricted the deployment of ABM systems to two areas in each country - around the capital city and around the ICBM site, with 100 interceptors for each site. It prohibited nationwide or regional homeland defense. The ABM treaty was probably more important because it ratified a vital strategic concept. The discussions in Moscow brought me back to 1967, when the controversial subject was first broached to the Soviets.

Victor and I accompanied Prime Minister Alexei Kosygin to New York for the special session of the UN General Assembly devoted to the aftermath of the Six-Day War in the Middle East. After delivering his speech in support of the Arab cause, Kosygin accepted President Johnson's invitation to meet in the home of the Glassboro State College President.

It was here that Defense Secretary Robert McNamara tried to win Kosygin over to the concept of curbing anti-missile defense. His argument carried logic: if a country obtains protection from nuclear attack, the adversary will be prompted to devise ways of penetrating it. New protective shields will become the destabilizing drivers of the nuclear arms race, feeding a vicious circle.

However, Kosygin saw the US proposal as weakening Soviet defense capabilities. My impression was that intellectually he accepted McNamara's point, but was held back by a psychological difficulty. Russia had a long history of foreign invasions. The notion of strong defense, from ancient Siberian log stockades to today's anti-ballistic missiles, was accepted wisdom. I listened to the debate sitting near the open door: squeezing a chair inside would have blocked the waiters' passage. The dining room was small and stuffy and this added to the heat of the debate. LBJ made occasional remarks to support McNamara, but Kosygin insisted: "Offensive weapons are immoral."

One could see the pros of the US proposition, but also the cons: the US was dodging the problem of offensive weapons, an area where it enjoyed a massive advantage. In contrast, the USSR was ahead in defensive missile systems, including a vast civil defense network of bomb shelters and emergency communications; it was not prepared to renounce all this.

Kosygin left Glassboro unconvinced. Back home, he consulted with Russian scientists. One of the vocal proponents of a curb on ABM defense was Andrei Sakharov, father of the Soviet H-bomb. In a few months, Kosygin was exchanging letters with LBJ on launching negotiations on both defensive and offensive strategic weapons - they began in 1969.

Nixon and Brezhnev discussed the Middle East, a "festering sore," as Nixon put it.

Brezhnev warned Nixon of the dangers: anything can erupt in an area where a million troops are concentrated. He proposed joint efforts; the simmering conflict was dragging Russia and the US into unnecessary confrontation. This should be avoided, if the two super powers were serious about building a stable relationship.

Nixon explained he was not compelled by the political situation in the US (he meant the Jewish lobby). On the other hand, his ability to influence the Israelis was very limited, particularly since they had been so successful in their recent wars. (Brezhnev frowned.) Nixon suggested that verbal broadsides should end, and the US and the USSR bring the sides in the conflict together. He expected that by September, when the party conventions were over in the US, both countries can "get to the nut-cutting part of the problem." This vernacular caused a ripple. Nixon wondered whether the expression could be translated into Russian. With a faint grin, Victor explained the connotation to Brezhnev. (I did not include "nut-cutting" in the final transcript. I usually dropped earthy language in my note taking – it carried no political significance. I saw it in the US version of the memcon.)

Economic issues took much time. Brezhnev considered them important, but "technical," which meant substandard in comparison with "political" issues. He was happy to let Kosygin handle them, especially the sensitive issue of Lend-Lease.

Kosygin took over. He would not relapse into sentimental life stories. For Nixon, he was a complete change from Brezhnev, and an unpleasant one. Kosygin knew his brief, and was in command of all details. When Nixon was a junior staffer in the Office of Price Administration in Washington, Kosygin dealt with Lend-Lease as Vice-Chairman of the Council of Peoples' Commissars, the then Soviet government. His American counterpart was FDR's Harry Hopkins.

The problem of Lend-Lease plagued the two countries' relations for years. The original arrangement was that US military supplies for Russia remaining at the end of World War II would be returned or compensated. All in all the USSR received around $11 billion in military equipment and food during the war (the UK received $31 billion). It was partly repaid. The US quoted the current debt as around $1.3 billion, but Nixon proposed repaying $951 million including $200 million interest.

Kosygin suggested repaying $300 million; the US charged the UK two percent interest over fifty years, he said. Podgorny suddenly chimed in, saying that the Soviet side "was prepared to raise the interest significantly." Kosygin gave him a murderous glance. He insisted that the USSR should enjoy the same terms as the UK, the full debt to be settled by 2001. "Ah, by 2001 you and I will be dead," Nixon murmured.

The discussion veered into areas of history and morality. "How much one can make on spilt Russian blood?" Kosygin asked. What about the delays in opening the second front in Europe and the huge losses the Red Army and civilians suffered? Nixon said he was aware of Soviet sacrifices; he was willing to pare the figure, but he pleaded for "a nominal sum" to quell the hawks in Congress. This was the essence of his position. The sum made no dent in the US budget - much larger loans were cancelled before, but he had to look back at critics at home. The problem was bigger than repayment of a debt and more important than the sum it involved. Nixon and Kissinger warned the Soviet leadership that US-Soviet economic relations hinged on resolving Lend-Lease - it was too political for Congress to ignore. It was an obstacle for the President to recommending that Congress grant most-favored nation (MFN) status to the USSR.

With help from aide Peter Flanigan and Secretary of State Rogers, Nixon tried to parry Kosygin's assault; it did not help. The latter addressed the Secretary several times as "Comrade Rogers" - as if a member of his staff who was not familiar enough with the subject.

Nixon suggested splitting the difference between the US and Soviet figures. They bargained on debt composition: military goods, naval vessels, merchant ships, cranes... Both men felt awkward: the debate was degenerating into an Oriental-bazaar haggle. At Nixon's reference to "Syrian rug merchants," Kosygin smiled for the first time. However, they were unable to resolve the Lend-Lease problem.

When Kissinger came to Moscow in September, Brezhnev took over. He felt the issue was close to resolution; he would take credit as a better negotiator than Kosygin. It was not easy: Kissinger patiently explained about postponements and the lump sum, which the Americans wanted. Brezhnev offered $650 million, but Kissinger turned it down, suggesting $750 million. At the wave of a hand, partly in jest, Brezhnev raised it to $651 million. Kissinger grinned: without Politburo authority? He was now versed in Soviet decision-making: he knew Brezhnev would need backing. He mused that the figures now resembled ICBM and SLBM numbers.

Brezhnev was impatient; after six hours of negotiation, he was losing face. He insisted that Kissinger get in touch with the President. He hinted that Henry was acting on his own. Time and again, he warned he would complain to Nixon, and did in all naiveté - without result.

Kissinger employed a diplomatic trick: he wrote to Haig requesting a flash cable to himself (he even drafted it) confirming that $650 million was totally unacceptable; $750 million was the absolute minimum.[11] With a straight face, he reported to Brezhnev the stern reply he received from Washington (though he had a fallback position). To Brezhnev's relief, he finally agreed to $725 million. Kissinger confessed later that his ignorance of the subject helped him negotiate. He was a good student of Gromyko: never give up the final fallback position (it was $700 million). He won by attrition.

Nixon hosted a dinner at Spaso House, the US Ambassador's residence, an ancient mansion in Moscow's downtown area. Bill Krimer sat behind Nixon and Brezhnev to handle interpretation. As guests, Victor and I enjoyed the food and wine. We were not worried about a missing memcon; Brezhnev would not venture into deep waters while eating. From Bill's brief account, we were right: it was mostly table talk bordering on gossip. Nixon was interested in personalities: he asked about Tito, Gomulka, and Mao Tse-tung and Chou En-lai. Brezhnev avoided harsh appraisals, but was sardonic about Mao: "A living God." Nixon evoked the Great Alliance of World War II and direct contacts between Roosevelt, Churchill and Stalin, and said he and Brezhnev should stay in touch through the private channel. Brezhnev supported this wholeheartedly.

After dinner, the guests listened to Van Cliburn's piano recital. We did not stay - we had to rush to the signing ceremony. The full Soviet leadership and the US party met around 11:00 p.m. in St. Vladimir hall of the Kremlin to sign the SALT treaties. Victor and I stood behind Nixon and Brezhnev. They signed the documents to applause. Champagne was served.

Before retiring at 2:00 a.m., Nixon conferred with Kissinger and Haldeman, and placed long-distance calls to Bebe Rebozo and Chuck Colson, his legal counsel.

A long working day means a long working night for the note taker. I took a Kremlin pool car to the Party Central Committee nearby. I dictated to a secretary from a thick pad of notes for three hours, checked the typewritten pages and made some edits. The girl was top Central Committee class: not a single typo in the twenty-four double spaced pages. I signed the record on the last page, opposite my name. I did not indicate my official position in the tradition of internal government memos, and put a "Secret" caption in the top right corner of the first page. I changed it to "Top Secret" - dramatize! This will be the most sought after document in the Soviet Union tomorrow morning, especially in the Politburo. I looked at my wristwatch; it was just past 4:00 a.m. A friend from the KGB Ninth Directorate (leaders' protection and logistics) told me later that Nixon took a night stroll in the Kremlin grounds at that very hour. He said a few warm words to a surprised soldier of the Kremlin Regiment. No interpreter was around.

Dawn was breaking. The black Volga sped me home on Moscow's north side.

The substantive part of the summit was over. In a historic first, Nixon and Brezhnev signed the Basic Principles of Relations, which included "equal security" and "equality." In terms of Russia's world standing, little better could be desired. The summit produced other groundbreaking agreements - in space cooperation, environment and health. John Warner, Secretary of the Navy, and Admiral Sergei Gorshkov, Commander of the Soviet Navy, signed a document "On the Prevention of Incidents on and over the Sea." It dispensed with low-level brinkmanship by gung-ho bomber pilots who made simulated diving attacks on each other's surface ships. Commands were issued to US and Russian submarine captains to stop tracking each other at close distances - there were several cases of minor underwater collisions.

The tone of Soviet press comments mellowed. Sugary documentaries ran in movie theaters and on TV about the Nixon visit, as if he was a leader of a neighboring Socialist country.

At the final plenary session, Nixon said he wished to invite the Russian troika - Brezhnev, Kosygin and Podgorny - to visit the US in 1973. Brezhnev thanked the President a bit too profusely. Kosygin and Podgorny did not respond: it was clear they would miss the next summit due to previous engagements.

I felt sorry for Kosygin. I enjoyed working with him on trips to India, Pakistan and the US. An unassuming person, he had a commanding presence. In 1966, he mediated between Lalbahadur Shastri and Ayub Khan at the Tashkent conference, which ended the war between India and Pakistan. The night the conference concluded, Shastri suffered a fatal heart attack. Kosygin arranged a dignified return of his body to Delhi and convinced Indira Gandhi that it was not a Pakistani assassination conspiracy. Victor and I accompanied him to the pyre at the Jamuna river burning *ghats,* next to the concrete slabs where the bodies of Mahatma Gandhi and Nehru were immolated years before.

I appreciated Kosygin's understanding of the interpreter's job, and his indifference to creature comforts. There was a memorable episode during a fleeting visit to Lahore. Late at night in the Governor's palace, I washed my socks in the huge bath that dated back to the Sepoy Mutiny — we were leaving Lahore early next morning. This was unwise: as I rinsed them, one disappeared down the drain. Nobody had an extra pair (we left our bags in the aircraft). Misha, Kosygin's burly good-natured bodyguard, brought me a black silk pair: "I took them from the boss's overnight bag, he wasn't looking." Next morning in the car, Kosygin stared at my ankles but didn't say anything. I returned the socks in the afternoon, after laundering them at the Embassy.

Kosygin suffered a political setback in 1967: he approved Stalin's daughter Svetlana's travel to India with the ashes of her partner Brajesh Singh, a Moscow publishing house translator. On the eve of her return flight home, she went to the American Embassy nearby to ask for asylum. Several years later I stayed in the same studio in our Delhi Embassy residential compound. A *choukidar* at the gate remembered the *memsaab* ordering a taxi.

Nixon's program in the USSR was not all work. He visited a local church and a farmers market. He reminisced about his 1959 tour of Moscow; his advice to American visitors was to see a vegetable market where, he claimed, the Russian spirit lived on. He took Pat to a Baptist prayer house. After the gilded opulence and burning incense of Russian Orthodox churches, it resembled a bare municipal council hall. Members of the congregation were few and did not look surprised. According to a Secret Service agent, "There were a lot of deacons packing hardware."

The Bolshoi ballet performance of Tchaikovsky's *Swan Lake* was, as always, enchanting. Nixon held his wife's hand. Tatyana and I sat behind them in the Imperial Box. I told her I will hold a ballerina's hand later - she chuckled. (I changed my mind after Nixon went behind stage: the exhausted ballerinas looked like sweaty construction workers.)

Just before the curtain went up a young woman in the pit stood up and shouted, "Freedom to Vietnam!" I peered down over Nixon's shoulder. Two young men in business suits escorted the woman to the exit. She turned out to be the wife of an Italian leftist paper correspondent. For the security men, it was like a nuclear bomb going off. Nixon did not flinch; he was used to heckling. He did not ask me what was going on. I did not volunteer an explanation: "Vietnam" sounds the same in any language. For the Soviet audience, the lonely cry of defiance echoed its bewilderment over the Kremlin's momentous policy shift: it stabbed the conscience of many. The lights went on again. Podgorny rose from his seat and applauded; the audience joined in. After momentary hesitation, Nixon rose and waved. This was the only incident that marred his trip. They never heckled him again in the USSR.

During the second act, Nixon suddenly turned to me, pointed his finger at the stage and said something that sounded like "yorrie." I had no idea what he meant. He repeated, "Yorrie, yorrie!" I was mystified, but faked comprehension. In the interval, I told Victor about it. He broke down laughing. He explained that at the start of the first act, he pointed out a dancer friend of his to Nixon. His name was Yuri.

WIRETAPPING AND LEAKS

Sitting a few feet away from the Soviet Union's most dominant person, I waited for the screeching sound of an automatic rewind of a hidden tape-recorder. I was concerned about the curious matter of the "Kremlin tapes."

On the first morning of the summit, Brezhnev's secretary Vika, a plump vivacious blonde in her late thirties, told me that in view of the event's importance the full-fledged delegation sessions (not the one-on-one meetings, she stressed) would be secretly recorded on tape. To provide a full transcript for the interpreters to check against, a backup, she said. This was the first time in my practice that this method was employed, possibly to emulate the SALT negotiations.

SALT was tape recorded by both sides from the very beginning in 1969 in Helsinki; the practice continued in Vienna and Geneva. The reason was the sensitive and complex subject matter. Neither side referred to wiretapping, though both were aware of it, a gentleman's agreement by mutual silent consent. Every night, delegation women translators transcribed the miles of tape running silently in the shoulder holsters of the interpreters. The taped records were essential for avoiding misunderstanding or missing important technical points. Each side could safely refer back to the exact language used by the other side at a previous meeting, ask for additional explanations or respond to questions. This assured accurate reporting to Moscow. Though cumbersome, the process provided the parties with a reliable picture of country positions. SALT was the most extensively recorded negotiation in history.

Parallel to taping, the interpreters took notes so they could later edit the full text, dropping irrelevant passages. The material was assembled into lengthy transcripts called "protocols." At the morning staff meeting of the Soviet delegation, the protocol was read aloud. The ensuing discussion helped prepare for the next round with the US delegation.

Pyotr, an interpreter new to the procedure, fell for a practical joke. The old timers warned him not to drop a single word from the protocol. At next morning's staff meeting, Ambassador Semyonov invited the interpreter to read out the text. Pyotr read out, slowly:

"Memorandum of conversation between V.S. Semyonov and G. Smith, Head of US delegation. Permanent Mission of the USSR in Geneva.
V. Semyonov: Before we begin, Mr. Smith, could I offer a drink of your liking?
G. Smith: With pleasure, Ambassador. Do you have bourbon?"

After the laughter died down, rosy-faced Semyonov remarked that there was no need for note takers "to go into such detail."

The taped version of the first Nixon vs. Soviet troika plenary session did not help; on the contrary, it slowed down memcon preparation. The typed Russian transcript put at our disposal the same evening was a small volume: 150 pages, double-spaced. Victor and I gave up after reading the first dozen pages. It was drivel. It contained everything: passages read out by Brezhnev from his brief, interjections from his colleagues, and whispered directions to the men's room. Here is one history-making passage.

"L.I. Brezhnev: We should have some *pirozhki* (stuffed pies) and tea. Could somebody tell them to bring food? I've been pressing this button but no one's coming."

At that moment, everybody looked at me. As the junior member of the Soviet team, I went to enquire. The same happened in Zavidovo the following year when Brezhnev ordered the elusive *pirozhki*. He pressed the bell - nothing happened. He told me to go and look for the wayward steward. This caused a three-minute break in my record, which I had to reconstruct later with Alexandrov's help. I did not include the *pirozhki* incidents in the memcons.

We told the Kremlin communications people the tapes were raw and the transcript useless. That night, we dictated seventy-five pages without using a single passage from the recording.

Why should a discussion in the Kremlin be recorded by a machine was anybody's guess. There was no permanent recording system in Brezhnev's office - he had no plans of publishing a thousand-page memoir. I doubt if Politburo colleagues longed to check on his handling of the negotiations. By the early 1970s, Brezhnev grip on power was near absolute. It grew along with his conviction that he could out-negotiate any foreign leader single-handedly. The taping may have had this objective in mind: to demonstrate his debating skills. The effect could have been the opposite. This was the major reason, I believe, for shutting the system down. As far as I know, no more Soviet tape recordings were made of his conversations with Nixon and Kissinger or Gerald Ford and Jimmy Carter.

Brezhnev was comfortable with memcons produced by our team: they were clear, logically constructed and reader-friendly. More importantly for Brezhnev, the coherent transcript was proof of his prowess as a negotiator. I am sure he was grateful we omitted clumsy turns of phrase and most of his heavy jokes. He felt pride in his newly found role, and gladly circulated the memcons to his Politburo comrades. As for government agencies that followed up, they preferred our ordered memcon to a "complete and un-abridged" one, where narration would go round in circles and obscure sub-stantive points.

There is no certainty that KGB listening devices did not record pri-vate conversations of the American team. Kissinger joked about this with Gromyko, pointing to a ceiling chandelier in the Kremlin. A diplomat expects any premises to be bugged, and no running water faucet or blaring radio can drown out voices completely. Technology to clean up background interference is continuously improved.

Nixon and his closest aides were not particularly fond of the opulence of the Kremlin - it was like living in a museum, among floor vases, Bokhara rugs and old master paintings. More importantly, the President and his National Security Adviser took seriously the specter of wiretapping bugs. Ever cau-tious, they conferred in the back-up Lincoln communications vehicle parked in the courtyard of their Kremlin residence. The sight was eerie: two figures huddled behind the bulletproof windows, talking animatedly and inaudibly, out of reach of Russian voice interceptors. Sometimes Bob Haldeman went to sit in the car, probably to dictate his daily diary.

A Secret Service agent told me the black limousine was the remodeled Lincoln Continental convertible in which John F. Kennedy was shot in Dallas in 1963. It now had titanium armor, bulletproof glass, and run-flat tires with aluminum rims inside. A permanent hardtop replaced the bubble top. It must have weighed several tons, which was comparable to the ZIL-114. I inspected the car; it looked brand new. This was now the safest vehicle parked in the safest place on Earth.

The scene in the Lincoln triggered a recollection about Premier Kosygin five years before in his Claridge's suite in London. The topic he discussed with Ambassador Smirnovsky was confidential; I pointed a warning finger at the ceiling. Kosygin dismissed my suspicions, "It's not worth the tape they might be recording on." The remark taught me about different perspectives on sensitive information.

At some point, we suspected that the US team electronically recorded Brezhnev's conversations with Nixon and Kissinger. No cast-iron evidence, no bulging breast pockets, but some signs were there: a briefcase placed in proximity to the speakers, a flower vase on the mantelpiece (in American premises). This could be expected, judging by the importance the White House accorded to the first super power summit on strategic weaponry.

My suspicions grew with the publication of Nixon and Kissinger's memoirs, which contained extensive quotes from private discussions with Soviet leaders. My research at the US National Archives and Records Administration (NARA) turned suspicions into conviction. The publication in 2011-2013 of Soviet-related documentation in the Foreign Relations of the United States series brought final certainty. The series is an impressive and highly useful archival collection. Most released documents carry the caption "Top Secret/Sensitive/Exclusively Eyes Only." The US classification grades are ingenious. They vary: "Exclusively eyes only" or "Top secret sensitive absolutely eyes only." In addition, "Retain no file copy, destroy all tapes," and even "Destroy all residues." They are less frenzied in the Soviet system: "For Internal Use," "Secret," "Top secret" and "Special importance."

It was clear that no human hand could have written down such detail of private conversations. The US memcons are extraordinarily exhaustive; as a trained note taker, I had no doubt about their electronic origin. The contrast with Russian memcons was striking: the latter were clipped, businesslike, to the point. The US version of the same meeting reminded one of a long

Chekhov play, with chitchat, asides, and theatrical interjections: "ah," "oh," "well" and "no-no." Friends who taped the SALT negotiations corroborated my conclusion: there was no way so much detail could have appeared in the US-version memcons without recording devices.

Comparing US transcripts with my memcons, I saw a pattern. If the venue was the US (Camp David, Oval Office, San Clemente) or a third country (e.g., Kissinger's suite at the Intercontinental Hotel in Geneva) the probability of taping was high. A taping system was easily installed. Taping was also likely if the meeting occurred in the Kremlin, Yalta or Zavidovo, but only if several US team members were present. At the dacha in Novo Ogarevo Nixon deliberately waited for NSC staff to arrive before speaking - they must have brought the tape recorder.

The odds of taping were low when Nixon or Kissinger conferred with Brezhnev alone, with only the Soviet interpreter present. The idea of them carrying a concealed tape recorder is preposterous. The risk of an embarrassing exposure will put off even the steely nerved. Who did the taping? My guess is Peter Rodman or Helmut Sonnenfeldt. It might have been Richard Campbell, A. Denis Clift, Winston Lord, Philip Odeen or Jan Lodal; probably Alex Akalovsky or Bill Krimer at a later stage, after Nixon, when American interpreters were admitted to sensitive conversations.

In private meetings, I saw Kissinger taking occasional notes. He was not a professional note taker. He could write down the main points; on the rest, he relied on his prodigious memory, which was not absolute. In a memcon transcribed from his notes, he refers to "an anecdote about the sex life of older men" told by Brezhnev.[12] He had not the dexterity to write it down fully. Of course, it was immaterial to the issue discussed. He did not take notes during a sensitive discussion Nixon had with Brezhnev in San Clemente in 1973 on China (I was the fourth participant, as interpreter/note taker), but there is an extensive US account unquestionably transcribed from a recording.

Some conversations were not taped, for example, the private breakfast meeting Nixon had with Podgorny in Paris in April 1974. The two Americans present were Brent Scowcroft and Alexander Haig - they prepared a short memo for the file. My memcon (I translated and took notes) is much longer and is the only full transcript.

Peter Rodman was my usual counterpart in note taking. He sat opposite me closer to the end of the table. We wrote furiously and at rare moments stretched almost in unison. I told him I wished we could compare our memcons at some point, when they were declassified. A good diplomat, he was evasive. I expected the texts to be almost mirror copies. I was wrong: the memcons were not similar.

I compared my transcript of the Kissinger - Gromyko meeting in Geneva on 16-17 February 1975, with Peter's version. He took notes. I did both: translated and took notes. His record is so detailed it reads like a movie script, with jokes and facial expressions mentioned in brackets. This was not possible without a recording device. Peter transcribed the dinner conversation, where we both relaxed taking no notes, because Gromyko spoke English and dispensed with translation.

On July 1, 1974, Brezhnev had a brief conversation with Kissinger in the Vnukovo-2 Airport VIP lounge, followed by a private word with Gromyko. This is the US transcript:[13]

"Brezhnev: We fixed up the house especially for you there [in Zavidovo]. It has six missiles under it.
Kissinger: I knew you were doing something there. Do the missiles have three or six warheads?
Brezhnev: Twenty! They are for the wild boars. (To Gromyko) How should we plan for our meeting this afternoon?
Gromyko: Well, I need to go to the dentist.
Brezhnev: How about 4 o'clock?
Gromyko: I could do that.
Brezhnev: (To the Secretary) Crimea is a very good place. I don't understand why you go to Acapulco.
Gromyko: Yes, and there are no sharks in the Crimea.
Brezhnev then talked privately to Gromyko and said there should be a short meeting in the Ministry of Defense at 2:30 p.m. Kosygin,

Podgorny, Grechko, Andropov, Ustinov and Gromyko should be there. Then at 3 o'clock, there would be a Politburo meeting. The group left the room at 1:45 p.m."

Did Sonnenfeldt record this? Hardly Ambassador Stoessel or Scowcroft. The Americans were not party to Soviet internal scheduling. None spoke enough Russian to write it all down. I know from Oleg Krokhalev, who translated the conversation, that the Soviet memcon was short, the essentials. Someone from the US team contributed to history by making the recording.

Not every meeting was taped. Take the memcons dictated by Kissinger after his many lunches with Dobrynin, and forwarded to Nixon. They are succinct and deal with essentials. If he tape-recorded the conversations, they would have run into dozens of pages. Kissinger also knew that shrewd Dobrynin would not appreciate a tape recorder. A single slip would disrupt the two men's close confidential relationship. Of course, Dobrynin expected that his almost daily telephone conversations with Kissinger were recorded - this was sensible. It was not done in Moscow: if Gromyko spoke on the phone with Kissinger, an aide listened in (if it was business) and took notes.

Some US memcons were prepared in the traditional way by experienced note takers. For example, the memo by Harold H. Saunders of the NSC staff of a meeting between Gromyko and Kissinger on June 23, 1973, was similar to a terse Soviet memcon. This would become practice under President Carter.

Once we witnessed a narrow escape. This happened during one of Kissinger's sessions with Brezhnev in the Kremlin. The General Secretary announced a short break. He rose and paced the room, talking to our team. Jan Lodal entered; Kissinger sent for him since SALT was the next agenda item. Brezhnev shook Lodal's hand, tousled his hair and advised a haircut. He walked over to Peter Rodman's chair, grabbed his briefcase and proceeded to the rest area through a door behind his desk. Peter dashed after him. With a mischievous grin, Brezhnev turned and walked back. Peter retrieved the briefcase and went back to his seat. His face was ashen; then flushed. I do not know whether it was an innocent prank or Brezhnev knew about the tape recorder.

I doubt he did. They never searched or x-rayed briefcases of people entering Brezhnev's study, or for that matter, the Kremlin compound. If your name was on the Spassky (The Savior) Gate guest list, it was free passage all the way.

I did not realize that one of Peter's chief tasks was collecting material for Kissinger's memoirs. He was a former student of his and a close confidant: many of the messages from the White House bore the words, "Please deliver in sealed envelope eyes only to Peter Rodman for H. A. Kissinger." "The unsung hero" of his tenure as Secretary of State - this was Kissinger's tribute to Peter, who transcribed the light exchanges of the summit years – they found their place in the three-volume recollections.

Even if the Soviets knew about the taping, they would not raise it with Americans, because among gentlemen tape-recording, like spying, would not be admitted. Both sides followed the best policy: "Don't ask, don't tell." On the plus side, the idyllic era of détente had the best coverage possible. For historical reasons, taping conversations with the Russians now seems vindicated. On the other side, bringing surreptitiously a tape recorder into a private meeting without the knowledge and agreement of the other side is a serious step, which raises the question of trust, a precious commodity in interpersonal relations. Such instances are extremely rare. In 2014, President Putin revealed that NATO Secretary-General Anders Fogh Rasmussen secretly recorded their private conversation in 2002, when he was Danish Prime Minister. Rasmussen denied the charge, but a Danish journalist who provided the mike corroborated it.

Brezhnev made a distinction between what was fit or unfit for writing down. I often failed to see his point. During a lull in negotiations, he demonstrated to Kissinger the "niceties of diplomatic language," which, he claimed, is chiefly about mutual admiration. He impersonated a telephone conversation with Gromyko about his wife Lydia's health. I laid down my pen, but Peter Rodman kept writing - it was too late to warn him. An irritated Brezhnev suddenly turned to Kissinger, "What is he writing this for?" Peter stopped. Kissinger's lame explanation was that his subordinate was in training.

I did not include this episode in my memcon, but it is there in the US version. It happened again the following year: Brezhnev warned Peter it was not necessary to write down what he was saying. Peter obeyed, but the exact conversation was later reproduced in full. Brezhnev was annoyed that Sonnenfeldt continued taking notes when Brezhnev stressed his words were "very private." He refused to accept assurances that it will not leave the White House - he knew it was impossible. We both laid down our pens. But again, the full version of the conversation was to appear in the US Foreign Relations series. Such instances ran into dozens.

Kissinger and Nixon thought their private conversations in Moscow were wiretapped. The suspicions were almost Freudian: "Pervasive bugging...by Soviets who were curiously unsubtle in this regard." Nixon quoted the story of his aide asking for an apple: in ten minutes, a Kremlin maid brought a bowl of apples.[14] Jokes like this abound in second-rate spy novels. In July 1974, Kissinger had a telephone conversation with Dobrynin about his impending trip to the USSR. He audaciously suggested that the Ambassador warn his people in Moscow to get all the recording equipment ready.[15] Dobrynin reacted good-naturedly and said all right.

On August 21 2013, the Nixon Library in Yorba Linda released the final installment of 94 secret White House tapes, covering the period from April 9 to July 12, 1973. This included the second US-Soviet summit when Nixon and Brezhnev met over six days in the Oval Office, the Cabinet Room, the Soviet Embassy, the President's San Clemente residence and aboard the Presidential yacht *Sequoia*. The recording of their private meeting in the Oval Office on June 18 is of poor quality; only the translator's voice (Victor's) comes through loud and clear. This was purported to be the only known recording of a US-Soviet summit. After the White House taping system was shut down, taping need not have ended. The transcripts of Soviet-American conversations during Nixon and Ford's Presidencies found in the Foreign Relations of the United States series are a testimony.

While maintaining the voice-activated taping system, Nixon was on guard for attempts to tape his private conversations by third parties. According to Bob Haldeman, he was worried about John Dean walking into his office with a concealed tape recorder: "Even the smallest ones are bulky enough...Where do you carry them? In your hip pocket or your breast pocket?"[16]

Haldeman recalled that Nixon recognized the problem of intentional or unintentional distortion or misunderstanding and became concerned about the absence of a record. He alluded to advisers who often came up with versions of their own and the President's positions on controversial military and foreign policy decisions. Kissinger's view on a particular issue was subject to change without notice, despite the President's assumption that a vital matter had been settled. The desire to have a precise record was a good reason for installing the taping system. What options were discussed? What were the arguments for and against? What were the decisions, exactly? How can they be refined, and who will implement the action? These ready questions arise from any important discussion in the White House or the Kremlin.

A taping system was one solution - several US Presidents made it their choice. Carried to extremes, it nurtured Nixon's suspicious nature. He was worried that a note taker busily writing down every word would inhibit his visitors. This may make sense, but permanent voice-activated recording was a big price to pay. No Soviet leader felt uncomfortable in the presence of an MFA note taker. This traditional method was near perfect in terms of accuracy and logical narration. It was reinforced by strict rules for handling classified documents.

Any comparison between the mode of operation of the Kremlin and the White House raises the question of security leaks. Suggesting such a possibility in the USSR was ridiculous, although there were lapses. The tight handling of government secrets was set into law and detailed regulations. They covered a multitude of subjects, from military hardware to last year's harvest and forest fires. Every other year Foreign Ministry staff was required to read and sign off the updated version of the little gray booklet which listed classified items. Despite our skeptical view of the contents, one broke the rules at the risk of a criminal inquest. The list was long, neigh impossible to memorize. No jotting down was allowed - the booklet itself was stamped "Top Secret."

Inevitably MFA officials, to be on the safe side, tended to keep their mouths shut on an even wider range of topics, some harmless. Open policy discussions were restricted to colleagues from government agencies: Party Central Committee, General Staff, military–industrial complex, KGB and some such. As a result, Soviet diplomats were proficient in self-censorship. This often led to loss of initiative and limited contacts with information sources: historians, journalists, and especially foreigners. Leaking to the press was unlikely for the simple reason there was no free press in the Soviet Union. As Gromyko used to say, "The question does not arise." In exceptional cases, a controlled leak was made in a "TASS Statement," in an article by a trusted columnist or a MFA official writing under an assumed name.

On the plus side, the stringent rules ensured a well-organized foreign policy staff. The unthinkable was achieved - a "leakless" foreign service. It is to this remarkable feature of the Soviet system that Nixon and Kissinger turned in their pursuit of truly confidential negotiations unhampered by government bureaucracy, Congress and the media. Their trust in Soviet diplomatic interpreters and note takers was touching, and we repaid it with discretion. Kissinger trusted Gromyko to hold secret discussions close to his chest. Soviet diplomats were never too talkative. They followed Gromyko's example.

Nixon and Kissinger reveled in secrecy. The specter of leaks was their rationale for relying on secret communication with the Soviets, the Kissinger-Dobrynin "back channel," or "special channel," as Nixon called it. The White House aired new ideas bypassing the bureaucracy, checking out new ideas, keeping secrets intact and saving time in the end. This sounded plausible. Still, conducting foreign policy by three or four people, albeit brilliant and empowered but not versed in the intricacies of complex issues, was fraught with risk. Practical negotiators were often left in the dark, bumping into closed doors or charging into open avenues they thought still existed. The double-layer negotiation of the first SALT agreements was a conspicuous example.

Kissinger adored clandestine negotiations. He wanted a single communications channel - his own, and was blunt about it. "We have delegation members," he told Brezhnev in September 1972, "whose sole desire is to receive the Nobel Peace Prize and save America from itself. They meet your people, talk about complicated ideas, then come back to us and present them as yours. You think these are our official ideas, and this creates confusion…" Interestingly, it was Kissinger who received the Nobel Peace Prize (together with North Vietnam's negotiator Le Duc Tho) in 1973.

Leaks were a constant theme of the Nixon Presidency. Before his trip to China, Nixon demanded that members of his staff and sensitive departments take polygraph tests if a secret document was leaked.[17] The atmosphere of mutual suspicion led to different branches of the Administration eavesdropping on the White House. The Army Signal Corps (under Melvin Laird) was tapping Camp David telephones;[18] the CIA was suspected in doing this as well. Leaks were often the butt of Kissinger's angry quips. To drive home his point, he denigrated the allies ("Consulting with the Japanese is like placing an ad in the *New York Times*") and Cabinet members alike. In their conversations with the Soviets, US officials from the President down demonstrated a startling propensity for indiscreet appraisals of members of the Administration, rages about the bureaucracy and plain gossip. Against this background, allegations of "leaks" were controversial, at least. True, the Nixon-Kissinger tandem was wary of leaving telltale traces of the private foreign policy they conducted. Kissinger was even tougher on leaks, because he thought they were seriously jeopardizing his clandestine negotiations. The rumor was that he was the source of some of them.

The suspicions Nixon and Kissinger nurtured went beyond the State Department. Cabinet members and Secretaries were not beyond the pale. In September 1972, Kissinger confided in Brezhnev that the Secretary of Defense "will not be long with us." The reason was serious: Melvin Laird objected to Nixon's policy on troop withdrawal in Vietnam. For Brezhnev, this sounded irrational: why was Laird appointed in the first place?

In the Soviet administrative setup, Ministers were not political appointees. As a rule, they were top experts in their own field. Kosygin, for example, was originally a textile engineer, appointed Minister by Stalin at the age of 34. Ministers were responsible for specific sectors of the economy and vast industrial empires. The Ministry of Medium Machine-Building, a euphemism for the atomic energy sector, employed three million people. Brezhnev received training as an engineer. He knew the workings of the unwieldy state-owned Soviet economy. He would not appoint a non-entity based on political allegiance to the chief. Sycophancy was not enough.

For a few exceptions (Kissinger was one), our impression of the Nixon Cabinet was of people not well versed in their areas of responsibility, though this was not as glaring as with some Senators and Congressmen. For example, Secretary of State Rogers, did not participate in important policy decisions. "Crybabies" in want of therapy, this was how Nixon described some of his appointees. There were instances when I laid down my pen deliberately to show I was not going to record embarrassing White House staff outbursts ("our meatball President" was among the worst). Whatever our private views, Soviet participants were always discreet.

Nixon appreciated the sterile Soviet environment - no country in the world placed so much on secrecy, and here he found an understanding and sympathetic audience. For a Presidential candidate whose private correspondence was opened by the CIA, this was a relief.[19]

Fear of leaks was the main reason Nixon and Kissinger decided to forego interpreting by State Department professionals and put them in cold storage. Perhaps American interpreters were not up to Nixon's standards of "loyalty." Kissinger confided to Brezhnev in Zavidovo that they did not use American interpreters because of the "confidential nature of both governments' relations." Brezhnev was not sure he followed such logic, but he appreciated this indirect reference to the discreet nature of his MFA staff. Incredibly, Nixon and Kissinger put their trust in the agents of the adversary, the Soviet interpreters. On several occasions, Kissinger asked for our memcons - apparently, they met his requirements. He could rely on their veracity and rational format, though the additional work of rendering them into English made a shambles of our careful job planning.

A Talk in Leningrad

Kissinger said, "Leningrad is an illusion." He cancelled the trip again, to bargain with Brezhnev and Gromyko over the final communiqué, especially the wording of Basic Principles, Vietnam and the Middle East. The only published memcons of those sessions are American - no Russian version was found. We did not usually write down the haggling over a communiqué's every line and stylistics. After all, the language was transitory. If a memcon was prepared, it focused on sticking points, the way they were resolved and the remaining issues. The painstakingly detailed US version is additional evidence that a tape recorder was used. Peter Rodman was present.

The morning meeting after the SALT signing ceremony started on a sour note. Gromyko confronted Kissinger: the *New York Times* published the SALT texts. The arrangement was, fumed Gromyko, to release them at the end of the summit. Kissinger was embarrassed: "Someone gave the texts to the press...I'm terribly sorry." Gromyko said, "You will submit tomorrow the name of the person. He will be crucified for this." Kissinger realized the Minister was pulling his leg.

They stopped the altercation at the sudden entry of Lieutenant-General Antonov, Chief of the KGB's Ninth Directorate, and a waitress carrying Kissinger's birthday cake. The girl kissed Kissinger on the cheek ("without orders," the General claimed). Gromyko pointed to sandwiches with huge servings of caviar. "Down with cheese," he said, "Long lives caviar!" Kissinger grinned: "I received more presents from the Soviet Foreign Ministry than from the State Department."

Humor wise, Kissinger met his equal in Sergei Antonov who oversaw security logistics for the Soviet leadership. A former UN diplomat, whose cover had been blown years ago in New York, Sergei Nikolayevich was bright and urbane, always ready with a smile and a repartee. Kissinger enjoyed badgering him: "Were you riding a motorcycle in the convoy, General?" "Couldn't this time," replied Antonov, "I was in civilian clothes." Kissinger asked for "a peek at my KGB file," confessing the General was one the few people he was afraid of. Antonov hemmed and hawed: "The file contains little Mr. Kissinger doesn't know already." I suspected the file was thicker than Henry imagined.

Kissinger enquired about a badge on a waitress's white blouse - she served breakfast in his residence on Lenin Hills. "Is that a Soviet Secret Service badge?" The girl blushed; it was her Komsomol (Young Communist League) badge. "It's a Secret Food Service badge," explained Antonov.

General Antonov could be tough: he turned down an American request to throw Kissinger's birthday party on 27 May in one of Kremlin's grand halls. As a concession for kicking out the NSC team, the Kremlin bakers prepared a large cake. Brezhnev sent a bottle of, appropriately, 49-year old Armenian brandy.

Antonov played a role in my career. On 16 June 1973, with an A-2 US visa stamped in my diplomatic passport I approached the steps to board the white IL-62 jet carrying Brezhnev's party to the US. A border control officer checking the passengers' list asked me to step aside. It was the General who quietly said, "Let him through." I found out later that a KGB Second Directorate (counter-intelligence) official crossed out my name shortly before departure, for a reason I will explain below. With a little help from my friends...

I accompanied Nixon to Leningrad - *Northern Palmyra* is its unofficial romantic name. The flight was less than an hour. The greeting ceremony at Pulkovo Airport emulated Moscow. They made sure crowds did not approach the passing motorcade. Nixon was resigned to the lukewarm reception, and did not grumble.

The itinerary included the Hermitage Museum adjacent to the Winter Palace, and a stroll in the Tsar's country residence at Pavlovsk. The German army deliberately destroyed it during the war. It now stood restored to its original splendor.

The visit began with a wreath-laying ceremony at the Piskarevskoye Memorial Cemetery, where most of a million Leningraders were interred during the 900-day siege. A visit to the cemetery is always heart wrenching. In the small museum, Nixon inspected the diary of a 12-year girl, Tanya Savicheva. She recorded family history: "Babushka died 25 January 1942, at 3 o'clock...

Uncle Vasya died 13 April at 2 o'clock... Mama died 13 May at 7.30 in the morning... The Savichevs all died... Only Tanya remains..." In the silent room a metronome ticked away the seconds. During the siege, 1,500 street loudspeakers transmitted the beat to Leningraders: the city was still alive.

I started translating Tanya's scrawl and choked - I thought of my grandfather. Nixon gave me a sidelong glance and waited patiently.

At the official luncheon, the Executive Committee of the Leningrad City Soviet (City Council), laid out generous fare: fresh caviar and Volga sterlyad in jelly, Russian *shchi* (sour cabbage soup), and trout. Nixon complimented the food and tried to steer the conversation to the political significance of his visit to the USSR. Mayor A. Sizov and other city officials were ill at ease: they were not qualified to discuss strategic arms limitations - these topics were the prerogative of the leadership in Moscow. The hosts mostly talked among themselves, and after several attempts at conversation, Nixon fell silent. The luncheon dragged on.

A waiter refilled his glass of *Mukuzani*, a full-bodied Georgian red wine. Nixon liked it. I told him it was a staple as caviar and vodka at government receptions. Did he want to keep the label? The waiter brought the damp square on a paper napkin. Nixon carefully folded the napkin and put it in his breast pocket. I asked the waiter, who was KGB catering section of the Ninth Department, to make a note of the President's interest. I checked later: a case of *Mukuzani* was delivered to the Presidential aircraft.

I sensed Nixon wanted to talk. It is the obligation of the interpreter to be proactive and try to trigger conversation with the hosts. My attempts failed. If City Soviet members will not talk with the President, then I will. Diplomatic interpreters do not usually do this, but this happens more often than people think. Foreign dignitaries feel at ease with interpreters who speak their language and often strike up conversations, if only to relax and get away from officials.

I told Nixon I was born in Leningrad and that my grandfather died during the German siege. He leaned over (I sat on his left) to listen to my story.

Our family moved to Moscow in 1939, after father accepted a job offer in the Peoples' Commissariat of Foreign Affairs. This probably saved his life. The Aluminum Research Institute planned to send him to Germany to continue studies; he spoke German and English. Now he was posted as Second Secretary at the Soviet Embassy in Kabul. In the early hours of June 22, 1941, war broke out. He volunteered for the front but they told him to stay put.

The Germans encircled Leningrad and shelled it methodically. Hitler's directive was to raze it to the ground, or starve the population to death. My grandparents did not evacuate in time; they were stranded in their apartment a few blocks away from the gilded spire of the Fortress of Peter and Paul.

"We saw it today," Nixon said.

Life got tougher after incendiary bombs destroyed the Badayev Food Depot. A quarter pound of rye bread a day was unsustainable. In the winter of 1941-1942, there was no electricity, running water, or sanitation. Granddad Vladimir had no strength left to walk to the railroad station, his place of work. Desperate for anything edible he laced his meager loaf with mineral oil and roasted it on the little fire stove. In a few weeks, he was gone. Babushka Maria piled his stiff body on a kid's sled and pulled it across town to the old Serafimov Cemetery.

"It's much smaller than the one we visited," I said. "Go on," Nixon said.

My mother knew nothing of her parents' plight. News coming from Leningrad was not good. A trickle of people, mostly women, children and wounded soldiers drove at night across the frozen ice of Lake Ladoga along the "Road of Life"- a lane cleared of snowdrifts. German aircraft bombed the truck convoys; hundreds perished in the black icy waters. Others were luckier: an aircraft carried Dmitry Shostakovich with his family and the Steinway to safety.

The Nazis were perilously close to Moscow, and we were evacuated to Kuibyshev (also known as Samara), a provincial capital five-hundred miles East. Some government offices and foreign diplomatic missions already moved to the fortified back-up capital.

Every morning, mother went to the market square to study bulletin boards with hundreds of paper messages about family members caught up in the migration. There was no news of her parents. One day she heard somebody call her name. It was Vera, a school friend. Her husband, an NKVD officer, was stationed in Kuibyshev. After hearing mother's story Vera said, "I'll help you."

Nixon was looking down at his plate, oblivious to the hum of voices around the table and distant laughter.

Several days later, somebody knocked on the door of Maria's apartment in Leningrad. She did not lock it anymore, so neighbors could carry her away if worst came to the worst. It was a young soldier. "Are you Maria Trifonova? We're going to the mainland. You may take a small bag." Maria was too feeble to care. The officer led her to a car. Its headlights were painted over leaving two slits enough to make out the road ahead. They drove to an airfield, and he helped her climb into a one-engine fighter plane. She squeezed behind the pilot's seat. The pilot laughed, "Keep quiet, girl: we'll sneak over the German lines. Hold for your life!" The engine roared, the plane lurched forward and she fainted. When she came to, they were in the air. In an hour, they landed in a military airfield near Moscow.

By that time father was sent to Halifax to look after Lend-Lease supplies and crews of Soviet submarines crossing the Atlantic. Shortly after, they appointed him Consul in Los Angeles and San Francisco. Arranging babushka's transfer to the US in the middle of the war was quite a feat. She told us what happened in Leningrad. Gradually, she reverted to her own composed self. She spoke at Russian Relief rallies and sewed dresses for my sisters. One day we found hoarded pieces of Wonder Bread under her pillow.

The city Mayor rose to propose a toast to peace and US-Soviet cooperation.

It was Nixon's turn. As I stood by his side, I whispered that every Russian at the table had a war story to tell, more tragic than mine. "I know," he said.

Holding a tall champagne glass Nixon said, "Each of us will carry a special memory from Leningrad. All will remember this splendid banquet, the delightful music, the new friendships and the spectacular beauty of this city, a city that refused to die... I would like to share one memory, of a twelve-year-old girl. I saw her picture at the cemetery today, and read several lines from her diary. She wrote how her mother, then her father, then her sister and brother passed away. "Only Tanya remains," she wrote. Tonight, I think of Tanya and all little Tanya's of the world, in the USSR, the United States, in Asia and

Africa. Therefore, I raise this glass to the Chairman of the Presidium, to the Mayor. But also to Tanya, a heroic symbol of your city, to her eternal glory."

During coffee, Nixon was pensive. He did not enquire about Tanya's fate. I did not tell him, to add to the gloom. In his *Memoirs,* he mentioned her being laid to rest in the cemetery. Actually, they found Tanya dying in the cold apartment, and transported her with a group of children across Lake Ladoga. She stayed in an orphanage on the Volga River. In the summer of 1944, she died of tuberculosis.

The memories of the Great Patriotic War pursued Nixon. In 1987, he paid a private visit to the USSR and went to the same vegetable market he saw in 1972. Several farmers recognized him. An old woman gave him two packets of sunflower seeds and said, "I lost two sons in the war; this is all I can give you. Please ensure there is no war." When Nixon returned to his residence he went for a walk in the park - he could not sit down to dinner. Again, he let his mask drop. If I didn't penetrate his façade by accident, I would not have believed it. He had so much self-control; he seemed so perfect.

We were back in Moscow in the evening.

The final plenary was set for next morning, to add up the results and say goodbye, but Nixon wished to have a last a fling with Brezhnev. A courtesy call, he said. He wanted to have as many publicized meetings as possible, better still with an undisclosed agenda.

Brezhnev was reluctant - he did not see the point of going over covered ground. Victor told me he advised Brezhnev to see the President after breakfast. Brezhnev brooded, "In the last seven years I never took my winter vacation, though I'm entitled. The others take leave twice a year. I am sick of approving their vacation requests. Meanwhile, Uncle Leonid slogs away!" He just arrived at the office - a quarter to ten - not your ordinary workaholic.

The short meeting extended to over an hour. Nixon took up the communiqué. He did not want the impression that irreconcilable positions remained: the Russian text mentioned differences "of principle" on the Middle East and Vietnam. They smoothed it over. On Vietnam, Brezhnev decided to sweeten the bitter pill: he suggested sending a "high Soviet official" to Hanoi to help end the war. He also insisted that President Thieu should resign at least two months before elections in South Vietnam. Nixon agreed, provided it was kept a secret (naturally, not from the North Vietnamese).

The "high official" turned out to be Podgorny. On June 15, he brought confidential "US concessions" to Hanoi - discontinuation of the bombing before the last American POWs were freed and discussion of political power sharing in South Vietnam. Bombing of Hanoi and Haiphong was suspended for several days while Podgorny was in town. Aware of Brezhnev's feelings for his hawkish colleague, a friend in the office hoped Americans would step up the raids instead. I did not like this cynicism about the war. By its end, almost four million tons of bombs were dropped on Vietnam, Laos and Cambodia. The pictures of B-52 carpet-bombing and of napalm victims in the villages flooded the media. It jarred the senses to listen to "confining bombing to present limits" or "suspending it for a while."

The result of Podgorny's trip to Hanoi was atmospherics. The new US proposals helped little. In reality, Moscow had no serious levers to apply. It tried on many occasions to talk the North Vietnamese into taking a conciliatory line. The latter always stood tough: they were grateful for military supplies, the MiG pilots and Soviet-manned anti-aircraft batteries. That was all; mediation did not work. Brezhnev and his friends were aware - without saying so much to Nixon and Kissinger - that the problem of Vietnam could not be resolved in Moscow: the warring nations had to settle it themselves. Whatever the outcome of their secret talks with the US in Paris, the Vietnamese knew they were close to a successful denouement on the battlefield. The ferocity of the bombing did not matter. Trying to break their resolve was a huge blunder the US paid for dearly.

Alexandrov's transcript of this final conversation was five pages long. Kissinger's was three. He omitted some substance. He forgot who translated - confusing interpreters and note takers was typical. Clearly, the conversation was not tape-recorded.

The final plenary in St. Catherine Hall on May 29 took less than an hour. The three Russian leaders enjoyed equal speaking time, with expressions of great satisfaction with the summit. Nixon said, "History has been made." In a magnanimous gesture, he asked Rogers if he wanted to make any remarks;

Rogers said all were fortunate to take part in a historic event. As they rose, Nixon said Rogers was leaving for the NATO Council, but the US will be "extremely circumspect in its consultations." Brezhnev said the Soviets would also be cautious. Both men exaggerated.

Nixon looked forward to the last leg of his journey, to Kiev, from where he was heading straight to Teheran. The official sendoff was from Vnukovo-2. Kosygin and Podgorny bade Nixon good-bye; we boarded the government IL-62. A colleague from Protocol said the visit went without a hitch.

In a few minutes, he received a nasty jolt: we had to vacate the aircraft.

We buckled our seat belts, ready for takeoff. The engines whined as if they would never stop, and died. I could see airport staff scurrying towards our plane across the tarmac, and a grim looking Kosygin climbing the aircraft steps. He entered Nixon's private compartment and said there was a "slight technical problem" - the party would have to proceed to a reserve aircraft. Boris Bugayev, Minister of Civil Aviation, stood meekly by his side.

"What do you think we should do with Bugayev?" asked Kosygin. "Promote him, by all means," grinned Nixon. "He found the trouble on the ground, not in the air." Nixon took the edge off the tension. He recalled several perilous incidents he experienced: a landing gear would not open and had to be cranked by hand; an engine going dead over the Sahara Desert; engines catching fire twice; his aircraft landing at the wrong airport blowing the cover of a confidential visit...

Bugayev knew he was spared. The story for the press was that an engine generator failed to attain the required frequency. They fed the same tale to Nixon. In reality, an engine support broke - a factory flaw.

The Presidential party, with Nixon and the First Lady in the lead, marched in view of the press to a back-up aircraft (the "*Spirit of '76*" had already left for Kiev). As they settled in the exact replica of the VIP cabin, there was another surprise. Since a technical fault with the Kremlin fleet was inconceivable, somebody along the line decided to save on food and drinks and did not stock the reserve craft with provisions. Bugayev was Brezhnev's personal pilot before his appointment as Minister. During World War II, he dropped supplies to partisans in the Ukraine. Arranging food supplies for Presidential aircraft turned out to be no less tricky.

I watched the flight attendants lug cardboard boxes from the main aircraft. In the confusion, they overlooked simple necessities. Nixon kept asking for plain water - he was denied this capitalist luxury. I went to the galley. A red-faced airhostess said there was a two-day supply of vodka, brandy, gin, whiskey, oranges and chocolates, but no potable water. I broke the bad news. Nixon could take a beating: he leaned back in his seat in resignation. Mercifully, it was just an hour's flight to Kiev. Soviet TV live coverage of Nixon's departure cut the embarrassing episode, but the aftertaste was bitter. In the Soviet leadership, it would be remembered as "The Day Kosygin Saw Nixon off." The Premier did not deserve it.

The American contingent swooped down on the beautiful city on the River Dnieper in four Presidential and two chartered planes from TWA and Pan American - I hoped they had drinking water on board. For some reason the accommodation list prepared by the Ukrainian authorities mentioned an "Official Party," which included Ambassador and Mrs. Jacob Beam and Henry Kissinger. All the others were lumped together in an "Unofficial Party," where one found Ambassador Emil Mossbacher, Chief of Protocol from State, Bob Haldeman and his aide Larry Higby, Ron Ziegler, Herb Klein, Dwight Chapin, John A. Scali and Rose Mary Woods. Speechwriters William Safire and Ray Price (he was to draft Nixon's resignation speech in 1974), were housed in Hotel Oktyabrskaya, an allusion to the 1917 October Revolution. Nixon and Kissinger's residential address was 4 Rosa Luxemburg Street, named after a German revolutionary murdered in 1919 after an ill-fated uprising in Berlin. Bill Krimer, "the interpreter without a voice," concluded the list.

The Ukrainian leaders headed by the Vladimir Scherbitsky, First Secretary of the Ukrainian Communist Party, were thrilled to receive Nixon. The First Lady, who seemingly subsisted on salads and yoghurt, had a hard time fending off Alexander Lyashko, Chairman of the Ukrainian Council of Ministers, who plied her with more food than her delicate frame could take. Sitting next to her at the official dinner in the light blue Mariinsky Palace, I fought a losing battle against the Ukrainian leadership whose clear preference was for the Rubens version of feminine form. "Please take some *borsch*," the Chairman insisted, "you are so thin." I tried my best to cushion this teapot clash of civilizations - it was fraying Pat's nerves. Unlike her husband who took the irritating aspects of a different culture in his stride, Mrs. Nixon could barely conceal her exasperation, be it police-controlled crowds, or lack of them, or Russians' fixation on rich food and hard liquor. Her experiences in the Ukraine were no better than in the Soviet capital where a security detail of thirty cordoned her off from American reporters.

Madame Lydia Gromyko, in a bright flowery dress usually accompanied Mrs. Nixon, providing contrast to her anorexic figure. The First Lady inspected the treasures of the Kremlin Armory and the Diamond Repository, listened to her guide describe the jewelry collection, visited a ballet school and a watch factory. She usually wrote a clipped "We are grateful for your hospitality" in the visitors' book. Her attempt to get friendly in the library of Moscow University on Lenin Hills was lost on astonished student readers whom she tapped on the shoulder and said "Hi." She rode the escalator deep down to appreciate Moscow Metro's palatial stations, visited the circus, and obediently attended official functions. Topping the list was tea with Mrs. Brezhnev and Mrs. Podgorny. Kosygin's daughter did not qualify for the party.

Tatyana told me the First Lady rarely asked questions but was always considerate to her interpreter. She retained a well-controlled smile throughout the trip. It eased at a fashion show set up by the hosts to neutralize her undiplomatic remarks about the way Russian women dressed. In a tweed Chanel suit, she sat by the catwalk, next to chubby Mrs. Brezhnev, who wore a loose printed cotton dress. Brezhnev's wife was uncomfortable: a family-loving homemaker, she shunned publicity and never went to fashion shows. Pat regarded a svelte model in a full-length snow-white fox fur coat with seven horizontal silver bands that matched the model's silver shoes. "I love that," she murmured. The first time she looked genuinely relaxed was when she visited the Bolshoi ballet school. Delighted, she clutched a tutu and a pair of ballet shoes presented by the young dancers.

I respected her unobtrusive support to the President in public, including brushing off American reporters' questions on Watergate (Russian reporters never raised the issue). Her curt replies were amazingly similar to the Russian official position: the big issues - détente and nuclear disarmament - were more important. Occasionally, she would say something nice and private about her husband. At the official dinner in Kiev, she turned to me and whispered, "Dick is so emotional, he always speaks from the heart." She gave me a side-long glance, as if watching for effect.

Nixon was not a magnetic speaker, a bit glib for my liking, but he struck the right chord with Russian audiences. He never read from notes; he did his homework and knew his history briefs. On the last evening in the USSR on 29 May, he touched the hosts with a laudatory reference to Kiev: "The Mother of Russian Cities is an appropriate place for my last dinner in the Soviet Union." "Dinner" and "supper" are the same word in Russian - *uzhin*. I was not sure of how the guests would appreciate the biblical connotation so I skipped the word "last." Kiev was also known, Nixon went on, as "The city of the Golden Gates," and, expectedly, likened it to San Francisco, "which visitors regard as the most beautiful city in America." He evoked the will of the people of Kiev to rebuild their city devastated by the Germans, an uphill task accomplished in seven years rather than fifty as some pessimists predicted.

Next morning we assembled at Borispol Airport to bid Nixon good-bye. I was last in a long line of officials. Nixon stopped, gripped my hand and said, "We're happy you were with us. I will never forget your grandfather. I hope it never happens again."

"What did he mean?" a TASS reporter asked me. I waved him away, "Nothing special; a private thing."

The personal touch and remembering family stories was a tool Nixon perfected to a great degree. My mother was overwhelmed when I told her about the conversation. Imagine, she said, President Richard Nixon mentioning granddad, thinking of the lonely death of a Russian railroad clerk in a frozen Leningrad apartment. She hoped to God her father was listening up there.

At 11.45 a.m., Col. Ralph Albertazzie taxied the white and blue Boeing 707 to the runway. We waved. The aircraft sped past, took off and gently banked south on the three-hour flight to Teheran.

CHAPTER 2

Brezhnev Goes to America, 1973

KISSINGER IN ZAVIDOVO

AFTER COMPLETING THE MEMCONS AND waiting for queries from the Kremlin and Gromyko's office (none came), I returned to London. My four-year tour of duty was ending. Ambassador Smirnovsky suggested I go for a fifth year, but I wanted more scope. A First Secretary position in the MFA disarmament section complemented my extracurricular activities for the Kremlin. Working under Kirill Novikov, Gromyko's closest adviser on UN affairs, was an exciting prospect.

After the 1972 summit, both sides had a clearer idea of the opportunities and confines of the path they took. After sizing each other up and settling scores on a number of divisive issues, the relationship moved into a structured pattern: there will be annual summits. Nixon and Brezhnev exchanged cordial letters, stressing the personal role they will continue to play. While Nixon's were in his own style, the letters from Brezhnev sounded as if a stranger authored them. That is exactly what happened: they were drafted by committee, usually by the troika of Gromyko, Kornienko and his deputy Victor Komplektov. A sprinkle of "sincerity" was thrown in to make them sound authentic, as if coming from Brezhnev's "heart." These passages sounded unnatural.

Sometimes the messages took the form of "Letters from the Soviet Leadership" - they were short and formal. They carried no signature, which was a veiled indication of a common Politburo stand. Perhaps neither leader wanted to swamp the other with personal letters. The White House reciprocated with "Messages from the US Leadership." The correspondence focused on strategic issues: nuclear arms control, the Middle East and Vietnam. Though satisfied with the state of relations with the US, Brezhnev emphasized that Vietnam was taking too much time. Both leaders wished the problem would go away. Another theme was US-Soviet economic relations, which were "only scratched" at the summit: grain purchases, credits for the Tyumen and Yakutsk natural gas project, Lend-Lease and MFN.

Nixon and Brezhnev confirmed that the Kissinger-Dobrynin confidential back channel would remain the central avenue of negotiations, and will operate from Washington. Only National Security Council staff will be privy to the channel. The State Department and other bureaucracies will be excluded. Henry Kissinger will continue as the one and only shuttle operator between the two capitals, with direct access to Brezhnev and Gromyko.

Our job of interpreting and note taking became less hectic. By now, we knew the American team, and were on first-name terms with all except Kissinger. We devised nicknames for the main summit participants, mostly by name and patronymic abbreviations. Brezhnev was "LI" (Leonid Ilyich) or "GenSec", Kosygin was "AN" (Alexei Nikolayevich), Kornienko - "GM" (Georgy Markovitch), and Dobrynin "AF" - Anatoly Fedorovitch. Gromyko was "Grom" (also Russian for "thunder"). Kissinger became "Kisa" - the Russian for "kitten," or plain "Henry." Only Nixon, probably for the almost single-syllable jingle, stayed "Nixon."

The KGB protection detail employed numbers. A plainclothes man would speak softly into his microphone warning his comrades, "17 left his room; walking to the car." That meant Brezhnev, or another dignitary. The numbers changed regularly; the list was top secret.

Kissinger was ideally suited for his Superman shuttle role: he was indeed faster than a speeding bullet, more powerful than a locomotive, could leap tall buildings in a single bound... And, he had a major advantage over Gromyko: he reported to one person only - Nixon, and this guaranteed a swift response to any Soviet initiative. However, his "Lone Ranger" galloping and decision-making was bound to fail somewhere along the trail, fouling up US-Soviet communications.

Brezhnev regarded Kissinger as the President's *alter ego*. He would involuntary address him as "Comrade Kissinger," as a member of the Kremlin government. Worldly and serious with Nixon, Brezhnev could be both serious and entertaining with Kissinger. He genuinely liked him as a sparring partner. Nobody spoke to him like this before. Kissinger had mastered the proper mix of cheek and flattery. Brezhnev liked playacting with Kissinger. He could be humorous, majestic, condescending, attentive, mischievous, hurt, ironic - all rolled into one. He claimed he was "just an engineer, not a diplomat." (He never admitted he was essentially a party organizer.) Taking the cue, Kissinger would protest, "The General Secretary is an outstanding negotiator."

In at least one sense, Brezhnev resembled Kissinger: both were unaware of modesty. I did not include in my transcripts such Brezhnev phrases as, "I am an objective and straightforward person," or "I don't bear malice towards anyone." Kissinger's reaction was always lowering his head in agreement.

For some obscure reason, both men chose Helmut Sonnenfeldt as the target for inoffensive jokes. Kissinger's closest aide was different from his boss. One could always expect a joke from Kissinger, but an impious observation from Sonnenfeldt, often on Soviet ways. Kissinger would offset the unpleasantness with a phrase repeated *ad nauseam*: "Sonnenfeldt is the problem the solution of which he pretends to be." Or: "With Sonnenfeldt, it's a race between the difficulties he causes and his indispensability." It was Helmut speaking, he claimed, "I just move my lips." He warned Brezhnev that Sonnenfeldt could read upside down. Brezhnev covered his papers with both palms, then lifted them and said he had no secrets: he can give away all his papers to the Americans.

Brezhnev chose Helmut as an object for mild teasing, probably because he knew his role in advising Kissinger and the respect he enjoyed. Kissinger felt Brezhnev liked the routine, and readily sacrificed Helmut. This could never happen with forbidding Kornienko (he was Helmut's counterpart in the Soviet team).

Brezhnev always watched Helmut's expression. "Sonnenfeldt didn't like what I said," said Brezhnev at a meeting on SALT, and suggested that instead of missiles, the two sides agree on "limiting Sonnenfeldt", or "counting him" in the warheads totals. "Could you move Sonnenfeldt to the back row?" he would propose, and Kissinger would take the cue: "We'll seat him under the table!" Helmut would fake a smile. He did not have Kissinger's prerogative of talking back to Brezhnev. He was Kissinger's colleague from Army days, but did I detect strain?

Sonnenfeldt demonstrated a powerful mind. Between us, we called him "Kissinger's Kissinger." Apparently, he shared Henry's condescension for everything Russian (Imperial or Soviet - it made no difference), but went further. This prompted Kissinger to claim that politically he was "to the left of Sonnenfeldt." His role in advising and guiding Kissinger along was certainly substantial. He approached the super power equilibrium in a geopolitical way, and granted legitimacy to the Soviet Union's security concerns. A "spheres of influence" analyst, he predicted that "an organic evolution" of the Soviet Union's relations with Eastern Europe might take a hundred years. Helmut's idea was that the US should not disrupt stability in Eastern Europe, and let the USSR consolidate its control in the region. Kissinger's reaction to the so-called "Sonnenfeldt Doctrine" reeked of jealousy.

The many sessions Brezhnev and Kissinger had in the Kremlin and in Zavidovo were lengthy and disordered - Brezhnev preferred them that way. He did not plan nor announce coffee breaks. In one drawn out session in the Kremlin the call of nature became unbearable. I whispered in Brezhnev's ear and he adjourned the session at once; I saw grateful glances. As Brezhnev's private restroom was going to be occupied by the host, I led the proles in a race down the corridor to the old wood-paneled restroom I knew - it seemed miles away. Kissinger panted and fell back. Sonnenfeldt, Hyland and I took the available three positions. The door opened, and we heard the deep bass, "If you guys were disciplined, you would stop." We cringed but held the fort.

Kissinger's commendable contribution to détente was educating Brezhnev on the American system of government. Dobrynin did that too, and Gromyko as well - unobtrusively. Hearing it from the horse's mouth was more effective.

This concerned the role of the Congress, a real problem for the White House. Kissinger advised Brezhnev that manner of presentation was important. During Lend-Lease negotiations in September 1972, he suggested agreeing on a lump sum coupled with a string of confusing interest rates. He said they would appear higher than in reality and help convince Congress to move on credits for Russia, MFN and the gas projects.

Brezhnev did not understand his American comrades' dread of the capitalist press. He was skeptical that Nixon would seriously heed an article in the *Washington Post*. He boasted he could order *Pravda* to criticize any Soviet Minister. Kissinger patiently explained the role of media reaction for the White House, though he admitted that the American public did not know the difference between SLBMs and the New York subway.

Kissinger's German-Jewish heritage and childhood memories of the Nazis nurtured a deep understanding of Russia's fears of foreign aggression and its preoccupation with Germany. Other high American officials required to be convinced, but not him. He once said there were people in the US who thought they could have peace and anti-Soviet policy together. [20] He regarded Soviet uneasiness and often intransigence in security matters not as propaganda but as a genuine concern linked to Europe's chaotic history. This proved his forte in relations with Soviet leaders.

In December 1973, Kissinger lunched with Gromyko. A professor of history talked to a practitioner who lived through it all. As conversation moved to prewar years, Kissinger said he always had respect for Stalin's foreign policy – the man had long-range vision. Kissinger thought the USSR was essentially right in concluding the 1939 pact with Germany (the Molotov-Ribbentrop non-aggression treaty). [21] There was very stupid leadership in Western Europe, he continued; you had no reasonable choice. Gromyko agreed: all Soviet attempts [to conclude mutual assistance treaties] with the British and French failed. Kissinger observed that "Stalin showed great courage, when we had the atomic bomb."

During a long session at the Kremlin, Brezhnev announced a break - he went to his private rest area to make a phone call to the Defense Minister. We rose to stretch our legs. Kissinger buttonholed Victor and me, and gave a sympathetic critique of Soviet foreign policy. He accepted the fact it fed on suspicions of invaders. Russia never had natural borders he said, so it was compelled to expand, hence its huge territory. The Mongols, Lithuanians, Poles, the French, the Turks - were all invaders... (I mentally added Truman's atomic blackmail).

Kissinger's keen grasp of the Russian preoccupation with security coupled with a healthy dose of mistrust toward Germans, permitted diplomatic breakthroughs that another member of the Administration could not achieve. Neither the 1971 agreement on West Berlin, nor the 1975 European Security Conference would have been possible without Kissinger's personal intervention. Possessive of intellectual brilliance and hypnotic power, he knew when to graciously cede a minor point, rather than score a propaganda victory. He hugely succeeded with the Soviet leaders, despite their suspicions of his feisty nature. He was the only US post-war foreign policy adviser who managed to instill deference to Soviet national concerns in an American President. He knew that traditional American simple-mindedness never grasped the complexities of the Eastern European world. He said he was criticized in the US for defending the Soviet Union, and Brezhnev believed him.

Kissinger did not expand, but here is what he probably had in mind.

In December 1974, soon after the Ford-Brezhnev meeting in Vladivostok, he made a remarkably candid presentation to American academic experts on Russia, including George Kennan. While defending US strategy, he produced arguments in favor of the Soviet stance that were more convincing than anything I heard from a Soviet official.[22] Détente was a two-way street, he stressed. The Soviets, he argued, concluded an agreement in Berlin. They were "not unhelpful in Vietnam" and "did not act irresponsibly in the Middle East." (His speaking style was contaminated by Gromyko's double negatives.) They settled the Lend-Lease problem. On the other hand, despite promises of MFN and a meager $300 million in credits over four years - during the Nixon era the sides were talking billions - the trade bill was tied to intrusive demands that we ourselves could not accept... He would not put up with it if Dobrynin came and made demands about Angela Davis... This was insulting for Brezhnev, but Jewish emigration rose considerably thanks to "quiet conversations," without public pressure... The US should look at the basic problems before using Sakharov and Solzhenitsyn "to hack away" at the USSR.

Kissinger defended SALT: the exchange of information on military capabilities like missile accuracy and deployment would have meant treason in the Soviet Union before. Thirty years ago, this information would not have been exchanged between France and Britain. He recounted a fascinating conversation with Defense Minister Grechko on US forward-based nuclear systems. The US position was that FBS could not reach the USSR, and therefore should not be added to the strategic equation. Marshal Grechko took him aside to show the lines and targets US Europe-based planes and aircraft carriers could reach in the Soviet Union. "It was done well," Kissinger said. "Then he said that would free your missiles to reach deep into the Soviet Union. The point is we are geared for a second strike and we tend to write off our FBS... For them it is not totally irrelevant."[23]

Despite the admission, Nixon and Kissinger were adamant about not counting FBS. This position never changed. For them, FBS had political significance: first, as projection of American power beyond the continental United States; and second, as reassurance for the West Europeans that the US will be there to protect them in an emergency. In 1974, during a private conversation with Nixon in a Crimean grotto, Brezhnev said the US warhead total was 16,498, not 6,100 the US claimed. Nixon did not dispute the figure.

Kissinger made an interesting confession on missile throw-weight, where the Soviets allegedly had a marked advantage. The Chairman of the Joint Chiefs of Staff assured him that if we want, we could put heavier missiles in the existing Minuteman silos; no need to use the 15 per cent silo dimension increase allotted under SALT. He lambasted domestic critics, including "mindless senators," who claimed the US made unilateral concessions - the Soviets did make major adjustments. Senator Jackson accused him of treating US allies as adversaries, and the USSR as a friend.

He added the US could not pile on conditions and conditions on the Soviets; he warned that theirs was not at all an irreversible policy. They are not irresponsible, though not creative. He said he had no interest in Brezhnev's survival as a person, but insisted that his group has a fear of war in their bones.

They behave with a timidity all out of proportion to their strength. Time and again, we have bluffed the Soviets when the objective correlation of forces was not in our favor. The younger generation might play the game a few steps further. Kissinger derided US responses to Soviet drafting proposals: "If there is no difference, we reject it on stylistic grounds. If there is a difference, we reject it on substantive grounds."[24]

George Kennan voiced agreement with Kissinger's explanations, saying that the Soviets' internal commitment to détente was very real: Americans underestimate the degree the Soviets are committed to their own propaganda.

Admissions like these were part of the internal debate in the US, but unfortunately, they had no decisive bearing on the American negotiating position at the summits.

Nevertheless, Kissinger wanted quick progress. Unlike Gromyko, he let his impatience show (a seasoned diplomat would never allow this). He often mistook Soviet inflexibility for "mediocrity." On one occasion, after several grueling sessions in Washington with Dobrynin he suggested that the remaining points the Soviets were after could be resolved at a later meeting with Brezhnev. He suggested conspiring with the Ambassador. He would "turn down" the Soviet proposal as for now, but will "give in" to Brezhnev in the Kremlin, "if the General Secretary played tough." Dobrynin reported the ploy to Brezhnev and Gromyko. It was played out as planned: Brezhnev stood his ground and Kissinger yielded. A delighted Brezhnev lost no time in recounting to his surprised colleagues in the Politburo how he "bound Ghenry head and foot" (this was how he pronounced his name).

Such tricks were employed more often than one would think. Ambassador Lev Mendelevitch, one of the best brains in the MFA, taught me, a young diplomat, a simple ruse. When negotiating, he said, leave two or three contentious issues for the Minister to address. He, in his turn, should leave a single one for the General Secretary. That last hurdle would be resolved, with flair, by the leaders themselves - "makes them feel good."

It remained unclear to me whether Kissinger's tactic was a sophisticated way of placating Brezhnev, or helping him against the conservatives.

In negotiating with the Soviets, Kissinger's approach was practical, in contrast to the Russian preference for the abstract, the philosophical and emotional, which rarely paid off in the longer run. Such was the fate of the painstakingly negotiated "principle of equal security," which meant to ratify the two nations' equal military status in 1972: it failed to survive into the early 1990s. Nixon and Kissinger tried to convince the Soviets, by providing cold figures and program outlays, of the uselessness of building up defense capabilities. Brezhnev and Gromyko often tried to convince the US not to increase defense expenditures and to stop modernization - with emotional appeals and hardly disguised threats. The tactics were different, but the sides managed to find a meeting ground. Kissinger accepted the limitations of American power: strategic advantage was no longer possible, given the relentless drive of the Soviet Union for military parity. Nixon shared the sobering realization. They could not help feeling respect for the Soviet Union's formidable war machine and ability to project its political influence in any corner of the world. Russia was now America's equal.

From this stemmed Kissinger's undisguised disrespect for "the others, the small countries." When Gromyko asked about his impressions of a visit to Warsaw Kissinger grinned: "The guard of honor couldn't get their boots in a straight line, but the military band played beautiful music." This off-hand attitude extended to some NATO members as well. In May 1973, Kissinger made a refueling stop in Copenhagen en route to Moscow. Police with submachine guns and dogs guarded his aircraft. The Danish Minister of Foreign Affairs wished to meet Kissinger at the airport. This was not his lucky day: he was told that Dr. Kissinger did not plan to disembark and will continue working.[25]

No love was lost between him and Michel Jobert, the sarcastic anti-American French Foreign Minister, for whom he felt a singular wrath: "If he makes any more statements like this, we'll have to turn some of our missiles against France." Jobert was known as "le Kissinger français," probably a worse sin. Gromyko confessed to Kissinger that he shared his dislike for Jobert: "He is flinging arrows at Moscow." They agreed that Jobert did not discriminate; he hated all joint US-Soviet actions. "Every time he attacks me," said Kissinger, "his polls go up three points in France."

Kissinger was often professorial. The problem with the French, he explained, lay in their education - just theory, no practical basis. The ultimate independence and freedom of action of a country depend on its weight, not its declarations. Brezhnev slapped the table in agreement.

To ingratiate himself with the General Secretary, Kissinger used Soviet and Marxist terminology. He spoke of "peace-loving peoples," and referred to Hegel's law of dialectics - quantitative change will turn into qualitative change. He used it to defend the US "partial steps" policy in the Middle East as opposed to immediately convening a Geneva conference with the participation of all countries of the region. He was not ideological in the abstract way: he regarded the USSR as a reincarnation of the Russian Empire. His and Nixon's meetings with the "Soviet comrades" showed that fear of Communism was outdated: it was really a competition of two powerful States.

One of Kissinger's less agreeable traits was making fun of Soviet officials and rejoicing in their discomfort. He often judged them by his own standards of portentousness and mistook traditional Russian reserve and ready emotion for shallowness and naiveté. Brezhnev was off bounds for his barbed tongue, though he barely resisted if given an opportunity. When Brezhnev said he received two messages from Japanese Prime Minister Tanaka, Kissinger asked, "One for each island?" (This was a reference to the long-standing Japanese claim to four islands of the South Kuril Chain.) In Zavidovo, the General Secretary's country residence, Brezhnev tried unsuccessfully to tear a dozen pages from a thick notepad. "It must have been produced by Smirnov," smiled Kissinger. Brezhnev did not think it funny and ignored the remark: to him, Smirnov personified the Soviet war industry.

Kissinger went to extremes to please Brezhnev. While reaching out to him, he never groveled. To Brezhnev, who was used to the toadyism of Soviet provincial officials, Kissinger's deference was refreshing. He was methodical in building his role of "By Appointment to the General Secretary Supplier of Creature Comforts." He knew exactly what Brezhnev would appreciate, like flying in spare parts for the Lincoln Continental Nixon presented to him in Camp David. Victor Sukhodrev remembered an urgent summons to the Kremlin where he found Brezhnev leafing through a catalogue of spare parts: he wanted to order some though there was nothing wrong with the car. The secret Kissinger/Dobrynin channel served these needs as well. On Kissinger's next visit to Moscow, Brezhnev took me aside and asked to convey his "sincere thanks for prompt service with the spares." Kissinger raised his arms: it was nothing, really.

We mimicked, in bass, a frequent phrase of Henry: "Mr. General Secretary, whatever is humanly possible, we will do." Kissinger's was a wise strategy. He deftly played on Brezhnev's weaknesses to lull him into complacency and extract real political concessions. Brezhnev often took flattery (actually, bait) at face value and could be dreadfully gullible. The aides tried to shield the General Secretary - not an easy task. At times, after listening to a worried Kornienko or Dobrynin, Brezhnev would admit that "Ghenry" did want to obtain advantage on the sly.

Not all Kissinger's quips were appreciated; they were regarded as "impolite" in Russian culture, or in bad taste. Sometimes their meaning was lost on the Soviet side of the table, except perhaps for Dobrynin, Victor and me. The Russian leaders were unsure how to react. As we took off from Vnukovo Airport, the aircraft's wheels retracted with a dull thud. "There go the dissidents," said Kissinger. He was surprised that nobody in the VIP cabin fastened their seat belts: "Now I know how Soviet leaders achieve rotation in office."

At a session in the Kremlin, Brezhnev produced a nickel-plated model of a missile nose cone. He looked at Kissinger and opened it. There were six miniature warheads; each contained a cigarette. Kissinger's reaction was instant, "Now our intelligence knows you have six MIRVs in your ICBMs." Brezhnev laughed: he loved jokes about spying - he was proud of the Soviet intelligence service.

In 1973 in Zavidovo, Kissinger rattled off a long list of Soviet aircraft and surface-to-air missiles the Egyptians moved closer to the Suez Canal. Brezhnev listened, commended US intelligence, and countered with Soviet information: Israel was recalling reservists, cancelling vacations for doctors, and deploying field hospitals for a thousand wounded. Kissinger grinned: he enjoyed this game. Brezhnev suggested pooling intelligence, to have a truthful picture of the war zone.

Kissinger's stories, told to anyone who would listen, were entertaining. He offset his arrogance, which he admitted, by a self-deprecatory attitude. At moments like this, he resembled an overweight wisecracking Woody Allen. "My megalomania is boundless" - this was his riposte to accusations of immodesty. His real problem was a persecution complex. "Not the Red under the bed type," he smiled. He had real enemies in government: "I look under the bed every night before retiring."

Books and writing about diplomacy were a recurring theme - he was sure he had few equals. "Do you know what one reviewer said about my book? He wasn't sure I was a good writer, but he said he was certainly a good reader... I liked that!" "He's supposed to be a genius, but you should read one of his books..." Or: "His signature is unintelligible, but his books are even more." Or: "Obscurity should not be confused with profundity."

At a meeting in Moscow, he claimed the US had a bomber that played the national anthem of the country it was flying over. Brezhnev loved the joke. He toppled over when Kissinger said, "If we make more concessions like this, you will have Alaska by next year."

He believed in his ability to arrange anything, from turning a newspaper columnist to making a deal with Le Duc Tho. Humility was something he read about but did not believe existed. "Every morning I pray to God to give me the wisdom to do the right thing during the day," he said. "Then I ask God if there was anything I could do for him."

It was not all fun. He was angry with a Secret Service agent who failed to rush to his side on a walk on Lenin Hills. The agent explained that Kissinger's self-esteem demanded a bodyguard trailing behind, irrespective of Moscow being a safe place. He was unreasonable when he accused, *post factum*, Russian servants of stealing his wife's shoes in the Lenin Hills residence. She liked walking barefoot on the plush carpet, and forgot to warn the Secret Service not to pack them for the airport. Nancy had to walk shoeless to the car. Kissinger never apologized.

His favorite target was the State Department. "We always send them draft Presidential messages for comments," he said, "but in truth to keep their ego afloat. In a recent one, we had a phrase, "Animals do not recognize national boundaries." The draft was promptly returned with a single edit: "some" animals…" A macabre story concerned a US diplomat abducted in Mexico. "They asked for half a million ransom; I have no one in State who would cost so much, so I declined." At this moment, he resembled a jeering Doctor Strangelove. Coming from a corporate diplomatic culture, I thought his jabs at professional diplomats unfair.

The jokes and stories came in cascades, in torrents; they echoed in Kremlin corridors as if possessing a life of their own. Perhaps they did: many wormed their way into newspaper reports I saw after hearing them weeks before in Zavidovo or Crimea. I wasn't sure Kissinger could keep track of what he told to whom and when - the supply was so massive. At moments, I felt the urge to say, "But you told us this last year at Camp David!" Unlike my NSC colleagues, I never included them in the memcons.

A bottomless supply of funny stories was one thing Kissinger and Brezhnev had in common. I suggested to Alexandrov once that he, as an aide, should record what particular joke Brezhnev told to which audience. He laughed and said he was too busy as it were. His view was similar to mine: most jokes should not be included in a memcon. His concern was that Politburo colleagues might see the General Secretary as a clown rather than a responsible statesman.

I enjoyed Kissinger's stories; there is nothing like an unexpected joke to defuse tension in the room and, for a note taker, to relax the tense neck and hand muscles. A brief break clears the mind and allows one to see the humorous and sometimes silly side of diplomacy. At a tense moment in negotiations, Kissinger could not find a document, and said, "Goddamn." Gromyko asked what the problem was. Kissinger explained: "I expressed an opinion about our legal adviser by damning a nonexistent entity in your philosophy." Gromyko burst out laughing: he liked this à la Gromyko explanation. Kissinger caught his style correctly.

At a grand reception for the diplomatic corps in the Kremlin on 29 May 1972, I stood behind Kissinger in case any of the Russian-speaking guests wished to chat. I told him I knew very few of the envoys. "Definitely not the Finnish Ambassador," he whispered after shaking hands with a large black person with decorations on his chest. "More likely Norwegian," I whispered back. He grinned. That was the way with Kissinger: he accepted repartees from people he had no control over. Victor and I, Soviet interpreters, were never at the receiving end of his stinging wit. We were safe: we were the keepers of the White House secrets.

Nixon's visit left some loose ends. A new agenda had to be prepared. Both sides made a hasty decision, as it proved later, to hold substantive summits every year - an uphill undertaking even for allied governments.

Kissinger travelled to Moscow in September, to discuss Lend-Lease and trade. At the start of the meeting Brezhnev wanted to make sure Nixon sailed in the Volga-10 hydrofoil he gave him (he liked to trace his gifts). Kissinger confirmed that the President took his friends out in the boat on the Potomac, but could not corroborate it with snapshots.

News was not encouraging. In July, Egyptian President Anwar Sadat, probably in a gesture to the US, expelled Soviet military advisers. His other reason may have been his secret war plan against Israel – he did not want Russians to talk him out of it. The autumn harvest was worse than expected; the country was in need of imported grain. Senator Jackson accused Russians of eating cheap bread made of American wheat (he was unaware of heavily subsidized food production in the USSR). To add to the troubles, dense smog from smoldering peat fields enveloped Moscow. Brezhnev needed new successes in foreign policy.

The Lend-Lease discussion with Kissinger was inconclusive. On trade, Brezhnev offered attractive prospects: a bilateral arrangement for 25 to 30 years to export trillions of cubic meters of Russian natural gas. Kissinger explained Nixon's difficulties with MFN. He could not deliver Congress;

opposition was too strong, though many Congressmen were aware that with-holding MFN was counterproductive, because it cost US jobs. (MFN was to be finally granted to Russia in 2012).

The good news was that Nixon was reelected in November in a landslide. In a telephone conversation, Dobrynin told Kissinger his Embassy staff was chanting, "Four more years!" Podgorny, as formal Head of State, was quick to send his congratulations. Brezhnev would not be upped: he wrote the next day and asked Dobrynin to read out his warm message to Nixon who was holidaying in Florida. He mentioned that Podgorny and Kosygin "also" expressed satisfaction.

Meanwhile, peace in Vietnam was truly at hand. The Vietnam Peace Accords signed in Paris on 27 January 1973, and ratified by the Final Act of the international conference on March 2, formally ended the war and the US combat role. The Kremlin heaved a deep sigh of relief; the coast was clear for a surge in US-Soviet relations.

In May 1973, Kissinger came for talks with Brezhnev. The Zavidovo round stands out by its substance, intensity, and good-natured hard bargaining. It is here, in Brezhnev's country residence ninety miles north of Moscow breakthroughs were achieved and groundwork prepared for Nixon's second summit conference and for the remainder of his Presidency. It was a *tour d'horizon,* covering all major issues. It was also a high point of Kissinger's vanity: taking on the leader of the USSR single-handed. He came on a five-day visit, twenty-one straight hours of which were negotiations. At the time, Kissinger did not fully appreciate Brezhnev's gesture - he was the first Western visitor at the secluded rustic retreat. He would never stay in the compound again. When he returned to Moscow in October, he was not invited to Zavidovo.

We arrived by car in the morning, to be housed in a prefab two-story building overlooking the parking lot. The receptionist handed me the key for a small room on the second floor. There was a bed, bookcase, small fridge, and a TV set. A glass of cool kefir by the bedside was refilled every evening. The Soviet party would take meals downstairs in the mess, the Americans in their residence.

I heard voices and leaned out of the window: Brezhnev and his body-guard were having a smoke below. I saw Gromyko approaching along an as-phalt path from a walk in the forest. Suddenly Brezhnev and the bodyguard stood at attention. They saluted and Brezhnev barked a report to the surprised Foreign Minister: "All is quiet, everything in order!"

Brezhnev played the perfect host: ten minutes after Kissinger and his NSC team arrived in the evening, he went to check if they were comfortable. Kissinger was effusive in praise, probably because he just received news from Washington that Haldeman and Ehrlichman had resigned. Kissinger's party stayed in a pseudo-rustic two-story cabin with large bas-reliefs of deer heads over the entrance. Brezhnev occupied an equally unappealing cabin.

The American team included Helmut Sonnenfeldt, Bill Hyland, Winston Lord, Lawrence Eagleburger and Peter Rodman. The rest of the twenty-two strong delegation stayed behind in Moscow. Kissinger again dispensed with State Department interpreters, apparently feeling safe with Victor and me, shining examples of diplomatic discretion.

The arrangement was for the two teams to meet every day in the morn-ing and afternoon. Although two sessions a day was Brezhnev's suggestion, he never kept the schedule. As energy slowly dissipated, he would lose interest in the proceedings and announce long breaks.

We assembled in Brezhnev's study on the second floor of his cabin, wait-ing for the host. I looked around. Varnished bookcases lined two walls, but books were few. A large TV set in a corner was showing a nature documen-tary. The picture was a poisonous green.

I asked Kissinger to sign a booklet of Russian texts of the 1972 summit agreements. Its circulation was an astonishing 100,000, at the price of 18 kopecks (25 cents) each. He saw Brezhnev's autograph on the cover. "With good wishes," he wrote and affixed his "double bed" signature under the brochure title in bold red, which read "Soviet Peace Program in Action." I showed it to Alexandrov. He suggested Kissinger suffered from political myopia. I said there was no harm in presenting SALT and the ABM treaty to our population as favoring the USSR - wasn't it true? Before he could reply, the door swung open and Brezhnev emerged from his bedroom. Dobrynin, who always felt at ease in his presence, asked about the TV picture. "You noticed that too," Brezhnev frowned. "I can't get rid of the green hue, nor can the repairman. It does get on your nerves after a while, don't you think?" (Earlier that year the USSR deposited a second Lunar Vehicle on the surface of the Moon.)

The conference table held notebooks, pencils in glass vases and two ashtrays, apparently for Brezhnev and Victor, who were the only smokers. As I rearranged the pencil vases - I knew nobody would use them - Brezhnev said he would do it himself.

Zavidovo. Left to right: Gromyko, Sukhodrev, Alexandrov, Brezhnev, Vavilov, Sonnenfeldt (partly obscured). Kissinger: "The General Secretary is a wonderful organizer!"(Vladimir Musaelyan)

Before the meeting began - it was close to noon - Brezhnev led Kissinger to the terrace balcony with its splendid view of ancient pine trees. Kissinger appreciated the balcony, but for another reason: during breaks, he used it for hushed conversations with Sonnenfeldt.

We sat down; I took my favorite place at the butt of the table to get a better view of the speakers. In case the room acoustics were faulty, watching the speaker's lips helped. Brezhnev sat with his back to the window. Suddenly he produced a large hunting knife and placed it next to the brief. He watched for effect. There was uneasy laughter.

Brezhnev had a strange attraction to knives. They gave him comfort. He would toy with one, or use a smaller one to cut an apple while talking. This fascination extended to guns, hunting rifles, small replicas of artillery guns, and of course, fast cars. He believed in "breaking the ice" with a little stunt, a joke or a story - he was frivolous at the start of a session. He made a suggestion: "Let's break off all communications for a week. The world will be excited - no Kissinger around!" Kissinger readily agreed: "My State Department colleagues will be celebrating!"

Brezhnev put the knife away and launched into a long presentation on the responsibility of the two countries' leaders: "We belong to a generation that must step over many phases and go faster than in the past."

Kissinger knew how to respond: he assured the General Secretary that President Nixon planned to spend more time on preparing Brezhnev's summer visit to the US than of any other foreign dignitary. He will feel comfortable in America.

The most important item on the agenda was the agreement on the prevention of nuclear war. Brezhnev proposed the idea to Kissinger in April 1972, before the first summit. Exchanges were going on for almost a year now, but made no headway. Brezhnev slapped the table: "Let's get down to business. The only thing remaining is this document on how to bomb everybody!" There was laughter. (I recalled this opening line in 1984, when President Reagan made a sound check before a radio address: "We begin bombing Russia in five minutes!") Brezhnev went on: "The struggle for peace will be so intense that all rocks will topple... Look at Alexandrov; he made a sacrifice for peace." Poor Alexandrov had his right arm in a cast: before coming to Zavidovo, he hit a bedstead while trying to shape a pillow. He learnt to write with his left hand, and trained by passing me amusing messages at the conference table - his handwriting improved with every note.

Brezhnev put on a serious face. He confided that not all Politburo members were aware of the secret project: "We are not telling our allies, not even

Poland and the GDR, where I am visiting soon." If the Americans swallowed his claim, they misconstrued relations in the Warsaw Pact. Feeding confidential information to the allies was the USSR's strong lever. (Alexandrov struck Brezhnev's phrase from my transcript).

Kissinger said, "On our side, only the President and those who sit at this table know about this. Your Foreign Ministry has an advantage over us; it read the document." The US will continue to consult with the allies, but "only on general substance." Sonnenfeldt grinned, and Kissinger's eyes gleamed sardonically. I believed him. Nobody in the Cabinet knows, Kissinger added. If they find out, he will have to apply for asylum in the Soviet Union. Brezhnev assured him of "a good life" if he did.

Both Kissinger and Brezhnev weaved a cloak of secrecy where none was needed. It was not a convincing show. This thought seemed to strike Brezhnev, and he corrected himself by saying that the two countries' relations should preclude any apprehensions on the part of the allies. "I wouldn't bet on that," mused Kissinger.

Brezhnev regarded the nuclear war prevention agreement so important that he attempted, though not in so many words, to make the next summit conditional on US acceptance. He said if Nixon signed it in the form presented by the Soviet side, he would go down in history as the greatest US President. Kissinger listened in silence.

The main point of dispute was the obvious anti-Chinese angle. The USSR and the US would commit not to use nuclear weapons against each other, but the possibility of employing them against a third party - China - remained open. Besides, if a conflict flared up in Europe, the US would be barred from a nuclear strike against the Soviet Union.

Kissinger put up resistance. He wanted to avoid anything resembling an anti-Chinese condominium. He produced a cable - just received from the President, he said. He read it aloud. Nixon's tone was shrill: he insisted that Kissinger "adhere strictly" to the President's guidance. Under no circumstances should he initial the text of the agreement, though he may give an assurance in writing that its substance would not be changed. "We are now at the limits of flexibility," Nixon emphasized. Kissinger handed the cable to Victor to translate it into Russian. Brezhnev fidgeted in his seat (he told us later Nixon's language was "rude").

Kissinger said there were no legal or language experts in the American party to study the final draft, while Gromyko had his Treaty Department a telephone call away. Gromyko pointed to Victor and me: "My language experts are here." However, he did not insist.

Though Kissinger thwarted attempts to steer the US into an anti-Chinese arrangement, he gave in on a critical provision. The final text of the agreement stated that the two Parties "will act in such a manner... as to exclude the outbreak of nuclear war between them and between either of the Parties and other countries." That was as close to a non-use clause as we could get. Kissinger was not always successful in watering down agreements: he accepted "act," rather than "do everything possible," as he insisted earlier.

Like a conjurer, Kissinger produced another telegram from the White House, and gave it to Dobrynin to render into Russian. It was on Vietnam. Looking over his shoulder I read the first few phrases: "The President wrote the following on the cable: be sure Brezhnev knows that any major hostile action by North Vietnam between now and the time of his visit could have a disastrous effect here..." Kissinger watched for Brezhnev's reaction - it never came. The scene was bizarre: Soviet officials never showed cipher cables to foreigners, and never, unless instructed, read them aloud. Brezhnev was suspicious: Kissinger's communication with Washington was too quick to believe. (Long after the episode, I learned that the President's telegram was doctored for the occasion.)

Noticing our surprised faces, Kissinger could not miss a jab: "Your experts must be already deciphering our codes." He expanded on the theme: "If we handed over all our cables, this would clog up your machinery of government. Our only line of defense is getting the other side to know everything; then they won't be able to distinguish truth from fiction." He had a point.

During a coffee break, Brezhnev led Kissinger to a corner desk to demonstrate two bound volumes of congratulatory messages on his recent award, the International Lenin Peace Prize "For Strengthening Peace among Peoples." He sheepishly pointed out some of the more adulatory letters for me to translate.

Kissinger commended the prize and politely leafed through the volumes. He was in a good mood. (He did not say he received news the President was thinking of appointing him Secretary of State. In three months, the appointment was announced. Probably Nixon wanted him as a human shield to fend off Watergate attacks).

The Lenin Peace Prize opened the floodgates of awards for Brezhnev: the Joliot Curie "Medaille d'or," the Karl Marx Prize "For Advancing Social Sciences," and the Gold Mercury Award for promotion of trade. By the end of his term he possessed four Gold Stars which were exclusive for Heroes of the Soviet Union (for outstanding war deeds) and to Heroes of Socialist Labor for peacetime achievement. Although Brezhnev saw combat in World War II, he was mainly remembered, quite warmly, as a morale-boosting "political commissar." His awards were now on par with other recipients of the Gold Star - Andrei Sakharov for developing the H-bomb, Igor Kurchatov, the father of the Soviet atomic program, and Sergei Korolev, the man behind Sputnik and Yuri Gagarin's space flight.

We saw Brezhnev tired quickly: he missed appointed hours of meetings as if he inhabited a different time zone. He muddled the day's program; the agenda was shifting all the time. He failed to give advance warning about his afternoon naps to the American team, or for that matter, to us. On the first day, we broke up at 2:00 p.m. for lunch. Brezhnev proposed to resume at five o'clock. When the hour came, I went to advise Kissinger to come at 7:00 p.m.

Somebody suggested a dip in the indoor swimming pool. I was the only one willing to go along with the US team. I explained the pool rules: change, shower, swim, shower again, rub down with large white towels, and relax in the anteroom by the electric samovar, with hot tea, honey and lemon. Without clothes, the NSC staff looked vulnerable. Kissinger should lose weight, I thought. I did a back flip from the springboard to show that Kremlin interpreters were versatile. There were surprised glances - the feat was unexpected. Kissinger did a clumsy breaststroke. He reminded me of Mao Tse-tung swimming in the Yangtze River.

In the evening, we assembled in Brezhnev's study. The bedroom door swung open - I caught a glimpse of a smiling nurse making up the bed. Brezhnev staggered into the room, and lurched. Dobrynin gasped and leaped forward to catch the fall. At the last moment, Brezhnev shot out his right leg and straightened. He beamed, watching for effect. Relieved laughter. Sonnenfeldt took a picture of the episode; he was the only one with a still camera. His photo collection of private moments with Brezhnev must be the largest outside of TASS.

Brezhnev did the little stunt on purpose, to prove his robust health. The intimate circle knew of his indiscriminate intake of sleeping pills. The habit was draining his power of concentration, but he ignored doctors' warnings. Periods of clear headedness gave way to minutes of restlessness and sometimes drowsiness. Smoking was another problem: he could not quit. He showed Kissinger a lean automatic cigarette dispenser, the size of a standard pack. His doctor set it to one cigarette a day. After Kissinger complimented him on the clever gadget, Brezhnev produced an ordinary pack from his pocket and lighted up.

That evening saw a keyed up Brezhnev - probably after a vitamin shot. The negotiating session lasted for five hours, ending past midnight. I wrote till my right hand ached. Victor chain-smoked as he translated in a progressively hoarse voice. The only other smoker was Brezhnev.

Usually Brezhnev invited Kissinger to start the session. However, he tired of listening to English for long stretches, and then to the Russian translation of equal length. He doodled, moved in his chair, looked at his watch, and glanced around, as if expecting someone to bang the gavel. He would interrupt the translator and resume speaking. One had to remind him that the translation of the previous passage was not done yet. When an agenda item was completed, he drew a line across his notes.

Brezhnev had no patience for technical details or legal issues, but was wide-awake when discussion turned to general goals and strategy. He reiterated his keen interest in channeling Soviet-American relations into a "secure riverbed." Kissinger echoed this; he emphasized Nixon's desire to achieve a fundamental change in relations, including trade. Trade is crucial, he said; it is currently restricted by the state of political relations, but now the latter will have to push it ahead.

Brezhnev grasped the opportunity: "Could you provide a two billion dollar credit?" Kissinger replied that, to his knowledge, the largest Export-Import credit of $1 billion was for Brazil, or was it Britain? There were never any deals like this before, he said.

Brezhnev turned to me and whispered, "So what, neither there were giraffes before." He charged into a mind-boggling description of a 40 to 50-year contract (he later reduced it to 25-30 years) to process flared gas from Russian oil wells. Billions of cubic meters are lost every year, he said. The USSR will initially pay with produce. Smiling slyly, he warned that Western Europe was forging ahead in economic links with Russia - "America will be late for its share of the cake… I thought America was a rich country, but it seems to be poor."

This was not an effective argument. I heard it a dozen times: it never worked. Kissinger had a nippy retort ready: "American businessmen are timid; contrary to Marxist theory they do not understand their true interests." He knew that the previous year's frost almost killed the Soviet winter crop; it could be reduced by a third. This will hit livestock. Russia failed to get quick loans from Japan and Western Europe. That's an area where the US could apply gentle political pressure.

The Middle East was already then (and half a century later) a problem with no end in sight. None of us expected it would explode shortly.

Brezhnev, despite his Jewish wife, was never a fan of Israel, and was suspicious of Kissinger's conflict of interests - if not complicity - on its side. He said he was aware of America's special relationship with Tel Aviv, but argued for steady pressure. Less sure of Soviet leverage with the Arab side, he was candid about his own stance on the Middle East.

"Please understand," he said, "I have to talk of American imperialism now and then, but this is for our public; my position is what I am telling you now." (The tongue-in-cheek references to domestic politics became a mantra with Brezhnev; he emulated Nixon.)

Kissinger agreed that avoiding a new war in the Middle East before Brezhnev's visit to the United States was a major American interest as well. He gave a CIA assessment of the situation: "Our people believe it's unlikely that Syria and Egypt would start military operations in the next six months. We also know from our sources that at high level you are urging restraint, but some of your lower level people are adventurous."

Brezhnev nodded, "That is true." He advised watching the situation closely. Gromyko was more direct: Americans were underestimating the danger.

Kissinger said he was aware of the situation. He told a story. "There was this scorpion that needed to cross the Suez Canal. He asked a camel to take him across on his back. The camel said, if I do this, and you sting me in the middle of the waters, I'll be dead. The scorpion said, we will both drown, so don't worry. The camel swam, and in the middle of the Canal, the scorpion stung him. Why? Cried the drowning camel. You forgot, replied the scorpion, this is the Middle East!"

Henry was warming up.

"An Arab was lying in the shade of a tent. Kids were playing around and shouting and the Arab could not sleep. Why don't you run to the village, he told them, they are giving free grapes. The kids ran away. The Arab lay awake and then jumped up: what an idiot, lying here while they're handing out free grapes in the village!"

Brezhnev grinned and struck back: "There was an old Soviet Jew who, after years of writing to the authorities, received permission to emigrate. But old habits die hard: on the eve of his departure he sat down and wrote his final anonymous letter, denouncing himself as a cover-up Russian."

A burst of laughter. Kissinger smiled weakly; the great ethnic joke battle ended in a draw. I did not include the jokes in the memcon, but wrote them down in my diary. Kissinger's stories were mildly anti-Arab, and Brezhnev's a shade anti-Jewish. He knew that Kissinger was no crypto-Zionist and would not be offended.

Brezhnev had a surprise in store, a hunting expedition. He chided Henry for being scared of wild boars roaming around Zavidovo. He advised him to be wary of the hunter who insisted on going first into the forest, since "boars always attack from behind, and the last hunter will be victim." He told stories of his lucky escapes. Once a boar charged up the steps of the hunting tower; another chased Gromyko; he shot one from the car... The stories were getting gorier. I put down my pen - I was never fond of hunting. Brezhnev admitted that hunters were the greatest liars. He invited all of us to inspect the large refrigerator where they kept boar meat.

Kissinger tried to wriggle out of the expedition. He never learnt how to shoot, he said; if he lands a boar, it would probably have died of a heart attack. Nevertheless, he took the plunge. Next morning he emerged outfitted in a Russian hunter's jacket and boots - they had all sizes on hand. He grinned: "I wish my organization could see me now."

After the brief hunt, Brezhnev presented photos. When Henry asked for an autograph, Brezhnev balked, "A thousand dollars each!" (At another time, he said he'd give him a photo only after the Vietnam War ended.) Dobrynin said they both looked like World War II partisans. "More like gangsters," Brezhnev suggested. Probably he was referring to Sonnenfeldt, who, on another expedition, got a black eye from telescopic sight recoil. Helmut's comment was diplomatic: he noted that lesser participants in the talks were careful to shoot smaller boars than the General Secretary did.

Brezhnev promised to send Nixon a Kissinger photo with the rifle. In turn, Kissinger warned he would send Nixon Brezhnev's photo with Bonnie Andrews. He kidded him about the NSC note taker, though I did not see her taking notes in Zavidovo. I assumed she was quite a dish. As were Galya and Vika, the pretty Brezhnev secretaries, with whom he joked during intervals, "to be in a better mood." Contrary to Kissinger's teasing, Brezhnev did just that, talk. Both girls were hard working and unassuming, with a nice sense of humor.

The hunt wore the General Secretary down. Victor told me that Brezhnev, after sharing a few vodkas with salami in the hunter's tower with Kissinger, again raised the Chinese problem. But the vodka stiffened Henry's resolve to avoid a discussion.

As Brezhnev napped, Kissinger and Gromyko proceeded to negotiate on their own. This saved time. They decided the format for negotiations on mutual and balanced force reductions in Europe (MBFR). The Soviets were not enthusiastic about losing their numerical advantage; the US hoped the new process would lead to loosening the Soviet grip on Eastern Europe.

The manner of deciding on prospective participants was casual. Gromyko, thinking aloud, suggested excluding Hungary; Kissinger did not object. He thought Italy could be dropped as well; the two nations' armed forces did not make a difference in the equation. Both men looked content. It was exemplary super-power coordination. No objections from client States were expected.

The Conference on Security and Cooperation in Europe (CSCE) was the next agenda item. Initially it was a Soviet idea designed to formalize, for all time, post-war borders in Europe. The issue of frontiers and the unlikely possibility of their change was part of the "first basket" - Principles - of the future Helsinki Final Act. The Conference assumed importance for the West as well - in the dimension of human contacts, the "third basket" of the agreement provisions. The conflicting goals of strengthening borders and piercing them at the same time assured that the process would be bumpy. The conservative branch of the Soviet leadership suspected it would eventually backfire, to nurture dissent and seriously weaken the Soviet system. Mikhail Suslov, the Party ideologue and powerful Politburo member called the conference a "landmine."

All the same, the CSCE was the next grand event on Brezhnev's international agenda. One of the remaining issues was level of attendance at the final stage. "Let's send Ministers if there is no success, and Heads of State if there is," suggested Kissinger and added, looking at Gromyko: "I expect your country's level will be Politburo, in any case." He had in mind the recent elevation of Gromyko to the supreme body, a move long overdue, which gave the Foreign Ministry the political status it badly needed. Before that, in the comparative pecking order of the two countries Gromyko was a rung lower than Kissinger.

For the US, the CSCE was of less importance than for the Europeans. Kissinger told Gromyko the US would not create difficulties. On human contacts, he did not mince words: he thought the West Europeans "were crazy." The US stood for improving things, but without getting involved in each other's domestic affairs. (He admitted on another occasion that the US Administration did not demonstrate "we can handle our own affairs.") He was aware that several European allies wanted to use the conference to reform the domestic system in the Soviet Union. He thought it was unrealistic: "They failed to do it in several wars." He promised to talk to West German Chancellor Brandt.

For Kissinger, it was not an American issue; whatever Moscow agreed with Bonn the US will accept.

The Soviet view was that Bonn's long-term strategy was reunification of Germany, which Moscow saw in terms of an Anschluss of the German Democratic Republic. France and Britain did not conceal their qualms about reunification. They preferred a divided Germany lest it grow into a domineering force on the continent. For Nixon and Kissinger, the GDR was a geopolitical fact. The US was willing to recognize the GDR once the Bundestag ratified the treaty between the two Germanys.

Many in the West saw the GDR as an aberration, a welfare state low on productivity and high on government control. The Soviet perspective was different: the GDR was a bulwark against NATO. This was one reason for stationing half a million Soviet troops and subsidizing its economy. The Kremlin pursued yet another goal, a deep cultural one. The existence of a friendly German Socialist regime was critical for dispelling deep hatred felt by Russians towards Germans after the most vicious onslaught on Russia after the Tatar-Mongols in the 13th century. It was vital for Russian-German reconciliation. It laid the basis for Russia's rapprochement with West Germany and later with a united Germany.

Realism on the part of the White House explains the extent of US-Soviet collusion on European security. Here's an illustration. An item of the CSCE agenda concerned exchange of information on major military maneuvers and troop movements. The West Europeans demanded 90-day advance warning of maneuvers of more than 12,000 troops in the 500 km border zone between the two military alliances. Gromyko ridiculed the demand: for Luxemburg, one regiment is a formidable force; for the USSR, five divisions going from winter to summer quarters would not be noticed. Kissinger smiled: "We don't notice them either, as long as they don't come west." He was sympathetic to Soviet concerns. He suggested a plan. Let the Soviet delegate publicly reject the US position, which supported NATO allies. The US delegate will inform them "the US tried its best, but…" He will then receive new instructions from Washington, agreeable to the Soviets. US delegate Ambassador Albert Sherer was unaware of this little plot. (The final agreement reached at Helsinki was 21-day notification of maneuvers exceeding 25,000 troops in the 250-kilometer zone, and voluntary notification of major troop movements.)

At the last day's afternoon session with Brezhnev, Kissinger shuffled his papers, and with a deep sigh, suggested discussing Vietnam. By that time, Brezhnev's dislike of the topic turned into revulsion. He delegated this increasingly irrelevant part of the US-Soviet agenda to Gromyko. He said it was getting late. He needed his nap to conserve strength for the farewell dinner - the US team was departing the following morning.

Gromyko listened sullenly to Kissinger's complaints about North Vietnam violating the cease-fire agreement, in particular by moving tanks to the South. Henry gave Gromyko a piercing look through his thick lenses: "We showed them the photos, but they claimed it were civilian goods. We insisted it's prohibited to carry civilian goods in tanks…" He droned on: "Hanoi is cynically violating the agreement… Hanoi has sent 400 tanks, 300 artillery pieces and 30,000 troops to the South. True, we sent quite an amount of military hardware, but that was before the agreement was signed… If they undertake a major offensive, we will be obliged to react, although we do not wish to embroil ourselves in a war again…"

The telltale expressions - "cynically violating," "a major offensive" (how major?), "will be obliged" to react, rather than "will react" - confirmed my conviction. I was thrown back a year to the confrontation at the dacha, when the entire Soviet leadership warned Nixon of "consequences" if the US continued the war. At that time, Brezhnev and his comrades were unsure of the course of the war, and were worried about its impact on the first summit and détente in general. This was history. They could not care less now: the tables were turned irrevocably. What they did not understand was Nixon clinging to the last vestiges of the South Vietnamese regime. After all, he already achieved his aim of ending the war.

Kissinger tried a philosophical approach. "We never expected," he said, "that with the signing of an agreement the people who strove for certain goals for twenty-five years would renounce them all at once. However, we thought that some time would pass, the agreement will stand, more or less, and then - other events would follow…"

I took down every word of this remarkable statement; it amounted to conceding surrender - with a face-saving grace period. Say no more, Henry Kissinger. The message was as clear as could be; the rest would be atmospherics. I wondered if Moscow would transmit my record to Hanoi tonight.

Gromyko looked down and doodled on his writing pad. Kissinger tried to catch his eye. He grasped at the last straw, "Marxists believe in the irreversible march of history, so why don't the North Vietnamese? They should understand the inevitability of the historical process… Why do they want to have it in a few days?" That was almost openly begging the USSR to ask the North Vietnamese not to overrun South Vietnam too fast.

North Vietnam's stance was ordained: no appeals to Marxism could change it. (The Soviet Ambassador in Hanoi once told me how difficult it was to make friends with the Vietnamese at any level: leaders, soldiers, intellectuals; it was easier speaking to Americans).

Gromyko was in no mood to argue. He listened stone-faced to Kissinger's pleading. "There is only one true version of Marxism," he said suddenly. "I have been told that in three different capitals," Kissinger muttered. "For three years we haggled with Le Duc Tho over which expression to use, "great efforts" or just "efforts…"

Gromyko interrupted: "Why don't you mention violations of the agreement by Saigon? The South Vietnamese are no saints."

"Yes, but their violations are of a minor, technical nature… Hanoi's violations breach principles. Moreover, the North does not release political prisoners. True, they released about 2,000 to the villages, but South Vietnam claims that 40,000 were abducted by the North. Well, one figure is obviously too low, the other too high…" Kissinger's voice trailed off.

There was silence. Gromyko gazed at a point above Kissinger's head and suppressed a yawn: "The USSR believes all parties should strictly comply with the Paris Peace Accords; the South should release all political prisoners." He added, as an afterthought, that the USSR as signatory of the Final Act of the International Conference on Vietnam supported this obligation.

Although Gromyko's tone was firm, his words carried little conviction. Knowing my boss well, I felt his remarks had no negotiating value, and were made strictly for my memcon and its readers in the Politburo. He saw no sense in debating the issue any longer. Although he studiously avoided mention of Watergate, he knew it tied Nixon's hands on Vietnam. The Paris settlement called for the eventual reunification of Vietnam, permitting the South Vietnamese and Vietcong troops to remain in place in South Vietnam - this was crucial. The 46,000 Americans killed in action, the arrangement to free American prisoners and to withdraw US forces left no basis for taking Kissinger's warnings seriously. As the POWs left in early 1973 (including John McCain, whose A-4 fighter was blasted out of the sky by a Soviet SAM missile) the fate of the war was sealed.

Gromyko enquired lazily, "When is Thieu leaving? His presence doesn't help." Kissinger retorted that even Le Duc Tho was not asking for Thieu's removal. Since they were on the subject, he said sullenly, [General Secretary of the Vietnamese Workers Party] Le Duan's presence was not helpful either. He pressed Gromyko to talk to Le Duc Tho when he made a stopover in Moscow on his way to Paris. Gromyko did not show he heard this remark. By all appearances, Kissinger did not expect an answer. Probably he also spoke for the record.

The topic was exhausted. Kissinger stretched - his suits looked too tight, ready to burst at the seams. He sighed: he was sure that in one or two years the Great Powers would disassociate themselves from Indo-China. He made a feeble attempt to compare notes on Cambodia, where, he claimed, Prince Souvanna Phouma asked for US bombing raids, but Gromyko did not react. (Neither expected that in two years the tiny country would become a killing field and that the Vietnamese army, as a savior, would oust the Khmer Rouge to tacit international approval.)

They turned to the last item, the set of principles of negotiations on a future SALT agreement. Drafts and counter drafts made the rounds. Kissinger warned against bare principles. The White House would be involved in a domestic debate for lack of concrete achievements. Principles, Kissinger lectured, always contain compromise language and become blurry; they sow the seeds of future misinterpretation and discord. Principles *per se* achieve little. The 1972 accord on basic principles of US-Soviet relations was possible only after negotiating SALT. The 1967 Security Council resolution on the Middle East established a principle, peace in return for occupied territories, but there is no concrete settlement in sight, he said.

I thought Kissinger's approach was sensible. Resolution 242 was a good example - I was involved in negotiating it in New York. Still, his disdain for signed political agreements was suspect; it was too close to disregarding international law. Brezhnev and Gromyko kept the pressure on principles: it was how their minds operated: from principles to specifics. Kissinger's mind worked from specifics to principles.

The Zavidovo round was nearing to a close, when Kissinger raised a delicate topic: the post-Nixon era. He spoke in confidence. "Everything must be done," he told Brezhnev, "to continue the current favorable trend after Nixon." He believed that Nelson Rockefeller's chances as President were high. He remarked, casually, that he was Rockefeller's friend, and could exert some pull.

Brezhnev's apparatchik mind started ticking, shifting cadres around: "Nixon should head the Republican Party - it will need an experienced leader." Kissinger glanced at Brezhnev to make sure he wasn't joking, and thought better of continuing a discussion on the American party system against the background of Watergate. I suspected Brezhnev thought Kissinger was talking about 1976, the end of Nixon's second term. He still believed his comrade was firmly in the saddle.

Zavidovo was the longest negotiation that Brezhnev was to have with Kissinger or any other foreigner: five working days and eight sessions. It was the most productive.

As we rose, Gromyko asked Kissinger whom he thought the most difficult negotiating partner. "Why, the Joint Chiefs of Staff, of course," he replied, "followed by the North Vietnamese. The Japanese - it's next to impossible to pry them from a set position." I realized later that he failed to mention Soviet negotiators. Long live détente!

Gromyko's reply to the same question was evasive: it depended on personalities, not nationality.

After Kissinger left for his cabin, Gromyko beckoned to Victor and me. We sat down in the empty conference room. He wanted to check his summing-up against our notes. He ticked off fourteen items, and referenced each in a phrase or two. I assumed it was a summary for Brezhnev's report to the Politburo.

- Helsinki conference preparations slow; we should expect no difficulties from US, they will talk to Brandt;
- Inviolability of frontiers: US have no problem, but we have to convince Brandt;
- Third basket: cultural ties to be linked to respect for national laws; US will not create difficulties;
- US will establish diplomatic relations with GDR after treaty ratification with FRG...

Gromyko did not bother to mention Vietnam. A very long negotiation was masterfully condensed into a set of bullet points, capturing the essence of positions and conclusions reached. There were no moral judgments. He asked us if he missed anything. I admired his powerful mind. For this, one was ready to gloss over his occasional mocking tone.

On the final night, 8 May, Brezhnev hosted an informal dinner for all participants in the Zavidovo talks. The hour was late; we looked forward to the well-earned *zakuski,* the Russian hors d'oeuvres, including smoked boar meat. There was no seating plan. Brezhnev sat in the middle of the table, his back to the windows, and invited Kissinger to take a seat on his right. Gromyko and Dobrynin sat opposite. Kornienko, Hyland, Sonnenfeldt, Philip Odeen, Richard Campbell, Peter Rodman, Victor and I plunked into available chairs.

The party was noisy. Kissinger toasted Brezhnev and his warm hospitality. Brezhnev toasted Kissinger and members of his party, and kidded Sonnenfeldt. He told stories. He was pleased: it was the longest negotiation he undertook single handedly. A splendid outcome - what more could be desired?

Gromyko was in a good mood. He turned to me, "Tell me, Vavilov, was President Roosevelt Democrat or Republican?" "Democrat," I said, thinking the Minister had one too many. Gromyko raised his glass to "Franklin Delano Roosevelt, the great Democrat who worked for Soviet-American relations!" "A great democrat," agreed Kissinger. "I'll drink to that!" Amidst laughter, he made sure it was a small "d."

The party broke up shortly after 2:00 a.m. A weary American team trundled to their quarters. "Wait!" said Dobrynin. He reminded Kissinger of Nixon's promise about the written assurance not to change the substance of the agreement on the prevention of nuclear war, after a review by legal and language experts. Moving his plates away, a tipsy Sonnenfeldt scribbled a few lines. Kissinger signed the paper and handed it to Dobrynin. (Back in Moscow, Brezhnev brandished the two-paragraph text, on White House stationery, to his colleagues as proof that he "out-negotiated Ghenry" and by proxy, President Nixon. He could not get an initialed agreement, but this looked even better.)

It was a quiet and sunny morning. Gifts were dispensed. Brezhnev received a pair of hand-painted porcelain plaques with American birds in foliage in gold leaf frames, and Gromyko a small silver bowl. Others had to do with propagandistic 1973 silver and bronze inaugural medallions. Mine was bronze.

Kremlin security said that packaged gifts from Brezhnev were already on board the helicopter. Departure was delayed for several minutes because of an altercation: Sonnenfeldt got a Zavidovo trophy, a stuffed boar's head, and Kissinger objected to having "that dirty thing" in the plane. Sonnenfeldt won, and they drove away to the helipad for the short flight to Moscow.

We returned to the main villa. It was almost 11:00 a.m. Brezhnev invited the Russian team to breakfast in the first floor dining room. The meal turned into a family feast to commemorate May 9, Great Patriotic War Victory Day. We took off our jackets. Victor and I sat with Galya and Vika. Brezhnev's old friend and aide-de-camp, Colonel Alexander Ryabenko, sat quietly at the end of the table. He was Brezhnev's chauffeur before the war, fought at the front, and returned to serve his boss after the war. Brezhnev's former tailor, Lieutenant-General Yefim Goldberg, now in charge of supplies in the Ministry of Defense, sat next to him.

Opposite me sat Nina, the comely nurse whom I glimpsed in the Secretary General's bedroom. Some said she was the source of smuggled sleeping pills. Dr. Evgeni Chazov, Head of the Fourth Chief Directorate of the Ministry of Health (also known as the Kremlin Clinic) spent a great deal of effort to evict her from the household, given Brezhnev's unhealthy reliance on her, mixed, I think, with genuine affection. Brezhnev kept most of his aides from old times: secretaries, cooks, valets and bodyguards.

Goldberg raised his glass and toasted "the Army officer who fought at the front." We stood and drank ceremoniously. Brezhnev's lips quivered; he thanked his old comrade. He reached over the table to clink glasses with everyone, and went around to plant kisses on women's cheeks. It was too early for Gromyko to have a drink, but others went ahead. The sense of relief was glorious. Brezhnev told funny stories. Vika made faces: "Andrey, we all laugh now - I heard that story at least fifteen times..."

We went to the porch to see Brezhnev off. He put on his sunglasses and squeezed behind the wheel of a dark blue Rolls Royce Silver Cloud with regular Moscow license plates. He looked dashing. An apprehensive Gromyko sat next to him, and Ryabenko climbed in the back. They did not buckle their seat belts. The car drove off at high speed.

Nikolai, a friend from the security detail, told me later that Brezhnev drove at seventy miles an hour along a highway cleared of traffic, and kept talking to his passengers. He almost veered into a ditch. For some reason he attempted, but was unable, to overtake the lead security vehicle. Upon arrival at the Kremlin, he summoned the fast driver and presented him with an Omega wristwatch - for "outstanding driving skills." Handing out small tokens on a whim was the General Secretary's forte, a nostalgic throwback to the times of the Tsars. The gestures left many pleasantly surprised and many more bewildered. From 1976 on, Brezhnev no longer sat at the wheel - the vehicle of State rolled on without the driver.

We followed Brezhnev's car at a safe distance in a black KGB Volga, and made a short stop in a forest clearing for sandwiches and beers. Approaching Moscow, we passed a run-down apartment building with three oversize portraits: Brezhnev, Kosygin and Lenin. I wondered what happened to Podgorny;

apparently, nobody cared. The country was slipping into a prolonged period of what people later called "stagnation."

Black Sea, off Crimea. Brezhnev serves beer to his aide Blatov and secretaries. Vika and Galya are in foreground. (Vladimir Musaelyan)

In next two twenty-four hours, Victor and I dictated 58 pages of transcripts of the Zavidovo talks and deposited them with Vika and Galya. They were the General Secretary's *lichnie devushki*, literally "personal girls." The term was no allusion to office romance but denoted female staffers who brought the most sensitive - "For Your Eyes Only" - documents for Brezhnev to read, or, as the office jokers put it, the "Burn before reading" grade.

GROMYKO STRIKES BACK

Brezhnev and Nixon would not have been effective without their foreign policy aides. Brezhnev suggested they trade them. Nixon thought it a marvelous idea. He pointed to Kissinger: "Mr. General Secretary, you are exporting Jews at present; import this one, you'll be less criticized."

Gromyko never wanted to emulate Kissinger. It was difficult to imagine him jetting around the world, dining and wining on the side. Besides, he was wise enough to clear important moves with MFA experts. Producing carefully formulated memos after consultation with other government departments - before applying to the Politburo for endorsement - was the standard operating procedure of the Foreign Minister. Several government members were no less powerful than Gromyko; he could not circumvent them.

Whatever idea the West had of Brezhnev as the unquestioned Number One, he had to, both by Party rules and by his nature of a consensus builder, turn to other Politburo members for approval. He remembered the fate of confrontationist Khrushchev who attempted to bypass the government and Party structure. Brezhnev had to muster support from the Party Central Committee (a body of some 400 members) to salvage the first Soviet-American summit.

Nixon and Kissinger may have regarded Soviet foreign policy as slow and cumbersome at times. True, it did not have the flexibility of a lean-apparatus White House operation, but it was solid, never hasty or badly prepared. It was done under Gromyko's watch.

His attention to detail was remarkable - he never missed a barely perceptible nuance. He was the only one in the Soviet leadership who really knew America (by coincidence, his Ph.D. thesis, before joining the Foreign Service, was on American agriculture). He was appointed Ambassador in Washington at the age of 33. Brezhnev was only half-joking when he told Kissinger that Gromyko was "soft" on the United States.

He was outwardly composed, but his quick temper with staff was legendary. He almost matched Kissinger in being curt, sometimes rude to subordinates. While Kissinger relaxed tension with a quip, Gromyko sulked, but was never vindictive. Perhaps both thought that staff bashing was good for morale. When I reported to him on a conversation Brezhnev had with a visitor, he told me, brusquely, "Vavilov, do you expect to grow a few more centimeters if you remain standing?" This was an invitation for me (of 5' 7") to take a seat.

One could be lashed on the flimsiest pretext. You could growl, but it would get you nowhere. MFA wisdom was "grin and bear it." Strangely, the Minister respected office courage, which few staff dared demonstrate. Never to acknowledge the slights he delivered, often unfairly, Gromyko would summon the aggrieved diplomat the next day to discuss a very different subject, pretending that nothing had happened. His towering stature as one of the world's most competent Foreign Ministers tempered one's occasional desire to slam the door in his face. You were not supposed to harbor hard feelings. This was not an easy thing; if brought to breaking point some staff talked back.

I translated for British Foreign Secretary George Brown when he negotiated with Gromyko in Moscow. Tired of whispered advice from the British Ambassador, Brown hissed: "Will you shut up, you idiot!" The red-faced Ambassador leaned back and remained angrily silent until the end of the session. I sympathized with the poor chap.

After escorting Brown to the door, Gromyko turned to me, "Well, Vavilov, you saw how a Minister can behave." He caught me at a bad moment; I was still recovering from a dressing down he gave me the day before on a matter not related to translation. "Andrei Andreyevitch," I said, "You're no better sometimes." I froze as the words were coming out of my mouth. Gromyko stared at me and said nothing. I never tried my luck again.

Once Gromyko was stuck for thirty minutes in the new elevator at the Soviet UN Mission in New York. He emerged without a word of complaint; there were no repercussions. The person formally responsible for maintenance at the Mission had a later career as Ambassador. Gromyko could be touchingly attentive: he used to ask me about my father, with whom he joined the Foreign Service in 1939.

As Deputy Director for Science and Technology at the MFA, I sometimes stood in for the department chief. I sat at a large desk reading mail and cables from Soviet embassies abroad. I watched the green telephone on my left, the Minister's direct line, dreading its ring. It did ring when technicians tested it at intervals, giving one a nasty jolt. Gromyko rarely telephoned department chiefs, and preferred buzzing his private staff. Whenever he called in person, it was with a specific query, usually on US or UN affairs, like what countries were current non-permanent members of the Security Council. Sometimes he asked peculiar things: did Thomas Dewey run against Truman in 1948? He expected short and concrete answers. I suspected he wanted to test his subordinates' memory.

Gromyko was as orderly in mind as in his habits. He was never late for meetings. One morning I drove with Victor to the Kremlin. "Idiots," he said, as we entered St. Catherine Hall, "we're thirty minutes early!" The lights were still dimmed, but I noticed a silent figure in a gray suit with a briefcase in a corner chair. We felt humbled.

Gromyko insisted on punctuality, notwithstanding traffic jams in New York. I talked his driver out of suicide when he pulled in at the UN main entrance three minutes late only to find that some delegate offered Gromyko a lift to the Soviet Mission. Fortunately, they talked business during the ride. An MFA diplomat once said Gromyko was the Russian version of Gloomy Gus. Never an extrovert, he seemed aloof and rarely shared his thoughts before hearing experts' opinions. Despite his reserve, he appreciated humor. His sense of humor was of a simple and inoffensive kind; he could not approach Kissinger in that department.

One day, we were driving to the UN when he suddenly pointed to a girl in bright green stockings walking along Lexington Avenue. "Vavilov," he asked, "have you bought a pair like these for your wife?" "No, Andrei Andreyevitch," I replied. "She'd never wear these, she's got conservative tastes." He grunted, pleased.

He was better with jokes on the rebound. In the Kremlin conference room, Kissinger shielded his notes and pointed to a ceiling chandelier: "That camera must have been put in by Ivan the Terrible."   "No," said Gromyko, "he installed the air conditioning." When they resolved the thorny issue of "significant increase" in ICBM silo dimensions (to mean not more than 15 percent), Gromyko smiled: "We are significantly satisfied, even more than 15 percent!"

When Kissinger warned, ironically, that a Soviet proposal could not be rapidly accepted, Gromyko said, "Why don't you accept it slowly?" In the summer of 1974, in a heated debate on the threshold nuclear test ban, Gromyko noticed Kissinger glance at his watch. He asked if it showed the time Kissinger was to get his paycheck, or maybe he already lived under Communism, enjoying everything without money? Kissinger jokingly confided that under the US system the government takes away according to his needs, and gives according to his ability. (He paraphrased the principle of a Communist society: "From each according to his ability, to each according to his needs." Of course, Karl Marx's phrase had Biblical origins.)

Gromyko had an agile mind, and loved comparisons: the US and the USSR are "like two ships sailing towards a common goal, circumventing islands and fogs, but staying the course." The Soviet Union is not an aircraft carrier, he added (alluding to US superiority in that area), rather a PT boat. In a tortuous 1974 discussion with Kissinger about prolonging the SALT interim agreement, Gromyko vented his exasperation. What Kissinger proposed, he said, was not unlike the USSR buying a horse: the buyer suddenly finds himself holding the bridle, but the horse is missing.

Gromyko reacted good-naturedly to people comparing him to Richard Nixon: both were tall, dark, same slim build, tough in negotiation, introverts, glum at times. They even spoke in similar baritone. Gromyko was aware Nixon noticed that too. He mused that next time on a dark night in Washington he will just try to walk into the White House. Once he confessed to Nixon, who called him a conservative, that he was slightly "right of center" in his political views, by Soviet standards. (This was much closer to center than political hawks like Podgorny.) Gromyko was relaxed in Nixon's presence: he never employed flattery, as Kissinger did with Brezhnev. In his regular meetings with Nixon at the White House, usually in the fall to coincide with the UN General Assembly session, he rarely joked, was businesslike and even cheeky at moments.

Quite old school in his dress tastes, Gromyko was. In New York, he would ask his assistant or Victor to look for a new hat: "I bought a Borsalino twenty years ago, but it's become a bit worn." He was used to dark gray double-breasted suits, straight out of a 1940's Humphrey Bogart movie.

Kissinger had deep respect for Gromyko - he felt he had to be on constant guard. He confessed that he can meet any Foreign Minister by his own decision, but he needed the President's approval to meet Gromyko. "Gromyko was, of course, extremely well informed," was his recurring observation in dispatches to the White House. He accepted that the Russian Minister's institutional memory and grasp of detail - of Soviet-American relations, United Nations, German problem, or disarmament - dwarfed his own fountain of erudition.

Gromyko was well read in classical literature and history. In May 1973 in Zavidovo, the conversation turned to protocol - Brezhnev complained he lost much time at official ceremonies and State dinners. A professor of history, Kissinger noted that during negotiations on the Treaty of Westphalia (to end the Thirty Year's War in 1648) they spent three weeks discussing the order of dignitaries entering the room. Gromyko confirmed it. He recalled the Congress of Vienna of 1815. He saw the doors through which the three European monarchs, including Alexander I, were supposed to enter the hall at exactly the same moment.

If prompted, Gromyko always had a story to recount. Kissinger knew that the Minister accompanied Joseph Stalin in Yalta in February 1945 - what was his view of the Soviet leader, his greatest quality? Gromyko said it was a strong intellect, strong character and willpower. Roosevelt, Gromyko said, looked healthy but tired; he had a faraway look. After calling on the President, Stalin told Gromyko, "He is a very good and able man; why has nature punished him?"[26] Kissinger appreciated historical anecdotes.

Gromyko's mastery of English kept interpreters on their toes. It was thorough but academic; he disliked words not found in the 1945 edition of the Merriam-Webster Dictionary. He was genuinely fond of the English language. His advice to a friend of mine taking up a post in the Soviet Embassy in London was, "Be sure to visit the churches and listen to the sermons; the English is excellent."

Gromyko preferred to have an interpreter by his side at official meetings for the sake of preserving a record. At private audiences at the White House, he would dispense with translation of the President's words, but wanted his own statements translated, for the extra time to think. Occasionally, he would question the interpreter's use of a particular expression, and recommend a version he thought was closer to his idea. He never gave ground on his understanding of English. I confronted him several times. Rather than acknowledge defeat he asked me to "later check with Sukhodrev," for him the final authority. When I told Victor, he shrugged: the Minister's request meant a dismissal of any doubts he had.

Gromyko always listened to the translation - were his thoughts put across correctly? He made short thrift with interpreters whom he regarded as substandard. Some colleagues were banned from his office and from Kremlin negotiations when the Minister was present. He would not deride an interpreter for a language slip - he knew this happened with the best experts. On one occasion, he mentioned a particular conference, and I erroneously said "peace conference." He turned to me: "I didn't say peace, just conference." He thought a little and then conceded, generously, "But of course, any international conference is a peace conference…"

Once, in Geneva, I made a slip in translation. Gromyko said that Kissinger's position on the Middle East was "unfortunate" ("*sozhaleyu*" in Russian). I said he "deplored" the position. I realized it was not the best word, but I felt the Minister liked my translation, because it added punch. Kissinger, who was usually tough-skinned, acted hurt. He wanted to know why Gromyko "deplored" his position. He kept harping on the word, which, he claimed, expressed moral condemnation and was far too strong. Master drafter Kornienko jokingly suggested a new verb, "reg-lore," combined from "regret/deplore." Gromyko backed down: he actually meant "regret." At this point, I admitted my mistake. Kissinger looked satisfied: he won the semantic battle. Gromyko passed the incident over; he understood the strain the interpreter is always under.

Gromyko did not hesitate to correct Americans. In 1974, as they drafted the joint statement on environmental warfare, he said he did not like the US phrase "to establish measures." Kissinger did not like it either. Sonnenfeldt suggested "to institute." Gromyko disagreed: measures cannot be "instituted," they are "brought about." He often drafted communiqués in English together with Kissinger. After the work was done, he would sit back and say, "It's a beauty."

Diplomatic folklore christened Gromyko "Mr. Nyet." In a particularly difficult discussion, Kissinger told him, "With you, Gromyko, the possibility of saying "yes" is remote." "Not true," parried Gromyko. "Whenever you say "no," I say "yes."

The Minister chose his words with extra care. Kissinger asked him point blank if Brezhnev still planned to come to the US in 1975 (with only two or three months to go before the appropriate time window). Gromyko did not give a straightforward answer - yes or no. He said, "We proceed from the understanding reached." This meant "yes, but." To us, it was clear that timing depended entirely on Brezhnev's state of health.

One thing that maddened Kissinger was Gromyko's love for double negatives. Instead of saying, "probably I will go to Cairo," he would say, "it is not excluded that I will go to Cairo." Of course, a double negative cancelled out into an affirmative statement, but no one could push Gromyko into simplifying the speaking style. Confronted, he would insist that the double negative was a shade milder than a straightforward statement. He told Kissinger he knew how to use triple negatives (quite a riddle for the note taker, I must say). His manner of speaking was addictive. When Kissinger said, "We do not exclude the possibility of cooperating with the Soviet Union in the Middle East," Gromyko shook his head in merriment: "This was an understatement with double negatives!"

Gromyko participated in the wartime conferences of the Big Three in Yalta and Potsdam, and signed the UN Charter in San Francisco in 1945. He served as Ambassador in London, Washington, and at the UN, and supervised all disarmament agreements with the West. He believed in détente and never considered it a tactical maneuver. This unique experience combined with, as one would now say, a computer mind and lethal negotiating skills in defending the Soviet national interest. "When I give way on a point," Kissinger said, "Gromyko regards this as a concession on his part... I do not mind being defeated in a negotiation; it is being tortured beforehand that I object to...

Shock treatment? I get it every day." For him, Gromyko was a concrete wall, never giving way, i.e., retreating to the fallback position before all negotiating methods were fully exhausted. Capacity for hard work, tenacity and determination in reaching a set objective played a key role in carrying this peasant boy from an obscure Belorussian village and his first job floating logs down a forest river to the pinnacle of the diplomatic profession.

In the fall of 1973, the Federal Republic of Germany and the German Democratic Republic waited to be admitted to the UN. In this connection, the four wartime allies decided to issue a declaration on their responsibility for Germany as a whole. The US saw it as reinforcing its occupation rights in Berlin. For the USSR, the declaration was an indirect way of supporting the GDR. The four powers wanted to ensure that any increased status of the FRG and the GDR not undermine their rights as victors in World War II. I travelled to Bonn, where Soviet Ambassador Valentin Falin secretly negotiated with Egon Bahr, aide to Willy Brandt, on the draft declaration. Endorsement by the Federal Republic was crucial. Getting approval from the GDR was easier - it usually followed Russian advice. I spent two nights at the Ambassador's residence by the Rhine. He introduced me to Bahr, who was surprised to see a language expert flown in from Moscow to check his and Falin's product (the text was negotiated by the Four Allies in English).

Naturally, Kissinger had a hand in drafting. Gromyko went over the US draft with a magnifying glass. He educated Kissinger on the historical origin of the problem and legal implications of language. He began by turning down all three paragraphs of the US draft. Kissinger assumed a straightforward statement was enough - that the two Germanys' admission to the UN did not affect the rights of the four powers. Gromyko insisted on saying that "it did not affect the question of their rights." He meant the question of rights did not arise at all. Kissinger did not grasp the hair-splitting difference, but agreed in the end.

It was fascinating watching both men negotiate. Kissinger's mercurial temperament and quest for quick results was difficult to match with the persistence of the Soviet Minister who was a master of attrition. In a particularly difficult session, Jan Lodal slipped Henry a note with additional argumentation. Kissinger read it and said aloud, "I can produce ten brilliant ideas myself, but what's the use?" At a protracted late night session, he leant back: "Let's stop. I see several of my colleagues had heart attacks that I've accepted your terms so quickly."

There was a deeper reason for Kissinger's fixation on Gromyko. He was aware that the Minister had a stabilizing influence on Brezhnev and Soviet foreign policy in general - it grew with his steady rise to the top. He avoided unnecessary confrontation with the US. Paradoxically, Kissinger's blunt rejection of some Soviet suggestions on SALT helped Gromyko to advise the Politburo to temper positions. He and Brezhnev had to steer a careful path; there was no fear of a military takeover, but opposition from the conservatives was always there.

Gromyko once told us, "You know what our military think: what is ours is ours, what is yours - we'll see about that." In a rush of candor, he told Kissinger a joke: a Soviet Army officer wanted a job with the General Staff. His friend said he was crazy. The aspiring officer said he heard it was a requirement for a desk job. Kissinger liked the story: it fitted with his and Nixon's low esteem of the brass.

Both men rarely used briefs, almost never took notes, and possessed the ability to conceptualize and explain complex ideas in short understandable terms. They often spoke without interpreters, in low voices. These encounters, at a cocktail party, or during a walk in the park, were most productive.

Gromyko recognized professionalism when he saw it, and was always loyal to his carefully chosen aides. This sense of loyalty led to errors of judgment bordering on gullibility. His private assistant had to fall flat on his face at a Warsaw Pact summit in Bucharest before it dawned on the Minister that the person had a drinking problem. Another case was serious. Gromyko refused to believe a KGB warning that Ambassador Arkady Shevchenko, the young UN Under-Secretary-General, behaved suspiciously. After the latter's defection in New York in 1978, Gromyko privately wondered if the Americans sprinkled some powder that affected his protégé's brain. He was incredulous when the KGB found that Shevchenko assisted the CIA all along. This was not held against Gromyko: as a close Brezhnev friend (they were on first-name terms), he was immune.

A realist in world politics, Gromyko had an irrational liking for grand policy initiatives, mostly in the field of disarmament. He adored the drafting the so-called *glavni vopros* ("main question"), a Foreign Ministry euphemism for a dramatic proposal sprung on the unsuspecting UN General Assembly. These were tabled every fall. In a third of cases, they did fire the imagination of developing countries. The greatest hit was the elimination of the colonial system in the 1960s. Most of the noble initiatives evaporated as the morning mist - for lack of wide support.

Obsessive secrecy surrounded every "main question." The conspiratorial approach produced a comic case. A secretary from the Minister's seventh floor typing pool felt slighted that she was passed over for the General Assembly delegation. She did an ingenious thing, typing her name into the final list already signed by Gromyko. Since the memo emanated from the Minister's private office, Personnel went into the usual motions, issuing the woman's travel documents and applying for a US visa. She would have surely flown to New York if she did not turn up next morning at the typing pool dressed in a military tunic with decorations. After a call to the Ministry clinic, it emerged she had a history of weird behavior.

NIGHTS OF CAMP DAVID

On 14 June 1973, two days before Brezhnev embarked on his first ever trip to the United States, I received a call from the Kremlin.

The General Secretary received a group of American reporters for an unprecedented three-hour question and answer session and a guided tour of his office. "You can ask any questions, no holds barred," he said. He showed them his battery of cream-colored secure phones. They inspected his huge desk. A drawer was open - it held his autographed portraits.

A huge vase with a realistic Brezhnev portrait in enamel stood in the corner. The long table held a high pile of books. I leafed through some of them: all were inscribed to Brezhnev by the authors, some effusively. None looked as if they had been opened. Some were war and spy stories.

With a sly smile, Brezhnev gestured to a large book cabinet behind his armchair. He pulled a handle and the door opened to reveal his private chambers. We went inside to inspect a Spartan room with a sofa, a table covered with a white cloth, two upholstered leather chairs, a color TV set, a fridge, cupboards and the omnipresent scrambler telephones.

Henry Shapiro of *Time* magazine, Jay Axelbank of *Newsweek* and others sat at the long conference table; Brezhnev faced them. I took a seat to his left. Brezhnev smoked American cigarettes. He was unaware that Nixon tried Russian cigarettes - it would have made a good story. (Twenty-five years earlier, in the same office, Stalin smoked *Herzegovina Flor*, a choice Russian cigarette brand. Judging from old photos, the office had not changed much.)

Shapiro asked about the hot line to the White House. Brezhnev explained that it was in another room in the Kremlin (actually, it was a teletype terminal in the basement). Was it used recently? Brezhnev thought for a moment. He couldn't remember. "Why," he said, "our relations are so good, there's no need to use the direct line so often." He spoke with Dobrynin in Washington the day before from his office phone.

Brezhnev explained that most of the time he stayed at his fifth floor Central Committee office at Staraya Ploshad. As Communist Party General Secretary, he chaired Politburo meetings every Thursday at 3:00 p.m. Yesterday, he said, they met for six hours to discuss his upcoming visit to America. He was very pleased with the present state of US-Soviet relations, but did not dwell on any specifics of the Politburo decisions. (To my knowledge, the meeting was devoted entirely to discussing the Soviet delegation directives for the US summit. The Politburo members also reviewed major speeches for delivery in America. This took inordinate time: they were read aloud since General Secretary preferred listening to reading.)

Brezhnev said he was fond of the Kremlin: it was an escape from the endless flow of papers. He could sit down and think. No aides to bother him; the door rarely opened. "I suffer a part of my life here," he told Shapiro, "write down this word, "suffer." He did not look it. (I suspected there was another, more important reason: the Kremlin was the ancient Russian seat of power, and Brezhnev was sizing up the place.)

He brushed off correspondents' questions about Watergate; he was not in a position to comment on an internal US issue. Was he taking his family along to the States? "I'm not," he said. "My wife is on a rigorous medical regimen, and my grandson is shortly passing his school exams. We will continue to meet with President Nixon for years to come. The family will have other opportunities to visit America."

He failed to mention his son and daughter; it was common knowledge they were slowly descending into alcoholism, as was his brother Yakov. His daughter Galina was in a strong lead. I saw her occasionally on the 14th floor in the Foreign Ministry building. She was employed by the Second European Department (British Commonwealth affairs), but rarely showed up. Brezhnev inquired about his daughter with Victor, who was the Department Deputy Chief, and suspected the guarded replies were meant to soothe his nerves. I recall a quaint episode when a post card addressed to Galina was received at the Department. It had a labor camp postmark: her friend, a flamboyant "Gypsy baron" and dealer in diamonds wrote to say hello. This light whiff of the Gulag created a stir in the Ministry corridors, but left Galina unperturbed.

Brezhnev's family would not have another opportunity to visit America. The reason he left them behind I found out at Camp David.

Only a few days remained till our travel to the US. Oleg Sokolov, USA Department Counselor and a friend from the class of 1960, offered me a comfortable armchair in his small corner office on the 13th floor to read and memorize the salient points of the Soviet position. The phrases I will use later when writing up our leaders' words will have to conform to the brief's language. Oleg puffed on his pipe and poured Sanka coffee.

Interestingly, on the eve of Brezhnev's US visit, the State Department produced a paper on lessons from Nikita Khrushchev's 1959 trip to the United States. High among them was the inadvisability of "provocative remarks" that would only produce angry retorts from the Soviet leader without contributing in any measurable way to the success of the visit. Other lessons learned were avoiding fatigue-provoking over-scheduled itineraries, as well as "displays which violate prudish official Soviet attitudes."[27] This referred to inviting Khrushchev to Hollywood to watch Shirley MacLaine and cast do a dance in *Can-Can.*

In a lengthy memo for the President, Henry Kissinger explained Soviet expectations of the visit.[28] It makes lively reading: it delves into Brezhnev's psychological makeup and his insecurities: "susceptible to flattery," "wants to be treated as an equal," and his overriding need for "concrete" summit achievements. In a parallel memo for Nixon, Acting Secretary of State Kenneth Rush suggested impressing upon Brezhnev that the US remained "both resolute and reasonable." He thought Brezhnev, while off home ground, would be "more susceptible to displays of defensiveness and bluster."[29] In the early 1970s, at the four-power talks on West Berlin, I saw Ambassador Rush; he seemed perceptive and prudent in judgment. Now, his almost Freudian analysis of Brezhnev was off the mark. For one thing, the General Secretary felt comfortable in America because he had no Politburo colleagues tugging at his sleeve. More importantly, his attention span would be flagging; he always found hard to overcome the jet lag. Strangely, the memo overlooked Brezhnev's state of health. The key conclusion of the US brief - it would have pleased the Soviets if they had an advance peek - was that Brezhnev was committed to better relations with the US. Reading the declassified texts three decades after the event, the similarity of expectations both sides had seems striking.

On June 16 at Vnukovo-2 Airport, I boarded the second plane of the fleet setting off for the United Sates. We made a brief refueling stop in Keflavik, Iceland. The aircraft taxied to the US-controlled area where we had our first taste of American hospitality: Coca-Cola and snacks at the military canteen. The Secret Service took over from the KGB the task of protecting Brezhnev. Transition was smooth; I always admired the quiet efficiency of Soviet and American security personnel. They met often to discuss protection procedures, which proved to be quite similar, and quickly established professional rapport. They will have much to do during the weeklong visit.

At around 4:30 p.m., the two main Soviet aircraft touched down at Andrews Air Force Base within minutes of each other. Secretary Rogers greeted the party - this was to be the peak of his personal involvement with the General Secretary. A dozen Embassy children in crisp school uniform and red kerchiefs presented flower bouquets. The low-key greeting ceremony was brief. The official White House welcome was scheduled for Monday, 18 June, when a reinvigorated Brezhnev returned from his two-night stay at Camp David fighting off jet lag and meeting Nixon privately.

I inspected my copy of a 106-page navy blue brochure, the program of the visit. Four maps showed the exact location of Brezhnev's aircraft after touchdown, the welcoming committee, the rope cordon, the "press area," the "crowd area," and the position of four US Army helicopters waiting on the apron to take the party to Camp David.

Victor went with Brezhnev to board Helicopter 1, and I raced to number 3. The engine roar was deafening. Sitting in a helmet beside the open hatch, I felt I was on bombing mission in Vietnam. In 35 minutes, we landed at the Camp David helipad. Not a single piece of baggage was lost: it was marked with "Special USA" tags with the State Department seal.

Brezhnev stayed in Dogwood cabin. Victor had to be on call inside the compound, but the Secret Service overlooked this contingency. Dobrynin offered him a couch in his cabin. Most of the Soviet party and the international news agencies checked into the Cozy Motel, a fifteen-minute drive away in Thurmont, Maryland. Kornienko's secretary Lera Borisova told me the motel was built in 1929; residents included Winston Churchill and Babe Ruth. She confessed she got the intelligence from a restaurant table napkin. Every porch in town flew American flags. The locals acted friendly; they peeked into our cars hoping to catch a glimpse of Brezhnev.

The one-on-one meetings of the two leaders were held in Aspen Lodge, Nixon's cabin. They were not extensive, just a general discussion of Soviet-American relations. Nixon wanted Brezhnev to relax, and, probably, to soften up; the stay in Camp David was mostly pleasure. He led Brezhnev to the panoramic windows in Aspen to see the swimming pool and golf course. Nixon was proud of the setting. He did not mind the KGB cream-colored telephone with a little round seal of the USSR (dialing number 22) in the Aspen lobby: suppose Brezhnev wanted to make an urgent call to Moscow?

To serve all locations that Brezhnev's party would visit, the KGB installed a satellite telephone exchange, suitably named *"Vizit."* Members of the delegation were assigned dialing numbers, from one to 99. Soviet military operators serviced the network, which covered Andrews and El Toro Air Force bases, the White House, Blair House, Camp David and the Soviet Embassy in D.C., San Clemente and various hotels along the way. Brezhnev called his family in Moscow and comrades in the Politburo. He was showing off to the Americans: Soviet worldwide communications facilities were advanced. I called several friends in Russia.

Before leaving the United States, Brezhnev offered the system to Dobrynin for Embassy use. "Thanks a lot, but no, thanks," was Dobrynin's reply. Maintenance costs would have been prohibitive. The real reason was the Ambassador's reluctance to be in daily telephone reach of the Kremlin. This was before cell phones and e-mails, which put all diplomats on constant call status.

As sensitive dictation had to be done in a secure place, we commuted to Washington. Back in my room 1221 at the Statler Hilton, conveniently next door to the Soviet Embassy on 16th Street, I switched on the TV. Although the Watergate hearings had been suspended for the duration of the visit, comments did not sound good. John Dean's face was on every channel.

I walked to the Embassy, the former Pullman mansion, passing through several police barriers. They looked at my lapel pin - a tiny enameled disk with green, black and yellow sectors - and moved the barriers away. We wore no photo IDs at the time: a special colored pin and face control were sufficient. I saw Jewish demonstrators in the distance.

Protests in defense of Soviet Jewry and their right to emigrate were a major worry for the KGB security detail, as well as the White House. Through contacts in the Jewish community, it tried to discourage large-scale demonstrations. The "hundreds of thousands" mentioned by columnists Evans and Novak never materialized, but fringe groups could be expected to make trouble. A Washington judge ruling helped: the Secret Service had legal authority to establish a secure 500-feet area around the Soviet Embassy. In case the area was relaxed, the State Department could restrict oral protests and leaflets distribution by declaring them "harassment," and thus illegal.

Kissinger made good on his promise. In May in Zavidovo, Brezhnev raised the issue, without mentioning Jewish groups. He reminded Kissinger that in 1972, despite American "vicious bombing" in Vietnam, the Soviet Union accorded President Nixon a warm reception. He would ignore small demonstrations - he did not expect Americans waving red flags in his honor. He hoped, however, that Nixon was concerned enough to avoid "inconveniences" during the US trip, including "direct actions." In other words, he was asking for reciprocity. Kissinger assured him that "absolute maximum effort" would be made to prevent actions by minority groups "inconsistent with the spirit of Soviet-American relations."

Nixon and Kissinger knew that whenever Americans at official level raised the so-called "Jewish question", Russian reaction was swift. The arguments were: the USSR saved millions of Jews from the Nazis (the Red Army liberated Auschwitz); it championed the creation of Israel and pressed Arabs to formally agree to the existence of the Jewish State. Besides, emigration was an internal matter for the USSR.

Nixon rarely mentioned the problem, delegating it to Kissinger. The latter, being a realist, tried to convince the Soviet leaders of the counter productiveness of restricting emigration. He wanted to lower the visibility of the debate in the US, and advised Congressmen that quiet diplomacy was preferable; they should not look at the problem in isolation, but as part of the full picture of US-Soviet relations.

Kissinger was wary of antagonizing Brezhnev, believing (rightly) that the carrier of bad news to a potentate's court deserved to be hanged. His usual way was to slip a State Department-compiled list of prospective émigrés, the so-called *refuseniks,* including hardship cases, to Ambassador Dobrynin. The latter always gave sound advice to American negotiators on how to handle the raw nerve endings of his political masters. He usually drew Brezhnev's attention to the fact of transmittal, but no more.

Every time Kissinger spoke to the press after talking to the General Secretary, he claimed Jewish emigration was "Issue Number One." That was stretching the truth. He did raise the matter with Gromyko, albeit in a perfunctory manner, evoking the tough position of Senator Henry Jackson and Congress. In a memo to the President on the thorny issue, Kissinger admitted that Senator Jackson's conditions "went far beyond... what any sovereign State would tolerate having another government say about its internal order."[30] He once told Brezhnev that Jackson, the grand anti-Communist, favored MFN status for China without any conditions. "Of course," he added impishly, "there are no Jews in China who want to emigrate."

Still, Jewish polls indicated the Administration faced real problems. Len Garment, Special Consultant to the President on Minorities and Arts, asked Kissinger for guidance; he thought there was no more self-serving group than the Jewish community. Garment suggested "a certain amount of theater to keep the lid on."[31]

Brezhnev appreciated White House reserve. Nixon felt distaste for the Jewish-controlled US media, which, he suspected, was hatching a Monster Plot to torpedo détente. In March 1973, he ordered, on Kissinger's advice, the US delegation to withdraw a draft resolution on free emigration submitted in the UN Human Rights Commission, for fear of Brezhnev's displeasure. "I think the bastard [US delegate] should be recalled", he told Kissinger.[32] All statements of Administration officials on Soviet emigration policy would have to be cleared with the White House.[33]

Dictation in the Embassy's secure room lasted into late evening, but I had to deliver the transcripts to Camp David for Alexandrov. Around midnight, I called extension 160, the summit motor pool. A young soldier in an olive green US Army sedan picked me up at the Statler's main entrance. We were quite a way out of Washington when I noticed that the driver - his name was Alan - peered at road signs. He confessed he was unfamiliar with the area. I had no option but to sit back and enjoy the ride. The sixty miles to the place took us over two hours.

We drove along unlit country roads, talking about science fiction. Alan was an ardent fan, and cited passages from stories by Robert Sheckley (whom recently I translated into Russian). He surprised me even more: he loved Stanislaw Lem, my favorite sci-fi Polish author. *Solaris*, a Soviet movie based on his novel, was a worldwide hit that year. I thought I would drop a line to Bob about a fan serving the world's most important meeting, to cheer him up. He had written to me from Spain saying that his work was breaking up and "his sanity was episodic at best."

We saw searchlight beams piercing the dense forest growth, and turned into a short stretch of road before a double fence with concertina wire. Trip wires snaked in front of the gate. A sign said "US Government Property, Do Not Enter." Armed men watched us; several wore civilian clothes. I recognized a KGB Ninth Directorate agent. A Marine with a flashlight approached the car.

"Keep your hands high on the wheel, Alan," I said, "they shoot without warning." He obeyed. The Marine saw the security badge on my lapel. He told Alan to open the trunk and peered inside; my briefcase was there, but he ignored it. He walked back to the driver's window and said, "You wait here, soldier. Hand over the keys." Alan climbed out of the car. He was distressed. He hoped to see the inside of the compound - something to tell his buddies over a beer. A Navy enlisted man climbed behind the wheel and proceeded at the prescribed 15 mph along the narrow asphalt road to Maple Cabin. Alexandrov was still up. He went through the memcons quickly, making ironic remarks about some non-substantive chitchat I left in the record. He made minor edits brushing up some of Brezhnev's phrases. The editing was lost on me, but I accepted there were turns of phrase that the General Secretary wanted his colleagues to see. Alexandrov did not change anything in my rendition of Nixon and Kissinger interventions.

I walked back to the main gate. Alan said he spent a dreary hour in the guardhouse sipping coffee and looking out of the window. He wanted to know if I saw the President. I looked at my watch: it was 3:00 a.m. He drove me to Thurmont.

Early next morning I was back at Camp David. Victor and I worked from a trailer office parked in the grounds. Though cramped, it served our purpose, which was to get the regular memcons out as fast as possible. The weather was nice, and we dictated to Vika on any available terrace in cabins occupied by the Soviet party. The tables were glass-topped but they held the weight of the Russian typewriter. KGB technicians swept all typewriters for bugs, and the secretaries never left them out of sight. They were mechanical, because electric ones were vulnerable - text could be deciphered from electrical impulses emitted by key strokes. I opened a packet of L&M Super Kings lying on the tabletop with a "Welcome to Camp David" sticker under the gold Presidential Seal. It was cigarettes, nothing else. I left the packet for Victor to enjoy.

After dictation, I walked to Dogwood Cabin to deposit a freshly typed memcon. Brezhnev was relaxing on the sofa. Old Brezhnev crony Konstantin Chernenko sat in an armchair. He was chief of the powerful and secretive Department of General Affairs of the Party Central Committee. He handled paperwork for meetings of the Politburo, kept its minutes, often handwritten in a single copy, and managed the private archives of the General Secretary. Brezhnev brought Chernenko to Moscow in 1964, after Khrushchev was kicked out in a bloodless coup. He was unobtrusive and efficient, a master of the private office: he brought order to Brezhnev's bohemian working habits, and rose along the bureaucratic ladder to occupy the strategic rungs. He submitted draft Politburo decisions for the General Secretary's perusal, commented on them and obtained his signature. He could propel a memo through the channels at the speed of light; he could also slow it down to snail's pace. Not a man of ideas, he possessed a finely honed brain that kept track of all important files and minutes that circulated in the Central Committee maze-like structure. He kept them in a tidy filing registry.

Chernenko was flicking TV channels. I helped him locate the main news programs. Though neither spoke English, they did not ask for translation.

The news clips about the visit were self-explanatory and friendly enough. Brezhnev liked the coverage; he thought Nixon had a hand in it. He wore an XXXL size navy blue Camp David windbreaker with the presidential seal on the right side and his name stitched on the left (Victor and I received similar jackets - perhaps they were a sign of trust).

Brezhnev did not think much of Camp David. Compared to the palatial government dachas on the Black Sea coast, always bathed in glorious sunshine, this place appeared confined and drab, under a buttermilk sky. He showed no desire to see the countryside or visit a nearby town. He was indifferent to mainstream America.

I recalled Kosygin during his 1967 trip to New York and Glassboro to meet with Lyndon Johnson. He was eager to see the people, the cars, the supermarkets; he walked the streets of Manhattan and shook hands with passer byes. At a cocktail reception, he tried a Whiskey Sour on my suggestion He liked it, but doubted it would beat vodka for the Russians. LBJ lent him *Air Force One* to fly to Niagara Falls. Kosygin sat with the pilots in the cockpit during landing. We drove through friendly crowds, and sailed under the spray in the *Maid of the Mist*. Kosygin wished to inspect the Niagara Hydro Power Plant. We went deep down to see a generating turbine, and lunched at John's Flaming Hearth Steak House. I liked translating for Kosygin. The biggest problem I had was fending off Mayor Lackey's questioning why the Prime Minister failed to bring his wife to the Honeymoon Paradise (she passed away earlier that year).

Brezhnev and Chernenko took meals in their quarters. We lunched in the Laurel Lodge mess. The table was simply laid out, the food basic but tasty and the stewards silent and efficient. Kissinger amused the motley crowd (Haig, Sonnenfeldt, Hyland, Assistant Chief of Protocol William R. Codus, Dobrynin, Victor and me) with his tales of World War II. He told us about his postwar experience in Germany, where he helped set up the administration of a small town (he also alluded to collecting intelligence for the US Army). One of the tasks was rounding up Nazis. He had a bright idea - to recruit volunteers with experience of police work. An elderly German said he had a police background. True to the admirable American quality of respecting professionalism, Kissinger signed him up. Soon the man delivered fifty bedraggled Nazis. Then it dawned upon Kissinger that "State Police" was *Gestapo* in German.

Another story was of a scene he saw in Germany in 1945 - of an allied army officer shooting a drunken soldier in disgust. As witness to Kissinger's life threatening outbursts directed at staff, I wondered about the episode. I felt uncomfortable listening to Kissinger's disparaging remarks about colleagues. Perhaps he considered some barely human. Bob Haldeman was now open game: "The German" resigned barely two months before. We entered the dim conference room in Laurel Lodge. The curtains were drawn. Kissinger groped for the light switches and flipped all of them. Nothing happened. He smiled broadly: "This was Haldeman's last charge!"

I was taking movie pictures by our trailer office with my Super-8 Bolex camera, when a young woman walked into my sights. She wore a black skirt and white blouse. A KGB security man accompanied her. He gestured to me, frantically, to stop filming.

I had seen the girl somewhere; she was certainly not American. Then I remembered: the flight from Vnukovo-2, the airhostess who stood at attention by the door as Brezhnev waved good-bye. The female flight attendants on Brezhnev's private aircraft qualified for a beauty contest. They were not the leggy, plastic-smile darlings of popular Western culture, but wholesome peaches-and-cream next-door young women, good-natured and surprisingly modest.

It was Lena, his favorite (I changed her name). She rarely left Brezhnev's cabin, after Mrs. Nixon, as I heard, expressed hardly veiled displeasure. Brezhnev introduced her to the President who came to pick up his guest for the short walk to the dinner party. Nixon thought she wore *Arpège*, but I was sure it was *Serebristi Landish* (Silver Lily of the Valley), a delicate Russian scent of early spring flowers. "Please take good care of him," he told Lena. He knew why Brezhnev was evasive about bringing his family along to the States.

"Pretty much of a ladies' man," was Nixon's later comment. He was right: power was an aphrodisiac for the General Secretary. In his younger years, he attracted women with his vitality, sense of humor and thoughtful signs of attention. Today, the energy was dissipating, though there were short bursts of playfulness.

That night, General Antonov told me Brezhnev was going to a picture show - he asked for *The Magnificent Seven*. Joined by Vladimir Medvedev, Brezhnev's bodyguard, we walked to Laurel Lodge. Lena held an unsteady Brezhnev by the arm: he could not see well in the dark. I took a seat between them. The Secret Service and their KGB comrades sat in the back. It was not an arduous translating job. I kept a rudimentary commentary on who Yul Brynner and Steve McQueen were trying to shoot at the moment. Our sympathies lay with Brynner, a forceful actor of Russian descent.

The two-hour long Wild West drama proved too much for Brezhnev. He was drowsy. After half an hour, he rose abruptly and said, "I'm turning in. I saw this several times. You youngsters please stay, enjoy the film." The situation was comic. I almost blurted out, "Sure, pop. Can we sit on the porch for a while after the movie?"

Brezhnev's entourage trooped out. I remained with Lena. We talked in whispers. She was not keen on the movie; neither was I. Two marines watched us leave the projection room.

The air was fresh and smelled of pine. There was no Secret Service in sight. If not for the smooth black tarmac, we may have been walking in a Siberian forest. She told me about her family; she was not married. She was sorry she couldn't see much of America. We avoided talking about the General Secretary. Lena wanted to know about my job, the mysteries of translation. "Mine is a completely different life," she said, and fell silent. I understood her appeal. She was unpretentious, intelligent. She listened. I saw her almost to the front door of Brezhnev's cabin. She pressed my hand, and walked on to the lit doorway. She turned and waved. I felt a pang - of sympathy or anger - it was hard to tell.

I never met her again. Once in Gorky Park, I saw a large TASS poster photo: Brezhnev waving from the top of the aircraft steps, off on another visit to distant lands. In a white and blue Aeroflot uniform, Lena stood by the door, saluting smartly.

Exchange of presents had become a summit tradition. The year before, Nixon gave Brezhnev a Cadillac Eldorado and received a Volga-10 hydrofoil speedboat. After refurbishing, Nixon sailed it in Biscayne Bay. Kissinger assured Brezhnev the boat represented Soviet naval presence in Florida. (In 2006, it was auctioned off on eBay.) This time the General Secretary received a blue Lincoln Continental Town Car with a commemorative bronze plaque on the passenger side of the dashboard. The model must have been a Nixon favorite; he drove one in San Clemente after resigning.

We stood in front of Aspen Lodge as Nixon described the car with enthusiasm. We were struck by the ambivalence of the scene: a franchised dealer was in the process of selling a car to a customer. I think Brezhnev was the only one oblivious to the connotation. The poster of Richard Nixon with a five o'clock shadow and the caption "Would you buy a used car from this man?" was US election lore not mentioned in the Embassy brief.

The General Secretary sat behind the wheel and gestured for Nixon to join him. Off they went, burning rubber - literally, as in the movies. In his memoirs, Dobrynin said he accompanied them in the car, but it was Victor, who jumped in the back seat in time. He told me Nixon almost bumped his head on the windshield when Brezhnev braked before a turn in the narrow lane. The President complimented the new owner's "excellent driving skills." At his next regular meeting with Gromyko in the Oval Office, he asked him to remind Brezhnev not to drive too fast.

Brezhnev was happy as a child whose dream came true. Several months before in Zavidovo, he told Kissinger that his wish in the United States was to drive an American car. He would take the red flag off the bonnet, put on sunglasses to mask his bushy eyebrows and "drive like an American" - he meant real fast. He also suggested putting a boar emblem on a Lincoln Continental

Mark III, a luxury model produced by the Ford Motor Company. Kissinger noted this special interest of the General Secretary.

As we waited for the leaders to return, my mind went back to an episode that demonstrated different cultural values. In 1967, Prime Minister Indira Gandhi came to Moscow for festivities to mark the 50th anniversary of the Bolshevik Revolution - I was her interpreter together with my good friend Yuri Klyukin. Indira's fiftieth birthday was in a few days' time, and Kosygin, Podgorny and Brezhnev (this was the pecking order at the time) presented her with a gorgeous diamond necklace. She was surprised, but accepted the gift. The Kremlin Armory Curator told me it belonged to the Tsar's family. Did it have a price? 19,000 Rubles, he said (about $25,000).

A few weeks later Indira invited the Russian Ambassador to her Delhi residence and returned the gift. As leader of one of the world's poorest nation, she could not keep it. It went against her values, she said. One could imagine the opposition's reaction if they knew. The Ambassador mailed the necklace to Moscow by diplomatic pouch; it was quietly returned to the Kremlin Armory. As if to compensate for embarrassment caused to her Russian friends, the following year Indira agreed to Kosygin's suggestion to share intelligence about Chinese intentions.

I tried to visualize Brezhnev returning the Lincoln...

The present for me was a pair of cuff links with the Presidential seal and a Parker pen with Nixon's signature. In 1972, it was a tin plate with the US coat of arms, a nice wall decoration. Another tangible fall-out from our stay in Camp David was Chernenko's emotive decision, in gratitude for Victor's and mine hard work, to double our *per diem* on the trip.

Aboard the helicopter back to Washington, I leafed through the US Protocol brochure. Ten pages were devoted to the description of an elaborate "Armed Forces Full Honor Arrival" at the White House. (Soviet Protocol was simpler and relied heavily on initiative from the staff lower depths. This sometimes led to disastrous results. On the last night of his visit to Moscow, Syrian President Assad (the father) decided to delay departure the next day by an hour. It was late, and the protocol coordinator decided to relay the information early next morning. Alas, he overslept. The full Russian leadership languished in the Vnukovo VIP lounge for an hour, cursing the hapless officer. He barely escaped being fired.)

A few minutes before 11:00 a.m. on Monday, 18 June, the President and the First Lady officially greeted Brezhnev on the White House South Grounds. The ceremony was grandiose with hundreds of spectators: the Diplomatic Corps, members of Congress, White House staff, guard of honor, military band and the press.

I need not have worried: Brezhnev looked steady on the podium. His bodyguard Vladimir was within reach in case he stumbled. Short speeches were delivered, to loud applause and typically American-fan screaming. After half an hour, we filed into the Blue Room to shake hands with Nixon and the First Lady. Both leaders reappeared on the White House balcony, where Brezhnev put on an act, whispering "confidentially" in the President's ear, the latter nodding happily. A girl from the White House staff asked me if Brezhnev spoke English; she thought he looked natural.

Victor accompanied the two men to the Oval Office. Both teams waited in the Cabinet Room. Kissinger was embarrassed: he was sidelined. Gromyko was unfazed. I whiled away the time by writing letters to friends on White House stationary as proof "I was there."

The leaders were away for an hour. Unlike the first somber one-on-one meeting in the Kremlin the previous year, the tone now was warm and relaxed. Mostly Brezhnev spoke. He offered excuses that his family could not accompany him to the United States. (In 1960, Khrushchev brought six members of his family to the US.) He delivered a private family letter for Tricia, who recently travelled to Moscow. Nixon was quick to invite Brezhnev's family to the US as his personal guests. Brezhnev said he will telephone the good news back home.

He spoke in long passages. Nixon tried to get a word in about "the two of us changing the world, since we have the key," but Brezhnev interrupted. He spoke of his meeting with American reporters: he would send Nixon the memcon (I made a note to tell Alexandrov to forward my memcon from Moscow). He expanded on personal relationships between leaders, and loyalty to any gentleman's agreement reached. He invited Nixon to come to the USSR in 1974 and in 1976, and confirmed he will visit the US in1975. He also warned the President he was going to take a nap in the afternoon.

Victor told me that Kissinger again asked him for an English translation of the memcon he dictated. He will ignore his request. Why doesn't he ask Nixon? Suppose the President didn't wish to inform him? I agreed it was up to the Americans to sort out internal coordination. The volume of work we were doing - without US interpreters - would double again if we succumbed to providing English translations of Soviet memcons.

The plenary meeting of the two delegations in the Cabinet Room dragged on interminably, ending past 3:00 p.m. The US team suffered pangs of hunger. We on the Soviet side were used to Brezhnev ignoring lunch hour. I ran out of paper; the White House writing pad proved handy.

That night, as I did dictation, the Embassy code clerk was curious why my notes were partly in English. I explained that I took notes in Russian or English whenever it saved time. This reflected the peculiarities of Russian phrasing: it takes 20 per cent more space than English. It would be "runway" in English, but "*vzletno-posadochnaya polosa*" (take off-landing strip) - in Russian.

Next day Brezhnev drove to Anacostia for a scenic sail to Mt. Vernon with dinner aboard the 104-foot Presidential yacht Sequoia. Nixon was fond of the yacht, which was fitted with anti-bugging devices. The Russian guests admired the overgrown riverbanks. Brezhnev told us that next year he would take Nixon along the Crimea coast.

To our relief, at the dinner in the White House Blue Room, State Department interpreters Bill Krimer, Cyril Muromcew and Dimitry Zarechnak served the main guests. I saw familiar faces: Van Cliburn, Shirley Temple Black and June Allyson, astronaut Frank Borman, William Randolph Hearst, Henry Cabot Lodge and Armand Hammer, Chairman of Occidental Petroleum and longtime friend of Soviet leaders. Apparently, the urge "to be there" was great. The guest list had unusual descriptions: "Escort of Mrs....," "Date of..." and even "Mother of..." The Johnny Mann Singers entertained the party.

On 19 June, Brezhnev met with Congressional leaders. We saw it coming: Jewish emigration. Brezhnev was prepared. He read out a brief, which proved the problem was being addressed. "95 per cent of Soviet Jews are free to leave," he said. Of the 61,000 applicants in 1972, over 60,000 received permission to leave. 300 wanted to return to the USSR, citing disillusionment with the social situation in Israel, bad living conditions and warlike atmosphere. A large number detoured to the US, Brezhnev noted. He looked at the audience and repeated the last phrase.

Brezhnev's data was at variance with US figures, which quoted almost 100,000 applicants, not all of them able to get their papers accepted, with only 31,500 actually leaving. Senator Jackson added to the confusion with his own and Israeli-inspired figures. The introduction of the "education tax" compounded things. Although higher education was free in the USSR, the émigrés were now required to pay compensation, from 5,000 to 12,000 rubles - a steep rate. Brezhnev did try to assuage the problem. At a Politburo meeting in March, he suggested suspending the tax without abrogating the law, as well as expanding Jewish newspapers, schools and concert halls. He wrote little notes to Podgorny and others in the Politburo: "Do we need the money at all? The stakes are higher." Kosygin supported him.

Brezhnev hated being in the spotlight on the Jewish problem. He was unable to explain the discrepancies in numbers. Discussions like this only served to increase his distrust of Jews who "always make trouble." In Zavidovo, he led Kissinger into a corner of the room to say that Jews were already a privileged group in the Soviet Union - in arts, science, even as politicians' wives. No facilitated emigration was allowed for other ethnic groups. People grumble that Jews are getting the best deal, he warned. Pressure from pro-Jewish sections of the American establishment may provoke a backlash in Russia, leading to a wave of anti-Semitism.

Nixon took this warning seriously; it fitted into his hatred of "East Coast liberals." The line Kissinger was to follow was to keep the lid on, procrastinate, use quiet diplomacy - it was in the Jews' long-term interests.

On June 21, Brezhnev hosted a banquet at the Soviet Embassy. It nearly turned into a protocol disaster. Three hours before the appointed time, the administrative attaché decided that the Viennese chairs in the Embassy's Golden Room needed sprucing up. A neighborhood hardware store delivered dozens of gold-paint spray cans, and staff went to work. An hour before the dinner the paint was still wet. I felt like King Midas as I touched a chair: my fingers were sticky with golden goo. The attaché's face was ashen. I went to check the chairs again ten minutes before the guests arrived: the paint was dry. This was either perfect timing, or heavenly intervention. The attaché's face was back to its ruddy hue; he told me he saved the Embassy from a mammoth cleaning bill.

The golden splendor of the grand room reverberated with toasts to eternal friendship, security and peace. Brezhnev read a prepared speech. Nixon had no text. He commended the Russian food and wine, mentioned William Roger's birthday, the thirty-third anniversary of his marriage to Pat, noted that 21 June was the longest day of the year, toasted Gromyko and Dobrynin and their spouses and the health of the General Secretary. He ended on a serious note: let us work together for peace rather than confrontation. Brezhnev was so moved by Nixon's words that he rose again to toast the President's health. He clinked his tall glass of *Sovetskoye Champanskoye* with everyone within reach.

The women's gowns glittered; their escorts exuded power. The invitees list was imposing: UN Secretary-General Kurt Waldheim, Vice President Spiro T. Agnew, Chairman of Chase Manhattan David Rockefeller, Chief Justice Warren Burger, House minority leader Gerald Ford, and Senators Fulbright and Scott. I caught sight of Armand Hammer. The dinner was a success. General Antonov arranged switching seats for Kissinger, who wanted to be seated next to Norwegian actress Liv Ulmann. Nixon went to the kitchen to thank the cooks and waiters and the Embassy wives who were drafted as kitchen help.

After the last American guest left, Embassy staff lined up in the hallway. Brezhnev went slowly round shaking hands. "Leonid Ilyich, thank you for everything you are doing for peace," said the *Izvestia* correspondent. Brezhnev turned serious: "Yes, yes, I'm doing all I can, how much more can one possibly do?" Bodyguard Vladimir led him to the limousine for a well-earned night rest at Blair House.

Brezhnev's less effective performance was a "dialogue" meeting with fifty-one American business leaders at his residence. Treasury Secretary George Schultz announced that he and Foreign Trade Minister Nikolai Patolichev were ready to sign two protocols: on establishing a Soviet-American Chamber of Commerce and on improved facilities for US executives in Moscow. President Nixon donated pens for the ceremony.

Brezhnev laid his red folder aside, and I braced myself for a "heart to heart" talk that could reach the mean minds of the capitalist moneylenders. He started by explaining the genesis of trade between nations, proceeded to political considerations versus trade, and then to World War II, which always made him sentimental. He swept through the emergence of nuclear weapons, the Cold War, his own life story and rise to the top - where "personal modesty is a must," he stressed. He switched to Richard Nixon's decisive role, and un-expectedly thanked the audience "for supporting the President." This remark was met with silence.

Time was running out: Alexandrov was desperately trying to attract the speaker's attention. Brezhnev noticed him at last, and said, "My comrades are pointing to their watches. They never give me an opportunity to finish my thoughts. I have to run off to sign another agreement. I would have preferred to burn th visit's schedule." He took a page from his notes, folded it accordion-fashion, and placed it in a heavy crystal ashtray. Producing a cigarette lighter, he set the top of the page alight. The tycoons watched with interest as the page burned down without a whiff of smoke. An old spy trick; it remained to flush the ashes down the toilet.

Brezhnev resumed. He said he invited the President to visit the USSR in 1974, and that he would return to America in 1975. He struggled valiantly with winding up his speech, but could not think of a proper ending. All of a sudden, he turned, apologetically, to Minister Patolichev on his left: "I have finished, Comrade Kosygin." (Victor ignored this in translation). He thanked the business leaders for their attention.

There was light applause. The speech took an hour and a half. There were no questions from the floor. I wrote down the speaker's closing phrases and shut my notebook. This was the first time I heard Brezhnev confusing the name of a close colleague, a bad sign.

On 22 June, Brezhnev was twenty minutes late for the White House ceremony where he and Nixon were to sign the Agreement on the Prevention of Nuclear War. Brezhnev did a little clowning with his pen and whispered in Nixon's ear. Nixon laughed. It was acting and gibberish, as usual.

The significance of the date was lost on Nixon, but it was a poignant reminder for the Russians: on this day in 1941, Hitler invaded the USSR. Both Brezhnev and Nixon stressed the agreement's "historical importance." In truth, it was toothless; its significance eroded over the years. Decades later, it stands like a gnawed rock tower in the Arizona desert beaten by the winds and rain, in the bleak landscape of American-Russian relations.

Henry Brandon of the *Sunday Times* tugged at my sleeve. We met in London a few years before; he was a reliable source, informed and shrewd. He suggested lunch. I politely declined, telling him I had to transcribe several conversations, which was true. Alas, I could not afford to be accessible. This was a typical situation on a State visit; we learned to steer wide of the press. I knew too much: I was in a cocoon, voluntarily incarcerated. The Soviet leadership and President Nixon placed trust in my comrades and me. In a different situation, I would have traded diplomatic intelligence with Brandon, but not on this trip. This was the wrong time.

I learned, after Brandon's premature death in 1977, that he was wiretapped by the FBI on Nixon's orders. He also worked for MI6. I shuddered to think of Kissinger telling Gromyko that a Soviet aide provided sensitive information to a suspect reporter. I had troubles of my own to afford this flap.

SAN CLEMENTE CELEBRITY CIRCUIT

The treat of the summit was Nixon's invitation to Brezhnev to spend time at his home in San Clemente, California. The General Secretary balked at the prospect of another long flight - to the West Coast - and cited "doctor's orders." Dobrynin persuaded him to accept lest he hurt the President's feelings. Brezhnev said he changed his mind partly because the Nixon's estate, La Casa Pacifica, meant "House of Peace." He liked symbolism.

We boarded the *"Spirit of '76"* at Andrews for the long flight to Marine Corps Air Station El Toro. The brochure placed on my seat said the aircraft was an Air Force VC137 remodeled from a commercial Boeing 707. Nixon had renamed it the previous year from JFK's truculent *"Air Force One."* The stateroom, staff rooms and the main passenger compartment were comfortable and tastefully decorated. (In contrast, the Soviet equivalent, Aeroflot's "Special Aircraft Group" that catered for the country's leadership, was austere. The interior design reminded one of a budget hotel manager's offices.) Complimentary sewing kits were provided, as well as razor blades, after-shave lotions and emergency raincoats. I picked up a light blue matchbook, which bore the omnipresent Presidential Seal and inscription, "The Spirit of '76 - Aboard the Presidential Aircraft," as a souvenir for my chain-smoking father.

The brochure explained evacuation procedures and gave advice on making telephone contact with the ground: "Passengers and guests are cautioned not to discuss classified information, as these conversations are easily monitored." It reminded me of Moscow rules. With KGB officers on board the advice was superfluous.

I fell into conversation with Ron Walker, Nixon's former Special Assistant and remarkable advance man, now Director of the National Park Service, the youngest in its history. Ron was my age, and we found talking easy. Although Nixon did introduce the first environmental legislation in Congress and established the Environment Protection Agency three years before, Ron's appraisal of the President's views on the environment was unenthusiastic. Somebody put an idea into his head that trees were a major source of greenhouse gases. He winked at the desolate landscape below, and said in deep baritone, "Killer trees…"

I knew that Nixon usually delegated dubious issues to his staff. In 1972, he appointed domestic affairs assistant John Ehrlichman to the high-level Conference on the Human Environment in Stockholm, giving him a free hand. Ehrlichman succeeded in watering down the conference outcome. On the eve of Brezhnev's visit, the Council on Environmental Quality asked Kissinger to raise marine environment, in particular the protection of whales - Russia and Japan were responsible for eighty per cent of the world's catch. It was not raised: protecting whales was not priority for the US or the USSR.

Nixon's suspicion of environmental issues had a deeper motive: our Enmod project. At the time, I was involved in developing a Soviet initiative to prohibit the use of environmental modification techniques as instruments of warfare. When the USSR first mooted the idea, Kissinger's reaction was negative. He and Nixon suspected the aim was to put constraints on methods the US Army was experimenting with in Vietnam: massive use of herbicides and defoliants, like Agent Orange, and artificial precipitation. Their assumption was correct. Russian experts did not discount the possibility of the US employing exotic techniques like artificial earthquakes and tsunamis. Years before he got entangled in politics, Andrei Sakharov suggested placing a nuclear charge in the North Sea: when detonated, it would engulf half of European NATO members in a gigantic tsunami. The Soviet leadership discounted such ideas, including "tectonic weapons" triggered by underground nuclear explosions as ineffective and a waste of resources.

In 1973, Brezhnev tried to interest Kissinger in Enmod, but Henry said he was not yet prepared. He used this excuse so often that Moscow was certain he held US foreign policy hostage to his dwindling resources of time. As Kissinger used to say, "There can't be another crisis because my schedule is already full." Gromyko pressed him citing Soviet scientists and military experts; he warned that if not constrained, artificial weather change techniques would have serious implications for climate. Perhaps, some sort of declaration could be issued by next year's summit in Moscow? Kissinger agreed to a joint study of the issue, but the Americans dragged their feet. On the eve of a Gromyko-Kissinger meeting in Geneva in February 1974 to prepare for the next summit, Sonnenfeldt and Hyland advised Kissinger to go slow on the

Soviet project: they preferred retaining possible tactical uses, like rainmak-ing.[34] The White House could have turned down the Soviet proposal so as not to "overburden détente," but it faced growing pressure from vocal Senators, es-pecially Claiborne Pell, and investigative reporter Jack Anderson. In the end, the White House gave in, most probably because it saw no sense in deluging and defoliating the Ho Chi Min trail. Carpet-bombing from high-altitude B-52s was more effective.

The Russian team had deliciously nothing to do in the muted comfort of the airborne White House. The hot barren landscape rolled below. Brezhnev dozed. Sitting in the rear staff section, I talked with Stephen Bull, the young Presidential assistant. Steve was immaculately dressed, alert and helpful. Enduring much of Presidential temper, he performed his responsibilities in a cool and cheery manner, which was not easy in view of the gathering domestic political storm. I appreciated his sense of humor.

As I passed the open door to the main private compartment, Nixon waved me in. He sat by the window, reading. His left leg was propped up on an ot-toman (phlebitis, they said). He asked me to take a seat. He wanted to know how the General Secretary was enjoying the flight. We were approaching the Grand Canyon, and Nixon wished him to see this marvel of nature. I prom-ised to tell Brezhnev. (I had no intention of disturbing his slumber. Lies were coming easily.)

Nixon took a long look through the window, and said, "Could you please ask Mr. Bull to come over?" I noticed his manner of referring to his aides formally by family name in front of strangers, always adding "Mr." In Russia it was different: the accepted way of addressing others was by first name and patronymic. This applied to all, from street sweepers to General Secretaries. We never addressed Brezhnev as "Comrade General Secretary," but simply "Leonid Ilyich." I liked the archaic way of addressing dignitaries in Russia. This went back to the olden times when one addressed the Tsar as one's uncle. It sounded homely.

I walked to the back of the aircraft and told Steve the President wanted to see him. Steve shook his head: "Can't come, tell him I'm busy!" He ran off and was back in a minute. Others joined us; the galley had a generous supply of drinks. I nursed a gin and tonic in a squat dimpled glass with the Presidential Seal. Steve beckoned to a gray-haired steward in a blue blazer, "Mike, we'll miss a glass." (Years later, Ron Walker, now Chairman of the Richard Nixon Foundation, remembered the episode. He was delighted that the POTUS glass, acronym for "President of the United States," was still in good use in Moscow.)

The genial atmosphere in the *"Spirit of '76"* was contagious. We compared notes about our jobs with risqué humor. Being on the breaking-news end of détente was heady stuff; the emotional release from Cold-War attitudes untied the knots and relaxed the sinews. I was surprised how easily genuine camaraderie broke through American distrust and Russian wariness. "If you're ever in Washington, call me at the White House; the switchboard will put you through," said Steve. I said sure, or we'll meet next time in the USSR in 1974 (which we did). I returned to the States in the fall, for the UN General Assembly session. By that time, Nixon had resigned and Steve departed to San Clemente with the transition team.

We touched down at El Toro at 6.48 p.m. A Presidential helicopter whisked both leaders away to Nixon's oceanfront estate. Victor went with Brezhnev. The rest rode in a large olive-green Army bus north along the San Diego Freeway, past the San Onofre Nuclear Plant to a point half way to Los Angeles. The bus turned into the appropriately named Avenida del Presidente, and into the Avenida Esplandian. We disembarked at the San Clemente Inn to a serenading Mexican band. A large billboard welcomed both leaders. According to the Inn's color brochure, San Clemente was renowned for "the world's best weather." It was stiflingly hot. Reception told me Mr. Brezhnev was lucky: he just missed a heat wave with temperatures running in the 100s.

I dropped my bag and went to check if Brezhnev decided to swing into negotiations. He did not. I walked around. Nixon bought the 1920s estate after taking the oath of office in 1968, and named it La Casa Pacifica. Though not large, it boasted a shaded inner courtyard, several comfortable cottages, manicured grounds and a pictorial view of the Pacific Ocean.

It was here in the "Western White House" that Nixon recently received several important visitors. South Vietnam's President Nguen Van Thieu came in April. The U.S. Marine Corps Drum and Bugle Corps serenaded him (probably as a send-off party: Nixon was fed up with obstinate Thieu who thought nothing of wrecking détente). The short description of the place provided by the Soviet Embassy failed to mention this bit of memorabilia.

The entertainment program laid out by our gracious hosts was meant for somebody else. There were actually team members who swam in the pea-shaped pool, dined to Spanish music in the candlelit tan and red leather El Dorado Room, and went on sightseeing tours. Our lot was the quick hamburger, a coffee mug resting on a confidential position paper, and breadcrumbs rolling off a transcript ripped out of the typewriter by an aide, who rushed off to prepare a condensed version for Gromyko to sign and cable to Moscow from the Soviet Consulate in San Francisco. The two nights in San Clemente whizzed by as a couple of hours. My only outing was a late-night dash for an aspirin to the Schultz Pharmacy at 100 So. El Camino Real.

A break we looked forward to on a late afternoon turned into a minor catastrophe. Seduced by a Secret Service suggestion to slip off to Disneyland, I asked Alexandrov, innocently, if a small group could check out the action on the beach.

Alexandrov was shocked that such an idea occurred during an important State visit. He almost burst into tears, and in a trembling voice commanded our errant group, including Leonid Zamyatin, Brezhnev spokesman, to use the "supposed lull" to prepare a digest of West Coast press reaction to Brezhnev's visit. This was unfair: a TASS contingent was doing the job round the clock. My first reaction was to remind Alexandrov of a 1959 incident when Nikita Khrushchev was denied a visit to Disneyland by the American hosts, albeit for security fears. Not again, this time by Leonid Brezhnev's chief aide? I held my tongue.

We were perusing the San Francisco *Examiner* and *Chronicle* when a meek Alexandrov entered and suggested that we disperse, maybe take some time off to do the sights. At this late moment, it was impractical. We held no grudge; in view of his boss's state of health the strain Alexandrov felt was enormous. Whenever strangers asked about Brezhnev's wandering focus we put on a brave face and alluded to his "peculiar sense of humor" or "eccentricity."

Or, as Alexandrov often did, laughed it off. The problem was getting worse. In September 1972, talking with Kissinger at the Kremlin, Brezhnev started reading from a US draft paper thinking it was ours (he quickly realized his mistake).

In the bar, Zamyatin poured two Bourbons on the rocks and said, "Andrey, the man is not behaving as a normal person would. There are signs..." He broke off. I agreed: something was seriously wrong. Thankfully, intelligent aides flanked the General Secretary; they were deft at disaster control. Besides, the memory lapses might be transitory; at most times Brezhnev seemed alert.

Zamyatin was not convinced. I ventured that the process would take care of itself at some point in the future. There was the bright side: no Congress to persuade in Russia, no politicians to win over and no press to spin. Unfortunately, the public was bound to know eventually about the "King's new clothes."

I felt sad about Brezhnev. My mind wandered back to my first diplomatic posting at the Russian Embassy in Delhi. In the string of Soviet dignitaries who visited India at the high point in the two countries' relations, one stood out. His position was Chairman of the Presidium of the Supreme Soviet, a largely ceremonial *ersatz* President of the USSR, who chaired anniversary rallies, pinned medals on the bosoms of actresses and awarded State Prizes. His name was Leonid Ilyich Brezhnev. In late December 1961, he paid an official visit to India. This was an opportunity to try my linguistic skills.

Comrade Brezhnev could have easily won a popularity contest. "The handsome Moldavian," Stalin used to call him. Though he did serve in a Party post in Moldavia, Brezhnev was Russian. Solidly built, swarthy and handsome, flamboyant and wisecracking, he loved working the crowds and making impromptu speeches. He listened respectfully to Indian President Rajendra Prasad and Prime Minister Jawaharlal Nehru. He went elephant riding. He created a stir by publicly welcoming the sudden occupation by Indian forces of Goa, Daman and Diu, Portuguese colonial enclaves. He had no time to consult Khrushchev in Moscow, but got approval *post factum*.

He endeared the audience at the Soviet Embassy Club in Chanakyapuri, Delhi's diplomatic quarter. The secretary of the staff Party cell introduced the guest of honor. Brezhnev interrupted him and said he knew exactly what the man planned to say: "We are honored by this visit of our respected and beloved member of the Soviet leadership…" The Party secretary's jaw dropped. But he was not to be thwarted by the Chairman of the Presidium, and blurted out, "Exactly, Comrade Brezhnev, that's what I intended to say!"

When laughter subsided, Brezhnev launched into a blunt exposition of the state of affairs in the Soviet Union: the bad harvest and rising milk and meat prices. He spoke without notes. He took questions until all were exhausted. He toured the newly built Soviet Embassy compound, at the time our largest, and invited senior diplomats to his birthday party - he just turned fifty-five. He toasted my close friend Oleg Hustochka, the Ambassador's chef, "Let me tell you, tonight was the best birthday dinner I attended." The Embassy wives adored Brezhnev.

The experience of other Embassy diplomats was different: it showed his less pleasant side. Lyonya Seleznev, the Economic Attaché, organized Brezhnev's visit to Madras. He double-checked the program prepared by local authorities and led the rehearsal of the Soviet national anthem. Out of breath, he welcomed the Chairman as his plane touched down. Brezhnev said, "Are you the Embassy official responsible for organization? You do not know your job. Where are my green parrots? You have thirty minutes to find them."

Security explained that Her Excellency Mrs. Naidu, Governor of West Bengal, gave Brezhnev two green parrots. They were brought to Madras but disappeared. Lyonya searched the rooms of Brezhnev's residence. The kitchen was the last place to inspect. A Russian maid was ironing Brezhnev's pants and another was opening a can of processed meat, just before a lavish State dinner. She explained Brezhnev was used to this fare since his war days. A strangely shaped object stood in the corner covered with sackcloth - it was the cage with the fugitive parrots. The maids said they covered it because the birds "squeaked disgustingly." The parrots were reinstalled on the balcony of Brezhnev's suite. At that moment, the Russian Consul entered with an identical pair of green parrots purchased in the bazaar, as a secret substitution. They were immediately set free.

I never expected to see Brezhnev again. Nor could I have predicted that in three years he would mastermind Khrushchev's ouster, and I would be taking notes for him at meetings with American Presidents. (In November 1973, Brezhnev paid another visit to India. He took Victor and me along. He conferred with Indira Gandhi, made public speeches, and toasted Indo-Soviet friendship. This time, he tired quickly. He did not meet with Embassy staff or exhibit any interest in Indian birdlife.)

Meanwhile, back at San Clemente. The conversation most important to Brezhnev occurred in Nixon's second story den. The meeting was private - just the President, Brezhnev, Kissinger and me. Kissinger had a yellow legal pad ready, presumably to take notes for the American record. In my memory, he did this two or three times. I braced myself for interpreting both ways and jotting down as much as possible, to prepare a detailed transcript afterwards. It was difficult, but manageable.

The conversation was one of the most fascinating I witnessed.

Nixon sat by the picture window resting his legs on an ottoman. Brezhnev relaxed in a reclining leather armchair. It was warm, and we took off our jackets. Brezhnev wore a white short-sleeved shirt; California was tropics for him. He put his legs on a footrest. He lighted a cigarette. I moved the ashtray closer to his seat and opened my writing pad.

Neither Gromyko nor Dobrynin joined us. Perhaps they wished to highlight the confidentiality of the encounter, but I do not exclude another reason: avoiding implication in what Brezhnev planned to say. He sometimes twisted and turned his talking points so they became unrecognizable.

Brezhnev's opening line was, "I speak frankly with you because you are my friend." (He thought that by dowsing Nixon with "personal sincerity" breakthroughs could be made.) He produced a paper and waved it in front of Nixon. He said it was a draft non-aggression treaty with China he sent to Beijing: he would publish it if the reaction were "propagandistic." He studied Chinese history. Mao and his colleagues were dishonorable, treacherous, crafty, sly, perfidious, spiteful, ruthless, and capable of destroying a whole nation. They oppress their own people. He evoked the Cultural Revolution, the mass trials and public beheadings, and even Soviet doctors' confidential reports on Mao's state of health. I mobilized my English reserve of abusive language to cover all the epithets.

Unexpectedly, Brezhnev asked Nixon for forgiveness for his strong words on Vietnam the previous year at the dacha. I felt I was in an Orthodox Church confessional. Nixon lowered his eyes.

Brezhnev told his brother's story. "The Chinese asked us to build a metallurgical plant in Mao's home town... My brother was the right man for the job, and I urged him to go, though he didn't want to leave his daughter... He was one of thousands of Soviet experts employed in China. Suddenly they started a great-power chauvinistic campaign against us..." Brezhnev looked at me: "Isn't it true?" A dedicated civil servant, I said yes.

Nixon listened in silence, unmoved by this piece of family history. Since he was not reacting, not even nodding, Brezhnev spoke in a louder tone to buttress my even-voiced interpretation. Probably he wanted more emotion. I raised my voice as well.

Kissinger took sporadic notes; he did not join the conversation. They wanted the General Secretary to drain his venom to the end. The tactic was to neither approve nor disapprove of what he was saying - to avoid a dialogue.

Manolo Sanchez, Nixon's valet, brought drinks and coffee. Nixon stuck to coffee, and occasionally puffed on a cigar. Brezhnev chain-smoked: his ashtray overflowed. He had bourbon on the rocks. I took water.

Despite undiplomatic language, Brezhnev's worry was genuine: while the US and the USSR were limiting nuclear weapons, the Chinese were building them up. The current balance was bearable; but what about 10, 15 or 20 years hence, when they speed up the development of their intercontinental ballistic missiles?

Nixon was non-committal. He had to be careful with Brezhnev: whatever he said the Soviets might use against the Chinese, at any rate relay it to secret Moscow sympathizers in Beijing. The opening to China was still a good card to play. Choosing his words carefully, Nixon said the US will continue to communicate with China, but will never do anything with China or Japan against the interests of the Soviet Union.

"Thank you," said Brezhnev. He added a veiled threat, though: the USSR cannot limit its arms while the Chinese were increasing their nuclear arsenal.

Nixon thought it unlikely the Chinese would be capable to reach ICBM levels comparable to the US or the USSR. Brezhnev was skeptical. He became irritated. He gesticulated and turned to me as if looking for help - I nodded to show he had an ally in the room. He went on another round of unmasking Chinese leaders. In 1963 at a Soviet Communist Party congress, Mao said that 400 million Chinese might die in an atomic war, but 300 million will survive. (Brezhnev got his dates and figures wrong: there was no Soviet Party congress in 1963. In his speech in 1958 at a Chinese Communist Party conference, Mao warned of the danger of imperialism unleashing a world war, which may annihilate 300 million; it would mean the end of capitalism. I had no quick way of checking the veracity of the quote, so I watered down the passage in the memcon.)

Brezhnev tried to provoke Nixon into an admission of guilt: "If you are planning to conclude a military pact with China..." Nixon replied, in an even tone, that military aid had not been provided, nor was there any intention to do so. Kissinger intervened: looking Brezhnev in the eye, he said the US never had any military discussions with China. Brezhnev cleared his throat and let the remark pass.

Nixon wanted to know the Soviet assessment of Chinese nuclear intentions. Brezhnev suggested it would take China ten years to reach the present Soviet levels, but incursions into Russian territory are occurring today. His final remark on China was ominous: "We are worried about the future lest it undermine our relationship...The peoples of the world will lose trust in us... We don't intend to attack China, but it will be different if China had a military agreement with the United States."

This was a direct warning.

Nixon made a dismissive gesture. He did not go beyond a general promise not to do anything inconsistent with the spirit of the agreement on the prevention of nuclear war. He committed to stay in touch with Brezhnev on China - "in total confidence." He suggested that the Soviet Union continue employing diplomatic means.

After two hours, neither side had anything to add on the topic of China.

Brezhnev could not sway Nixon, who gave no guarantee of the future mode of America's relations with the 800-million-strong nation, be it sales of military hardware or assistance in weapons production. He saw that his attempt at "personal diplomacy" was not working. He seemed at a loss; the energy pills were wearing off.

There followed a brief discussion on Vietnam. Nixon asked for Soviet restraint on arms shipments. Brezhnev looked away: "Don't worry about this - probably we sent rifles... The Chinese are the source of fairy tales about Soviet arms shipments." He promised to speak to Prime Minister Pham Van Dong and General Secretary Le Duan the following month in Moscow "to urge them to adhere to the Paris Agreements."

Brezhnev stood up; the conversation was over. We went down the stairs. He beckoned to me. Lowering his voice to a whisper he said, "Please dictate the transcript to Viktoria Mikhailovna (Vika, his private secretary), and give it to me personally, nobody else." This meant he had transgressed his brief and would edit the memcon. I did not mind.

Down in the courtyard, Gromyko asked me about the conversation. I told him it was about China, and briefly recounted what the General Secretary said and Nixon's reaction. I said that Brezhnev asked me to hand the transcript to him personally. Gromyko stared at me and made no comment. Nobody else from the Soviet party asked me about the conversation in the den.

After dictating the memcon to Vika, I went to see Brezhnev in his room. Bodyguard Vladimir was keeping vigil at the door; he told me the General Secretary "was busy" and on no account should be disturbed. I had several explicit visions of what that meant, but settled on a late afternoon nap. I went back to Vika and explained the situation. "Don't worry, Andrey, give it to me," she said. I knew it was as safe with her as in the Kremlin vault. When Brezhnev emerged, I told him that the single copy of the memcon was with Vika. "Good," he said.

Thirty years after the event, it transpired that Kissinger was informing the Chinese about conversations with Brezhnev. The following month, Kissinger met Ambassador Huang Zhen in the Map Room of the White House. He said, "The meeting was between Brezhnev, the President, myself and the Soviet interpreter. We have told no one in our Government of this conversation. It must be kept totally secret."[35] Not only did Kissinger give his own rendition, he embroidered it to please the Ambassador. In his words, Nixon repeatedly said that he was not interested in hearing Russian views on the Lin Biao incident (China's number two died in an air crash in Mongolia in 1971 while fleeing to the Soviet Union). Likewise, he was allegedly "not interested" in exchanging information on the Chinese nuclear program.

Kissinger's account of this meeting in his *Years of Upheaval* was imprecise. My recollection is that Nixon displayed keen interest in Brezhnev's anti-Chinese sermon. Many years later, reading Kissinger's declassified memo for the President's file, I realized it was tape-recorded. Kissinger sat next to me and made few notes; he had a faster brain, but not a faster hand. The US memcon (its classification was "Top Secret; Sensitive; Exclusively Eyes Only") contained my exact translation of Brezhnev's words. However, he struck some of Nixon's comments on China and edited others. He indicated, wrongly, that the interpreter was Victor; remembering more than three faces in a meeting was beyond his power.

In November the same year, Kissinger called on Mao Tse-tung in Beijing. Mao spoke of a possibility that the Soviet Union wanted to attack China. Kissinger jumped at the opportunity: "I used to think of it as a theoretical possibility. Now I think it is more a realistic possibility... I think they above all want to destroy your nuclear capability."[36] Kissinger could not have said this without the President's approval. Kissinger warned Dobrynin that China might be able to deploy its first ICBMs in 1977. If this was not meant as a provocation for the Russians, it was dangerously close. No wonder Mao poured cold water on Kissinger's exuberance. He said, "[Soviet] ambitions are contradictory to their capacity." His sense of history was sweeping but realistic: it would take "30 or 50 years" for China to reach the Soviet nuclear capability.

He was right; wrong were the lesser mortals, Brezhnev and Nixon. By 2013, China had no more than 75 ICBMs and about 250 nuclear warheads, not necessarily deployed. In comparison, the US had 7,700 warheads (2,150 deployed), and Russia 8,500 warheads (1,800 deployed).[37] Besides, China followed a proclaimed non-first-use policy for nuclear weapons.

Kissinger's fixation can be traced to the secret US-Chinese talks in Warsaw. In December 1970, he told Bob Haldeman the Russians would attack China "by April 15." [38] There was a 60 per cent chance of a Soviet strike, he said. A skeptical Haldeman asked him why not 65 or 58 per cent, but was swayed by news of US aerial photos of "hundreds of Soviet nuclear warheads stacked in piles," with "eighteen thousand tents in nine feet of snow."

In May 1973 in Zavidovo, Kissinger was under the impression that Brezhnev, in a private conversation in the hunting tower over a bottle of vodka and sausages, hinted about a Soviet preemptive nuclear strike against China. Although the Soviet leadership was deeply concerned with Chinese intentions, this was a gut reaction to the Cultural Revolution, anti-Soviet propaganda and Mao's predictions of a worldwide atomic war. I doubt that anybody in Moscow seriously contemplated a first nuclear strike. The conventional firing power of the Soviet Army deployed at the border was colossal. At the height of confrontation in 1969, the Chinese overran Damansky Island, a grassy strip of land in the middle of the Amur River. It took a brief "Grad" artillery bombardment to push the Chinese back. The loss of lives - 58 on the Soviet side and close to 3,000 on the Chinese side - showed the USSR had no need to resort to nuclear weapons. China did not fit the doomsday scenario.

Was Brezhnev blissfully ignorant of these backdoor contacts with the Chinese? Did he believe Kissinger's "cross-my-heart" oaths that he never discussed with the Chinese issues affecting the Soviet Union? I suspect the Soviets had inside sources in Beijing that nurtured Brezhnev's suspicions.

Soon after the 1972 Moscow summit, Kissinger travelled to Beijing. On his return to Washington, he called Dobrynin. He was angry about an article by Joseph Alsop who claimed he went to discuss military measures against a Soviet attack. "Absolute outrage," he said.[39] He sounded defensive. The US China policy was secretive; it was also befuddled. Back in 1963, it was the Chinese threat to India that troubled the White House. President John Kennedy pondered a nuclear strike against China and the USSR if India was overrun.[40] In the triangular game the White House was playing, positions changed 180 degrees.

Kissinger told things to the Chinese opposite to what he told Brezhnev. To make matters even more confusing, he told the Indians (a Soviet ally) that in the case of a military conflict with China the US would support India.[41] Perhaps Kissinger was entangled in his elaborate tactics. He told Nixon that he followed the strategy of telling Dobrynin things which, "if they got leaked back to the Chinese, would appear like a provocation and therefore highly improbable."[42]

Brezhnev's behavior in San Clemente was unpredictable. His naps made a shambles of protocol. On the last night, when Nixon had gone to bed, Brezhnev insisted they wake him up. It was three o'clock in the morning, and he wished to discuss the Middle East. His aides could not talk him out of it. Victor told me that as Brezhnev spoke about Israeli withdrawal from occupied territories, a sleepy Nixon hinted that he had better think about Soviet proposals in the morning: "We have to break up now." "Perhaps I am tiring you?" Brezhnev asked nonchalantly, and continued talking - he could afford to sleep late. Nixon kept his cool but he boiled inside. The next day Brezhnev announced that he and Nixon "worked till the early hours of the morning."

An unrelated bizarre incident happened that night. Brezhnev's bodyguard Vladimir encountered a sleepwalking First Lady. There was no Secret Service around, so he picked her up gently and carried her back to bed. His impression was the agents were used to it.

Always receptive to conspiracy theories, Kissinger decided the nocturnal visit was a ploy to catch the President off guard, and to wear down US resistance. The true explanation was simple: Brezhnev kept his schedule to the Moscow time zone. That included wearing two wristwatches, one showing Moscow time and the other the local hour. He demonstrated the watches earlier to Nixon, who observed it was the only way one could tell when to go to the bathroom.

At a poolside reception on Saturday, I stood in the receiving line between Brezhnev and Nixon. Most of the one hundred and fifty guests were from the entertainment industry. Brezhnev shook hands with Gene Autry, who came in white-topped cowboy boots, Cyd Charisse, Burl Ives, Dan Rowan, Barbara Stanwyck, Red Skelton, Frank Sinatra… Nixon had a few words for every guest. I helped Brezhnev with introductions - I knew the actors by sight. Kissinger approached, escorting Jill St. John. I leaned close to Brezhnev's ear to explain: the James Bond girl in *Diamonds Are Forever*. "Was scantily dressed," I added as an afterthought.

Brezhnev was pleasantly surprised: "Well, well, Ghenry!" He gave Nixon a nudge. Nixon laughed: "You can't beat Henry!" Jill and Henry stopped, holding up the line. Jill was radiant. Wally McNamee of *Newsweek* captured the amusing scene at the poolside. With an old lion's glint, Brezhnev stared at the slim divorcee moving away to shake hands with Mrs. Nixon and from his life into the crowd. She was a beautiful picture. Kissinger's ability to attract glamorous women added a human touch. Whether it matched their genuine interest, I do not know. (Brezhnev was never bashful about his women. He noted Kissinger's interest in glamorous escorts. At the next summit in Russia, he accused him of ogling the girls at Crimean beaches. This was not true - none were close.)

Poolside party at La Casa Pacifica. I tell Brezhnev Jill St. John was a James Bond Girl in Diamonds Are Forever. (Wally McNamee)

Wally McNamee sent me the photo and asked if I could get it auto-graphed by the General Secretary. I showed it to Alexandrov in Moscow. He said Brezhnev saw the movie, where Jill played Tiffany Case opposite Sean Connery. He thought the photo hilarious, but advised against sending it over: "His wife and colleagues wouldn't understand."

I sent Wally a liter of choice "Moskovskaya Vodka" along with my regrets. (Recently, we reminisced about the episode, which became part of his lectures on photography. I am grateful for his permission to use the photo for this book.)

At the party, Nixon and Brezhnev made lighthearted off the cuff speech-es, to loud applause. A woman with a face-lift told Nixon, "You must do this more often." I could not place her - she looked too young for my time.

Brezhnev's eyes glazed over from staring at the half forgotten faces of the silver screen. He whispered in my ear that he wished to retreat, unobtrusively, to his residence. I whispered, in turn, to Nixon. We walked Brezhnev a few steps and deposited him with Vladimir. I returned to the party and found Victor by the transparent screen on the ocean side; he was talking to Frank Sinatra - he knew him from Khrushchev's US visit. He introduced me to "Ol' Blue Eyes" and commandeered a waiter with a drinks tray. We drank to Soviet-American friendship.

If I rewrote history in my memcons with caution, politicians did it with flair. In November 1981 Ronald Reagan sent a letter to Brezhnev, reminding him of the conversation they had in Casa Pacifica. It said, in part, "When we met I asked if you were aware that the hopes and aspirations of millions of people throughout the world were dependent on the decisions that would be reached in those meetings. You took my hand in both of yours and assured me that you were aware of that and that you were dedicated with all your heart and soul and mind to fulfilling those hopes and dreams..."

The only flaw in this moving account was that most of words were never uttered. The jovial and obviously fit 62-year-old Governor explained the tech-nical details of carrying fresh water from the Sierra Nevada, and congratu-lated Brezhnev on the summit. The latter gurgled sympathetically. Reagan was a blurry face in a beeline of Hollywood celebrities. (In September 1976, in Kissinger's suite in the Waldorf Astoria, Gromyko confessed he never saw a Reagan movie. Kissinger said the President of Universal Studios told him Reagan would not withdraw from nomination at the Republican convention-to remain a second-rate actor for 30 years required a monumental ego.)

I heard of some guests' impressions of Brezhnev. The best was Red Skelton's: "I asked him if he was a card-carrying member of the Communist Party."

Victor and I consulted on the short exchanges Brezhnev had with guests, and decided there was nothing worth putting on paper. We were wrong. In late summer of 1978, the phone rang in my 10th floor office in the Foreign Ministry. It was Victor: he received an airmail letter from Frank Sinatra. I took the elevator to the 14th floor. The letter had a Las Vegas postmark. Sinatra wrote he never felt better in his life, physically; Barbara, his wife, was wonderful. He was planning a tour in the Soviet Union. Then, "My dear Victor, I don't want to be a pain in the neck, but would like to ask you for a small favor. My daughter Nancy is doing a book about me. If a daughter asks her daddy something, can you refuse?" He wanted to know what exactly Brezhnev told him at the reception in San Clemente back in 1973. I remembered the short exchange; Sinatra was a favorite. Still, I had to get approval for the quote from Alexandrov (by that time, some Brezhnev's utterances needed editing). Never a slow poke, the aide OK'd it.

Soon after, Victor and I attended the UN General Assembly session in New York. Sinatra was in Florida, and contacting him took a while. His wife Barbara took the call. There was loud music in the background. She shouted, "Frank, will you turn the goddamn thing down?" Sinatra came on the line; he was delighted. He took down the text and asked Victor if he could do anything for us. "What about a couple of signed albums, Frank?" suggested Victor. Next day a parcel was delivered to 136 East 67th Street, the USSR Permanent Mission to the UN: ten autographed double albums of Portrait of Sinatra: Forty Songs from the Life of a Man.

So what did Brezhnev tell him? I knew Sinatra was accused in the early 1960s of aiding American Communists through his defense of screenwriter Albert Maltz. Later, he became a Nixon supporter. He was 57, just back from retirement. As he and Barbara approached, I only had time to whisper in

Brezhnev's ear, "Famous American crooner." Brezhnev thought for a moment and said, "May your songs continue to bring people closer together." He shook Sinatra's hand firmly. Comrade Brezhnev, I thought, you can say that again! The phrase failed to make the Bartlett Dictionary of Quotations, but Frank Sinatra got a truthful account.

Brezhnev met the Skylab astronauts who splashed down 800 miles southwest of San Diego, to be picked up by aircraft carrier *USS Ticonderoga*. The slightly wobbly but happy Pete Conrad, Paul Weitz and Joseph Kerwin presented Brezhnev with plaques carried on board the spaceship. He drove an electric golf cart around the grounds, a cigarette dangling from his mouth, with Nixon in the passenger seat. (Later that year, his office imported two carts for the Black Sea dachas.)

Brezhnev recorded a televised address to the American people in the "Western White House," a makeshift structure passing for a Presidential office. The text was printed on large teleprompt cards. Fifteen minutes before the recording Dobrynin proposed adding a new paragraph. Alexandrov was acerbic: how did he expect to do it?

I volunteered. Grabbing a thick black marker I quickly wrote three calligraphic lines of new language on an empty card (I was a skilled draughtsman in high school). Alexandrov said the paragraph in the middle of an empty card looked like something out of an orphanage. Dobrynin disagreed. I supported him, hating to lose my work. After a brief discussion, a wise decision was taken to stick to original text. I realized later that none of us thought of consulting the speaker.

Brezhnev slowly read his statement for the cameras, stumbling over Russian tongue twisters - *"viyigrat voinu"* and *"viyigrat mir"* ("winning the war" and "winning the peace"). It took three takes before he mastered the paragraph. He asked us how it went. Somebody said his gestures were imposing.

Led by a Secret Service agent, Brezhnev, General Antonov and I walked to Nixon's study. It was empty. Brezhnev turned to me: "Where are the children?" I was puzzled. He explained he promised "Ghenry" to meet David and Elizabeth. Nobody warned me: I rushed off and found the two kids cringing in the corridor. Brezhnev embraced them and planted kisses on their foreheads. He turned to us and lowered his voice: is it all right to give them pens embossed with his name? General Antonov whispered back it was OK. His pens looked suspiciously similar to the Nixon gift Parker pen - probably came from the same supplier. The General Secretary uttered appropriate words, how "intelligent" the kids' father was, and "please always behave." David suddenly stood to attention and said in a clear and loud voice, "Thank you for everything you are doing for peace!" The kids reminded me of Soviet Young Pioneers (missing were the red kerchiefs and Lenin badges). Their father beamed in the background - I suspected who the drafter was.

Next day at the San Clemente Inn, I rose early, had a quick breakfast and put my bag outside the door for collection. The buses were leaving at 7:30 a.m. for El Toro for the flight back to Andrews. We boarded Brezhnev's IL-62 just before he and Nixon alighted from the Presidential helicopter. From the window, I watched an athletic feat performed by Chuck Connors who came to see Brezhnev off. The 6 foot 5" movie actor gave him a present the day before at Nixon's home, a pair of matching Colt .45 six-shooters, and showed how to twirl them. Brezhnev was a fan of *The Rifleman*, an American TV series. He shook Chuck's hand and hugged him. Suddenly, Connors grabbed Brezhnev by the waist and lifted the 200-pound General Secretary off the ground. His feet dangled in the cool desert air. The bodyguards gasped. Chuck slowly lowered him, and both laughed at this extraordinary demonstration of US-Soviet friendship. The episode brought out the best in Brezhnev, his love for good-natured theatricals, like bear-hugging people he liked. He invited Chuck to visit him in the Kremlin, perhaps shoot a movie in Russia. Chuck said he would, with pleasure. (He did, later in the year.)

I watched the two men hit it off and tried to imagine other leaders being bodily lifted in this way. Harold Wilson? Afraid not. Giscard d'Estaing? Mais non! Nicolae Ceausescu? The Siguranza would have shot Chuck between the eyes before he could raise a hand. With Brezhnev, it seemed natural.

He did not hug Nixon, but they shook hands like old friends: "Meet you next year…" (None of us saw Casa Pacifica again. After resignation, Nixon returned there to nurse his wounds, accompanied by a small group of faithful followers - Bull, Brennan and Woods among them. Here he wrote his memoirs and was interviewed by David Frost. In 1980, the former First Family moved to New York to be closer to their children. The new owners told a visitor to the grounds that Nikita Khrushchev stayed there in 1973. So much for institutional memory….)

We were airborne. Despite lack of sleep due to the late send-off staff party hosted by the Secret Service, I asked Brezhnev's secretary Vika to sit next to me. As soon as the plane leveled at 15,000 feet, I started dictating. We worked for the best part of the flight. A cheerful Brezhnev came down the aisle. He was happy with his stay in California. Relations with the United States were now as cordial as with France and West Germany. He stopped by our row, and I reported brightly, "Leonid Ilyich, all your pending memcons will be ready before landing at Andrews." The reaction was unexpected: his lips quivered, he wiped a tear away, and patted me on the shoulder: "*Ochen horosho* (very good), young man, thank you!" Maybe, I thought, I overdid the reporting; should be more reserved next time lest we have to comfort a sobbing General Secretary. Vika sighed: "Let's get on with the job, Andrey."

Brezhnev had unfinished business in Washington, an unpublicized private meeting with Henry Winston, Chairman of the Communist Party USA. Minister-Counselor Yuli Vorontsov took his car to personally deliver the General Secretary from Blair House to the Soviet Embassy. The Secret Service cordoned off the block. They asked tenants in buildings across the street to shut windows. Embassy diplomats were screened on entry to the mansion. A tall middle-aged man caused a flurry - he brandished a Soviet passport and said he wanted to enter. He was a visitor from Tallinn and just wanted to register. They showed him the way to the Consulate down the street.

I doubt if Brezhnev's prepared statement to the American Communists increased their awe of his person. Nevertheless, the 1970s saw Party membership grow to an impressive 25,000, including (so the Embassy thought) a strong contingent of FBI informers.

The US trip went smoothly; eleven new agreements were signed. The Soviet team was happy. With the uncontrolled environment of America, anything could have happened. Soon after, a brochure with texts of agreements and speeches was published in Moscow with a circulation of 150,000. The Chinese reaction to the second summit was expected. "Hegemony," they said.

During the long flight across the Atlantic we had a lively party to celebrate the success of the trip, plus two birthdays. It was a sunlit afternoon when we landed at Vnukovo-2. A border control officer came onboard to stamp our passports; there was no customs. It was easy getting used to VIP treatment. As we walked down the ramp, I saw lovely Inga waving from a waiting car. Victor turned to me and said in English, "Andy, look! I still got the same wife!"

YOM KIPPUR WAR IN THE KREMLIN

On Friday, October 19, 1973, I was driving home from a brief stay at the MFA clinic for a regular check-up. A Voice of America news report was coming in on my car radio: Henry Kissinger had just left for Moscow "on the invitation of the Soviet leadership." I smelt trouble; my plans for a brief vacation were dashed.

The call came at noon: Gromyko's private assistant asked me to be on hold "and for God's sake not to disappear," a move I was actually contemplating. I phoned Victor; he had similar orders. The two-man team was on the road again.

The "Yom Kippur War" started Saturday, 6 October. Egypt and Syria attacked Israeli positions in the Golan Heights and the Sinai Peninsula in a coordinated surprise attack. Israel declared its first nuclear alert, with armed missiles and aircraft. Caught by surprise, the US and the USSR were quickly drawn into the conflict by respective client states. The Israelis counterattacked: they crossed the Suez Canal and encircled the Egyptian Third Army; it was trapped. No protective barrier remained between Cairo and the Israeli army. It was also twelve miles from Damascus. The US opened an air military supply route to Israel. Pleas from President Sadat led to a massive Soviet arms airlift to Cairo.

Kissinger's plane touched down in light rain at Vnukovo- 2 at 7:00 p.m. A haggard Bill Hyland waved in greeting, "We thought we'd get a breather." Two hours later, we all met in Brezhnev's office in the Kremlin. Kissinger used to say he never negotiated after a long night flight: the jet lag put his brain at a disadvantage. However, he had to accommodate to the General Secretary's life style.

The American team (Assistant Secretary of State Alfred Atherton, his deputy Joseph Sisco, Sonnenfeldt, Lord and Hyland) looked as if they were trampled over by a bison herd. Kissinger wore a black blazer. He greeted me with a smile and a warm handshake, something he did not do before. He needed time to size up the relative importance of Soviet officials.

Brezhnev was expansive - he always performed better in the evening. In a light blue turtleneck and dark blue blazer with two gold stars on his chest, he looked the embodiment of leadership. He had a sore throat ("Don't think it's because I am weak," he warned Kissinger). Towards the end of the session, his voice returned to the original rich baritone, almost the same frequency as Kissinger's. He was not vindictive: he did not remind Kissinger of his warning in May in Zavidovo that a conflict might flare up in the Middle East after his summer trip to the US. (Kissinger confessed later that Brezhnev's was correct in his prediction.)

Expectedly, the General Secretary started with a joke: "Ghenry, I have a proposal: let the Arabs occupy Tel-Aviv, and the Jews Cairo; then we'll have peace!" Everybody laughed. We took our places around the billiard-green felt covered table. As usual, I sat at the end of the short Soviet row to Brezhnev's left, next to Kornienko.

Kissinger said he brought greetings from President Nixon. Brezhnev thanked him, but failed to congratulate Henry on 1973 Nobel Peace Prize shared with Le Duc Tho, as announced three days earlier. So undiplomatic; perhaps he simply forgot. (Le Duc Tho turned down the award. Two years later, Kissinger followed suit: he returned the prize and reimbursed the Nobel Foundation. Both laureates cited reasons that reflected their acrimonious debates in Paris.)

Brezhnev proceeded to say he saw no sense in analyzing the situation on the ground, who suffered the heaviest losses, and where the armies were now: "We are not the General Staff."

However, it was clear that the evolving situation at the front was Kissinger's ace. As Brezhnev paused for breath, he intervened. He said the President regarded the problem as serious: small countries should not drag us into a clash of our own interests crucial to the world; an immediate cease-fire is in order; the on-going competition in supplying arms to the belligerents must stop.

Brezhnev agreed, except on the last point: the USSR was implementing a four-year agreement on military supplies. "It seems you want to implement it in two weeks," remarked Kissinger. Brezhnev raised his voice: "President Sadat says we failed him by not providing enough arms to destroy the Israeli army." Kissinger smiled gleefully: "It's difficult to destroy an enemy army when your own forces can't move ahead."

Brezhnev raised his hand to stop Henry's mockery and suggested seeking a realistic solution. He was aware of Nixon's initial inclination to enforce a peace settlement on the warring sides, but he suspected Kissinger opposed a bilateral initiative (this turned out to be the case). The Kremlin was in favor of US-Soviet guarantees of a cease-fire, plus reiteration of the 1967 UN Security Council resolution 242. Kissinger admitted the approach was constructive, but his preference was solely Security Council guarantees. He and Nixon did not want anything that looked like a condominium. Brezhnev doubted the effect of another UN resolution and of Secretary-General Waldheim's role in securing peace. "Our two countries guarantees will not be taken lightly," he insisted. He understood, of course, that the US motive was diluting Soviet influence in the region. (That evening, Vladimir Vinogradov, Soviet Ambassador in Cairo, sent a cable reporting on his conversation with President Sadat, who was surprised to hear about Kissinger's visit. He claimed Israel would not hold out for long; the Soviet leadership must show firmness. Believing this bluster was a mistake.)

It was close to midnight. Brezhnev rose from the table and invited everybody "to taste some *pirozhki* (cakes)." This meant a full-fledged dinner. It was my turn to translate, since Victor needed rest. Kissinger yawned repeatedly. His party was exhausted; the only American to demonstrate stoicism was Joseph Sisco, the Middle East expert. Sensing that Kissinger's body defenses were down, Brezhnev accused him of reneging on a promise to deliver a cowboy belt with two holsters promised by Chuck Connors in San Clemente. Kissinger feebly blamed the bureaucracy in Washington.

As the night wore on, Brezhnev was energized, as if he fed on plutonium - the effect of his afternoon sleeping pills wore off. He ate the meat cakes with relish, advised his guests to have "more of this nourishing Russian food," and told stories. He demonstrated his new Russian-made electronic watch. He said only two have been made; Erich Honecker had the other one. He suggested an exchange: "Let's swap without looking." Kissinger refused; his watch was evidently pricier. (Brezhnev had a fascination for watches. At earlier meetings, he presented Soviet watches to Kissinger and Sonnenfeldt. Stoessel, as a worthy Ambassador, wore a Soviet watch - he said it was excellent.)

Brezhnev proposed a toast to the health of the President, and walked around clinking glasses with everyone in the room. At 1:30 a.m., he suggested we disperse and reassemble next morning at eleven. I dictated the memcon until 4:00 a.m. The Politburo was in session from the early hours, discussing how to extricate Russia's ally, Sadat. News received overnight from the battle-front was grim. Sadat was in panic; he was ready to accept a Security Council cease-fire resolution, and he needed it now.

We reassembled at noon in Brezhnev's Kremlin study. This time he wore a business suit, but with the same medals - his valet re-pinned them every time he changed, or maybe they were dummies. He slid a typewritten page across the table to Kissinger, a draft UN Security Council resolution. He suggested a new tack: the US and the USSR should propose it together in New York.

Kissinger said that in response to "the constructive Russian draft," he had a shorter version consisting of three paragraphs. He handed me the paper and I rushed out of the room to dictate a typed translation into Russian. After two minutes, Brezhnev's secretary came to enquire why it was taking so long. I ignored him, knowing well that my text would go to the Politburo. More importantly, it might become a Security Council resolution to end the hostilities. There was nobody to revise my translation. Time was lost already, because the Chief of the MFA Near East Department did not have the Russian text of resolution 242, which was referenced in the eighty-word draft. I would have fired him, if I had the power. The secretary came again, pleading for "anything that was ready." I was adamant. At moments like this, the rule is to produce a quality document, whatever the intimidation. As I brought the translation into the room, Brezhnev was telling a humorous story; others were drinking coffee.

I handed the page to Brezhnev. He put on his reading glasses, but relapsed into another story, and then another. Time was running out for the Egyptian forces. For some reason, he described the characteristics of his ZIL limousine, which he said resembled a Packard. In the 1940s, Soviet leaders drove around in black Packards. The ZIL was sturdy and fast, with a lower center of gravity, so it would not overturn if a bomb exploded underneath.

Brezhnev read my text, and proposed going paragraph-by-paragraph. It was odd to see both teams engage in collective drafting. Brezhnev liked the new experience: his editing skills were getting better by the hour. Some edits were hair splitting. Gromyko and Dobrynin insisted on the words "practical implementation," because it reinforced the message. Kissinger said the word "practical" was superfluous. The compromise was that the word would stay in the Russian text but not in the English version. (When the final text in two languages was received at the US and Soviet Missions in New York, Ambassador John Scali promptly called back about the discrepancy in translation.)

All through the editing process, I was composing a rolling text of the emerging resolution in Russian, to finalize it by the time they agreed on the English version.

Kissinger was not aware that Brezhnev was ready to accept a text without mention of resolution 242, in view of Israeli opposition. To our surprise, Kissinger volunteered mentioning 242 "in all its parts." This was a bonus. Naturally, Brezhnev agreed.

He announced a short break. He went to a corner to consult with the Russian team. Kissinger walked over to Victor and me and said, "The insanity of the situation is that when the Arabs rejected a cease-fire they were in a much better situation; now they're accepting when they're worse off. We knew what it'll come to." We did not argue: as interpreters, we were not supposed to express political opinions, because we were a service, not the decision-makers. Kissinger did not expect any reaction; he just vented his feelings.

He returned to his seat and leaned back. Pointing to the large clock on Brezhnev's desk in the shape of a ship's steering wheel, he enquired if there was a microphone inside. "If there is one," said Victor, "it was installed in Washington - it's American-made." The small plaque at the base said it was a Chelsea Claremont Ship Clock, a present from Ambassador Dobrynin. It is visible on photos of Brezhnev at his Kremlin desk.

Negotiations resumed. The next hurdle was reference to "negotiations between the parties concerned under appropriate auspices." Brezhnev agreed, if it meant US and Soviet attendance at all key stages, in the beginning, the middle and the end. Kissinger's interpretation was different: attendance, but not all the time, and not necessarily at the same table. After some bickering, Gromyko and Kissinger drafted an interpretation, which both initialed with "A.G." and "H.K." "Auspices" will mean active participation of the US and USSR in the beginning and thereafter in the course of negotiations. We won a crucial point.

Next was the timing of the cease-fire. Brezhnev proposed "immediately." Kissinger stalled: the later the Security Council issued the call, the better for the advancing Israeli army. The polemic was delaying the cease-fire already. Kissinger said delivering orders to field commanders took time. He would need an hour to write a cable to Washington; and allow for two hours for encoding at the US Embassy. It would be on the President's desk not earlier than four hours from now - he had to get Nixon's formal approval (he was sure he would get it). Brezhnev grimaced. He said he needed twenty minutes to speak to his comrades in the Politburo; they would certainly approve.

Kissinger turned to Gromyko: the Security Council would need additional time to convene. One could not fool Gromyko. He said, "I personally convened the Council in half an hour; the maximum time needed is an hour for the members to drive downtown to the UN." Kissinger thought better of arguing with Gromyko on UN procedure.

They settled on twelve hours, from the moment the Kremlin negotiation concluded. Kissinger suggested the Soviets establish a direct telephone link to John Scali in New York, so he could transmit voice instructions. Brezhnev surprised everybody by rushing to the front office to tell his secretary to start putting up a link. He returned and said the line will operate from Kissinger's residence on Lenin Hills. Kissinger reminded Brezhnev that the instructions would have to be identical with the ones the Kremlin transmitted to Jacob Malik, the Soviet UN Representative; that would take additional time. He won on this point.

I watched the small group orchestrating a Security Council enforcement action thousands of miles away, while the world waited. Soon, good news came in from New York: the text was introduced in the early hours of the morning on October 22 by the US and Soviet Ambassadors. The Security Council approved what was to become resolution 338. The Chinese delegate did not vote.

It guaranteed, as Brezhnev believed, Soviet participation in the final Middle East settlement. Resolutions 242 and 338 remain the basic international agreements on a problem that was never expected to last into the 21st century.

The American team left. Victor and I lingered in Brezhnev's study. He shared impressions of what exactly transpired. At moments like this, we occasionally received instructions regarding the transcript. At least listening to the discussion was useful. Points were stressed that were important for the Soviet side, and this could be highlighted in the memcon. Though our preparation was thorough, we were not party to Politburo debates. Sometimes Brezhnev would telephone one or two Politburo colleagues to describe the battles of the green felt in his folksy way - they were eager to hear the latest news.

Andrei Kirilenko called. The intercom was on. He listened to Brezhnev's story and congratulated him, "Incidentally, Leonid Ilyich, my doctors recommend a check-up; do you mind if I take a couple of weeks off?"

"Sure, no problem, go ahead," Brezhnev said. "What about Pitsunda on the Black Sea, or Crimea?" He pressed a button and turned to us: "Did you hear that (expletive) going off on a holiday? Suslov called me yesterday, just back from his vacation. With all these negotiations, I had four hours of sleep, and just managed a quick bowl of soup. I work till three in the morning every night, with no time to rest, and these (expletive) enjoy their vacations!"

There was nothing left but to murmur words of sympathy at the inhuman treatment the General Secretary endured from his loafer colleagues.

We got word later in the afternoon that following the marathon negotiating session the doctors advised Brezhnev to rest. He promised to get in touch with Kissinger later at his residence on Lenin Hills. The call came through late that night. According to Kissinger, "It was one of the ordinary interpreters on duty. When the guy heard the voice over the phone he stood to attention, stuttered and couldn't relate a single word of what the General Secretary was saying."

Before making that call, Brezhnev chaired a Politburo session. I was still in his office dictating, when Kosygin entered and asked if "Leonid had managed to settle all the issues." A silent Andropov appeared, in shirtsleeves.

Victor and I left the room, discretely, and settled down in the anteroom. It was a long wait; the pangs of hunger were unbearable. A kindly steward led us into an adjoining kitchen, where he served us ham and cheese sandwiches and strong black Georgian tea. After another hour, Alexandrov emerged to tell us that Brezhnev, for some reason, forbade giving my memcons to anybody (Alexandrov took them straight from the typewriter).

I was surprised to see the edited version, done by unnamed staff in Brezhnev's Central Committee offices. More than a case of bad editing - the version contained errors of substance. I made quick corrections and sent it back to Alexandrov. He told me later that the previous night some participants made edits. "They lost so much time," he complained. "You or I would have done it faster, but they never let go of the transcript." I was at a loss for the reason. Did Brezhnev spruce up the record so it would explain the ease with which he agreed to Kissinger's draft?

Brezhnev reappeared; he looked haggard. Seeing us in the anteroom, he groaned, "I haven't slept for two nights. Had no food today; must get some chicken soup. My head feels like a ringing church bell. I can't go on like this, it's impossible!" We looked down.

He called for a stenographer and started dictating a letter to Nixon. The expressions were elaborate; I fail to recall the wording except for several references to his "personal relationship" with the President. I was sure Alexandrov and Gromyko would rewrite it later to make it unrecognizable.

Brezhnev completed his dictation and walked over. He said he saved Egypt's Third Army. He patted me on the back and said, "Well done, young man." He turned to the steward: "Get Victor a glass of vodka." I nudged Victor: "It's like I am getting a medal and you a cash prize." He agreed that a sign of distinction received in kind was preferable. The steward brought in a full glass of vodka for Victor and small celebration tumblers for us.

Presents from Kissinger were delivered. I received a heavy bog-colored earthenware vase with a lid, of uncertain purpose. A friend said it looked like it came from a crematorium.

The negotiators met briefly next morning. There were mutual congratulations and references to World War II allied friendship. This was the first time a UN crisis resolution was tabled by the United States and the Soviet Union together. They stopped the Yom Kippur war.

Still, things were not going smoothly: the Israelis continued their advance. Brezhnev sent two ominous messages to Nixon complaining of Israeli treachery. Both countries were guarantors of peace in the area, he said; Israel must implement resolution 338. He proposed to dispatch US and Soviet military contingents to enforce the cease-fire. Kornienko wondered if Watergate was not on Nixon's mind as he pondered the proposal; a joint super power move might help his political image. Kissinger's advice was to turn it down. Nixon yielded, but Brezhnev would not give up. A veiled Russian warning of unilateral action triggered a US forces worldwide nuclear alert (DefCon III, highest when attack is not imminent). Since the Kremlin meant this as a warning only, it ignored the American response. No Soviet action came. It took time for tempers to cool. Later, Nixon wrote a pacifying letter to Brezhnev; he said, "Perhaps it was our mistake, perhaps yours."

The crisis faded, but the aftertaste was bitter.

Did Brezhnev know about the impending war? The following year he admitted to Kissinger that he knew less than three days before the outbreak; too late to do anything about it. Kissinger thought the USSR dared not pass the intelligence to Washington for fear of an Israeli preemptive strike.[43] The Middle East had serious domestic implications for the Administration in view of the Jewish lobby. Kissinger advised Brezhnev to restore diplomatic relations with Israel; he would then deal with them directly, thus easing his burden.

He was right. I remembered how back in 1967, after the Six-Day War, First Deputy Foreign Minister Vassili Kuznetsov summoned Ambassador Katz to inform him the Soviet Union was breaking off relations with Israel. The Embassy must close down and all staff to leave as soon as possible. Katz was numbed. He only asked Kuznetsov what "as soon as possible" meant in terms of time. Kuznetsov smiled faintly, and repeated the words, and I repeated the translation. I saw the Ambassador out. He turned to me: "Two weeks?" I thought it was a fair time frame, but kept silent. It was almost a family story: my father was instrumental in establishing relations with the new State back in 1948. I saw their rupture. The break eliminated any influence the USSR had with the Israelis, and helped little in our uneasy relationship with the Arab world.

Nixon's strategic goal was to weaken Soviet influence in the Middle East. Of course, he denied this. "Baloney," he said, responding to Brezhnev's complaints about US intentions. Brezhnev accused Kissinger of a secret deal with the Arab countries to exclude the Soviet Union from the peace process - the bilateral "auspices" agreed the previous October. Kissinger brushed off the accusations, "The notion of a secret deal with the Arabs is a contradiction in itself." He was like an eel: he gave a different interpretation of "auspices." The Soviet Union's Arab clients increasingly realized that the key to any lasting solution lay in Washington. Russian influence in the region gradually waned. It never recuperated.

CHAPTER 3

"A true comrade": Nixon's Last Summit, 1974

Shooting from the Hip

IN THE COLD MONTH OF December, Chuck Connors followed up on Brezhnev's invitation. Brezhnev did not forget his spontaneous act of friendliness in California. He carried Chuck's Colts on hunting forays in Zavidovo and demonstrated shooting from the hip: bang, bang.

My office phone rang: Alexandrov asked me to come to the Kremlin for the meeting.

I took the subway to Revolution Square Metro Station and walked to the Kremlin Spassky Gate with the great tower clock. I presented my maroon leather-bound Foreign Ministry ID to a guard. He ticked off my name in the list. I walked along the red brick wall to Entrance 6, right beneath the dome of the 18th century Senate Building, with the Red flag on top battered by the icy wind. Another guard checked my pass against his list. Sometimes they asked where one was heading, and you replied, "Leonid Ilyich's office." I went up to the second floor by a wide circular staircase, and after a final, third, check, was ushered into a landing with two corridors extending right and left. Never remodeled from the times of the Tsars, the corridors were long and straight: one could study the artist's perspective. Nobody accompanied you; the guards expected the visitor to know the direction. I walked along the red carpet and reached a heavy oak door. The gold letters on a magenta glass plate said, "Leonid Ilyitch Brezhnev, General Secretary of the Central Committee of the Communist Party of the Soviet Union." A male private secretary stood up from a battery of cream-colored telephones.

"Could you entertain our guests for a while?" he asked. "Leonid Ilyitch is watching an ice hockey match. It's ending soon. Perhaps you could explain, ah, that he's in conference?" No surprise to me. I was used to Brezhnev's peculiar schedule: sleeping late, working late, taking meals at irregular hours, watching soccer and ice hockey games on TV during office hours.

In a few minutes, Connors and Faith Quabius entered, accompanied by an officer. I led them to an adjoining room where we sat down at a round polished wood-encrusted table. A waiter served us tea and cookies. Chuck asked me about the buildings' layout and history. He was overwhelmed by the Kremlin; his girlfriend was speechless.

Chuck Connors calls on Brezhnev in the Kremlin. (Vladimir Musaelyan)

After fifteen minutes, the private secretary said comrade Brezhnev was ready to see us. Philip Yermash, Chairman of the State Cinematography Committee, was waiting by the study door. I guess his role was to be on call in case the meeting produced a joint film initiative; this was known to happen.

Brezhnev stood up from his desk, delighted to see his "cowboy comrade." They embraced - this time Chuck refrained from hoisting him. The General

Secretary waved to the pair to sit down and pulled a desk drawer. It jammed and I went over to help. Together we pried it open. I expected to see the Colts, but it overflowed with Brezhnev photos. Some were framed and signed. He looked handsome on all. He presented one to Chuck.

Brezhnev was choosy about his photos and personally approved them for publication. Photographers sent him photos to sign - he ignored those that caught him at an awkward moment. He liked his image as manly and responsible: in sunglasses in a speedboat, hunting, or signing an important treaty. With time and advancing age, his control slipped. The photos the public saw in his autumn years were of an ailing person.

The General Secretary was relaxed; this was not a negotiation. He recalled the meeting with Nixon in California and stressed the practical results of his (which I changed to "ours" in the memcon as a gesture to the Soviet troika) encounters with the President in Russia and the US. He asked Connors, if he met the President, to convey this feeling. He expected to solidify the strategy laid out in 1972 and 1973; their future meetings in 1974 in the Soviet Union and in 1975 in the US would be even more fruitful.

Chuck promised to convey the feelings to the President. He was excited: being involved in high diplomacy is thrilling.

Brezhnev smiled: people asked him about meeting Chuck in San Clemente. "I explained that you were so tall I found it hard to reach up to kiss your cheek, and you hoisted me up. When I returned home, I saw the scene on film. I looked up your biography. I know yours is a worker's background; you succeeded in becoming an actor. As for your souvenirs, the two Colt revolvers, I always carry them when I go hunting."

Connors was moved. "I am often asked about how we met, why is that you noticed me? I reply that history touched me by chance. Human moments occur when two direct men feel sympathy. Yes, this was a sincere, human moment. For most Americans our encounter was important in the sense that you emerged as a humorous person, not just a political leader."

Yes, Brezhnev said, the reaction in our country was similar. (He was stretching a point: the episode was not reported in the Russian media; I will have to edit this part of the memcon.)

Connors said the Colt Company managers asked him to tell Brezhnev that they were making a pair of custom cowboy Colt .45s, specially engraved. It would take about six months to deliver. They were also sending two revolvers that serve as cigarette lighters; one can use each a million times. The Colt people wished to establish trade ties with the Soviet Union.

This news pleased Brezhnev; he expected the Soviet industrial Ministries would be interested.

Connors said he left two movies at the US Embassy, *Geronimo* and *Ride beyond Vengeance,* as presents for Brezhnev. Brezhnev loved cowboy films; he saw *The Magnificent Seven* at least seven times. He sighed: "Our "Hollywood" is not as rich as yours." "But you have a rich heart," Chuck said. At the end of the meeting, Brezhnev presented a Soviet watch to Chuck and a souvenir (in a closed box) for his girlfriend, "as a token of our friendship."

That evening at the MFA, I dictated the memcon to a secretary. I put the date and signed it: "Recorded by A. Vavilov." I added the standard phrase, "Memcon not reviewed by L.I. Brezhnev." I deposited it with the Minister's private office for delivery to the Kremlin by KGB messenger. Brezhnev's comrades in the Politburo would be on the circulation list. Similar to Kissinger, modesty was not Brezhnev's strong point, so I killed most of his non-essential remarks to shield the old man. I thought Chuck made an excellent diplomatic debut. He reinforced later it with a 90-minute documentary entitled *Peace and Friendship.*

Connors and his guns captivated Brezhnev. When Kissinger came to the Kremlin for another round on the Middle East, Brezhnev, who was also Supreme Commander, pointed a miniature artillery gun at him. When Henry said a General Secretary never shot at him before, he trained it on Sonnenfeldt. Gromyko advised pointing it at himself, rather than at Americans. Brezhnev loaded the gun with something that looked like a tiny shell and pulled the lanyard. When nothing happened, Brezhnev said he would ask Sadat for spares. Kissinger observed that Sadat probably had them in the wrong guns.

Brezhnev was pleased with his marksmanship: he claimed he had not missed once since he got the Colts. He grinned: "I'm like Chuck Connors." (I am grateful to Helmut Sonnenfeldt for recording this exchange. It was dropped from the Russian memcon.)

APRIL IN PARIS

After de Gaulle retired in 1969, Nixon asked Vernon Walters to deliver a letter of encouragement to Colombey-les-Deux-Eglises. "He is a true comrade," said de Gaulle upon reading the letter."[44] Nixon valued this mark of high esteem, coined in the days of the French wartime resistance. In three years, the Soviet leaders placed him in the same category, to make the most of a beautiful friendship.

In March 1974, Kissinger travelled to Moscow to discuss the agenda of the third Nixon-Brezhnev summit. I do not know if he expected it to be the last; Nixon had less than six months to go. The backdrop to the meeting was Watergate. Impeachment proceedings were in train. John Mitchell, Bob Haldeman, John Ehrlichman and several others were indicted on charges of conspiracy, obstruction of justice and perjury. Senator Jackson reinforced his demands on Jewish emigration and fought any new concessions to the Soviets.

The talks were held in the Kremlin - not in Zavidovo, as promised to Kissinger earlier.

I was in Brezhnev's office when he took a call on the intercom; a Politburo colleague wished to know how the negotiations were going. "Ghenry is shifty," Brezhnev complained. "I planned inviting him to Zavidovo to talk without protocol, but that's too much honor. We'll negotiate in the Kremlin in a formal atmosphere." "You're right," said the voice on the intercom. "He hasn't deserved it. If he was forthcoming and bared his soul…" "Exactly," said Brezhnev. He was upset.

It would have been a bizarre experience listening to Kissinger "baring his soul," if he followed this Dostoyevskian advice. He might have enjoyed knowing about the little plot to downgrade his trip.

As an introspective Russian, Brezhnev could not rid himself of a sense of guilt: he did not live up on a promise. He must make amends. His lame cover story was bad weather, rain and fog in Zavidovo; it would have been risky for the helicopter. Everything was ready for the American party - too bad it didn't work out. Brezhnev's voice was hoarse; he was not good at lying. He topped it with a joke: next year during the summit, he would take Kissinger to Zavidovo again for boar hunting, but he would have to stay in a cabin with six Soviet missiles underneath!

Kissinger did not mind: he said the wild boars must have been grateful this time. I'm sure he didn't miss Zavidovo; it was too far from US Embassy communications.

A weight lifted off Brezhnev's shoulders. He enquired about Kissinger's children, David and Elizabeth, who travelled to Moscow. David loved the Young Pioneers Club, Kissinger said, and Liz admired the present Brezhnev sent her. Brezhnev rubbed his palms together. He knew how to offset the bad aftertaste: discuss the dates of President Nixon's summer trip to the USSR. They quickly agreed on June. Brezhnev said he left the length of the visit to the President. Six weeks would be fine, because Nixon already has a residence in Moscow, the Kremlin. Let Congress take a rest! Seriously, seven or eight days would be just right, to include trips to Crimea or Lake Baikal. "Or Yalta - Roosevelt stayed there," Brezhnev said. "Any place in the USSR the President wishes to visit."

Brezhnev, Gromyko, Dobrynin, Alexandrov, Kornienko, Sokolov and I sat at the window side of long table, facing Kissinger's team. Bottles of mineral water, *Essentuki* and *Borjomi,* and regulation crystal ashtrays were positioned at equal intervals.

Victor sat at the smaller butt table - Brezhnev occupied it when he chaired meetings. It held a flip calendar, an electric alarm clock, a cut crystal ashtray, and the "MIRVed" cigarette case shaped like the warhead nose cone of the "Satan" missile. There was a large photo portrait of Brezhnev and other generals of the Belorussian front taken at the Red Square Victory Parade in 1945 by my old friend Yakov Halip. I saw no red Kremlin folders with papers to sign.

Brezhnev turned serious. He said he appreciated Nixon's firmness and resolve at home; he had the full support of the Soviet leadership. I had a feeling Kissinger was glad he did not expand on the awkward topic of Watergate.

Brezhnev looked at me down the table: "This will be off record." I showed him I was putting down my pen. This generation of Americans, he said, never experienced war on their territory, or for that matter, an advance of the enemy as far as the Volga, to Stalingrad. They had not lost twenty million lives. (I corrected it to twenty-six million in my transcript.) He was "dumbfounded" by calls in the US that Washington should speak from a position of strength, and by demands for new military appropriations.

I saw no reason for this to be off the record. Brezhnev was not looking, so I resumed writing. They proceeded to discuss SALT. The two sides had conflicting objectives: the US wanted to constrain Russian deployment of MIRVs; the Soviet Union wanted to keep doors open for catching up with the US. Kissinger said the USSR was developing four new missiles. Brezhnev dismissed the accusation: they are improved older ones. Henry grinned: if it were only an improvement, he would hate to see what a new system looked like!

The issue was complex, and Brezhnev stumbled over numbers of launchers, submarines and MIRVs. Kornienko, who sat next to me, had to walk over several times and whisper in his ear. It was then that Kissinger asked mockingly, "What are 3,000 MIRVs among friends?" Brezhnev took this in good humor, and corrected himself. He decided to assail Kissinger with Soviet intelligence on US weapon systems. With a sly smile, he claimed US MIRVs had 12 warheads. Kissinger said 10. Brezhnev kept insisting on 12. (It turned out he was right. Kissinger confessed later that the original Trident submarine test was for a 12-warhead missile, but the Navy settled on 10 in the end.)

Next on Brezhnev's list was the B-1 bomber: if the US renounced it, the USSR will reciprocate by not deploying the new Tu-160 aircraft. Kissinger said he was skeptical of the B-1, and advised the Soviets to demand rapid B-1 deployment - the US would go bankrupt. He confessed to ignorance about Tu-160. (Still in design stage, the world's largest supersonic bomber was a response to Rockwell's B-1; it was deployed in 1987, and still flew sorties against Islamic State positions in 2016, as did Tu-22M, the famous "Backfire".) Brezhnev asked Kissinger to report to the President, who "would understand." Giving him a stern look, he said in a barely audible voice that he was making these concessions "in view of the domestic problems and political difficulties the President is experiencing." It was the first time I heard Brezhnev try Watergate as a pressure tool. He never did that again.

Moscow thought that new dramatic ideas would facilitate the summit's success. Brezhnev suggested, with a straight face, to withdraw US and Soviet nuclear weapons from the Mediterranean.

Kissinger shook his head: "Absolutely unacceptable." Although he did not explain, the reasons were clear. First, this encroached on US forward-based systems. Second, Nixon held firmly to gunboat diplomacy: few things are as dramatic as the massive hulk of an aircraft carrier in the morning fog. A snow-covered silo with a "Satan" missile thousands of miles away in Siberia did not have the same psychological effect. The Soviet Navy had no realistic plan of matching US aircraft carrier construction. The proposal stayed on the US-Soviet agenda for a while, until it died a natural death.

Kissinger was reticent about Brezhnev's idea of ceasing production of chemical weapons and their destruction. The USSR doubted their effectiveness. They were dangerous to store and indiscriminate: wind and rain quickly dispersed poisonous concentrations. A bigger reason was concern with the US chemical industry's edge in "binary weapons," safe components that produced a deadly concoction when mixed.

Kissinger cited verification problems. Brezhnev countered that the 1972 biological weapons convention had no foolproof verification clauses. Kissinger was frank: the US preferred to retain the chemical weapons option for retaliation purposes.

Brezhnev was dissatisfied with progress on CSCE. He admitted the US was not putting up obstacles, but he expected real help. He complained about Holland, Belgium and Luxemburg who kept presenting "absurd" proposals on confidence-building measures (advance warning of troop movements and maneuvers). Kissinger understood the problem, but he wanted to avoid siding openly with the USSR. On the third basket - human contacts - he said he never thought the Soviet system would change by opening a Dutch cabaret in Moscow. He advised to tie obligations to Soviet domestic legislation. He gestured frantically (no, no!), when Brezhnev suggested giving the US several more Solzhenitsyn's in line with free movement of people.

When Kissinger mentioned the possibility of joint US-Soviet projects in new alternative sources of energy, Brezhnev looked worried. Probably, he saw the new ventures - liquefied coal, shale oil and energy saving - as undermining the growing Soviet oil and natural gas empire, a muscle-flexing tool, especially in Europe.

Brezhnev's performance was passable, but he digressed often from his brief. He felt unsure of his expertise, a fact he tried to gloss over with excessive joking. He was frustrated: he wished negotiations did not take so much time. But, presenting convincing arguments was not enough; they had to match the interests of the other side.

At the luncheon in the Palace of Receptions on Lenin Hills overlooking Moscow, I translated Gromyko and Kissinger's brief toasts. Kissinger spoke of President Nixon's strong commitment: "Our greatest goal is that over the next three years, we can make the relationship that has grown up between our two peoples and our leaders irreversible."

The next three years - he meant 1977. He was reaching for the future as if it would help Nixon. The speech may have been drafted in our MFA office. The notion of "irreversibility" of détente was the watchword of the Russian delegation at the European Security Conference. The West Europeans regarded the notion as solidifying Soviet control over Eastern Europe. Nixon thought otherwise. The more he felt boxed in at home, the more he tried to reach out to those who "understood" him, and that were his comrades in Soviet Russia. For him, "irreversibility" was a magic password to solidify his political defenses and make him indispensable, to help maintain the US-Soviet relationship and the main political actors. Nixon needed more meetings with the comrades.

In March 1974, French President George Pompidou flew to Pitsunda on the Black Sea for a meeting with Brezhnev. De Gaulle praised his intention to meet his Soviet comrade. It would be the last time: Pompidou confided to the General Secretary that he had terminal leukemia. In less than three weeks, he was gone. In an unusual gesture, Brezhnev sent a letter to Nixon recounting his conversation with Pompidou.

Close to eighty foreign leaders converged on Paris for the State funeral, including President Nixon. Some time back, he criticized protests by American Jews against Pompidou in New York for selling French fighter aircraft to the Arabs.

Brezhnev asked Nikolai Podgorny to attend the services; he did not feel well enough for an avalanche of bilateral meetings with other leaders. I accompanied Podgorny. He dutifully attended the ceremonies at the Notre Dame de Paris. An urgent message came in from the American Embassy: Nixon wished to meet him at the US Ambassador's residence on April 7 at 10:00 a.m. For this, he would be ready to postpone his departure from Paris.

By touching base with Podgorny Nixon would demonstrate "continuity" of his personal relationship with Soviet leaders. Apart from a good press opportunity, he could probe Soviet views two months before his third summit with Brezhnev.

The message from Nixon produced a storm in a teacup. Podgorny was angry; he regarded the invitation as a "summons." He told the Soviet Ambassador he saw no reason for driving over to meet Nixon: "If he wishes to see me let him come here, to the Embassy." But there was a hitch: the Secret Service (so the Russians were told) advised Nixon not to leave his residence except for the memorial services. It took several hours before the Ambassador and Minister-Counselor Vladimir Kizichenko persuaded Podgorny to consult with Moscow. The reply, signed by Brezhnev and Kosygin, came quickly, "Nikolai, you ought to meet Nixon." To appease Podgorny his Politburo comrades advised him to propose a luncheon format.

Since Nixon's departure was scheduled for noon, the Americans suggested an 8:00 a.m. breakfast. "Too early," thundered Podgorny. "Make it at least a half hour later." He thought he was defending the status of the USSR, in effect, Brezhnev's. I am sure this was how he explained his initial intransigence to colleagues in the Kremlin. Kizichenko had another theory: Podgorny did not dare meet Nixon without a clear go-ahead from Brezhnev.

So be it: a Sunday breakfast at 8:30 a.m. at 41, rue du Faubourg Saint-Honoré. I tried to make small talk with a sulking Podgorny in the Embassy car, but he was uncommunicative. Nixon walked to the car with outstretched hands, smiling broadly. It was quite a turn out by the international press. The American Ambassador was nowhere in sight; the Soviet Ambassador was not invited either. It would have diluted the importance of the meeting.

To balance the participants (to make it three against three) Kizichenko joined the meal. His French was excellent, but it was not needed. Nixon's two assistant generals, Alexander Haig and Brent Scowcroft, sat silently throughout the meal. I did not see them taking any notes. Kizichenko offered to take notes to relieve me for the translation. I was grateful to the World War II veteran turned diplomat. As I expected, no American interpreter was present. (Years later, a two-page note on the discussion, probably dictated by Scowcroft, was released by the State Department. The brevity was a sure sign no tape recorder was used. My memcon was five times longer.)

We were served orange juice, omelet, coffee and marmalade, and, unexpectedly, black caviar on toast. Nixon pretended irritation that there was no caviar, and told the waiter to bring some: "They don't know that people in Moscow are used to eating caviar." "We don't eat it at breakfast," said Podgorny. Nixon insisted, "Ordinary people don't, but you in the Kremlin do. I want Russian, not Iranian caviar!" he shouted to the departing waiter. I prayed they would get off the subject, lest Podgorny become edgy. He never touched the delicacy, but I helped myself. It was impossible to tell its origin. Both brands come from the Caspian Sea, and they pack them in small round Russian glass jars.

Nixon was in a relaxed mood. If he wished to escape the killing fields of US media, it was in the company of Soviet leaders. In their clumsy embrace, he sought solace and a sense of security that reinforced his emotional shell. Podgorny felt the warmth and thawed. Nixon said he was impressed by Khachaturian's *Spartacus* he saw in 1959 in Leningrad. After agreeing on the merits of the Bolshoi Ballet dancers and La Scala opera singers, both men turned to serious things, the upcoming summit in Moscow.

Nixon recalled the first summit, which came, he stressed, after an abnormally long period of the Cold War. Podgorny responded that the third summit would outstrip 1972 not only in substance but also in Russian people's hospitality: "You will feel a completely different atmosphere in the country."

This was balm on the US President's frayed nerves. He wanted to know about places in the Soviet Union worth a visit, and Podgorny gave him an oral tour of Georgia, Azerbaijan and other spots. "I'll go anywhere you invite me," said Nixon. He tried a little flattery remarking that Brezhnev, Podgorny and Kosygin "spoke with one voice." Podgorny agreed, ignoring the fact that the comparative strength of the three voices was now very different from 1972.

Nixon wanted to know if the talks would be held in the Kremlin, and his guest assured him that this was the best place in terms of communications and TV exposure. "Ah, the TV," Nixon muttered. He then plunged into the issue of leaks. He talked as a person harassed. Little beads of sweat appeared on his brow. He said he enjoyed talking to Soviet leaders because no leaks were tolerated in the Soviet Union. One could always speak in confidence - unlike with some people in the US and with "the so-called allies." Podgorny noted that some US allies and members of the Administration did have loose tongues; they babbled about conversations the President and Dr. Kissinger had in the USSR. Why, Kissinger was obliged to refute some statements he supposedly made!

Nixon smiled: "Some of his critics say he was upset with the way things were going, and got married to get over it." (On 30 March, Henry Kissinger married Nancy Maginnes.)   "There are people in the US, I'm sure in your country too," he went on, "who are not tuned in and don't want the new summit to succeed. Take Senator Jackson and the American press... Sometimes our hands are tied, but we're trying hard."

Podgorny nodded: "As far as the USSR is concerned, there are people like Solzhenitsyn and Sakharov, but they are dissidents and don't play an important role... The absolute majority of Soviet people support détente and strengthened ties with the United States."

Nixon said he would like to explain his own plans, "to lay it on the line, cold turkey." First and foremost, he intended to go forward on trade, which will be one of the great steps. No swift results are expected, but our children will benefit. Although big business is behind him, the problem is still with granting MFN status to the Soviet Union. He shook his fist: "The Jews are blocking it. They are out of their mind. Before our visit to Moscow, 200,000 were leaving annually; last year the numbers dropped to 35,000. Many do not wish to emigrate and some return to their communities. What do they want?" "It's a shame," agreed Podgorny. "They all say they are emigrating to Israel but for some reason settle down in Austria, Italy and especially the US; we have detailed information about that."

"I know," Nixon said. "Kissinger is a Jew. I instructed him to work with the American Jewry on MFN. When I return to Washington I'll invite leaders of Congress and tell them the truth: our countries' future relations must not be destroyed by failure on MFN." Podgorny agreed: MFN was not exclusive status; it was the accepted format among regular trading partners.

Nixon did not exaggerate when he warned of forces "against détente." Apart from Senator Henry Jackson, a kaleidoscope of enemies crouched in the shadows. He understood the strength of these groups: from anti-Soviet conservatives (he was supposed to be one, he once told Gromyko), to labor leaders to liberals who wished détente would fail, clutching at anything to strike Nixon down. Ominous warnings from Moscow about enemies of détente in the American establishment were not much off the mark. Jim Angleton believed that détente was "a sham, a tactic." After resigning from the CIA, he told friends that he was "done in" by Kissinger in retaliation for his outspoken doubts about the U.S. policy towards Russia and China.[45]

Podgorny mentioned the principle of "equality." Nixon tried to allay his concerns regarding the USSR's world status. He dismissed Podgorny's remark that some members of the Administration call for America to be Number One: it is just that Americans refuse to be "number two." This does not affect our relations. Repeatedly Nixon stressed that equality should remain a principle, although by reasons of geography, Russia is entitled to a larger land force, and America to a larger navy. "We must find ways of reducing the burden of danger, otherwise 70 million Russians and 70 million Americans might perish in a nuclear exchange," he said.

This remark led Podgorny to the problem of China, and Mao's willingness to sacrifice 300 million Chinese in a nuclear war. The USSR was convinced that China must participate in arms reductions in the future. Nixon was receptive: he thought they should "drag" the Peoples' Republic of China into the process of disarmament. However, both agreed they had few means to influence it, and the only hope lay in a new generation of leaders. The current ones "are not eternal," Nixon remarked.

The conversation switched to SALT. Both men noted that their defense establishments were eager to go on MIRVing missiles. Nixon said he knew the problem of MIRVs: "the USSR is light years ahead in throw weight." The summit will not succeed without resolving these issues. At any rate, he had no intention of leaving negotiations to Kissinger. He complained about the attitude of the US military ("more difficult than the Jewish lobby") that create problems in arms control, and asked Podgorny if he experienced the same difficulty. Podgorny admitted that Russian generals did not like nuclear disarmament either.

I looked at Kizichenko: he was writing furiously, but I must have a full record in my own style later.

After dispensing with the diet food, we rose from the breakfast table. Nixon suggested a stroll in the garden. He said he wanted to have a confidential exchange on the Middle East.

US Ambassador's residence in Paris: Podgorny, Nixon, Vavilov. (White House photo)

While we were sitting, I was comfortable in jotting down notes and translating. A stroll is a different story. Interpreters who tried it will agree that taking notes in movement is quite a feat: one has to rely on memory alone.

We walked in the immaculate grounds of the former Rothschild mansion, taking in the warm April air. Nixon stopped several times to stress a point. He put his arm around his comrade's shoulders. He wished to dispel the impression that Kissinger schemed to exclude the Soviet Union from a settlement, in particular, from the Israeli-Syrian negotiations on disengagement. Both countries had a role to play in different ways, he said. The US was not trying to sidestep the USSR: if that were so, the Soviet leadership would have had "a legitimate beef." True, Israel tried to exclude the Soviet Union. Podgorny retorted that "the American sugar daddy should learn to stomp his foot occasionally." Nixon sighed: "It's hard for Soviet Jews; it's harder for the US government." He suggested that Russia continue to work with Syria and the US will continue working with Israel: "those people" should not continually drag us into confrontation.

Podgorny did not look convinced.

The topics were exhausted; the breakfast meeting took two hours, more than planned. Nixon turned to me and said could I fall behind - the photographers will take pictures of the two men. I warned Podgorny and stepped back. The two men talked animatedly, not understanding a word. As usual, the acting was realistic.

We went to the cars. In the courtyard, Nixon grabbed Podgorny's arm and pointed to several snipers on the residence roof. Podgorny let Nixon speak briefly to reporters, and we drove back to the Soviet Embassy in Rue de Grenelle. I joined Kizichenko in drafting a brief cable for Podgorny to sign. The full memcon will go to Brezhnev by diplomatic pouch.

The next day, Russian newspapers reported that the meeting was "businesslike and constructive." Nothing earth shattering, around 1.0 on the Richter scale.

The Nixon-Podgorny conversation was my only charge in Paris. I joined my interpreter colleagues in a memorable but uneventful tour of the city's nightlife. We entered the Trinité Metro station at one in the morning; the ticket booth had just closed. In an expansive gesture, the attendant waved us through the gate: "C'est offert par la Trinité." A nice ending to a long day.

I heard that Brezhnev was jealous of the meeting; it meant chipping off his exclusive prerogatives of dealing with Nixon. The fact that he personally dispatched Podgorny to the memorial services in Paris was beside the point. In three years, Podgorny was unceremoniously dismissed. Brezhnev added the latter's post to his Communist Party title. In effect, he became the authentic President of the Soviet Union.

DRIFTING IN YALTA

On the eve of the third summit, Soviet newspapers carried a photo of a smiling Nixon on the front page. The *Crimean Pravda* published a short biography with a terse mention that "R. Nixon launched his active political career in 1946." It stressed the summit will transform Soviet-American relations into a permanent factor for peace.

The number of US security personnel increased. When the KGB asked the US liaison officer the number of Secret Service agents arriving with the President, he was sheepish: "Less than a hundred." It was 99. 107 cars were put at the disposal of the US delegation.

The *"Spirit of '76"* landed on a quiet June day at Vnukovo. This time Brezhnev greeted the President on the tarmac. Premier Kosygin was also there; I stood by his side. Nixon walked briskly down the aircraft steps. He shook Kosygin's hand warmly, and turned to me: "You're both, ah, from Leningrad. Most of your family died there. I remember your grandfather."

"It's amazing you remember the little things, Mr. President," I said.

"I don't," he said. "I remember the important things."

The Kremlin dinner started an hour late because Brezhnev's private meeting with Nixon extended beyond the appointed time. He was never a stickler for protocol, especially if it clashed with his private schedule, which changed every hour. Kosygin, Podgorny, Suslov and Defense Minister Marshal Grechko stayed in an adjoining room: they did not wish to be seen waiting for Brezhnev. Leonid Ilyich was steadily building on his "more equal than others" status. At last, the two leaders appeared, and we sat down at a table laden with *zakuski*. I sat on Nixon's left and Kosygin on his right. Brezhnev sat opposite. Brezhnev's wife Viktoria Petrovna made a rare appearance; Kosygin and Podgorny's daughters were there, as well as Mrs. Nixon and Mrs. Gromyko. No starlet for Kissinger this time.

Nixon skipped the *zakuski* - he was un-Russian in his eating habits. We dined on ice-cold *okhroshka* (beet soup) and lamb cutlets. They printed the menu in three different colors in two languages on silk. Nixon told me he liked the idea: "OK if I take them?" I folded all three menus, and he put them in his pocket. He struck up a conversation with the Premier. "The fate of the world is in the hands of the USSR and the US," he said. "The other nuclear states - England, France, China and India - are nothing. However, in twenty, no, fifteen years, the situation will change. The others will forge ahead fast. This is why we should see eye to eye now, or it may be too late." Kosygin agreed: "Let's act together, but we don't want publicity lest it offend other countries."

One topic proved awkward. Nixon noted the expanse of the two countries, "from sea to shining sea." Kosygin recalled a swim he had with Fidel Castro during a visit to Cuba in 1967, after his meeting in Glassboro with LBJ. "We swam out so far I warned him he might be picked up by the US Coast Guard." "Castro is an intelligent statesman," Kosygin added. Nixon smiled weakly. "Do you really regard him as intelligent? My impression was different. As Vice President, I had to receive him in 1959. Eisenhower refused to talk to him." That was as far as Nixon wanted to go in discussing Cuba; he did not want to spoil the meal. (Kissinger once warned Gromyko that Nixon "was emotional on Cuba.") Nixon felt dislike for Kosygin. Probably he was uncomfortable in his commanding presence - no chance playing on his emotions or vanity. His intelligence, tenacity and ordered mind were a turn-off. Paradoxically, Nixon felt at ease with Brezhnev, a Party apparatchik, rather than with Kosygin, a no-nonsense CEO of an industrial corporation, the impression he produced.

As usual after the meal, Nixon went to the kitchen to thank the chef. The cooks, kitchen help and waiters were bowled over and happy to shake his hand.

I asked Kosygin if he wished me to write down Nixon's words about other nuclear States: he actually echoed Brezhnev's warning in San Clemente the year before. Kosygin said no. I suppose that rather than circulating a memcon touching on strategy, he wished to mention this tidbit to Brezhnev personally.

June 28 began with wreath laying at the Grave of the Unknown Soldier, at the foot of the high redbrick Kremlin wall. Podgorny led the ceremony. As we approached the eternal flame, I read out the names of Hero-Cities cut in slabs of red granite topped with gold stars: Moscow, Leningrad, Kiev and Stalingrad... Novorossiysk was recently installed - Brezhnev saw action there as political commissar. Nixon bowed his head, listening to my reading the bronze inscription, "Your name is unknown; your feat is immortal."

As we walked back to the cars, Mikhail Georgadze, Secretary of the Supreme Soviet, asked the President's military aide, Lieutenant Colonel John Brennan (he was Major in 1972) about his decorations. They were getting needless attention, I feared. The day before, Brezhnev slapped Brennan on the back. He appreciated the marine's swarthy looks, his ready smile, smart uniform and the medals: "*Molodetz* (good fellow), a real hero!" Surely, the General Secretary did not mean Brennan's Purple Heart received in Vietnam. Did he think young Brennan fought in the Ardennes? My fault: I failed to warn him. I ignored Georgadze's question, and Brennan sensed the awkwardness. By this time, he knew that sporting war medals would not win him a popularity contest in Russia. Emotions of your man in the street over Vietnam ran no less high than in America.

Nixon got into the ZIL, I sat next to him. We drove with the American flag flying on the bonnet. He decided it was the moment to work the crowds. I told the chauffeur to stop. We halted twice in Revolution Square: near Hotel Metropole and by the Lenin Museum. The early morning strollers were startled but acted friendly. The throng quickly grew. People were running in our direction; they wanted to see the American President. The crowd surged and heaved me against Nixon, and both of us against the stone barrier of an underground passage. The Secret Service and the KGB were pushing people back. Nixon smiled broadly and raised both hands high in his trademark V-sign. He tried to climb on the parapet but bodyguards restrained him: it was a fifteen-foot drop to the granite steps below. "I know how you suffered in the war!" he shouted. "Let's work together!" I shouted the translation. Amid the cheerful faces and cries of "Peace," "Friendship" and "Come again," Nixon was euphoric.

Refreshed by the unplanned reception, he fell back into the car seat. I scrambled inside, the limousine door clunked shut. I said we could have been crushed, but he waved my words away. "Just seeing you here, Mr. President,"

I said, "people feel relieved. It's as effective as signing treaties." He liked my harmless flattery: "I know." "I know" meant he agreed. He was recharged for another round of talks in the Kremlin.

In a telephone conversation later that year with Reader's Digest Editor Hobart Lewis, Nixon claimed he did not like Moscow.[46] He said, "There were no babes in Moscow, not even pretty stockings... Moscow is a grim city... Look at the faces... In Leningrad the faces were a little happier." My impression was different: Nixon loved mingling with the Russian crowd, and had a way with women in the street. He did a few dance steps with a young brunette who kissed him on the cheek. For her, the reason was less Nixon's personality than the sense of release from confrontation with America.

At the Bolshoi Theater, the First Family was treated to a potpourri concert of finest Soviet performers, with ballet pieces from *Swan Lake* and *Carmen*, opera airs and Russian, Ukrainian and Georgian folk songs. The concentration of talent was brought to a crescendo by the Red Army Song and Dance Ensemble, which sang an American song in English. The night before I was at the Foreign Ministry dictating my notes, when the duty officer transferred a frantic call from the Bolshoi. They were printing a program in two languages for the gala and urgently needed the spelling of a song's title. Over the phone, it sounded like "Suomi." I wondered why they would choose a Finnish song. Could they sing it to me? They did the first few lines. It was *Swanee River*.

But back to negotiations. The long motorcade entered the massive old Borovitski Gates and sped across the wide cobbled square to the *Gorka*, or "Hill," as they called the private entrance to the General Secretary's quarters. The short flight of covered steps to the high oak doors is across the square from the steel and glass Palace of Congresses built by Khrushchev in 1961 to replace the Old Kremlin Armory. We took an elegant ancient elevator to the third floor. Brezhnev was waiting in his study by the desk; he briskly walked toward Nixon and shook his hand warmly. He also seemed recharged.

At this meeting, and later in St. Catherine Hall Brezhnev was the sole speaker. Although Podgorny and Kosygin flanked him, few vestiges were left of "collective leadership." He listened intently to Nixon referring to "highest level" meetings. He expanded on the theme. He proposed that high-level meetings (he did not say "highest level" in deference to his silent comrades - a diplomatic touch) should be held as the need arises, as working sessions, and address not more than two or three issues at a time.

Nixon warmed to the idea. Talking with Brezhnev was a balm to the soul. It must have reinforced his resolve to fight the Watergate prosecutors. He advised Brezhnev not to wait for a year for another meeting. "If we feel a single subject comes up that is worth an exchange of views at highest level, we do that," he said. "We might have another summit growing out of that meeting."

When Brezhnev said he wanted him reelected, Nixon responded with force that he would do it in the next two and a half years (I was perplexed: did he mean 1976, a third term?). He emphasized that personal encounters between the leaders of two most powerful states are important because they lead to progress on truly major issues; they can solve many matters only at this level. He took up the subject again in his dinner speech, stressing thrice that "all this would not have been possible without our personal relation-ship." My mind went back to 1972, when in his first messages to Brezhnev Nixon stressed the importance of direct personal contacts, later to bloom into "a personal relationship." Initially Brezhnev avoided developing the theme in deference to his Politburo comrades. After the hierarchy was established, he went for it full steam. A *Pravda* announcement on the meeting mentioned Dobrynin, Alexandrov and Kornienko as participants, but omitted Brezhnev's two closest comrades. It was generous towards the American party: it acknowledged Kissinger, Haig, Stoessel, Scowcroft, Sonnenfeldt and Hartman. I asked my TASS friend Misha, who supplied official copy for the media including mention of participants, for the reason. He smiled mysteriously and pointed upwards - orders from the top.

The General Secretary read from prepared text. Taking notes was easy, because I could always check against his brief later on. I had to be on my guard: he deviated from his notes several times. It was not clear whether he was developing a point, or veering off on a dangerous tangent? I relied on my hunches. I suspected he didn't do his homework. The impression got stronger with every conversation he had with Nixon. It was no contest in terms of preparedness.

Nixon was less voluble. He did not expect much from the third summit. He focused on generalities: its importance and close personal relationships. He decried lack of progress on MFN, and admitted difficulties of trade between private and socialist economies - "they are like oil and water." He looked forward to breaking the logjam at CSCE, but did not go beyond expressions of hope; no promise of active cooperation, as Brezhnev wanted. Nevertheless, he commended the "non-security" bilateral agreements, because they provided incentive to maintain détente. He admitted some US experts downgraded them unjustly; they were not getting much play in the press.

The Middle East problem was in limbo. Nixon objected to convening a Geneva conference, favored by the Soviets because it would strengthen their hand in the region. He used an ingenious argument: we should not be seen as opposing each other in a great public forum, but rather proceed step by step, working bilaterally, in closest consultation. Brezhnev pondered this explanation and seemed to be taken in. Gromyko was quick to confirm, in a loud voice, that the USSR was against substituting the conference (with all parties in the region, including the Palestinians) for bilateral talks.

Moments before Nixon's party arrived at the Kremlin, I watched Brezhnev. Gesticulating, he outlined to his colleagues the case he would place before Nixon in simple terms: "Chase the Jews beyond the Suez Canal." Kosygin and Podgorny listened in silence. They did not nod. I took some movies; too bad, I did not have sound.

We looked forward to Crimea, the jewel of the Black Sea. For me, it beat the French Riviera in natural beauty. A few months before, Nixon told Ambassador Dobrynin that the two countries must restore the "spirit of Yalta," when great powers did not permit small nations to interfere. "We shall not let small matters like Hungary do us in," he said.[47] The year 1945 fascinated him. Repeatedly, he evoked the great wartime leaders - Stalin, Churchill and

Roosevelt, and the agreements they negotiated. He thought he and Brezhnev could do the same, [48] but publicly it had to appear different. Nixon had second thoughts about spelling out the next leg of the trip as "Yalta." With growing criticism at home, he did not want another problem: Yalta held memories of confirming spheres of influence in Europe. The two sides agreed to refer to "Crimea" or "Oreanda."

I checked into a luxurious room on the first floor of the Lower Oreanda Sanatorium. A mischievous Alexandrov locked me in; his sense of humor was eccentric. My calls for help brought Galya, Brezhnev's favorite personal secretary (she stayed with him until his death), who unlocked the door. Alexandrov wanted Victor and me and the girls to finish the transcripts quickly and go to the "First Dacha," Brezhnev's private beach, for a night swim in the Black Sea. I was reluctant, Alexandrov or not. It was almost one o'clock in the morning, a bit late for a dip followed by staple Kremlin brandy. Thankfully, it started raining and the party broke up.

Brezhnev invited Nixon for a sail in a Soviet Navy yacht by the steep cliffs rising from the clear blue water. He certainly upped the Potomac cruise on the "Sequoia" the previous year.

The KGB stewards wore smart sailor suits, but unsure footing gave them away. When the boat swerved, Brezhnev fell into a chair, and the silver crashed to the deck. The Black Sea was choppy that day.

My recollection of the meeting in Oreanda is of pervading nervousness on the part of the US team. Brezhnev invited, or rather pulled Nixon into a grotto by the sea, "to have a few words" before the main session. Victor went along. The two teams, including three General Staff Generals, lounged by the pool. Nixon went alone, so no American would make a record of the conversation. After an hour, Bill Hyland turned to me, "They'd better come out soon before they wreck anything." After two hours, he was in a state of mild panic.

Kissinger and Gromyko relaxed in wicker chairs in the shade by the poolside, conversing in low tones. They did not show any signs of worry. One could not help admiring their nonchalance; in conservative suits, wearing somber ties and sunglasses they looked like two aging contract killers stalking a quarry. They had the capacity for a long wait. They exuded confidence: any wild scheme their masters might hatch in the grotto will not see the light of day.

At last, Nixon and Brezhnev emerged into bright daylight, blinking. Victor looked dazed. Brezhnev said they "decided everything" - his usual bluff. We joined the two leaders, this time with experts. The grotto was in reality a comfortable arched room, with nine or ten chairs. There was not enough space, so I took up a position at a miniature table by the door leading to a windowless kitchen.

The topic was SALT. In a historic first, the Soviets quoted figures for their strategic nuclear arsenal. Two General Staff aides, Kozlov and Afonsky, were so nervous that one tripped over the other's foot, and files with columns of figures and charts spilled over the floor. The red-faced Generals dived down; I helped collect the top-secret documents.

A KGB steward brought in light refreshments. He was unaware of the American habit of consuming innumerable cups of percolated coffee when talking business. Nixon rose while Brezhnev was speaking and squeezed past me on the way, I thought, to the rest room. He turned and asked me in a low voice, "Where's the coffee man?" "Should be inside," I whispered back, "I'll check." There was no other exit from the kitchen - a mystery. The steward emerged from the bathroom. I said he kept the American President waiting. He almost fainted. I told him to bring in fresh coffee and sandwiches at half hour intervals.

There was a long discussion on MIRVing. The launcher numbers for the two sides, as suggested by Brezhnev, came close: 1,100 for the US and 1,000 for the USSR. He said the 100 US advantage would make a fair and balanced agreement. Kissinger objected, because the greater throw weight of Soviet missiles made a big difference in potential MIRVing (it did not with one-warhead missiles). Nixon was impatient: the summit was weak on substantive agreements. He said, "When we get into numbers of this magnitude it is almost beyond comprehension. It really does not mean much. The fundamental thing is to reach an agreement." He was almost quoting Brezhnev.

The sun sets quickly in Crimea. Victor and I tiptoed below Brezhnev's bedroom windows and almost bumped into a sentry dressed in black with camouflage paint on his face. He held a snub-nosed Kalashnikov. I asked him to inform other posts that we were a friendly group on our way to the beach.

The night swim in the sea proved to be the only one we managed in Crimea. Victor told me what happened at the one-on-one conversation in the grotto. "You wouldn't believe this, but our man proposed a mutual assistance treaty against nuclear attack." Since the only imaginable case of attack was by China on the Soviet Union, the treaty was tantamount to an anti-Chinese axis. I asked about Nixon's reaction.

"Just a moment," said Nixon, "do I get this right: you actually propose…?" "Exactly," said Brezhnev. He warned Nixon: in a nuclear war, the white race will be wiped out, to leave the yellow and black races. Nixon listened, and then said, "This is revolutionary." He promised to think for a couple of months, and revisit the proposal.

Nixon told Kissinger only briefly about Brezhnev's idea and I can picture Henry's horror. I also know that the Americans do not have a memcon of the grotto conversation. Kissinger never asked us for one, because he knew it would not be freely given. Victor's memcon went under lock and key into the Kremlin safe. Judging from what he told me, good riddance.

At 8:00 a.m. on July 1, we got ready to leave for Simferopol Airport for the flight to Minsk. Brezhnev decided to accompany Nixon in the car, although the latter preferred to be alone with Pat during the long drive. I ran to look for my car. The black Volgas looked alike; car 21 was nowhere in sight, and the motorcade was pulling out. My rule is never to be left behind at any cost; if necessary, gate crash any passing car (in 1966 in Tashkent, I flagged down Kosygin's car as he drove to the airport in the cortege carrying Indian Prime Minister's Shastri's coffin). I saw Ronald Ziegler waving from a rolled down window. This guy knew the problems staff faces in a mile-long motorcade where assigned vehicles are never at the promised spot. I jumped in. It turned out to be a most enjoyable hour and a half drive.

Ron, then 33, was in high spirits. He was thrilled at his first contact with an alien civilization. The evil totalitarian empire proved friendly on closer inspection, and he was pleasantly surprised with Brezhnev. He had problems initially with Russian security who regarded the American press a nuisance, but things were straightened out. As White House spokesperson, he did not have a particularly difficult job to do in Russia. He helped American media with access to events and press conferences. He provided rudimentary information identical to the terse reports articulated by Zamyatin. Both planted friendly questions among members of the press corps. Kissinger approved the expected questions and replies for US newsmen; at most times, Ron was ready with a response.

We talked about how we got into our respective professions. Ron worked for an advertising agency and for Haldeman. He corresponded with Nixon after his defeat to Pat Brown in the 1962 California governorship elections. The angry farewell speech - "You won't have Nixon to kick around anymore because, gentlemen, this is my last press conference" - must have produced an indelible impression on Ziegler, laying a solid foundation for his disdain for the press. He was the youngest press secretary hired by the White House. He looked handsome with his dark-hair and sideburns. I told him of my childhood in California; we both loved the West Coast.

While Ron talked a lot, he knew how to listen. He was a voracious consumer of information, absorbing, processing and storing it for future use. I knew of his imprint on the profession. "This story is no longer operative" was the famous euphemism. Some regarded him as abusive and pompous, but I saw him in another light.

Ron was modesty embodied. We did not discuss politics. We heard and saw more than one person could handle, and were bound by dedication to our political masters. Ron felt at ease in the balmy Crimean air. The trip was professionally challenging but pleasant, the closest thing to a political paradise. There were no leaks, bad publicity or press accusations. The household names of the growing scandal back home did not ring bells in the peaceful and controlled journalistic environment of the USSR. Russian reporters never asked awkward questions about Watergate.

This time Ron asked questions. Freed from the political sieges of Washington, his inquisitive mind fluttered around diverse topics, like current rules for admission to the KGB, Russian history and ballet. He confessed he never heard of Anna Pavlova or Galina Ulanova, but was willing to learn. He never saw any resort as alluring as Crimea.

I enjoyed talking to Ron, and, myself a government servant not appreciative of meddling reporters, I liked him. He was doing his job, arranging impressions. He presented Nixon as Brezhnev's prime international negotiating partner; their relationship was the linchpin of world peace. Consequently, the continuation of the Nixon Presidency was vital for world peace. In fact, Kissinger told Brezhnev in March that his rapport with Nixon "was unusual" among leaders of great powers because it guaranteed stable relations between our countries.

In Yalta, Ron asked Victor and me to stand five yards away as they photographed the two leaders strolling by the seaside. Whenever possible, I steered clear of such photo opportunities: it adds to the leaders' image if they are seen in no need of assistants. Nixon wore a maroon jacket and slacks, and Brezhnev a light blue windbreaker. Both wore red ties, as if the two men had Commie leanings. They talked animatedly. Brezhnev gestured and Nixon nodded, thoughtfully.

The "personal relationship" was staged. The chemistry was superficial: they were poles apart in every respect. Besides, they could not speak each other's language. The public saw Brezhnev whispering in Nixon's ear on the White House balcony, and Nixon grinning in reply. Nixon laughed at a Brezhnev remark during a signing ceremony, not understanding a word. Today, they strolled by the seaside in Yalta, deep in discussion. Both men valued the acting scenes and their effect on an unknowing public. The human touch was a symbol of a bond that never existed. A personal relationship at the top is a rarity. It can promote intergovernmental relations to a limited extent. With time, the novelty wears off, and hard facts of national interest dampen the glow. Between leaders of two opposing political systems, it was nigh impossible.

Ziegler was jumpy when Russian newspapers omitted two references in Brezhnev's speech to his strong personal bond with Nixon. Representations were made to the Soviet side - Ron knew it could not have happened without explicit orders. Kissinger sided with Ziegler; he sensed a plot against Nixon. He was wrong again. Brezhnev's aides thought the repetitious reference could impair the carefully maintained facade of "collective Politburo leadership."

Brezhnev and Nixon had a vested interest in building each other's image. For this reason, Brezhnev avoided references to Nixon's domestic troubles, and Nixon ignored his state of health. As Watergate moved toward a denouement, Nixon increasingly saw Brezhnev as the administration's lifeline to justify his continuation in office. Worried about his image, he was careful to shield Brezhnev, who must not appear a loser, unable to secure MFN and Export-Import Bank credits. And, heaven forbid, an ailing man. He wanted to uphold his comrade's image as a robust leader firmly in command; his health problems had to be concealed. Even without this, Nixon and Kissinger had a difficult job battling on several fronts - right wing Senators, the Pentagon, the Jewish lobby, the Watergate witch-hunters, not to forget the Soviet negotiators.

MINSK: "THE ENEMY WILL BE DEFEATED, MR. PRESIDENT!"

On July 1, Victor and I accompanied Nixon on a day-trip to the capital of Belorussia. Our colleagues - Edouard Zaitsev and Oleg Krokhalev - stayed behind to translate for Gromyko and Kissinger who finalized the summit outcome documents.

From Matchulichi military airfield, we drove to the government residence at Zaslavl. From there, to a wreath-laying ceremony in Minsk, in memory of a fourth of the republic's population decimated in World War II. In the limousine, Nixon read. His diligence in preparing for negotiations with Brezhnev never ceased to impress me. I saw him silently shuffling small rectangular cards at free moments, in cars and airplanes. He read, analyzed, memorized, and kept himself in a state of total preparedness, ready to respond to any question. He brought to my mind the Soviet Young Pioneer motto, "Always prepared!" I did not see Brezhnev similarly engaged.

Pyotr Masherov, First Secretary of the Communist Party of Belorussia, joined us. He descended from a wounded French soldier, who remained in Russia after the retreat of Napoleon's Grande Armée (his family name originated from the French "*ma chère*"). He was a war hero: at 24, he commanded a partisan group that raided German convoys and troop trains. Nixon explained the US position on SALT to Masherov. I had the impression he was rehearsing his future intervention when Kissinger was not around. Masherov, as candidate member of the Politburo, received regular reports on the progress of negotiations, but did not follow the nuances. He would not engage in a discussion conducted by Brezhnev.

There are few things so moving in Belorussia than memories of the Great Patriotic War. Victor, Alex Akalovsky and I went for a short walk to the picturesque Zaslavl Lake, when we saw Masherov. He told us he wanted Nixon to visit Khatyn. This village is a sacred shrine for Belorussians. Like the devastated villages of Lidice in Czechoslovakia and Oradour-sur-Glane in France, it stands as a reminder of Nazi barbarity. In 1943, collaborationists of OUN-UPA (Ukrainian Rebel Army, currently honored in Ukraine) burnt alive all 152 inhabitants, including 76 children, in retaliation for the shooting of several Wehrmacht soldiers. Almost six hundred villages suffered the same fate in Belorussia.

A guide led Nixon among the ruins. He lowered his head before the large bronze figure of a father carrying his dead son from the smoldering ruins. The prototype was Iosif Kaminsky, the single survivor of the massacre.

A writing desk stood in the middle of a green lawn at the entrance to the site, with an open visitor's book. Nixon sat down and produced a pen. The sun shone on his stooped figure. He was in pain from his bad leg. He wrote for a long time. To the American team, the message of the scene was unmistakable. I heard a military aide whisper a caption, "Nixon out of office" - to a glacial stare from Rose Mary Woods.

At a State luncheon given by the Belorussian leadership on the lakeshore, Nixon listened to Masherov's story of three daring girls who, on a September night in 1943, blew up Wilhelm Kube, Hitler's ruthless *Hauptkommissar* of Belorussia. Nadezhda Troyan and Maria Osipova, young members of a partisan group, performed the operation. Maria carried a British-made anti-personnel mine in a basket of forest berries through several German check-points, before delivering it to Elena Mazanik, Kube's house cleaner. Elena planted the mine under Kube's bed mattress. By the moment hapless Kube was putting on his pajamas the girls were being spirited away to a partisan airfield deep in the forest to be flown across the frontline to Moscow. They were awarded Hero Stars of the Soviet Union.

"Are they still alive?" Nixon asked. "I'd like to shake their hand." "Oh, yes," said Masherov. He asked me to get in touch with his assistant to try to reach "the girls." "Terribly short notice, I'm afraid. I hope we can get hold of Maria."

Nixon raised his glass. "I thought at first that Mr. Brezhnev chose Minsk for my itinerary because a little girl was born here, Olga Korbut…"

There was a nodding of heads and smiles. In 1972, Nixon received the diminutive Belorussian champion gymnast in the White House. He thought her Olympic performance (she did the women's first ever somersault on the balance beam) did more for reducing political tensions with the USSR than embassies were able to do in five years.

"...After talking to my friends here, the President, the Chairman of the Council of Ministers and Party Secretary (for Americans here I will explain that they are, in Belorussia's scale, "Podgorny, Kosygin and Brezhnev") I understood that courage in battle had been the reason. Both my neighbors at this table lost their mothers during the war. Minsk is the appropriate place to speak of peace. Looking at the young and handsome waiters serving us today, I am wondering whether they will live in peace or war...The General Secretary and I are working for one goal: to prevent the squandering of our young men in wars."

At the airport, I saw a middle-aged woman in the crowd. She wore a little gold star on the lapel of a simple gray jacket. Masherov, who rarely wore his own Hero Star, led her to Nixon: "Here she is - Maria." Nixon shook her hand and patted her on the shoulder. I felt he wished to embrace her, but did not. "You are a real war hero," he said. "I wanted so much to tell you this in person. Thank you for coming all the way to see us."

Maria Osipova was unperturbed. She saluted and suddenly responded with words imbedded in her memory since her partisan years in the swampy forests of Belorussia, "Thank you Mr. President; our cause is just, the enemy will be defeated, we will prevail!"

When Nixon heard my translation, he started. His back straightened: if a wizened little lady was prepared to battle the enemy, so was he. Cornered and betrayed, he will fight on!

The powerful memory evoked by Maria touched us all. Back in the aircraft, I told Nixon about the origin of the phrase. Stalin coined it in 1941, and it became the battle cry of the Soviet Republic. He was surprised, but did not comment. (In an odd coincidence, sixty years later, President George W. Bush Jr. used the phrase on another dramatic occasion, 9/11: "Our cause is just, we will prevail!" The hard-hitting short phrases the Soviet leader drafted seemed to have a life of their own, sneaking into the minds of alien speechwriters of another era. As to Olga Korbut, she would emigrate to the United States, to be caught in a mesh of financial and family problems.)

We landed in Moscow in late evening. The next day in the afternoon, the two teams held a two-hour round of talks.

Nixon spoke live for twenty minutes on TV to the Soviet people, with a satellite link to the US.

He hosted a farewell dinner at Spaso House, the elegant residence of Ambassador Walter J. Stoessel in the old Arbat area. Nixon drove from the Kremlin in his Cadillac. The two flags on the bonnet - American and Soviet - were draped. The car stole silently along Moscow streets in view of unsuspecting passer byes. Victor and I jumped into the empty Presidential ZIL-114. A security car followed.

We arrived at Spaso House a quarter of an hour before guests started pouring in. The Soviet troika arrived; Kosygin and Podgorny looked subdued. Most of the eighty Russian guests were Party and government officials.

In the Chandelier Room, a columned hall on the first floor, Eugene List treated us to a piano recital. As a young US Army performer, he played for Truman, Churchill and Stalin at Potsdam in 1945. Perhaps Nixon wanted symbolism. List waited, smiling patiently, as Brezhnev walked to the grand piano and tinkled on the keys. Somebody hushed.

Nixon took Brezhnev's jest as a cue for his speech. "I have just learnt that the General Secretary and I studied music. I wonder what would've happened to the world if we became successful musicians." A ripple of laughter. A US Embassy official told me that Nixon was a passable piano player fond of classics. I said Brezhnev loved community singing.

Sitting in the first row on this last day of the third Nixon-Brezhnev summit, I wondered about the careers the two men chose: politics over music. Détente was bound to happen eventually: nuclear parity had inexorable logic. Its basis was Russia's persistent drive to achieve a balance that, finally, would guarantee its national survival against any odds. I had no certainty what Watergate would mean for the US. The future political evolution of the USSR was not too clear either. History could take different directions (it was four weeks to Nixon's resignation, but we had no way of knowing.)

Nixon went on. He referred to his "personal relationship with the General Secretary," three times in a short speech. Out of the corner of my eye, I saw Sonnenfeldt and Hyland exchanging glances. A Russian proverb says, "You cannot spoil the gruel with butter," but this time I could not agree.

Turning to Victor, Nixon said what a great job he did as interpreter for several American presidents. He listed the lot, starting with John F. Kennedy, but missed a name. An ordinary interpreter could have done two things: translate "as is," or correct the President as unobtrusively as possible. In any case, he could not whisper a reminder in Nixon's ear in full view of the audience. Victor did a third thing: he stopped and smiled at Nixon. The latter looked back querulously. Some in the audience noticed the omission. At last, Nixon slapped his forehead: "Of course, Lyndon Johnson!"

We dined on Striped Bass Supreme, Roast Prime Sirloin Beef and Grand Marnier Mousse. The wines were Robert Mondavi Fumé Blanc, 1972, Mirassou Pinot Noir, 1969, and Schramsberg Blanc de Blancs, 1971 - all Nixon years. Victor was at the main table, next to Brezhnev. Bill Krimer sat behind two non-English speaking Russian Ministers. "Way down the food chain," was his wry explanation. He did not receive the commemorative bronze medal placed in front of each guest, with a thumping Nixon quotation: "We stand on the threshold of a new era of peace in the world."

Tatyana was aiding Mrs. Brezhnev. Incredibly, I was off the hook. I went to the overflow area. My neighbor on the right was Marjorie P. Acker of White House staff - she worked for Rose Mary Woods. I did not fathom the psychological strain these women experienced. On my left was a US Embassy administrative attaché. He complained about White House smart alecks who requisitioned the Embassy copiers and typists. We toasted each other: the work was over.

The dinner ended close to midnight. As the long northern dusk turned into night, the First Family bid farewell to the last guest and drove to their Kremlin residence.

In the morning, Nixon told Steve Bull to arrange a photo opportunity with the KGB bodyguards, the motorcycle escort, and the First Family's three Russian interpreters. He spoke a few words to each group. "Thank you for taking care of us," he told the surprised motorcyclists: the last time any leader spoke to them was 1971, when Pierre Trudeau grabbed a police bike and sped across the Kremlin courtyard.

The Soviet troika arrived; Steve ignored them and positioned us to best angles. Our masters waited under the covered entrance of the Kremlin residence.

Tatyana, Victor and I stood in bright sunshine. Nixon held Tatyana's hand and grinned, "You translated for my wife last year when you were a little girl."

First Family's team: Tatyana Ovchinnikova, Andrey
Vavilov and Victor Sukhodrev. (Yakov Khalip)

At the last plenary session on 2 July, Nixon chose to take up Vietnam, clearly a lost cause. He referred to North Vietnam's military buildup: it was proceeding at a faster rate than was permitted by the Paris agreement at a time when the US was shipping less materiel to South Vietnam. His litany continued: the key to "a semblance of peace" in the area was showing restraint; it would be "a tragedy" if the situation got out of control. Finally, the key phrase: "This region is less important for our strategic interests to be dragged into confrontation, as we feared might happen in 1972." There could be no other interpretation of these words: the coast was clear for Hanoi.

(The end came after Nixon's resignation. In mid-April 1975, Gerald Ford literally begged Brezhnev for a temporary ceasefire in South Vietnam. He wanted safe evacuation for local collaborationists and US citizens. In a message to Ford, which Dobrynin read to Kissinger over the phone, Brezhnev indicated the Vietnamese "reacted positively." In the morning of May 1, a "Most Urgent" telegram arrived at the Soviet Embassy in Hanoi. The Ambassador was ready to depart for a meeting with Prime Minister Pham Van Dong, but waited for the message to be decoded. It was a congratulatory letter from Leonid Brezhnev to General Secretary Le Duan. Victory was final. The previous day, in a swift tank assault, North Vietnamese forces overran Saigon; it was renamed Ho Chi Min City. The Premier hugged the Ambassador and told him they will publish the messages from Brezhnev and Mao Tse-tung side by side. The Ambassador failed to tell him that Moscow would not make Brezhnev's letter public. It wished to spare American feelings - a little bonus for his US comrades. Vietnam was a chapter in super power relations that never made pleasant reading. The book was closed.)

Brezhnev summed up the third summit. He said both nations moved closer to the greater goal, preventing confrontation. He referred to their "joint active role" in the CSCE and the Middle East. The exaggeration was deliberate, to remind Nixon of unfinished business. He turned to Kosygin and Podgorny: did they wish to say anything? They added a few words.

Nixon echoed the General Secretary. He stressed that "the greatest danger" lay not in bilateral misunderstandings, but in being dragged into confrontation in other parts of the world. Events there should never weaken our relations, he said.

With dozens of high officials flanking them, Nixon and Brezhnev signed two major agreements.

In the protocol to the ABM treaty, Nixon agreed to the Soviet proposal to forgo one of two permitted national ABM designated areas. The USSR chose the area around Moscow, its command center. The US chose the Minuteman base in Grand Forks, North Dakota. When I asked an American friend about the choice, he smiled: nobody likes Washington! During negotiations, the only proviso Brezhnev asked for was that the US protected area not be where Kissinger's home was.

(In 2002, George W. Bush Jr. abrogated the ABM treaty for almost the same reasons Kosygin initially defended before LBJ in1967. This dealt a heavy blow to real disarmament.)

The other agreement restricted underground nuclear weapon testing. Brezhnev let Kosygin deal with it - the Premier was proficient in technical details. The US objected to the Soviet idea of a comprehensive ban, but Nixon was ready to consider a threshold; say, a 100 kiloton yield ("half a loaf," he said, but let us do what is possible now).

Kosygin, a crafty bargainer, said that meant we wanted "to continue testing." No, no, objected Nixon: that means we want "to limit testing." If I agree to your idea, he said, people back home would say I am giving away the store. Kosygin suggested a higher threshold, at least a megaton (the Soviets trailed behind the US in underground testing and employed bigger charges). He also proposed a two-year option to resume testing if "others" did not join (he meant China). Nixon resisted.

The Soviet desire to obtain an agreement was so strong that Brezhnev and Kosygin overruled Gromyko. They suddenly proposed a concession, to limit tests to a yield of 150 kilotons. A worried Gromyko whispered to Brezhnev that he already agreed on 200 kilotons with Kissinger. Kosygin turned to the Foreign Minister, "You just sit there and listen; we are proposing this." Gromyko fell silent. He was unaware that at a morning meeting, the Politburo decided to agree to US terms, judging there was little difference between 200 and 150 kilotons. This also involved a minimum number of tests, calibration shots, and exchange of geological data for test sites. Both sides had the technological capacity to cut down on massive charges; smaller ones were as effective. Besides, it looked good to the world. A lower threshold would have involved on-site inspections, never favored by the Soviet military. Another reason which made possible a quick agreement was the growing ability of both countries to conduct computer-simulated testing without the use of nuclear charges.

An understanding regulated so-called "peaceful nuclear explosions." The USSR used PNEs for natural resource excavation and digging canals. The US was concerned about clandestine weapon tests. On Kissinger's insistence, advance notification and presence of observers were agreed. He smiled wickedly:

he had several candidates for the explosion sites. (With time, the PNE issue lost its significance as the Soviets realized their limited industrial value.)

As to SALT, progress stalled. US forward-based nuclear systems remained a headache for the Russians. Nixon knew, though would not admit publicly, that the US had an enormous advantage in warheads, about 3.5 to 1.

They failed to agree on new figures for the strategic triad. Nixon was worried about reaction in the US. "Sophisticates in the press and political world will zero in," he said. "Critics will say the summit was a flop." He and Brezhnev were unable to solve everything at one meeting - this is why annual meetings were important. We are not going to wait one full year before discussing this again, he stressed. There was metal in his voice: "I consider it a highest priority that before meeting again in Washington or Camp David, we will have bitten the bullet on this by then. We must have something more definitive than a prayer." Kissinger added it was important that the third summit was not seen in the US as a total stalemate. He suggested declaring that both sides agreed to find "a new balance of quantitative and qualitative aspects of strategic arms."

I liked this elliptical way of explaining failure. Dependence on US public opinion and the press always struck the Russian negotiators as fanciful, because they were never under pressure from the Soviet public or the national media. Reacting to an unacceptable American proposal, Gromyko would occasionally claim, "Our people will never understand it." Brezhnev would warn, "The Supreme Soviet will never ratify this." Nixon and Kissinger did not take the references seriously. They knew about decision-making in the Soviet Union.

Agreements were signed on cooperation in energy, urban construction and artificial heart research. The two leaders joked that "artificial heart" must be Gromyko's and Kissinger's future responsibility: they were akin to robots for their inhuman stamina. As to the 10-year agreement on economic, industrial and technical cooperation, it was lame without Congressional approval of MFN.

Brezhnev and Nixon signed a non-legally binding 130-word statement on the dangers of using environmental modification techniques for military purposes. This was a culmination of a long and difficult discussion between US and Soviet experts. Gromyko wanted a "ban," but Kissinger suggested softer language: "to deal with," "control" or "eliminate the dangers of." Ever the expert, Gromyko explained the ambiguities: "control" could embrace use, including increased use. Gromyko, Kissinger, Kornienko, Dobrynin and the interpreter debated wording in English and Russian. Kissinger agreed to "overcome the dangers," with the interpretation of the term to be determined later.

(The follow-up to the 1974 Statement became my purview in the Foreign Ministry. A Soviet-American draft was negotiated in 1977, as basis for the Enmod Convention. It entered into force with wide international backing the following year. I felt satisfaction to be guardian of a small part of the Nixon-Brezhnev legacy, and reflected on it in a thesis. The sobering thought was that dubious military utility is the chief reason for renouncing a weapon system.)

Brezhnev hosted a farewell buffet lunch in the Kremlin's St. George Hall. Nixon kept a brave face. He even tried expanding links with the Soviet military. Alexander Haig invited Defense Minister Andrei Grechko to visit the United States by enticing him with a game of tennis. Grechko, who did play tennis, looked uncomfortable - things were moving too fast for the Soviet military-industrial complex. He asked me to respond in non-committal terms.

A KGB friend told me the Secret Service visited *Voentorg,* the Defense Ministry store in downtown Moscow, to wipe up a year's supply of Soviet Army leather belts with massive brass buckles with the hammer and sickle. The belts were famous for their occasional use in drunken brawls near Russian military bases.

Of the Soviet troika that saw Nixon off at Vnukovo-2 Airport, only Brezhnev seemed genuinely sad to see his comrade depart. A bond was to be broken: both leaders pondered the uncertainties ahead. Standing in a line on the tarmac, we bade farewell to Nixon. He shook hands with everyone. He was a good actor: he was pleased and confident. It did not look as the last goodbye. He waved from the top of the aircraft steps, then beckoned to Victor and tossed him an autographed Parker fountain pen. It was a neat catch. At 5:20 p.m., the *"Spirit of '76"* zoomed off into the evening sky, on its non-stop flight home.

Last photo with Brezhnev and Nixon. US Secret Service agent Bill Duncan looks on. (Yakov Halip/Vladimir Musaelyan)

Victor and I went straight to the Foreign Ministry to dictate the remaining memcons. We tallied the result. The transcripts of private Nixon-Brezhnev conversations and full-fledged plenary sessions totaled 121 pages double-spaced (we dictated 175 pages at the first summit). My work log reads, one-on-one meetings - four memcons in Moscow and Yalta: 8 pages; plus 8; plus 1; plus 17. Full plenaries: 28 June morning -18 pages; 28 June afternoon - 20 pages; 29 June morning - 14 pages; 2 July morning - 13 pages; 3 July morning - 5 pages.

I sat down in Gromyko's private office to check and sign the memcons. I noticed that the four face-to-face memcons plus the one of the Yalta grotto conversation were not on the Politburo circulation list. No reason was given.

The third summit was substantive, but uncertainty over Nixon's future cast a pall. Watergate affected his freedom of maneuver. He made long daily calls to the White House. At the meetings, he spoke less than at previous summits, preferring to listen and letting Kissinger do the talking. The year 1974 was a watershed in Soviet-American relations, a high point never to be repeated. The prospect of annual summits extending into the bright future failed to materialize.

"Watergate is a plot!"

Inevitably, this narrative has to include Watergate. Nixon's resignation was three weeks away, but it was not yet a certainty for the Soviet leadership. What did Brezhnev make out of it? Oddly enough, he did not comprehend the dangers the mushrooming scandal held for Nixon. Ambassador Dobrynin confessed that he himself initially misjudged its seriousness, and was baffled by White House involvement.

While in the US, Brezhnev seemed oblivious to the stream of distressing headlines on the affair. A day after he left for the West Coast in the "*Spirit of '76*," the *Washington Post* reported Vice President Spiro Agnew promising, somewhat hastily, "to continue President Nixon's foreign policy" (no wonder Nixon has been trying for two years to get rid of Agnew). Watergate Special Prosecutor Archibald Cox was building his task force. A front-page article by Carl Bernstein and Bob Woodward claimed that White House Counsel John Dean had classified papers that implicated Nixon's aides. I doubt the reports caught Brezhnev's flagging attention; the priority for his entourage was keeping him in shape during the last leg of the historic visit.

My explanation is that the reason for Soviet complacency lies in ideological and cultural factors. In a country where democratic process was viewed with suspicion, whether by the Russian Tsars or the Communist Politburo, it was difficult for the leadership to figure out the storm over a nocturnal break-in into an opponent's election office, almost a prank. Preposterous! Soviet leaders appraised the developments through the prism of "class interests." This was not surprising: the Politburo, with its superficial understanding of Marxism, saw Republican Nixon as somebody handpicked by the "realistic" faction of the American bourgeoisie that opted for saner relations with the other nuclear super power.

The reasoning ran something like this. Nixon wanted détente with the Soviet Union. Was not curbing the nuclear arms race much more important than censuring him for a minor infraction? *Ergo*, he was hounded by the American far right and big business aligned with the military-industrial complex, possibly the CIA. Watergate is a plot, and Nixon a victim of lynch mob tactics! Russians will always sympathize with a victim. This analysis might seem primitive, but some Nixon aides did claim that Watergate was an attempt by the "dark forces" to undo the real achievements of the Nixon Presidency.

The American political system confounded Brezhnev, who lacked proper education in history. Once he asked Kissinger, who were the enemies of improved US-Soviet relations? Kissinger listed them: 1) Anti-Soviet conservatives of the John Foster Dulles type of the 1950s; 2) the Jewish community, which expects unlimited support for Israel and emigration from the USSR, and considers US-Soviet Middle East policies "too close;" 3) the anti-Nixon intellectuals. To Brezhnev's surprise, there was no mention of big business. He liked Henry's joke that they were on one side and Senator Jackson, "our common enemy," on the other. Kissinger added the US military to the list later.

Long beyond the tipping point, the Kremlin persisted in its disbelief about the crisis, and hoped it would be contained. Brezhnev sent Nixon signals of encouragement. In his many conversations with Kissinger, Brezhnev expressed his conviction that when years will have passed and "second- and third-rate circumstances" transpired, Nixon will prove right.

Weakening Nixon would have dealt a serious blow to the security configurations erected by both super powers. With this in mind, Moscow desisted from attempts to use Watergate as a bargaining tool in the elaborate chess game both sides were playing. It may have seemed tempting to exploit Nixon's weakness, but such a move could have upset the whole cart. The Soviet leaders were clever enough not to succumb to the urge. They knew Nixon's freedom of action abroad, especially in Vietnam, was restricted, but they did not precipitate his difficulties.

Kissinger had no sensible explanation of Watergate for Brezhnev and Gromyko. Just before Christmas 1973, he told Gromyko that Watergate did not affect the day-to-day conduct of US foreign policy. Paradoxically, he said, it provided greater freedom of action, because domestic opponents are afraid to attack everything. Gromyko hoped Nixon would carry through. At a meeting with Kissinger in April 1974 in Geneva, he asked for his opinion on the probability of impeachment. Kissinger, a lover of percentage points, said there was a 52 to 48 chance against it in the Senate; he did not see how the opposition could get a two-thirds majority. Yet, Gromyko, who knew the vagaries of American politics, was worried: he saw Brezhnev placed his bet on an individual who tottered on the brink.

For the Soviet leadership, the mere thought of a new face in the White House was heresy. The Soviet media avoided anti-Nixon themes on orders from the Propaganda Department of the Central Committee. When Brezhnev reminded Nixon of their annual summit arrangement, his concern was obvious. He would feel betrayed if his comrade disappeared from the scene. To pacify Brezhnev, Kissinger suggested lightheartedly that Gromyko end his speech at the UN General Assembly with a resounding "Four more years!" He could wear a Nixon hat - "Nixon's the One!" Gromyko confessed to Henry that in his thirty years dealing with US affairs he could not have predicted impeachment. Late in the affair, Nixon wanted to know the Russian reaction. Kissinger told him of Dobrynin's only query: why they did it out of the White House.[49]

Brezhnev followed the unfolding drama with incredulity. The first Watergate transcripts were a shock for those intimately involved in summit conferences: Nixon, a polished and unruffled diplomat and a cursing and vindictive conspirator. Victor and I closed our minds to the revelations: we were doing a job that did not require apportioning moral blame.

At last, Brezhnev saw that disaster was imminent. At the end of May 1974, Dobrynin delivered Brezhnev's highly confidential letter of support to his besieged comrade: "We do not understand much of what is happening in the United States... I do not identify the opponents with the majority of the American people. One needs tenacity and firm spirit - this the President has. Some may think you will give way, but we are pleased to note that you will not provide them satisfaction."

Nixon was deeply touched, and was silent for a minute before commenting to Dobrynin. Of all world leaders, he said, including US allies, only Brezhnev found simple personal words of support. He wanted Brezhnev to know he would not forget it. Despite our differences and strong domestic opposition, he was determined to strengthen Soviet-American relations.

These words, which Dobrynin wrote down, are missing in the version of the conversation as it appeared in the US Foreign Relations series. It quoted Nixon as saying that "the important thing was not his problems - they will pass - but the legacy of peace that we will leave... Tell Brezhnev not to worry about me and my health." [50]

In the evening of Thursday August 8, Ambassador Stoessel requested an urgent meeting with Brezhnev. It was set for next day at 10:00 a.m. in the Kremlin. The Ambassador informed him that Nixon was to resign the same day effective noon Eastern Standard Time, and that the transition of power to Gerald Ford will be smooth. Brezhnev was flabbergasted: "But he is the Commander-in-Chief!" It was as if he expected Nixon to crush a coup d'état. Twice during the conversation, he left the room to make phone calls. To Gromyko? Dobrynin? The Minister of Defense? He looked lost. Was he worried about the fate of comrade Nixon, détente, or a new face in the White House? He definitely was, on all counts. As an emotional person, he felt compassion.

That night, a despondent Brezhnev listened to Nixon's resignation speech. Judging by its length, phraseology and emotion, it might have been drafted in the Kremlin. The similarity of writing style was one of the lesser fall-outs of Soviet-American détente. Nixon had a few subdued words for the USSR: "We must continue to develop and expand that new relationship so that the two strongest nations of the world will live together in cooperation, rather than confrontation."

Nixon resigned to avoid impeachment, and several of his aides served brief jail sentences. Ironically, a pall of perjury hung over his head for the 18 ½ erased minutes of a crucial tape recording. At the high point of Watergate, Alger Hiss, the man Nixon helped convict for perjury back in 1951 (he protested accusations of spying and no evidence was found in Soviet archives), suggested that no one should be sent to jail. Not even Nixon and Agnew, he said. "Jail doesn't do anybody any good." [51] Perhaps deep down he felt satisfaction: what goes around comes around.

CHAPTER 4

The Long Goodbye, 1974-1979

FIELDING GERALD FORD IN HELSINKI

HOWEVER DEJECTED BREZHNEV FELT ABOUT his comrade's fate, his summits with American Presidents were not over. Gerald Ford sent him a letter, where he referred to the man he pardoned: he was committed to follow Nixon's course. He invited Brezhnev to visit the United States in 1975; he will stick to Nixon's summit schedule.

The confidential back channel remained. Brezhnev and Gromyko were pleased that Henry Kissinger stayed on to guide the new President. This was the best sign that Nixon's foreign policy focus, irrespective of Ford's closeness to Congress, would be maintained. Kissinger's importance for the Soviet leadership increased, and he basked in the new glory. It affected his behavior at meetings with the Soviets: he felt unfettered. He told Brezhnev that his personal impact on the political scene in the US was now perhaps more than of the President. He was optimistic about Ford, who did not argue with his advice and did not edit his draft messages to Brezhnev. He thought the new President's position was growing stronger by the week; by the time he left in 1981, the two countries' course will be a permanent feature of the world scene.

For Moscow, détente remained vital. At staff conferences, Gromyko insisted, "Keep up the momentum; keep up the momentum!" Did we detect a hint of worry? Ford might dampen Nixon's view of Brezhnev, steer away from a discredited Administration's strategy, and demonstrate his own grasp.

Troubling reports came in that Ford was not happy with the overuse of the term "détente."

In the fall of 1974, I was in New York at the UN General Assembly session, when Victor called about a Brezhnev-Ford mini-summit in November. I asked him to get me off the hook. A Counselor from the Ministry's USA Department went to Vladivostok to take notes. This was the only Brezhnev US summit they allowed me to skip.

The Kremlin faced a serious problem, Brezhnev's deteriorating health. His capacity to conduct vigorous negotiations dwindled. On the eve of Vladivostok, Kissinger sent Ford a five-page appraisal of Brezhnev, his strong and weak points.[52] The Soviet leader emerged as a chain-smoking warm person who appreciates physical contact with his interlocutor and humorous stories. He lacks in thorough preparation, but relies on his aides for rectifying mistakes in presenting the Soviet position.

Strangely, Kissinger failed to warn Ford that Brezhnev was undergoing personality change – this was impeding serious negotiation. The smooth translation of his interventions masked his increasingly stilted way of speaking. Alexandrov and Gromyko patiently rectified misleading statements he made and prompted him to raise points he forgot. He had problems with MIRV numbers. He insisted that British and French nuclear weapons be included in the general count - Dobrynin had to remind him it was past history. These were not whispered conversations; Brezhnev's hearing was impaired. State Department interpreter Alex Akalovsky rejoined the negotiations to perform an unusual function: to listen to discussions in the Russian team during short breaks. They happened often.

In Vladivostok, both leaders found it hard to focus on the small print of a new nuclear balance. In exasperation, Kissinger told Kornienko that both their bosses "were too dumb to grasp their own advantages." Kornienko smiled imperceptibly.

Ford was no Nixon: Kissinger led him through a labyrinth of issues. He told him about a disturbing trend, swift Soviet technological advance. Replacement of current missiles with MIRVed warheads went at a faster rate than the US anticipated. Given their larger throw-weight, they matched

American capabilities. Kissinger also arranged with Ford that if he met Brezhnev alone, a record was to be made. There should be no replay of Nixon concealing private discussions.

Kissinger and Gromyko helped the leaders negotiate the framework of a future SALT-2 treaty, with limits on each country's strategic triad: 2,400 delivery vehicles each, including 1,320 MIRVed missiles on ICBMs and SLBMs. Each side would be free to decide the composition of the mix; no new ICBM launchers (silos) would be built; a new treaty would be negotiated to last until 1985.

Brezhnev explained to Ford his old idea of a mutual assistance pact. In October, he reminded Kissinger of his grotto exchange with Nixon, who promised to think about it, but evidently could not because domestic events took over. Again, as in the grotto, Brezhnev claimed it was his personal hush-hush project; he never showed the memcon to anyone in the Soviet leadership. This was hard to believe, as was Kissinger's assurance that none except President Ford will hear of it.

When Brezhnev claimed an idea was his personal project, he switched on his emotions. He would say, "I am absolutely frank with you, I am an emotional man; I have been through the war; the older you get the wiser you become..." He thought references to sentiment were effective with even hard-boiled politicians. Nixon found it difficult to argue with waves of emotion, so he voiced interest, nothing more. Kissinger was more direct; he steered Brezhnev back to the agenda.

Ford was forewarned, and followed Nixon's style. He was non-committal, and suggested that Kissinger and Gromyko continue discussing the project. Brezhnev kept referring to his positive experience with Richard Nixon, but Ford chose his words carefully. Political reaction at home was high on his mind, and this he tried to explain to Brezhnev. He also reassured him that détente should be made irreversible.

By the time of Vladivostok (the name of the city is translated as "Rule the East"), the Chinese assuaged their belligerent stance towards the USSR by proposing a non-aggression treaty and disengagement of forces in disputed border areas. American analysts like Bill Hyland correctly predicted that the

Sino-Soviet conflict would not be a permanent state of affairs. Kissinger advised Ford that the US should support the Chinese for ten years, and afterwards it may have to join the Soviet Union.[53]

Brezhnev suffered a mild stroke on the last day of the meeting. Grechko and Podgorny's refusal to support the agreement with Ford might have been the trigger. Brezhnev talked to obstinate Podgorny on the secure line for a long time.

Ford invited Brezhnev to visit the United States in 1975, and Brezhnev reciprocated with an invitation to Moscow. Neither trip materialized.

In February 1975, Victor and I split responsibilities. The original plan was to accompany Gromyko to Geneva for a round of talks with Kissinger in preparation for the next summit. Gromyko acquired a primary role in foreign policy decision-making, although as a disciplined functionary, he would never compromise Brezhnev's formal stature.

British Prime Minister Harold Wilson was coming to Moscow to meet Brezhnev, who wanted Victor to be at his side. I accompanied Gromyko. I asked the Minister's office to include an additional interpreter to help out. Gromyko agreed, but when we arrived in Geneva, he said he wanted me at his side at all meetings. This meant both translating and note taking. As usual, doubling the workload did not affect pay.

On the first night, the full American team came to dinner. They admired the Soviet Mission's location: it stands on a hill across the road from the Palais des Nations, the sprawling UN Office. As aperitifs were served, Gromyko invited Kissinger to a private room, where he briefed him about the Wilson visit to Moscow. It was nothing dramatic, since the role of Great Britain diminished in Soviet foreign policy. Notably, the "Great" part of the country's name was dropped in MFA interoffice correspondence, a slight probably not noticed by the British.

They laid the table for fourteen. The food was excellent; the caviar supply generous. Holding a small vodka glass, Gromyko toasted Kissinger. He rarely took alcohol; this time he was eager to create a good atmosphere. He wished to discuss the European Security Conference. "Kissinger," Gromyko said, "let us set the date of its final, highest level, stage." He suggested April or May; Kissinger preferred late July to early September. The Kremlin was frantic: the window of opportunity for Brezhnev's meaningful participation could close any day.

Brezhnev's post created a protocol problem. It was not spelt out in the Constitution, which only referenced the Communist Party's "leading and guiding role." Kissinger quizzed us on who will lead the Soviet delegation to sign the Final Act, envisaged as a legally binding document. Gromyko's answer was ingenious: "Anyone who is entrusted with the mission can lead the delegation." True, the leader of the thirteen million-strong CPSU enjoyed sufficient rank to join any top-level meeting. It was safely assumed that General Secretary Leonid Brezhnev would represent the USSR at the Helsinki summit.

Gromyko wanted to know whether the June date for Brezhnev's visit to the US still stood. Kissinger looked surprised: of course, it did. He suspected that Brezhnev's health was a major worry in the Politburo. President Ford received confidential reports, mostly hearsay. A secret White House memo mentioned an improbable bit about Brezhnev extracting his painful dentures and smashing them on the floor in a Kremlin corridor.[54] Washington thought that his slurred speech and persistent cough indicated radiation treatment. The rumors were wrong.

The remaining unresolved issue in the Final Act concerned the possibility of peaceful change of frontiers in Europe, one of the ten principles under negotiation. Kissinger repeated it was a matter between the USSR and the Europeans, especially the West Germans. He shrugged: "We are not the problem."

Gromyko educated him on the fine points of difference. The USSR wanted each of the principles to "be observed" or "be of equal validity." He could not agree to the FRG formula: "Each is equally valid and interdependent." Kissinger asked why. Because, lectured Gromyko, if a party says one principle is not observed (say, on human contacts), it will be free not to observe any of the others. Like wheels in a watch, he explained: if one stops revolving, everything stops. Suppose someone is denied an emigration permit from the Soviet Union - should it be grounds to nullify the principle of the inviolability of frontiers?

Kissinger confessed the abstruse debate eluded him. He could not be seen as letting US allies down; on the other hand, he wanted progress with the Russians.

The peculiar linguistic formula, which Kissinger and Gromyko finalized, read: "[States] consider that their frontiers can be changed, in accordance with international law, by peaceful means and by agreement." Since I was involved in finalizing the English text, I know the first coma was against rules of grammar. However, deliberate punctuation mistakes yield to politics if negotiators say so. The idea here was to highlight the norm itself (frontiers can be changed) and cases when it would be feasible. Kissinger later confessed he never fully grasped the operational significance of commas placed around a clause.[55] The passage agreed was critical because it paved the way to German reunification, a theoretical possibility that most thought would never happen in their lifetime. It did, in 1990.

Champagne was served. They exchanged brief toasts claiming friendship and determination to follow the path set by the two countries' leaders. Gromyko evoked Brezhnev, but Kissinger failed to mention President Ford.

The next day we reassembled in Kissinger's suite at the Intercontinental Hotel. He took Gromyko aside to a corner room with a view of the Palais des Nations and Lake Geneva beyond. I was surprised to see Peter Rodman. He would be taking notes for the Secretary instead of an interpreter from State: the NSC still ran the show. Peter waved, took out his yellow legal pad, and I produced mine, a white Kremlin one with a dark red edge. It was not easy: sitting in a spongy leather armchair with my back to the high windows, I had to translate and take detailed notes at the same time.

They sailed through a list of issues, comparing notes. In Cyprus, the Greek military government deposed Archbishop Makarios two weeks after Nixon left Moscow. Turkey invaded the island and established a secessionist "Turkish Republic of Northern Cyprus." Kissinger's sympathies lay with Turkey, a member of NATO; the US was worried that Archbishop Makarios could become "a Castro in mufti." For this reason, Kissinger was evasive. We do not have a position yet, he said, though "we object to Turkish occupation and regard Cyprus as a single state..." Gromyko was forceful: "Turkey is carving up the island with a knife." Kissinger vented his frustration with Makarios: "He should be more realistic and watch his deputies who'd sell him cheap despite constantly addressing him as "His Ecstasy" (of course, the Cyprus leader's official title was "His Beatitude").

For Gromyko, the problem of Cyprus was important because of implications for Soviet influence in the Middle East. His disappointment was understandable. In a letter to Ford, Brezhnev advised joint US-Soviet (or UN Security Council) guarantees for Cyprus sovereignty. Ford, under Kissinger's influence, did not promise anything beyond "consulting" with Moscow. The US planned to increase its role in the Middle East. Kissinger said that with his experience of the region, he "was qualified to run a lunatic asylum." He parried Gromyko's claim of excluding the USSR. He also warned against placing too much confidence in Arab leaders. "The feeling of gratitude," he remarked wryly, "was never a driving force in the Middle East - countries here changed sides many times in the last 25 years."

For some reason they started discussing the Royal Saudi family. Gromyko first met Prince Faisal in 1946 - he led the Saudi delegation to the First Session of the UN General Assembly. Saudi Arabia was one of the first countries to recognize Soviet Russia. This remark provoked a Kissinger story. "No one can fool the King. He told me the Soviet Union was in collusion with Zionists: the USSR actually started the 1967 war in cooperation with Israel. I remember being shoved into a hundred-yard long reception hall by three men who looked like slaves. The King was at the far end. I walked 99 yards, and the King walked one yard to greet me. He then broke into a 45-minute speech about Jews and Communists. He claimed that Jews overran Russia, and were sent afterwards to Israel. In the end he presented me with a painting of the Holy Oasis, which he said the Embassy could keep for three months."

Gromyko grinned; he was aware of the Saudis' paranoia towards the Soviet Union.

I did not include Kissinger's story in the memcon, but wrote it down in my diary. It was beautified in the US transcript.[56] (On another occasion Brezhnev told a similar story, of a Minister from Libya, who, in the middle of talks with Premier Kosygin in the Kremlin insisted on a prayer session. He fell to his knees and prayed under the portraits of Marx and Lenin.)

Gromyko wanted to know if the US had military contacts with the Chinese. Kissinger said it was not in the US interest to build up their war machine: "We're not fools. For five years it's anti-Soviet; in five to ten years it'll be both anti-American and anti-Soviet."

At the end of the meeting, Gromyko's orderly mind needed a clear idea of issues agreed or left in abeyance. With no notes in front of him, Gromyko summarized, asking probing questions and jabbing a finger into Kissinger's protruding chest. Kissinger's forte was argumentation, always interesting, sometimes unusual. However, he was averse to confirming promises he gave out freely, especially on timing.

My transcript reads (it was shorter than the US version):

"A.A. Gromyko. You promised to consult your allies on confidence-building measures. When can we expect your reply?

H. Kissinger. We will respond in two weeks.

A.A. Gromyko. The sooner the better. What about peaceful change of frontiers? We want a clear answer. If problems persist, we will revert to our previous [hard] position. When will you give us a reply?

H. Kissinger. Within ten days, hopefully.

A.A. Gromyko. The date of the CSCE final stage. I do not like the June/July target at all. You promised to consult and reply before Monday.

H. Kissinger. You will get our reaction on Monday, end of day.

A.A. Gromyko. On Cyprus: you did not mention dates, but wanted to discuss the situation, and get in touch with us shortly. We want this fast; blood may be spilled.

H. Kissinger. We have certain problems.

Gromyko. Of course, but it is an international issue. I do not see any insurmountable obstacles to resolving it.

H. Kissinger nods.

A.A. Gromyko. I intend to say [at the press conference]: "On the Middle East, we exchanged information and views on the Geneva Conference." Mind, we do not want to be invited to rubberstamp the decisions and enjoy a photo opportunity. We are ready to participate in talks leading to a conference, but will not go around begging with an extended hand.

H. Kissinger. I appreciate what you said. We are at the end of a string of partial steps. I will consider our possible joint efforts more seriously. We do not have any specific proposals yet; as soon as they emerge, I will get in touch with you. Perhaps we will need to meet again.

A.A. Gromyko. We expect more specifics from you as soon as possible."

So went the rapid machine-gun questions and defensive answers. One could not miss the tone: this was the USSR talking to America. Kissinger squirmed in his chair like a suspect under interrogation in the Lubyanka Transfer Prison. The reason was Rodman's presence; his transcript of promises made by his boss would be on record for the State Department bureaucracy to see. Kissinger was not used to this mode, but his aides had to plan and prepare responses to the Soviets. The Secretary of State position was different from that of a free operator; things had to change in Kissinger's conduct of office business - he needed diplomatic discipline.

They went over the draft communiqué of the meeting and edited the English text. I did not have to translate. It was a treat watching them dissect wording for nuances that an ordinary reader would miss. Gromyko enquired why Kissinger wished to omit reference to the "only" legal government in Cyprus. Kissinger explained that "only" sounded provocative, as if there already was another government. Gromyko agreed. He said he intended to mention to reporters his "personal impression" that views of both sides on convening the Geneva Conference on the Middle East "are converging."

Kissinger intimated he would be a bit more opaque: "an understanding was reached" on the issue.

(In May 1975, Kissinger finally agreed to convene the conference, but without Palestinian participation at the start, lest it create insurmountable problems. In time, it will reach that point, he promised. Gromyko's apprehension was that it was just a "cover," but Kissinger assured the Minister that the US does not want a cover, or a cover-up. We are not so good at "cover-ups," he added. "We will go a modified hang-out route." The allusion to Nixon's belated - and unsuccessful - Watergate tactics brought smiles.)

We crammed into the elevator going down to the lobby of the Intercontinental where the press was waiting. As the doors slid open, I was blinded by klieg lights and lost my way in the throng of hotel guests eager to catch a glimpse of the two diplomats. Gromyko started speaking in Russian. He asked Kissinger if he saw his "namesake Andrey anywhere." Kissinger said he last saw me in the elevator: "Perhaps he got stranded?" He suggested that the Minister make his statement in English. I pushed through the crowd to pick up the short statement in translation. Gromyko told me he and Henry "spent a lot of time looking for me" - it was his kind of humor. He was in a good mood as we drove the short stretch to the Soviet Mission at 15 Avenue de la paix.

The Minister went to his suite to write a short cable to Brezhnev, and I settled in the secure room to dictate the memcon. Two excited girl secretaries were on night shift. Thoughtfully, they laid out coffee and sandwiches. I looked forward to sleeping in the plane next day.

The second stage of the CSCE was a marathon session in Geneva involving thirty-five countries. Since the negotiators worked on an English rolling text, Soviet delegate Deputy Minister Anatoly Kovalyov wanted a reliable language expert to watch over the perfidious British, our American comrades, and the revanchist West Germans, lest they try to juggle unacceptable linguistic nuances. He asked Moscow "for Vavilov or Sukhodrev." Victor was eager to go.

That suited me, since I was engrossed in UN affairs at the Center. To Victor's chagrin, he was told to stay in Moscow in case his master called.

My two-week mission stretched to six months. Apart from linguistic services, Kovalyov put me in charge of the special working group on the organization of the CSCE summit stage. He assured me that any cable I drafted on seating arrangements in Helsinki would go directly to Brezhnev.

Kovalyov cut a strange figure: chain-smoking and mysterious-looking, he was also a consummate poet, who published the only ode in the world's literary annals devoted to CSCE negotiators. His German was passable, his English rudimentary. His Russian was incoherent - few aides could make him out. A cunning diplomat with a furtive desire to beautify the USSR, Kovalyov wrested a promise from the Party Central Committee to stop jamming foreign Russian-language broadcasts.

Kissinger and Gromyko met again in Geneva on July 10 and 11. Victor accompanied Gromyko. The two envoys thought they met to deal with the only important outstanding issue: the date of the third stage. Instead, another problem blew up in their faces.

The last-minute hurdle was erected by the tiny island of Malta. Prime Minister Dom Mintoff insisted that Iran and the Persian Gulf countries be invited to Helsinki. He also tabled an unpretentious proposal to withdraw the US Sixth fleet from the Mediterranean. The USSR would have loved that, but the proposition was anathema for the US and NATO. Governed by the rule of consensus, the negotiators could not initial the draft Final Act without Malta's approval, and thus finalize the date of the third stage, the summit.

I knew Mintoff. A smallish figure, he was leader of Malta's opposition Labour party, who travelled to London in the late 1960s. He slipped into Harrington House, the Soviet Embassy, to explain the situation on the island and meekly ask for support. I often accompanied him to see Ambassador Smirnovsky in the Embassy garden room. He peered over his shoulder and smiled nervously. Perhaps he was tailed by MI5.

In 1975, he was self-assured as a rock. Since a great logistic effort was at stake, the Finns were panicky: they had to know the exact date of the summit in advance. However, no amount of cajoling helped. The Finnish

Foreign Minister telephoned Valetta. The response was the Prime Minister was unavailable: "He went horse riding on the beach." Malta quickly became the delegates' focus for anger and jokes, some nasty. A British delegate wrote a masterful spoof on the Final Act. One of the kinder provisions was pouring asphalt into the Mediterranean to turn it into a parking lot. I provided an "official translation" into Russian. We gave both versions pseudo-genuine document numbers and distributed them among delegates known for their sense of humor.

Kissinger and Gromyko were desperate to break the impasse. It was a rare occasion when a single country provoked the wrath of both the US and USSR, and of over thirty others. Kissinger frowned, "What can be done with this man Mintoff? Assassination, maybe?" All laughed. Gromyko grinned at the allusion to the CIA assassination plans uncovered by the Rockefeller Commission.

They discussed more humane methods of getting Mintoff aboard. Sonnenfeldt objected to the idea of sending a joint telegram as counterproductive, because "it would inflate his ego." Gromyko agreed. Kissinger volunteered another proposal, "Float Malta down to Libya and anchor it there."

Unknown to both teams at the Intercontinental, Yuri Dubinine, a perceptive member of the Soviet delegation, convinced the Maltese delegate that the presence in Geneva of Kissinger and Gromyko could be his best - and last - chance to include some reference to the Mediterranean in the Final Act. The delegate produced a slip of paper from his wallet (it was the fallback position) and gave it to Dubinine who rushed to the Intercontinental. I read out the translation to Gromyko. He made the most of it: the Russians managed to extract a concession from the Maltese. Kissinger was surprised: "There's no allusion to the Sixth fleet?" "Nothing," said Gromyko. He asked Kissinger and me to sit together and check the wording. The text was innocuous: contributing to peace in the region, reducing armed forces, strengthening security, lessening tensions… Kissinger and Gromyko congratulated each other on this latest round of super power solidarity.

Positive signals were coming from Moscow: Brezhnev was alert enough to attend the third stage in person.

The CSCE assembled in Helsinki from 30 July to 1 August. Essentially, it was a speech-making affair plus the signing ceremony of the Final Act. The thirty-five heads of State and government spoke for fifteen minutes each, mingled in the foyer, and met for dinner at the Presidential Palace. As Kissinger pondered the seating arrangement in the conference hall, he thought the Finns deliberately moved the USSR delegation to the back of the room, and the US contingent up front. He wondered if it meant "revenge of Finnish protocol for decades of Soviet pressure."[57] This was far from the truth: the seating formula was decided beforehand. Otherwise, how could Erich Honecker of the GDR occupy a seat in the first row? At any rate, the Russian delegation was happy with the arrangement, since the back rows had a larger overflow area for the security detail, aides and Dr. Chazov.

Apart from the CSCE negotiators, the Soviet delegation included the old *Amerikanisti* team. The *Europeisti* colleagues will handle the ceremonial consummation of the conference. Our assignment was substantive, a two-day Brezhnev-Ford meeting on the margins.

As we boarded the overnight special train at Leningrad's Finland Station to Helsinki, we found there was a new delegation member. Every Soviet diplomatic delegation had an administrator who saw after day-to-day organization, cars, accommodation and hospitality. The person to manage delegation logistics was Konstantin Chernenko.

His appointment raised eyebrows: by any stretch of imagination, one could not visualize him compiling car lists and listening to MFA officials whimper about their wretched perks. Chernenko quickly appointed a deputy - for the menial chores - and focused on what he did best: collecting and filing the most treasured outcome of the CSCE, the memcons of the Chief.

On the first day of the conference, I had a talk with Chernenko on the art of maintaining records. He set me thinking. Had I been right in my impetuous juggling with the spoken word of my political masters? Did I varnish history and omit the tiny jewels that historians would miss and curse the heartless note-taker? Chernenko taught me a lesson: no conversations between leaders and no remarks are too trivial to be recorded for posterity (actually, this was close to the American way of preparing memcons). Listening to his arguments, I nodded, but in my mind, I disagreed. MFA interpreters were hardened professionals who followed an established *modus operandi*.

Dignitaries who filed past Brezhnev's seat prompted our discussion. They lingered and some felt obliged to murmur brief words of greetings. Prime Minister Olof Palme told Brezhnev he met his son when he was Soviet Trade Representative in Stockholm. Brezhnev said he was happy to hear this, and fell silent. Palme spoke Russian, but it was hard for Brezhnev to sustain a conversation.

When later that day I told Chernenko about this example of an inconsequential exchange not worthy of a record, I got the coldest stare this side of the Polar Circle. "But you must write it down," he said. When I opined that this was small talk with no policy implications and would look weird as a memcon, Chernenko struck a deadly blow. "Do you realize," he puffed, "That this might well have been the only time they met at the Conference? Your memcon can be the basis for a news item back home." He was right; I had not thought of this angle. I dictated a paragraph. The next day it was reproduced in both *Pravda* and *Izvestia*. I made a mental note to be more attentive to Chernenko's wishes. I remembered Gromyko telling a group of young MFA interpreters: negotiations lose any importance without a record; history only recognizes a written memorandum.

President Urho Kekkonen hosted a dinner for the thirty-five heads of State and Government. The Finns were deft in dealing with political sensitivities. Choice seats went to Gerald Ford, with silent Erich Honecker and ebullient Helmut Schmidt of the two "Deutschland" on his left. Further along sat UN Secretary-General Kurt Waldheim, Yugoslavia's Josip Broz Tito, Brezhnev, Turkish Prime Minister Suleyman Demirel and Gustav Husak of Czechoslovakia. Harold Wilson and Valéry Giscard d'Estaing faced the main row, presenting their distinguished backs to other guests. President Urho Kekkonen sat in the center under a statue of a goddess brandishing a sword, with a vicious looking lion at her feet.

The Finns seated me on a chair behind my master. I missed the food, but was consoled by the fact that Brezhnev was not eager to eat. Just before dinner, he said he would not go, let Gromyko take his place. Dr. Chazov reasoned with him: he cannot offer his seat at the main table to another person - it was a leaders' assembly.

Brezhnev looked exhausted. A KGB logistics sergeant, dressed as a Finnish waiter, filled three cut crystal glasses in front of his plate, for white wine, red wine and champagne. They remained untouched.

Brezhnev's neighbor on the right was Tito. He did not utter a word throughout the dinner; he was 83 and looked unwell. Demirel on Brezhnev's left made a brave attempt to strike up conversation. Turkey had just demanded the closure of US bases in retaliation for an arms embargo. Demirel wished, by talking to the Soviet leader, to demonstrate his "Soviet option." He said the best brand of wheat ever introduced in Turkey was *Bezostaya-1* bred by Soviet geneticist Nikolai Vavilov. He recalled that the frost-resistant variety "fed the USSR." Brezhnev said he knew that. His good humor evaporated when Demirel complimented Dmitri Polyansky, a Politburo member in charge of agriculture, who visited Turkey recently. Polyansky was fast becoming a political non-person, to be banished shortly to an Ambassadorial post in Japan.

After half an hour, Brezhnev leaned back and whispered to me that he was tired. Would it be all right if he slipped away? I assured him it was not a problem - I will express regrets discretely to the host. To help him rise required effort: he was twice as heavy as I was. I inspected the table to pick up anything left behind, odd papers, notes, or pens. This time it was reading glasses. I led Brezhnev to the door and handed him over to his bodyguard Vladimir. Brezhnev was the only guest to leave early, in full view of the room. This would fuel speculation about his condition, but he was past caring.

To make amends for seating me behind Brezhnev, Finnish protocol invited me to a buffet in the adjacent room. Three KGB Ninth Directorate officers were having a working supper with Finnish security. Waiters brought us fare served for the VIPs and excellent port in small glasses. My robust colleagues, used to generous after-work servings of ice-cold vodka, downed the port and asked me to negotiate a refill.

The Ford-Brezhnev mini-summit on the margins of the CSCE took two sessions. Brezhnev appreciated Ford's clear reiteration, in a message, of the invitation to visit the US in the near future. Spring was suggested. The White House wanted an early indication of the date. Unknown to Ford, Brezhnev was reluctant to travel by air, so Moscow was cagey about timing. Kissinger, in his conspiratorial fashion, thought the Soviets held back for political reasons, to press the US on SALT and trade.

Meanwhile, news from the US was disturbing. In February, Henry Jackson announced his candidacy for nomination for President from the Democratic Party. The trade bill collapsed under Congressional opposition. A logjam was building up in SALT and MBFR.

New problems arose. My friend Sasha, an Embassy First Secretary, suffered serious eye damage, according to Soviet doctors, from focused microwave radiation - his first-floor desk faced 16th Street. The US accused Russians of radiating the Embassy in Moscow. Several bilateral commission meetings were cancelled. Rightist groups claimed that civil defense planning in the USSR meant the Kremlin seriously contemplated a first nuclear strike.

On July 30, shortly after 9:00 a.m., we drove to the US Ambassador's residence in Helsinki. Ford greeted Brezhnev at the door. We were ushered into a modest whitewashed drawing room with an open fireplace and wall crystal chandeliers between the tall windows. There were cigarette packs and matches with the Presidential Seal and Ford's signature in gold; the blue matchbooks had a nice velvety feel. Four ubiquitous ice water jugs were positioned on the polished rectangular table. Throughout the détente years, Brezhnev never touched iced water; he worried about getting a sore throat.

The Soviet Embassy informed the hosts we would be six: Brezhnev, Gromyko, Kornienko, Alexandrov, Sukhodrev and I. Facing us, with their backs to the windows, sat Ford, Kissinger, Scowcroft, Stoessel, Sonnenfeldt and Rodman. Bill Hyland found a place by the window. The White House team was still in command, but it became more open, judging by the presence of Ambassador Stoessel. I was glad to see State Department interpreters return from the cold. Alex Akalovsky sat in the back but did not translate. He listened to the discussion, especially to private remarks among Russian participants. These were many, since Brezhnev found it hard to grapple with the subject matter and asked for explanations from aides.

US Embassy, Helsinki. Left to right: Gromyko, Brezhnev, Sukhodrev, Alexandrov, Vavilov; Rodman, Sonnenfeldt, Kissinger, Ford, Stoessel. (Vladimir Musaelyan)

Ford looked fit, as a former football player should. He had a thick briefing book in front of him. He smoked a pipe and glanced at Kissinger as if checking if he was on the right track. Brezhnev had a much leaner file. He never opened it. He smoked cigarettes. It was a warm day, and towards the end, everyone was in shirtsleeves except Kornienko. The iced water was a relief.

Brezhnev contemplated Ford, a "replacement comrade" for Nixon. He liked Ford's looks and his uncomplicated manner of speaking. He appreciated that the new President would be steered to a large degree by Kissinger, the person who held quasi-legal rights to détente.

Brezhnev started speaking without invitation, as was his habit. He informed Ford that his weight "stabilized at 78 kilograms." Kissinger could not miss a joke opportunity: before Ford could react, he said his own weight was "stable within a ten kilo range" - everybody laughed. Brezhnev had some friendly asides at Kissinger, whom he threatened with "a little bomb in my pocket," and at Gromyko. "They are the only ones against détente," he said.

Cutting the flow of jokes, Ford looked at his speaking notes. He emphasized the importance of détente; his desire was to continue with Nixon's foreign policy. His White House tenure was dependent on its continuation, despite unnamed "critics in government" and elsewhere, who wanted his term to be no longer than 1 ½ years. He was confident his tenure would last for the next five and a half years.

Brezhnev protested, "Why not eight?"

Ford wished Brezhnev would come to Camp David this year, in the fall, say, second half of October. Brezhnev's eyes misted over: "Ah, Camp David, quiet and relaxing." He would like to come one or two days in advance, as in 1973. He did not confirm a date.

Brezhnev evoked the importance of the Vladivostok understanding on SALT; Ford nodded. The discussion unwound at a lazy pace. Alexandrov scribbled me a note: "They are squeezing words out of each other as from toothpaste tubes; each side wants the other to talk."

When the discussion turned to the Middle East, Gromyko had to prompt Brezhnev. After a while, he decided to take over. In a clipped tone, he outlined the Soviet position: a comprehensive solution to be addressed by the Geneva conference, as opposed to piecemeal American steps. I never saw Gromyko so irritated with Brezhnev, who was fouling up a carefully planned negotiation.

Brezhnev turned to Gromyko and talked in a loud voice, as if they were alone in the room.

Victor stopped translating, and I put down my pen. Ford waited. Kissinger asked, "Is it a private fight, or anyone can join in?" I chuckled. Victor did not translate the question. Brezhnev started, turned to face Ford and feigned attentiveness. Ford grinned. I thought Kissinger was getting bolder by the day.

I did not write down the altercation because it was not material to SALT, the subject they were discussing. I made a mental note just in case. There is a fairly accurate account of this episode in Kissinger's memoirs.[58] He did not take notes (he rarely wrote down anything). Peter Rodman knew by now that he should stop writing at embarrassing moments. I looked at a large vase with flowers and hanging creepers on the mantelpiece.

There were surprises in store for Brezhnev. Ford took up Jewish emigration - a marked departure from Nixon's agenda.

Brezhnev winced: "If you wish, we can add Solzhenitsyn to the list." Kissinger was on his way to the washroom. He stopped in his tracks: "Let no one think I'm leaving because Solzhenitsyn's name has been mentioned." Brezhnev did not smile. He failed to understand the American media's affection for the angry nationalist writer who believed that pro-Western Jewish intellectuals masterminded the 1917 Socialist revolution in Russia. Ganging up with AFL President George Meany and Senator Jackson, he has been creating difficulties for the White House with his rhetoric.

Brezhnev produced a paper and started ticking off figures of Jewish emigration applications and actual departures. "We are reaching the point of tragedy," he said. "What are we to do? Talk people into leaving?" Dozens of his friends were Jews. Was he to talk Veniamin Dymshits, a Deputy Prime Minister, into leaving because he was Jewish? The number of applications was decreasing: from a peak of 26,800 in 1972 to 14,000 in 1974. 6,000 left in the first six months of 1975; 116,000 left since 1945. The rate of permissions granted runs to 98.4 per cent; security cases are an exception. Besides, many Jews went elsewhere, rather than Israel. In 1,000 cases, people asked to be repatriated back to the USSR.

"A good batting average," agreed Ford, but "more encouraging" figures would help with legislation he intended to recommend to Congress. Senators Javits and Ribicoff could use any good argument for revising current laws harmful to the continuation of détente.

As Ford spoke, Brezhnev got impatient. He wished Nixon were there: that man was an understanding comrade. Besides, listening to Ford's statement in English was wasting time. While Victor translated, Brezhnev would turn to Gromyko and converse with him in a low voice, not looking at Ford or even simulating interest. However, he expected other participants to listen to his Russian. When he noticed Kissinger whispering into Ford's ear, he stopped and called out as to an errant schoolchild, "Ghenry, Ghenry!"

As we trooped to the cars, Brezhnev buttonholed Ford. Lowering his voice, he said the Soviet leadership was interested in his re-election and would employ all means to make that happen. A fittingly serious Ford thanked Brezhnev: he said he expected to be re-elected and would do everything to strengthen détente and make it irreversible. When Victor told me about this tête-à-tête, I said it was a good bargain: wishes for re-election in exchange for irreversibility of détente. Ford's confirmation of this particular goal was important. It was a marked progression of relations: from America as "second to none," to parity with the USSR, and on to irreversible détente.

Back in Finlandia Hall, Brezhnev delivered his statement, which was simultaneously translated. I loitered nearby his seat in case some dignitary wished to talk. Victor arrived with the typed memcon of the private conversation with Ford. Brezhnev read it, tore it up and absentmindedly placed the pieces in an ashtray. After we left the conference room, Jan Lodal retrieved the pieces and reconstructed the page. The partly legible text was translated and supplemented by Alexander Akalovsky who overheard a fraction of the conversation. Good marks for Jan and Alex - the things we do for our masters! However, professionally speaking, it was a bouquet of lapses on both sides:

- Brezhnev involuntarily destroyed a record.
- His aides failed to retrieve the pieces after he left.
- Ford failed to dictate a memo, so his aides were saddled with the Russian version.

The second Brezhnev-Ford meeting on August 2 took place in the imposing Soviet Embassy. The Americans provided an official list of their team: Secretary Kissinger; Ambassador Walter Stoessel; Brent Scowcroft, National Security Advisor; Helmut Sonnenfeldt, Department of State Counselor; Arthur Hartman, Assistant Secretary of State; Bill Hyland, Director of the Bureau of Intelligence and Research at State; Jan Lodal, Director of Program Analysis, NSC; Peter Rodman, NSC; and Alexander Akalovsky, State Department.

Chernenko, General Mikhail Kozlov, Deputy Chief of the General Staff, and SALT expert Nikolai Detinov joined the basic Soviet team.

Ford complimented Brezhnev on his speech; it set the right tone, he said. Brezhnev thanked him for support in ensuring the conference summer date. The inference was clear: he could not have made it later. He did not comment on Ford's intervention, which was almost botched and later blamed on NSC staff.

It was not their fault. A bright and witty lot, they worked under pressure and against severe constraints of time. The adrenalin-charged atmosphere of nervous hilarity helped us all in tense situations where anything could go wrong. It did, right in the middle of the conference. Just as President Ford took the podium in Finlandia Hall, the conference secretariat started distributing the printed version of his speech. I heard shuffling of papers. A puzzled Olof Palme who sat two rows in front of us was trying to locate the line the President was reading - he could not find it. He looked up at Ford who was not speaking *ex tempore*. I rose and walked to the door. Bill Hyland stood there, lost in his private thoughts, evidently not listening to a speech he read a dozen times before. I told him there was something wrong; the delegates did not have the correct version of Ford's speech. He groaned, "Oh my god, we did it again!"

It emerged that Kissinger kept making changes to the President's statement until the last moment. Frantic staff were cutting and pasting new passages and feeding the reconstructed pages into the copier, which was churning out a thoroughly garbled version. Two hundred copies were rushed to the Conference secretariat for distribution.

"Now's the moment to defect to the Soviet delegation, Bill," I said. "Not a bad idea," he replied, "If you want some speeches corrected." I can fathom the blood spilled when Kissinger realized what had happened with President Ford's first major international appearance. He failed to mention the episode in his *Years of Renewal*, stressing instead Ford's "powerful speech," and "eloquent affirmation... The concluding section was especially strong."[59]

Meanwhile at the Soviet Embassy, the two leaders tried to flesh out the SALT framework they agreed in Vladivostok. The discussion was the most confusing I ever witnessed at summit conferences. It was now a pattern: Brezhnev started with generalities, but moving to complex specifics, he was quickly lost. It was hard for Ford as well. Gromyko and Kissinger took over, while the two leaders looked on helplessly.

The problem for the USSR was that the US led in long-range cruise missile development. Moscow wanted to cap them for as long as possible. The crucial issue for the US was Soviet sea-based cruise missiles with a range between 300 and 500 kilometers. Kissinger said they could hit forty per cent of American cities along the coast. The US is unable to counter since most Russian cities are located deep in the land mass. The alternative, Kissinger went on, was either to allow for more US long-range cruise missiles or move Russian cities to the coast. "This was actually proposed by our Secretary of Defense," he added mockingly. "Move Russian cities!" (The reference to Melvin Laird was not included in the US record of the conversation.)

"Put them on barges, or what?" laughed Brezhnev. "I expected you to propose moving our own cities inland," said Kissinger. Geography and national history complicated negotiations.

Another problem was the Soviet "Backfire" aircraft. It bedeviled negotiations for years. As Nixon did before, Ford insisted it was a heavy bomber. Brezhnev repeated it was a medium bomber. The Americans were less than candid about the aircraft (Tu-22M). It could reach the US only if refueled in mid-air. Gromyko once shamed Kissinger: taken to extremes, even a fighter jet could be termed strategic if it was refueled three or four times in flight.

In a highly technical discussion, Kissinger kept saying that range depended on speed, altitude and load. General Kozlov patiently explained that at 18,000 meters with minimal load the radius would be only 2,200 kilometers. With a tailwind, probably 2,400 kilometers. Kissinger tried to argue with Kozlov, but stopped in time - he was facing a military expert.

Brezhnev was annoyed. He repeated what Kozlov said. Ford referred to his intelligence analysts. Brezhnev said Soviet intelligence tells him the US is converting light missiles into heavy ones. He suggested that intelligence experts should negotiate "instead of us."

They were going around in circles. At last, Kissinger decided to relax his obstinate position. He suggested a formal reiteration of the plane's performance at optimal speed and altitude, and that the airframe would not be changed - all this to be signed by the General Secretary!

Brezhnev almost blew his top. To check the aircraft's true range, he said, let us put Sonnenfeldt on board, fill it up and try to fly it to New York. As to the airframe, we will build a fuselage stretching from Archangelsk to Washington! He turned away, fuming.

American arguments held no water. Soviet experts suspected that the US held the Backfire issue for a trade-off at some later stage. This proved correct. In a memo for Kissinger, Bill Hyland advised him to hold firm on counting the aircraft in the aggregate strategic weapons levels "if only to preserve some bargaining leverage."[60] In September, Kissinger admitted to Alexis Johnson that including "Backfire" was "an outrage, a fraud;" if it was strategic, then any one-way mission system is strategic, including FBS, and the Soviets gave up on that.[61] (Ford yielded in the end; "Backfire" was not counted against the total number of strategic delivery vehicles.)

All through the heated discussion, Chernenko, who sat on my right, remained silent. He started when I asked Ford to autograph a stamped commemorative CSCE envelope. I already had signatures of Harold Wilson, Giscard d'Estaing and Brezhnev. Chernenko asked me if I could get him an autographed envelope too. I handed Ford an extra envelope to sign. He obliged. Chernenko was delighted. I thought this little favor would do no harm to our future relations.

The shift in the US position was evident; White House transition was taking its toll. During a coffee break, Brezhnev buttonholed Kissinger and said he complained to Ford that Henry ignored a Soviet proposal on cruise missiles. In his best acid tone, Kissinger replied he did it on his own, in total violation of the President's instructions; now he was in deep trouble. He quickly added, "Since Gromyko became Politburo member he's more difficult to talk to." Gromyko let that remark pass. For the Soviet team, the bleak conclusion was that the new Administration's attitude was hardening. (Kissinger was telling foreign visitors that US strategy was "to weaken the Soviet Union."[62] If that was true, the Soviet military build-up seemed a sensible response.)

The mini-summit in Helsinki showed that the USSR was getting less from détente than it expected. MFN and credit arrangements were collapsing. The harvest was bad. The USSR was being sidelined in the Middle East. SALT stalled (it was one reason why Brezhnev postponed his trip to the US). The Soviet Union made massive concessions on FBS and verification, but the US refused to meet it half way. In Moscow's opinion, after Vladivostok the US went for a new arms race.

The two hard-working teams found a moment to relax at a strawberry and cream and champagne reception hosted by President Kekkonen on Luonnon-Maa Island. The Soviet delegation boasted of specialists in every European language - they followed Brezhnev around like a wolf pack, led by Alexander Ignatiev, the MFA's ablest Finnish interpreter. Some never saw Brezhnev before and were jittery. I gave them quick advice on handling the General Secretary. Our Hungarian expert Nikita Darchiev's sidesplitting impersonations of some high officials also helped.

Brent Scowcroft, Bill Hyland, Jan Lodal, Victor and I sauntered from the bar to the lawn and toasted the conference success. After listening to a few humorous stories about our masters, Bill looked around: "This détente has gone too far, where are our allies?" Bi-polar super power mentality was thrilling; we belonged to a restricted club. In the meantime, we might as well make our job socially gratifying.

As I walked back from the bar with a second gin and tonic, somebody touched my sleeve - an American colleague with whom we long shared a tongue-in-cheek attitude towards our leaders. He gently pulled me aside. Lowering his voice, he said he wanted to talk about SALT. "Sure," I said, "Why don't you tell me your fallback position?" "Andrey," he said, "Henry will kill me for this, but you should know..." A faint smile never leaving his face, he proceeded to describe Kissinger's tactics for next day's discussion, which was to focus on controversial Soviet weaponry - heavy missiles, the "Backfire" bomber and sea-based cruise missiles.

My first thought was, "This can't be happening." I turned around slowly: nobody was watching. A roar of laughter from a small crowd surrounding Brezhnev and Giscard d'Estaing - I heard the voice of Nikolai Afanasievsky, our French interpreter (future Ambassador to France).

I asked my friend to repeat the figures he quoted; he did, adding that he thought the Soviet side was getting a raw deal. The information was startling enough, no less than the informant. Our conversation took no more than three minutes. He walked away. I finished my drink. I realized I did not thank him; but there are situations when a "thank you" sounds out of place. Collecting intelligence about the intentions of the adversary is vital for developing negotiating tactics. This work went around the clock, and summit conferences were no exception. A morning briefing for Brezhnev by the Chief of the local KGB *rezidentura* was the rule in all our travels. All the same, I was an unlikely conduit.

I took the conference shuttle van to town. The white five-deck *Mikhail Kalinin* moored at the pier was luminous in the setting sun; the high stack displayed the golden hammer and sickle on a wide red band. The young sailor at the gangway saluted as I showed him my pass. I walked by the deserted swimming pool and down the narrow corridor to cabin 201, where I took off my tie and changed into a sweater. I went to another section of the ship and knocked on Victor's cabin door. We went to see Georgy Kornienko. He might be in bed, but this could not wait. He shrugged off the remains of sleep and, never voluble, said, "Interesting." He asked me to repeat the figures.

Next morning at the Soviet Embassy, Brezhnev and Gromyko stalled on figures. Kissinger was angry: he had to back down. I do not think the episode perceptibly changed the dynamics of the negotiation - the stakes were too high, but it was a point won by the Russians.

I saw my American friend; we smiled at each other as if nothing happened. He was perfectly at ease, so I gathered he did not speak on impulse. I was at a loss about motives for the indiscretion. Was a stool pigeon trying to worm his way into our secret chambers? Was it genuine desire to let Russia play a level field, or sympathy for the USSR? Sweet revenge in office politics? Kissinger's staff was too independent to show the other cheek every time. His insolence towards subordinates was embarrassing; he did not mind the presence of strangers. I sympathized with them. Once he lambasted a staffer in my presence: "I'll kill you for this!" He watched me for effect and grinned. I smiled back. Surely, he was kidding - were his rages genuine?

I don't think open or thinly veiled threats were always hurled in vain. Kissinger liked the devious move, the cloak and dagger.... As Vietnam and Chile showed, queasiness was not regarded as a virtue. In 1969, he was so desperate about winning in Vietnam that he lobbied for using a nuclear bomb.[63] In late 1972, when South Vietnam's president Thieu was getting obstinate, he warned, "We'll kill the s.o.b. if we have to." Strangulation was mentioned. (Soviet leaders would have welcomed the option.)

I reflected on yet another explanation. The gravitational attraction of the two superpowers was felt most at the top. It was a peculiar feeling, placed as we were close to the leaders: we belonged to a single team striving for a common goal. In the exhilarating atmosphere of newly found solidarity, the desire to achieve quick results tended to obscure formal barriers and traditional rules.

I did not enquire if there was a follow-up to the episode. I doubted it. Diplomats walk a thin high wire occasionally, and the degree of indiscretion one is willing to show is in proportion to information obtained from the other side. What happened here was a voluntary act, without anything asked in return. The story nagged me for a long time: was I talking to the original Deep Throat, or Deep Throat-2? Some things figured, some did not. Over the years, the Watergate whistleblower's identity remained a mystery. Dozens were under suspicion, narrowed down to a handful close to Nixon: even Ron Ziegler and Steve Bull were mentioned by self-appointed sleuths. When W. Mark Felt, FBI Associate Director, made his confession in 2005, I noticed an odd coincidence: he started supplying information to *Washington Post* reporters Bob Woodward and Carl Bernstein in May 1972, just as Nixon embarked on his epoch-making trip to the USSR. Felt never had access to summit briefs and was not involved in negotiations. I was intrigued when the two reporters claimed that "many other sources and officials" assisted them and other reporters for the hundreds of stories published in the *Washington Post* about Watergate. Curiously, when Woodward wanted a meeting, he would position an empty flowerpot with a red flag on his balcony.[64]

In the ensuing years, I followed the career of the person who approached me at the cocktail party, and wished him well. I was anxious about the wiretapping Kissinger practiced on White House staff.

The signing ceremony of the 30,000-word Helsinki Final Act was the peak of Scandinavian organization. The dignitaries sat on the stage in Finlandia Hall in a long arc in alphabetical order. Secretariat officials carried the thick leather-bound document and placed it in turn before each to sign. Each page had the names of two countries with the leaders' titles in the six official languages of the conference, i.e., German, Spanish, French, English, Italian and Russian. The two Germanys signed first: Chancellor Helmut Schmidt of the Federal Republic and Erich Honecker, First Secretary of the Central Committee of the Socialist Unity Party of Germany. The FRG had its way: the two states sat next to each other.

After the ceremony, I peeked at the volume: the leaders were denoted by first and family name; only Brezhnev was a terse "L. Brezhnev." The British Prime Minister had a lengthy string of letters attached, "The Rt. Hon. Harold Wilson, O.B.E., M.P., F.R.S." - a riddle for uninitiated. Tito would have beaten Wilson in any contest of titles and war medals; he chose not to. Prime Minister Dom Mintoff failed to show up – perhaps he got wind of Kissinger's radical proposal to solve "the Mintoff problem." The Maltese Ambassador signed the Final Act instead. He crouched between the rows of seats collecting autographs for Mintoff. Some delegates did not mask their disgust.

The night before, I went to Finlandia Hall to oversee typing of the authentic Russian text. I saw a young West German delegate. With typical German precision, he made sure the loaded coma (in the frontiers principle) stayed in the Russian version. He also tried, at this late stage, to tinker with the Russian name of his country, Federal Republic of Germany - "*Federalnaya*

Respublika Germanii" (possessive case), by putting it in nominative case - *"Federalnaya Respublika Germania."* I told him this was not possible either politically or grammatically (it translated back into English as "Federal Republic Germany"), and warned of terrible consequences. He withdrew.

Chinese reaction to the Final Act was tactless: the *People's Daily* said it was "empty and worthless." The USSR thought differently: the Act solidified the territorial status quo in Europe, including the border between the two German States, i.e., the dividing line between the Socialist and the capitalist world, and between NATO and the Warsaw Pact. This was a Soviet objective of long standing, based as it was in fears of a revanchist Germany. The West was pleased as well, having obtained strong obligations on a freer movement of people and ideas. For this, Mikhail Suslov wanted Soviet delegate Kovalyov fired. He received a medal instead on Brezhnev's insistence, as did we in the MFA team.

We packed our bags and prepared to leave. I had several memcons to complete, but I planned to do them in Moscow. There is nothing like the exhilarating sense of release after an exhausting assignment. Victor and I looked forward to a relaxed cruise to Leningrad in pleasant company on board the *Kalinin* - it had become a home.

Chernenko raised objections to the plan: Sukhodrev and Vavilov should not travel together: suppose they both perish at sea? Can we risk losing Comrade Brezhnev's unfinished records still fresh in their memory?

It is difficult to argue against a point out of logic. What if Brezhnev sailed on the *Kalinin* and suffered a similar fate? My carefully phrased opinion was ignored. I confessed I took most of the notes. An obedient civil servant, I boarded Brezhnev's IL-62 in dreary official company. Victor headed for Helsinki Port with the girl secretaries and MFA friends.

After landing at Vnukovo in the afternoon, I drove home, dropped off my bags and headed for the Ministry to dictate the remaining memcons. It took me a full day. Early next morning, on a stiflingly hot Sunday, I called Chernenko's office at the Central Committee in Staraya Ploshad. They confirmed the boss was in. I went by Metro to deliver the transcripts in person. It was quicker than dispatching them through the Kremlin messenger service.

Chernenko might have questions - he better read the memcons in my presence. The dictation amounted to 45 pages, double-spaced. The thirty-minute ride downtown in the cool and spotless underground was refreshing.

I showed my Communist Party membership card to the KGB guard at the staff entrance. This was standard procedure: unless you were an employee of the Central Committee you had to show your Party card to gain admission - a Foreign Ministry pass was not enough. My name was on the list. The guard leafed through my card, a thin maroon booklet, pretending to check payment of monthly dues (three per cent of salary). I knew he looked for a typographical oddity, a tiny letter slightly different from the card's miniscule font. This was a nifty way of checking if the Party card was genuine. It was the Russian "я" (pronounced "*ya*") on a certain page. The guard saluted and waved me in.

I took the elevator to the fifth floor. It was deserted but I could hear signs of activity in a nearby office. A male secretary swung open the door of a spacious Spartan study. Chernenko rose in greeting. His hand was limp; he wheezed (he suffered from asthma and emphysema). He looked disapprovingly at my light orange bush shirt; he was in long-sleeves and tie. His expression changed when I handed him the light blue Foreign Ministry folder with the memcons. He looked as if he was receiving a priceless gift; he handled the folder with care. He offered me tea with lemon and small bagels. He was a quick reader. He had no questions and shook my hand again. I walked down the stairs, showed my Party card to the same guard, and stepped out into the August sun. The Old Square looked peaceful on the weekend; there were few cars. Muscovites had left the smoldering city for their dachas, the forests and river beaches. I felt a free man.

QUIET DAYS IN CRIMEA

Ten days after the Helsinki Conference, on the second day of my well-earned leave, a call came from Brezhnev's office. The General Secretary agreed to meet a group of US Congressmen at his summer residence in Yalta. The Central Committee logistics department has already arranged my travel.

The flight took two hours; I had a reserved seat in the front row of the forward section. Special treatment came in the form of drinks. The captain asked if everything was OK. He suspected I was on an important mission.

To my dismay, the treatment did not extend to my arrival at Simferopol Airport. Nobody to meet me; there was no car. I could use the trolleybus connection to the coast about sixty miles away (the world's longest line), but I would not find Brezhnev's residence. It would look strange asking for directions at the bus stop. I walked to the VIP pavilion and asked for the KGB duty officer. He made calls on the secure high frequency line to the Yalta Mayor's office, the Crimea Regional Party Committee, and to several government dachas. He said he did not have Brezhnev's dacha number - perhaps he was telling the truth. At last, I got hold of a Gromyko bodyguard I knew. He reached the Chief of the Crimean KGB in his car. After a few minutes, the Deputy Regional Head of Crimea called me, with profuse regrets and terrible oaths to punish the culprits; his assistant will drive me to the coast.

The assistant, an unruffled gray-haired war veteran, told me not to worry: "Leonid Ilyich is not some needle in a haystack." From the deserted Yalta Mayor's office (it was a Sunday), he reached Brezhnev's dacha. They confirmed my status; a car will pick me up in the morning. I checked in at the Yalta Hotel. Perhaps my travails were indicative of the administrative sloppiness growing like a tumor around the ailing Brezhnev, compounded by traditional Russian indifference to the possibility that things may go wrong.

Brezhnev received the Congressmen in "Small Dacha 3." The two-story structure is perched high above Yalta, hidden in the shady cool of a cedar forest. Its southern glass wall overlooks the Black Sea in the distance. They used the place for mid-summer conferences of East European leaders, who also spent part of their summer holidays in Crimea (Ceausescu skipped the meetings).

The conversation was nothing spectacular. Brezhnev dutifully read the talking points prepared by the Foreign Ministry about the prospects of US-Soviet relations, the need for expanded trade (the Jackson-Vanik amendment as the main obstacle) and the continuance of détente. Questions posed by the Congressmen were straightforward enough: restrictions on Jewish emigration and Russian arms sales. Brezhnev parried those sluggishly with standard replies.

At the end of the meeting, Congressman Sidney Yates raised his hand: "May I ask Chairman Khrushchev for an autograph?" His colleagues giggled. I did not correct Yates and Brezhnev did not notice. Another Congressman reached over and gave him an *Apollo-Soyuz* cigarette pack to sign. The Philip Morris/Glavtabak venture commemorated the 1975 joint US-USSR manned space mission. Others followed. Yates asked me if there was any significance in the General Secretary signing cigarette packs. I said I did not think so: the white packs were lying freely on the table, and were as good as anything was for an autograph. Yates asked no more questions.

I dictated my notes to Brezhnev's secretary and returned to the hotel. The three-hour job done, the Mayor of Yalta offered hospitality "for as long as I wished." Since I was technically on vacation, I stayed for another three days to loaf on the beach and swim in the sea. Resort hotels were cheap in the USSR, often free for trade union members, so I did not strain the Crimean budget.

In January 1976, Kissinger came to Moscow to work on a backlog of issues, because Brezhnev kept postponing his US trip. I was skiing in the Caucuses and hard to locate. Victor shared some tidbits from the talks. Several times Brezhnev addressed Kissinger as "Comrade Kissinger." Henry said calling him like that will not be without impact on the primaries - Jackson and Reagan would be grateful. Brezhnev suggested sending him to Leningrad. Kissinger clapped his hands in delight: "In a "Backfire" bomber!" Brezhnev reminded him that it did not have the range to return. "But it can be refueled in midair," Gromyko said.

The General Secretary presented a Russian watch to Sonnenfeldt. Kissinger warned his associate that the Russian dentist who treated him might have put a transmitter in his tooth. Brezhnev broke out laughing. The watch, Kissinger continued, must be for picking up conversations if the tooth failed. I know it sends, Kissinger said, but can it also receive?

Meanwhile, the US-Soviet scene deteriorated. Angola became a factor straining relations. Despite pressure by Kissinger, Gromyko refused to assume responsibility for the Cuban contingent fighting on the side of President Agostinho Neto, although he admitted Moscow shipped a few tanks to the legitimate government. By spring of 1976, Ford had second thoughts about the term "détente." Despite Kissinger's advice, he stopped using it altogether in his speeches. He broke with his initial embrace of "irreversibility." Perceptions in Moscow changed: Ford was lukewarm to détente and weak regarding its enemies in the US. In November, Ford lost the election to Democratic candidate Jimmy Carter. Brezhnev's second trip to America was shelved altogether.

In the years that followed, I did occasional translating for Brezhnev but felt like a leftover from the Nixon years. Victor had the same impression. We concentrated on our substantive subjects - disarmament in my case and the British desk in his. The Russian *Amerikanisti* team stayed the same, with perpetual Gromyko at the head, Dobrynin going into his third Ambassadorial decade in Washington, and Kornienko watching over US-Soviet relations at home. They did not let Victor and me far from the circle; there never was total respite.

Brezhnev's health continued to deteriorate: it was sad watching the once vigorous and magnetic person slowly turning into a physical wreck. Sometime in 1974, I was walking in the Kremlin grounds with his secretary Vika. She told me Brezhnev had almost stopped working (he was 67) and was holed up for weeks in Zavidovo. His colleagues hesitated to call him. Vika said, "I was at the *pominki* (remembrance meal) in the Kremlin for his mother. She was close to 90 - Leonid Ilyich often said he wished to live to that age. All guests, from cabinet members to gardeners, assembled in three large adjacent rooms. He talked about his mother and proposed a toast to her memory. His words were transmitted by loudspeaker in all rooms. Then he proceeded to the adjoining room and spoke again, in almost the same words; and to the third room where they were repeated. It was weird."

I could trace Brezhnev's lapses back to 1972. He failed to find the memo he wanted to read out to Kissinger in September. He would deviate from his brief and confuse dates and figures. At one session, he insisted the US had deployed ten thousand MIRVs. Kissinger was incredulous and kept repeating, "Ten thousand MIRVs?" Brezhnev did not explain. He was impatient. Nixon and Kissinger always listened closely to his long passages, but Brezhnev would often interrupt to react to a statement he did not like. He tended to replace hard bargaining with frivolous conversation.

One morning in August 1978, my office phone rang. It was the Deputy Minister of Foreign Trade: would I be available to fly with Dr. Armand Hammer, the industrialist and art collector, to Crimea for a meeting with Brezhnev? He quickly added that the General Secretary's assistant did not object to commandeering me.

Hammer was 80, a small, wiry and ambitious man still on the go. His wife Frances, an alert and inquisitive woman, was twenty years his junior. I picked them up at their five-room apartment in a quiet street off the Tretyakov Art Gallery. We had coffee. Russian old masters adorned the walls. As we rode in a black Chaika limousine to Vnukovo, Hammer told me that in the last two weeks he dined with the King of Morocco, joined Prince Charles at an exhibition in Edinburgh and opened a chemical factory in Odessa. His next appointment, after meeting Brezhnev, will be with Colonel Qaddafi in Tripoli. Names like that never failed to impress me. He talked with pride of the recent inauguration of the world's biggest fertilizer terminal in Grigorievka on the Black Sea, a hundred miles from the city of Kherson, the birthplace of his father. It was part of the largest East-West business deal in history - $20 billion - involving a swap of Soviet ammonia, urea and potash for US super phosphoric acid.

Hammer had a standing invitation from generations of Soviet leaders starting from Lenin. Perhaps one might call him an agent of influence. The FBI probably regarded him a fellow traveler. He was astute and careful to play both sides to his own gain - political and financial. Brezhnev respected him.

We flew in a Russian executive jet to Simferopol. It was red carpet treatment: a ZIL-114 limousine drove us to the coast for less time than the flight lasted, slightly over two hours. Highway police stood at attention, having waved hundreds of cars to the shoulders: Brezhnev's hospitality extended to traffic control.

Yalta had poignancy for Hammer. It was here that Olga Vadina, a Russian cabaret singer, swept the 23-old American doctor off his feet. Olga died several years later, leaving him a son. Today, the Soviet Navy took Armand sailing along the beautifully rugged Crimean coast. We disembarked at the pier, amidst scantily dressed and perplexed sunbathers. We drove around. Hammer said he could not recognize the town. We went wine tasting at the Massandra vineyards, where Hammer instructed me in vintage brands.

We stayed in a palace built high above Yalta for Tsar Alexander III as a pleasure retreat. The Hammers were assigned an elegant suite, and I a bedroom with ornate heavy furniture. After a light brunch, palace caretaker Masha, a prim woman with a healthy tan, came to see me. She lowered her voice: "Andrey Mikhailovitch, they ate very little. I hope they liked the food; it is fresh and nutritious. Another thing, Mr. Hammer is rummaging in the closets and inspecting every plate and saucer. Will you please tell him there's nothing of value here?" I promised to do that. Did she enjoy her palace job? "Well, I am almost fifty, and still KGB Sergeant," she said.

I told the Hammers the story of the place. After the 1917 Revolution, it was requisitioned for a Government rest home. In 1941, the Germans occupied Crimea and turned the palace into a Wehrmacht officers' hospital. Fleeing the Red Army, they carried away the paintings, crockery and even some antique furniture. After the war, the palace was stocked with government-issue replacements.

Unable to resist, Hammer lifted a saucer and peered at the bottom. The plate was bone china but obviously not good enough. He put it down. Back in the 1920s, he bought priceless art objects from Lenin's government at the cheap: the country needed food and medical supplies.

Around 6:00 p.m., as we were getting into the car, a motorcade swished by with a police Volga in the lead: a Mercedes, a Volvo and a Rolls-Royce. I saw the last two cars in Zavidovo. "That's your host," I told Hammer. We drove several miles up a winding mountain road to the same glass-walled dacha where Brezhnev received US Congressmen in 1975.

Leonid Ilyich stood in the hall waiting for his guest. He looked unwell. The two old men embraced in silence and sat down at a large oak table; they were pleased to see each other. I sat next to Brezhnev. After a few welcoming words, Hammer launched into a tirade of brazen praise. I put down my pen: this should not be on paper. He spoke about his meeting with Lenin in 1921. I heard this opening before: he employed it with all Soviet leaders, possibly except Trotsky and Stalin. This time he improved on the story: "Lenin impressed me so much that if he told me to jump out of the Kremlin window I'd have gladly done so!" (Fortunately, the idea never crossed Lenin's mind; he appreciated young Armand circumventing Western trade restrictions. Hammer was surely aware that Lenin's second floor study was not exactly a sheer cliff drop to the lawn below).

Hammer delivered the punch line, "You, Mr. Brezhnev, are the true successor to Lenin. Not Stalin or Khrushchev, but you!" Brezhnev brooded for a while, and neither confirmed nor denied this remarkable proposition. He drawled defensively, "Whatever people think about Stalin, he did a lot for his country."

Hammer turned to his current pet project: arranging a Brezhnev-Carter summit meeting. "You are both at a disadvantage - there's no personal contact," he explained. "Carter is a good man but naïve. He was a farmer; his hometown has a population of five hundred. If you talk to him as you do to me, he will believe you and tell Congress that you desire peace. Frances and I had breakfast with him just before leaving the States, and he told me he was ready to meet you any place you wish. An early meeting is important to get you to know each other... How about Poland? Gierek is ready to invite both of you to Warsaw." Evidently, Hammer was delivering a White House message. The signals started reaching Moscow several months before.

Despite his mounting weariness, Brezhnev parried Hammer's assault citing the need to create "necessary conditions" for a summit, in particular, by bringing more shape to the SALT-2 treaty. "However long we discuss this," he said finally, shifting uncomfortably in his chair, "I can't deviate from my formula."

High points for you, Leonid Ilyich, I thought, you are true to the brief.

Hammer was distraught, but he was amply rewarded a minute later. Brezhnev suddenly announced that Francis Crawford, an International Harvester executive arrested for currency speculation on the black market, would be deported following his imminent sentencing by a Russian court. (The case attracted much press in the US, and the State Department sought to use Hammer's standing in Russia to resolve it amicably. The previous month, he wrote to Brezhnev stressing the volatile publicity that a trial would bring. He suggested that the authorities simply throw the man out for the sake of détente and bilateral trade. The Crawford case was linked to the arrest of two members of the Soviet UN delegation on espionage charges. The arrangement was to release them after serving short stretches. Several dissidents would be permitted to leave Russia.)

Hammer clapped his hands in delight. "This is the best piece of news I can carry from the Soviet Union! Crawford is a crook; I saw the evidence. Do invite reporters to the court hearing. I'll tell Carter about this!"

A waiter brought in a tray of small glasses with strong *Zubrovka* (Bison Grass vodka). This was not a good idea. We drank. Suddenly, Brezhnev turned to his aide Anatoly Blatov and, pointing at me, whispered, "Who is this?" "Our comrade from the Foreign Ministry," whispered Blatov back, calmly. There was a flicker of recognition in Brezhnev's eyes, but they clouded over again. He fumbled with the metal band of his wristwatch and accidentally unclasped it. Blatov helped to clasp it back.

I was dumbfounded. I thought of a story our French-language interpreter told me about Brezhnev in Rambouillet, illustrating both his loss of memory for faces and language prowess. Towards the end of a grand *dejeuner,* the palace waiters went round with coffee. The Russian Ambassador, in a desire to serve beyond the call of duty, grabbed the tray from the waiter and leaned over Brezhnev's shoulder. "Coffee, Leonid Ilyich?" he asked in Russian. The General Secretary turned, stared at the Ambassador in astonishment and gasped, in German, "Nein, nein!" (He did not speak German, but had a collection of short phrases in the major languages, which he used to please his hosts. His English was restricted to "Very good," "OK" and "Goodbye.")

Brezhnev produced an illustrated history guide to Alexander III's palace. He read it aloud, stumbling over jaw-breaking words not chosen for their brevity, like *mramorovidniy izvestnyak* (marble-like limestone, or semimarmo). He finished reading, laid the booklet aside and beamed at Hammer. Hammer beamed back.

The magic moment came: exchange of gifts. At Hammer's signal, a baroque leather bag was brought in with a set of golf clubs. This seemed like a joke in bad taste. The other present was more proper - a box of commemorative coins to mark the 1980 Olympic Games in Moscow. "We're going to mint 150 million," said Hammer.

The *pièce de résistance* was a red Mercedes-Benz 280 (not brought in). Hammer explained the symbolism: red is the color of Revolution, and Brezhnev is leader of the world's revolutionaries. The interior is black leather, he added.

The thought of driving a fire-brigade vehicle across Red Square seemed to trouble Brezhnev, and he turned to Blatov: "What shall we do?" Blatov whispered back, "Express our gratitude." Hammer's tactful reaction was quick: "The car is still in Germany, and can be repainted." Brezhnev nodded, as if giving consent to the job. He presented his guest with a jewel box incrusted with semi-precious stones from the Ural Mountains. Hammer lifted the lid - it was empty.

Hammer produced a thick volume, his biography written by Bob Considine (*Larger than Life*). "Could this be published in the USSR in Russian?" he asked.

Brezhnev did not react.

"It may be abridged."

A pause.

"I'll pay for publication."

Brezhnev nodded. (Excellent negotiating tactics, Leonid Ilyich!)

After Hammer left, Blatov asked me what I thought about the publication proposal. I said Brezhnev's word should be honored. (In 1981, "Progress Publishers" printed 50,000 copies of the Russian translation in abridged form. After Brezhnev's death, Hammer updated it in line with changes in the Soviet leadership. They printed 100,000 copies in 1988. Little remained of Brezhnev, but Mikhail Gorbachev figured prominently.)

The two men spent three hours in conversation, and were tired. Brezhnev accompanied Hammer to the car. Hammer supported him on one side and a bodyguard on the other. The industrialist could not resist a parting pleasantry: "I achieved everything I wished in life. I do not need money. I donated a cancer research institute. My only objective is to establish good relations between the US and the USSR. If God grants you another thirty years, you may turn the world around!" They kissed each other on the cheek, Russian fashion. The Hammers left for the airport. I stayed behind to dictate the memcon.

On arrival in London, Hammer told the press "he never saw Brezhnev in better shape." He brought a scoop: hapless Crawford will get a light sentence and possibly be deported.

Back at the palace, Masha laid out a simple supper and asked if I minded spending the night alone - she was eager to get back to her family. She showed me the trip wires across garden paths. There would be a sentry outside the gate. A car would pick me up in the morning. She led me to a well-stocked fridge; I assured her I could prepare my own breakfast.

It was past ten, on a moonlit night. I inspected the palace. The furniture was nondescript, heavy oak and cedar *circa* 1950s; the regulation Uzbek carpets were the same as in the Kremlin or any other government office. The paintings on the walls belonged to recent artists: mostly nature scenes. In his memoir, Hammer was exuberant about the palace; he loved dramatizing. He told me once that his life's dream was to buy "Arm and Hammer," the baking soda company with the realistic logo, but they refused to sell.

I went for a stroll in the garden, stepping over the wires. The view from the second story balcony was magnificent. A hundred years ago, Alexander III must have stood here, gazing at the mountain crest sharply outlined against a rising moon.

In the morning, a KGB driver put a box of fresh Crimean peaches and apples into the car trunk. When I protested, he explained this was government property and would perish if not consumed by local staff or friendly agencies. Traffic was light to the airport.

Hugging Jimmy Carter in Vienna

While nobody missed Gerald Ford in Moscow, there were varied opinions about Jimmy Carter. Younger MFA staff leaned towards giving the new US President the benefit of the doubt. We were aware that American politicians artistically managed youthful vigor. Carter's face was lined, but he ran up the steps of the Presidential aircraft carrying a garment bag and a briefcase - perhaps they were not entirely empty. The aging Soviet leaders never carried briefcases, bags or files. They expected personal aides and even bodyguards to do bellhop duties. The interpreters were not immune, although we shunned the menial tasks: imagine holding a briefcase, interpreting and scribbling notes while standing. On trips to Asia, I carried a supply of small transparent plastic bags filled with rubbing alcohol to be handed unobtrusively to the leader when he put his hands behind his back. He crushed the bag - the hands were disinfected.

In New York, I watched the TV anchormen heating up to the Presidential race. I suggested a poll in the policy section of the Soviet Permanent Mission. Betting was a dollar per head. Proceeds would go to a post-election office party on the sixth floor overlooking the NYPD 19th Precinct. As the results came in, I opened the ballot box (they used it for the New York Party Cell elections) and announced that the overwhelming majority of staff voted in favor of Carter. Two junior diplomats were sent to Kasey's Kitchen, a corner diner on Third Avenue, for beer and sandwiches. As we drank to new expectations, the Deputy Permanent Representative suggested that our vote for Carter did not mean we preferred him to Ford; rather it showed our expectations of the election results. As always, he was right. Carter's fascination with the plight of dissidents in Russia was to solidify positions on both sides and was counterproductive. His mother's visit to the Vatican to ask the Pope to pray for them antagonized even the dissidents in the Russian Orthodox Church.

Back in Moscow, I attended a meeting in the Foreign Ministry's conference hall to listen to Gromyko. His expositions were instructive. They set out foreign policy priorities and were useful for briefs diplomats would prepare in the months ahead. He spoke without notes. The size of the audience was in opposite proportion to his candor. His discourses before large audiences were tedious. In intimate surroundings, he made incisive observations, including on the role the MFA should play in the power game against domestic adversaries, especially in the Ministry of Defense. He spoke about Jimmy Carter. "We in the Politburo," he said, "watched him closely and expected new language regarding the Soviet Union; we got used to a Republican Administration. Carter's policy carries some continuity from the previous government, but he has introduced new elements that complicate, rather than ease, our relations with the US... American positions on a number of issues have hardened. There are attempts to gain unilateral military advantage, which complicates disarmament negotiations. Despite assurances, there is no tangible progress on trade. The problem of human rights existed before, but Nixon never gave it more attention than it deserved. Carter raised it to priority level, and turned its sharp point against us... There was no such problem in US-Soviet relations; you will not find single American diplomatic note on the issue in the archives. Now the file is overflowing. I wonder what Carter would say about Iran where human rights are being violated, and where the CIA has hundreds of agents; or Chile, Southern Rhodesia, Namibia, South Africa..."

Gromyko let the biting remarks sink in, and continued. "Still, the Carter Administration is a fact, and the USSR must build its foreign policy accordingly; we cannot engage in "a wall-against-wall fight" (the allusion was to an ancient Russian village sport of a "wall" of fist fighters battling another "wall"). Curbing the arms race is a "first category" issue; it has important repercussions for the basic cultural, political and economic interests of all countries, and is crucial for life itself. Carter's views are different: he regards nuclear non-proliferation and the test ban as "peripheral" treaties of limited significance. The Western powers are not willing to stop the arms race; they are not ready to resolve the historic contest between the two systems in peaceful competition; in essence, they are against arms control based on equality."

Gromyko had barbed comments about other NATO countries. He said West Germany "loved to teach others how to behave, which is a German trait," but our relations with them are a priority in Europe. He admitted that the FRG complied with the Helsinki Final Act. He said France entertained strong suspicions about West Germany, and did not want reunification though would never say so publicly. Frenchmen "remember Germans marching on their land." France has a strong interest in maintaining stable relations with the Soviet Union. We managed to convince them that our common interest lies in cooperation, rather than military confrontation. He commended French leaders who "in matters of principle" continue the policies of de Gaulle and Pompidou.

Gromyko's view of Britain was condescending: the British were dismally failing to speak with an independent voice and served American interests. The UK raised the flag of human rights while shooting people in Northern Ireland and supporting Rhodesia. "The British don't have the strength to stand up to us. But we're not in a hurry; we can wait for relations to improve."

He reserved derisive language for China: relations were as strained as in the times of Mao. Direct border clashes gave way to "unbridled anti-Soviet propaganda." Let us proceed, he continued, from the objective interest of China to improve relations with the USSR, and, while not condoning belligerence, let us try to ignore propagandistic attacks. The Chinese understand little of what is happening in their country, so we should aim at normalizing relations, however difficult it may be. (In fact, gradual normalization started the following year.)

Turning briefly to the Middle East, Gromyko suggested Egyptian president Anwar Sadat renounced Nasser's bequest by signing the Camp David agreements - "he opted for American dollars and Israeli support." Let the Arabs sort out their national interests for themselves...

As usual, the Minister called on staff "to show initiative" in finding new avenues and exploring new ideas. He stepped down from the podium to reserved applause. We were in for troubled times.

In September 1978, Brezhnev received members of the American-Soviet Trade and Economic Council. The group was led by Armco Steel Chairman C. William Verity. It included Michael Forrestal, whose father, the US Secretary of Defense, was a Cold War icon. In 1949, hounded by visions of a

Communist invasion, he flung himself from a sixteenth-story window of the Bethesda Naval Hospital.

I arrived early in the Kremlin. The warm rays of the autumn sun streamed through the high double windows of Brezhnev's spacious study and made patterns on the Samarkand carpet. There was no sign of recent activity. Brezhnev's desk was tidy: no "In" or "Out" trays. The Chelsea Claremont Ship clock was still there. Next to it were a compact East German alarm clock, a desk calendar and two trays filled with paper clips, badges, keys and small change. The telephone console to the left of the armchair bore a sign in large letters: "PLEASE LIFT RECEIVER." Brezhnev kept forgetting to do this, and visitors were occasionally exposed to private conversations.

The door to the rest area opened and Brezhnev walked in accompanied by Alexandrov; he greeted me like an old acquaintance. The American party was ushered into the room: smiles all around.

Verity said he knew of the General Secretary's "love of gadgets," and produced a strange contraption that resembled a nickel-plated mushroom. He said it was an "innovative clock." He pressed it: the clock chimed the hour and then the minute in a higher tone (handy for the vision-impaired, I thought). He also gave Brezhnev a beautifully crafted silver scale model of the Yankee Clipper, which, he said, led the way to trade between the two countries 150 years ago. Photographs were taken. We took our seats, the Americans facing the windows.

Verity slid a book across the table, the English edition of Brezhnev's biography. He wanted to have it autographed for President Carter. Brezhnev looked helplessly at Alexandrov, who whispered in his ear, "It's alright, Leonid Ilyich, just an autograph, they don't need a message." Brezhnev took the book and slowly signed his name with a black felt-tipped pen. Part of the scrawl intruded on the black portion of the cover. Carter would need a photo developer to decipher the signature.

The General Secretary held his notes firmly. He forgot to put on his reading glasses. He lost the line he was reading, but tracing a finger down the page, he located it. He read a paragraph twice. I translated it once. The Americans thought I omitted something important, but thought the better of asking. Translating was easy. I had before me the copy of the three-page script, with simple and short sentences typed in large bold. I did not expect Brezhnev to deviate from the text, and he did not. Alexandrov passed me a note: "A.M., please speak louder." The General Secretary had problems with hearing as well.

Brezhnev read mechanically, without conviction. The figures he quoted proved that US-Soviet trade trailed behind Finland. He said US discrimination was driving it even lower, with various Congressional amendments and political obstructions. He asked his guests to assure President Carter of Russia's desire to improve bilateral relations. It was boring, not a single new point.

Verity said he was frustrated with the US government, which used trade as a political tool. He was critical of the Jackson-Vanik amendment to the Trade Act of 1974, which linked trade to Jewish emigration. (It was to be repealed in December 2012.) It hurt emigration by provoking a Soviet backlash and precluding progress in trade. He showed interest in Russia's proposals of two dozen lucrative trade deals.

Brezhnev rose and shook hands with all of us. I turned at the door: he was standing by his desk smiling. Bathed in the soft electric light his face looked tanned. The long white silk curtains fluttered gently in the light draft.

The American visitors were sure to report to the White House about Brezhnev's frail condition. Yet, he had unfinished business to attend to, the SALT-2 treaty, which was close to completion.

Brezhnev met Jimmy Carter in Vienna at his fifth - and last - summit with an American President, from 15 to 18 June 1979. Alexandrov oversaw the drafting of position papers. A day before leaving for Vienna, he called Kornienko to say there was a problem with the *rechevka*, the talking points. Oh no, it was excellent, but too lengthy for the General Secretary in view of an "articulation problem." (Paradontosis and sleeping pills made his speech an effort.) Could

Kornienko please cut it by half? It took Kornienko twenty minutes to tighten the text. We thought striking a dozen words was barely possible.

By now, in addition to Communist Party General Secretary, Brezhnev was Chairman of the Presidium of the Supreme Soviet. By a twist of fate, he regained his old title of the 1960s. Combining the two positions made him, in effect, President of the USSR. Old habits die hard: we still referred to Brezhnev as *GenSec*. "Chairman" smacked of "Chairman Mao."

Brezhnev's four-engine IL-62 landed at Schwechat Airport on a drizzly Friday morning. He drove to the tree-lined Soviet Embassy compound in Reisnerstrasse 45-47. The two dozen members of his party checked into the Imperial Hotel in Kärntnerring. A few minutes after I opened the door of room 425, I almost broke my neck.

I threw my bag on the bed, and went to have a shower. As I lowered myself on the bath's edge to take off the shoes, I tumbled backwards: the bath was recessed. My head hit the wall and my shoulder grazed the water tap. Cold water spurted from above drenching me to the bone, as I lay dazed in the bath. After nursing my bruised shoulder and swabbing a bloody gash in the back of my head, I sat in an armchair for several minutes and looked around, cautiously. It was an old and respectable hotel. There was a double bed, an ancient creaky wardrobe and a TV set. I changed into a dark suit.

I studied the logistics brochure the Embassy attaché gave me. He told me that Adolf Hitler stayed at the Imperial with Eva Braun in March 1938 in the giddy days of the Anschluss. The brochure did not mention this. It contained the essentials, from telephone numbers of the Chancellor's office to taxi stands, the clothes pressing service and advice on how to sign bills at the restaurant ("You are not required to tip; the Embassy will be billed for all expenditures incurred"). The annotated summit program was crammed with "Reserved" and "Free" time slots, some several hours long. A confidential Embassy memo read, "The Austrians have renewed their invitation to the Opera, but this time they put it differently. If for some reason Comrade Brezhnev would not be in a position to accept the invitation, perhaps Comrade Gromyko might be interested in attending, as well as the Defense Minister, if he arrives. President Kirchshlager and Chancellor Bruno Kreisky will attend." The Opera was scheduled from 7:30 p.m. to 10:15 p.m.

According to the memo, dinner for twenty guests hosted by Jimmy Carter might present a problem: "The venue has not been agreed; Americans insist on the Ambassador's Residence, which is eight kilometers from our Embassy; they claim their Embassy lacks a proper dining room and kitchen." Suspicions ran strong: was it an American plot to wear out the General Secretary by the long car drive? Tactfully, the memo failed to mention Jimmy Carter's hobby: that morning he jogged sixteen laps around the Ambassador's residence. The General Secretary walked 120 meters (as protocol warned) from the aircraft to the car.

The memo took my mind off a bad headache. I left the room shutting the door carefully. The ghost of Herr Hitler must have aimed at bigger fish; I got off easy.

The first day in Vienna was ceremonial, laying a wreath at the Schwarzenbergplatz monument to Soviet soldiers who died liberating the city in April 1945. Brezhnev and Carter had a thirty-minute audience with the Austrian President and the Chancellor. The General Secretary wore all four of his gold stars, three small gold medals awarded for various contributions to peace and a tiny red enameled flag.

Carter wore a gray herringbone business suit. Unlike Nixon, there was no miniature American flag pin on his lapel. He was at pains to be deferential to the Soviet leader, and complained to the Austrian press: "I hope I can keep up with Mr. Brezhnev's tempo."

The opening session took place on Saturday morning at the US Ambassador's residence. I watched Brezhnev appear at the entrance of the three-story Soviet Embassy and slowly descend to the waiting ZIL-114. The security detail blocked him out of sight of any unauthorized onlookers. At 10:48 a.m., the limousine navigated the narrow ramp and pulled out of the compound for the ten-minute drive. Victor and I jumped into our car and followed at close distance.

A smiling Carter walked down the steps to greet Brezhnev; they shook hands silently. The General Secretary walked with a slight limp; the steps must have seemed like the North Face. An American protocol officer escorted Brezhnev to a large conference room, and eased him into a comfortable chair in the middle of a long oval table. The polished surface was bare except for large ashtrays, bottled Austrian mineral water and heavy crystal glasses. Simple rectangular cardboard name-cards were placed before each of the ten seats on both sides of the table.

Carter's style was different from Nixon's: he wanted to involve as many aides as possible. There was a brief struggle for chairs on the Soviet side of the table; I held on to mine at the far left end. I also commandeered a bottle of water and a glass. Next to me sat Leonid Zamyatin, Brezhnev's spokesperson. He was in great strain: any story he gave out to the press about Brezhnev's health had to be a cover-up (he sympathized with Ziegler). I opened my writing pad.

Presidential assistants Hamilton Jordan and Jody Powell sat opposite. They were excited - most probably, they never met a Soviet before. I shared my mineral water; they were grateful. I waved to Bill Krimer at Carter's side; he waved back. State Department interpreters were done with the Nixon era, released for active duty by the new White House. Bill, the civilian version of the Sad Sack, looked upbeat. He interpreted and took notes. Jody Powell was also taking notes, as well as Reginald Bartholomew of the NSC and Ambassador Malcolm Toon. National Security Adviser Zbigniew Brzezinski, Secretary of State Cyrus Vance and Secretary of Defense Harold Brown wrote as well. I hoped the White House had one official memcon in the end, rather than nine different versions. (I was unaware that Carter's memcons were now different from Nixon's style. They resembled the Soviet model: descriptive and focused on essentials. Apparently, the White House gave up tape recording.)

I kept the definitive record for the Soviet side; it would be the only full version for the Kremlin. Kornienko jotted down a few notes for his own use. He turned them over to me later; he knew the nature of my job and was always helpful.

I had a strange feeling that Henry Kissinger might pop in any moment.

Carter beamed his photogenic smile, and the flashes went off. All Americans, except the top brass, wore striped business suits in various shades of blue. The Russians wore dark gray. The American team was conspicuously young, including the 54-year-old Carter. I thought of a group of boy scouts facing a veterans' club.

Brezhnev was 72. His team had an impressive backlog of experience: Andrei Gromyko, Defense Minister Dmitri Ustinov and Chief of the General Staff Nikolai Ogarkov. The workhorses were there: Kornienko, Dobrynin, Zamyatin, Victor and me. The only outsider was Konstantin Chernenko. I decided his role was to provide moral support to the leader (I was wrong: he was in training). He sat on Brezhnev's right, fingering a US Embassy notepad.

Security escorted the photographers out of the room, the hubbub died down and negotiations commenced. A smile never leaving his face, Carter welcomed Brezhnev at the American premises and suggested he start as the host. Unexpectedly, Brezhnev put on his glasses and opened his folder. He spoke for twenty minutes, ignoring Victor's half-hearted attempts to interrupt for interpretation. At last, his stamina ran out. After regrets that he forgot about translation, he leaned back and removed his glasses. He peered at the American team. The President kept his smile; other faces were inscrutable.

Brezhnev read his speaking notes almost verbatim. This made the task of translating much easier, since Victor and I had a carbon copy. This late-life manner of the General Secretary was a boon for the note taker; I would use the notes for writing up. At one point Brezhnev asked Victor if he should read the "long version" of a passage or the "short one" (this was conditional on Carter's response). In a low voice, Victor advised him to read the shorter version, and indicated it with his finger. I saw markings in the notes when Brezhnev was to turn the discussion over to Gromyko. At such moments, he looked relieved. He was too tired to argue or engage in meaningful debate.

Brzezinski, who knew Russian, looked on impassively with a tight smile. His eyes were slits: he looked like a Chinese cookie that refused to open.

Carter listened with his arms crossed. When Brezhnev mentioned Russia's desire for peace, he jotted something down, probably to impress the Soviet leader that his words were important to be recorded by Presidential hand. Brezhnev noticed this, and pointing a finger at Brzezinski (the only other familiar face in the American team), said, "He's the one who doesn't want peace." He waited for a moment. "Since no one objects, it must be true." Everybody laughed, including Brzezinski.

Carter chose the right tone with Brezhnev; he spoke as the junior partner in a law firm. Brezhnev was an elder statesman; he addressed him as "Mr. President." He sprinkled his speech with references to world peace, which Brezhnev liked. "The world looks upon us as leaders; we should not let other countries or leaders hold us back," Carter said. Brezhnev appreciated his allusions to nuclear parity and the two powers' special status, the cornerstones of US-Soviet relations.

Listening to Brezhnev, I watched for departures from prepared text. Apart from an exclamation that "God will never forgive us if this meeting fails!" his only substantive deviation was a remark about the US military budget, which he called "unprecedented and excessive." He turned to Gromyko, seeking his support. It was a strange sight: Brezhnev was trying to draw the Minister into the discussion, but Gromyko resisted. He was used to such meanderings, and tried to steer Brezhnev back on track. The issue was not in the brief. Debating it served no purpose: the true size of Soviet military spending was never disclosed. Civil and military industries intertwined and prices were calculated from a much lower base than in the US. There was no reliable method of comparing expenditures.

Carter noted that in the last fifteen years the Soviet Union increased its defense budget more than the US. "We're looking at America," said Brezhnev. "We're looking at each other," said Carter. "We need more consultation and information. Secrecy is counterproductive. It is human nature to exaggerate actions by the other side. This is why we both sometimes take unnecessary actions." It sounded reasonable; Brezhnev did not object.

Carter argued that encrypting telemetry data from missile tests increased suspicion. Verification was central to the viability of SALT-2, but US experts faced a problem. Judging from satellite observation of craters the accuracy of Soviet missiles was higher than suggested by telemetric data picked up. They suspected it was either encrypted or deliberately distorted.

Gromyko intervened to say this was the Russian understanding as well: no encryption of parameters "pertinent to the treaty." The latter term, of course, was open to interpretation.

Brezhnev interrupted Carter; he wanted to speak off the record. "No notes to be taken," he said, looking around. I laid down my pen, preparing to memorize whatever was coming. Again, he took up the US military budget. Brezhnev's concern had a deeper motive, which he did not articulate. His constant worry was that the Soviet economy would be bled white. Alexandrov recalled a meeting in Brezhnev's office where the top military brass, in reply to a direct question, conceded that, if arms control talks were broken off, the USSR could not win the arms race and thus guarantee the country's security.

After another long intervention, Brezhnev became restless. He looked around and suddenly said in a loud voice, "I'm fed up with this, when is the lunch break?" He was under the impression that the SALT signing ceremony would follow lunch. The Soviet team froze. Carter looked quizzically at Bill Krimer, who gazed ahead.

Gromyko murmured soothingly in Brezhnev's ear: the ceremony was two whole days away. Victor said he had not finished translating. Brezhnev slumped in his chair. I did not include the embarrassing incident in my transcript. In Bill Krimer's memcon, Brezhnev is quoted as saying, "Lunch time." As a true professional, Bill glossed over the embarrassing incident.

We broke up at 12:30 p.m. Carter gripped Brezhnev's arm to steer him down the steps. Back at the Soviet Embassy, Brezhnev seemed disoriented; he could not grasp the sequence of the program. He asked Ambassador Mikhail Yefremov about the next event on the agenda. We stood in a circle unable to help. I thought of creeping amnesia. Our biggest worry was that Brezhnev might stumble and fall at the SALT-2 signing ceremony. Worse still, he might not be able to affix his signature to the treaty. Alexandrov was on edge, his hands trembled and his glasses steamed up. If not for his slight frame, he would have bodily carried Brezhnev to the Hofburg Palace. Alas, he was no Chuck Connors. Brezhnev slowly walked to the long-awaited meal at the Ambassador's residence, followed by four hours of "leisure time."

After downing vegetable soup and cutlets at the Embassy canteen, I took the elevator to the code room where a young secretary braced herself for her first-ever dictation of summit talks. I assured her I would speak slowly.

The first day of the summit proved exhausting for the General Secretary. The night's performance of Mozart's *Abduction from the Seraglio* failed to bolster his staying power; he stole from the opera during the first act. After a decent interval, President Carter also left. A shrewd move: the audience would think the two leaders headed to a round of late night consultations.

That evening, we received a message, handwritten in large block letters on a yellow legal pad page. It read,

"Personal message to President Brezhnev.

Mr. President,

SALT-3 is important. Deep cuts, 5 per cent a year - as agreed to be mutually beneficial, safe havens, etc. I will discuss this with you tomorrow… Respectfully yours, Jimmy Carter."

I Xeroxed several copies, dictated a translation and delivered it to Alexandrov. Dobrynin thought it was an attempt by Carter to try out an idea on Brezhnev without springing it on the Soviet team at next day's plenary. Was Carter attempting to inject personal diplomacy into the negotiation? He should have known better: Brezhnev was past the point when "a personal relationship" à la Nixon was effective. Under the circumstances, Ustinov and Chernenko vetoed any immediate reaction to the President's proposals, though they did look promising.

Driving back to the hotel, I reflected on Carter. He was well briefed and comfortable discussing technical issues. Probably for this reason, Brzezinski was less visible than Kissinger at Nixon's side: in fact, he did not speak at all. Unfortunately, however Carter tried, he could not reach out to Brezhnev in a dialogue. The Brezhnev of 1979 was a person quite different from the one who joked and argued with Nixon and slapped Kissinger on the back.

The second meeting, on Sunday, took place at the Soviet Embassy. The conference room was large and brightly lit by dozens of electric candles. Brezhnev sat with his back to the huge fireplace. The table disposition was similar to the previous day at the American residence, except that the mineral water was Georgian *Borjomi.* Stop corks were placed next to the bottles, in case the participants wished to conserve the bubbling spirit.

Soviet Embassy, Vienna. Alexandrov looks over Brezhnev's shoulder to check the brief. Carter beams. (Vladimir Musaelyan)

There was a dramatic discussion of MBFR. For a long time negotiations stalled over conflicting numbers. Brezhnev read from his brief: the Soviet Union would reduce its land forces in Europe "quite considerably," in response to a "just" stance by the Americans. Gromyko interjected: the American estimates exceeded the actual force levels of the USSR and its allies by 150,000. "We simply don't have those troops," he said. Simple steps, reducing a division on the Soviet side and a brigade on the American side, and so on, can avoid the difficulties with numbers. "Otherwise," he concluded, "the problem is stuck."

This was the only moment Carter let his exasperation show: "The matter can be resolved today! Let Secretary Brown and Marshal Ustinov go to another room where we will explain frankly and fully how we arrived at the figures. Do you agree? Brown will speak on behalf of the President. You will then understand."

Brezhnev looked down; he did not respond. I looked at Ustinov. The Defense Minister remained silent, his eyes downcast. One could cut the tension with a knife.

Ustinov was two years Brezhnev's junior and a close friend. A few days before the war, Stalin appointed the clever 38-year old engineer People's Commissar for Armaments. He nearly fired him when his passion for motorcycle racing resulted in a broken leg. Over the years, he amassed vast power and became unquestionable Tsar of the Soviet Union's military-industrial complex. A workaholic with an ascetic life style, he demanded the same from staff. The military empire he built competed with the United States and elicited fear and wonder. In the last decade, he supervised, with Marshal Grechko, Admiral Gorshkov and Leonid Smirnov, the biggest expansion in Soviet strategic might. Ustinov had the final word on Russia's security, his passion. However, he saw the world in black and white, rather than as a multicolored mosaic. If there ever was a Soviet strategist who truly followed Mao Tse-tung's maxim that "power grows from the barrel of a gun," it was Dmitri Fedorovitch Ustinov.

In Vienna, sitting among a group of men wielding ultimate power, Ustinov pondered his response. He decided to remain silent. He would not reply to Carter. He did not want to, period. The negotiators on both sides of the table looked at Ustinov, and then at Brezhnev, who was doodling on a page of his brief. The Soviet side was reluctant to admit responsibility for any discrepancy in conventional forces. Once again, the Soviet military showed it held a veto over all matters of security. Whatever the smiles and agreements, the United States was still the main enemy, and all means were fit to confound it. The time for disclosure of military secrets had not yet arrived.

After a silence I thought would never end, Brezhnev gestured as if inviting the session to resume. Gromyko cleared his throat and suggested proceeding to the next agenda item. He went into a half-hearted explanation of the Soviet position on banning "radiological weapons," an esoteric topic lazily discussed by the disarmament conference in Geneva. It was one of my charges, so I scribbled a few notes to include in the memcon; I knew the countries' positions.

Brown and Ustinov did sit down together for a short while, but it was a pure formality. There was no meeting of minds. The episode put an end to American hopes that Defense Chiefs could sort out numbers and hardware in a parallel negotiating channel.

Brezhnev hosted a lavish dinner at the Soviet Embassy in honor, as the beautifully engraved invitation said, of "His Excellency Mr. James Earl Carter, President of the United States of America." Soviet Protocol was unbending; no "Jimmies" to be treated to Kremlin fare - Fresh Caviar, Pheasant and Consommé with Siberian Pelmenis (meat cakes), Baked Sturgeon à la Russe, Roast Suckling Pig, and Strawberry Plombiere Ice-Cream.

Early next morning, June 18, I was at the resplendent white and gold main hall of the 13th century Hofburg Palace. I chose a place near the podium with my amateur movie camera. Jimmy Carter sat on a sofa in the first row surrounded by the Secret Service; his wife and daughter Amy were in the audience. He waited for Brezhnev. At 12:57, Brezhnev appeared in the doorway; bodyguard Vladimir carefully maneuvered him to the podium. He was only seven minutes late. A secretary from the Central Committee wiped tears from her eyes: she did not expect the deterioration to be so evident. Dr. Chazov had brought the art of short-term gerontological revival of Politburo members to dizzying heights, but this time he was helpless.

Carter must have felt a surge of sympathy for the Russian leader. After putting his signature on the last page of the agreement, he stood up, walked to Brezhnev and embraced him. The latter reciprocated with an unexpected kiss on the President's cheek, and a second kiss on the other cheek. The curious episode, which both teams witnessed with mixed feelings, added a human touch.

Afterwards, Brezhnev confessed he felt uneasy the chumminess went too far, but Victor told him it looked natural. I agreed: "A kiss is just a kiss…The fundamental things apply, as time goes by…" The kiss sealed an achievement; SALT-2 was a significant step forward. If SALT-1 froze strategic weapon numbers for five years, the Vienna accord set new numerical limits, both quantitative and qualitative. At the staff conference the previous year, Gromyko erred on the side of caution. Maybe Carter did want to go further. He even alluded to recognizing Soviet fears of a strategic threat from China. (SALT-2 was not ratified. US domestic opposition was too strong. On Christmas Eve 1979, the Russian 40th Army entered Afghanistan. US-Soviet relations plummeted.)

On the last day of the summit, I drove to the Soviet Embassy to finish dictation, collect my papers and pick up my *per diem*. Entering the accountant's office, I saw a strange scene: cellist Mstislav Rostropovitch was pouring a bagful of Austrian schilling notes onto the bookkeeper's desk, honoraria from a concert in Vienna. Soviet artists were obliged to turn over the bulk of their concert fees to the State, which reimbursed them at a rate higher than the regular pay all Soviets received abroad, plus hotel expenses. Rostropovich looked miserable. The severe-looking bookkeeper with a beautiful name Sofia asked him "to arrange the notes neatly stacked and to submit a proper receipt." (Not surprisingly, in 1991 Rostropovich was seen in Moscow's Dzerzhinsky Square hugging an AK-47, ready to storm the KGB Headquarters.)

We left Vienna in the afternoon, after Brezhnev's brief pep talk with Austrian Communist Party leaders. Our German interpreter told me it was a bad idea; the Austrian comrades were dismayed by his condition.

It was the last time I saw Brezhnev up close.

CHAPTER 5

Transitions

TRYING TO LEAVE

PITFALLS COME UNEXPECTEDLY IN AN interpreter's life. At the Gromyko-Kissinger meeting in Geneva In February 1975, tempers ran high. They tossed figures, acronyms and formulas across the table like playing cards. At one point Kissinger, with a sarcastic glint, asked Gromyko, who Brezhnev had in mind when referring in his speech to "travelers peddling soporific tales in the Middle East?" The US Secretary of State?

"Have you seen the full text of the speech?" asked Gromyko. Kissinger said no. I translated, "No, I have not." I should have said, "Mr. Kissinger says he has not." Gromyko was as exhausted as I was, because he suddenly pounced on me: how could I, a Ministry official, not have read the latest speech of the General Secretary? It took a few minutes before I managed to convince the Minister that Kissinger was the culprit, rather than I, who read the speech. Kissinger's confession helped.

During a break, Gromyko steered me to the coffee table and asked in his inimitable way, "Vavilov, are you alright?" (He meant my arguing with him over the translation). "Just tired, Andrei Andreyevitch," I replied, resignedly. "Perhaps I've overstayed in the interpreting business." He grunted and turned away.

As the decade of the 1970s ended, the nagging feeling of imprisonment turned into conviction: I wanted to focus on my substantive brief, arms control. The summit meetings became a rut, high-level conversations a *déjà vu*. They paralleled the downturn in Soviet-American relations, which were slowly reverting to the ice age. I was not the only one disheartened by the trend: the USSR was steadily losing the economic and military race with the US. On a dreary December afternoon in 1979, Oleg, my old friend from the USA Department, invited me to his office to break the news: Soviet troops had just entered Afghanistan. It did not bode well for his desk. He poured two tumblers of Armenian brandy, but it failed to dissipate a sense of foreboding.

It was difficult to explain my desire to leave: I was trying to get out when some were trying to get in. Victor Sukhodrev felt the same; he was on the lookout for candidates eager to serve the top leadership and shine on television. However, we were too close to the center of power. Brezhnev, an aide told me, "felt comfortable with his regular interpreters." It was harder for Victor; he was ready to accept an Ambassadorial post, but Brezhnev wanted him to stay close. What gave me hope was the large number of people willing to sacrifice their nights and energy for the job of note taking for the Politburo. They danced around the Kremlin negotiating schedule like swarms of hungry bees looking for drops of nectar. The problem was they were not particularly welcome.

Being on constant call, plucked at any moment by the leadership was interfering with my main job. I negotiated the bilateral environment modification agreement with the Americans, the basis for an international convention. In the Conference of the Committee on Disarmament, the chemical weapons agenda was picking up steam under our astute negotiator, Ambassador Yuri Nazarkin; I wished to see the process through.

Too many interpreters passed the point of no return and were condemned to stay in the business until retirement. Speaking for my country with my own voice brought me more satisfaction than putting other people's thoughts, however important, into a foreign tongue and writing them down for future generations. I had my share of translating history; it could proceed along its warped path without my aid.

Gromyko ignored my pleas. His private assistant thought I was mad. Brezhnev's aides were of the view was that his note takers were supposed to stay on to the grave (if they went first). In desperation, I made sure to be away at arms control negotiations in Geneva or New York in the hope I would be forgotten.

Soon, I faced a personal problem. My sister Irina, an actress in a leading Moscow drama theater, married a distinguished French author - unfortunately, a NATO country citizen. This made the MFA Chief of Security unhappy; he was preoccupied with senior-level penetration of the Foreign Service. However, efficient bureaucracies tend to hold together, and my colleagues did not let me down. Harmless name-dropping also helped. I made a cautious supposition that my namesake, Andrei Mikhailovitch Alexandrov, Brezhnev's perennial foreign policy assistant, would "humbly disagree" with any rash move to oust me. This turned out to be best policy: I found I never left the gravitational field of the General Secretary.

Though the vigilante succeeded in blocking my foreign travel, my security clearance was not withdrawn. The case might have made good material in the purges of the 1930s, but did not look credible today. I continued to receive foreign diplomats, drafted instructions for negotiators and went to foreign Embassy cocktail parties. On occasions, when I stood in for the department chief, a somber looking person would silently glide into the room carrying a brown leather folder. He produced a KGB or GRU cable from New York, Vienna or Geneva bearing on the department's sweep of the UN agenda. He waited while I quickly read the cable and ticked it off. Occasionally, a memo would arrive from these agencies with views on nuclear terrorism, illegal trafficking of radioactive materials, or the spread of HIV/AIDS. I fail to recall anything that required follow-up by my office.

Henry Kissinger was among the few who understood Russian suspicions of foreigners, a strange trait nurtured by the country's convoluted history. The Empire's immense territory was difficult to defend. Over centuries, the wide-open steppes invited repeated invasions, the last one in 1941, which devastated half the country and took a terrible human toll. In 1697, at the start of his reign, Peter I travelled with the Great Embassy to Europe to study shipbuilding and other trades. He was listed in the 250-men group as "Peter Mikhailov, bombardier." The average Russian of the time regarded foreign travel close to treason. Early in the 18th century, Catherine the Great issued a *ukase* "On maintaining secrecy by officers of the Collegium of Foreign Affairs and on visiting the homes of foreign envoys exclusively for official purposes." Deep suspicions of *chuzhaki*, or "aliens," were prevalent. It was fertile ground for government secrecy that neither time nor social upheavals could fully erase. The Socialist system in Russia espoused Dostoyevsky's maxim that all adults must be treated as children, shielded from the pleasures and vices of the decadent West.

One day, Evgeni Chazov asked me if I would take a part-time consultancy, on nuclear weapon issues, with the Soviet Chapter of the International Physicians for the Prevention of Nuclear War (IPPNW). I agreed. In three weeks, I was on an Aeroflot flight to Rome, accompanying Dr. Chazov to a meeting with Dr. Bernard Lown, the other co-founder of IPPNW. As the plane took off from Sheremetyevo Airport, I felt the secretive bureaucratic hurdles falling away like the supporting gantry of a *Soyuz* space rocket. A Central Committee official called the MFA Chief of Security, reminding him that the Party had final authority in any issue, and would he please not meddle in affairs above his station. By stroke of bad luck, it transpired that the person was also involved in petty speculation deals, which led to his dishonorable discharge. Probably he came under scrutiny by a more covert counter-intelligence department. My consolation was that the other side was not immune to paranoia. In a classic example, CIA's Jim Angleton suspected Harold Wilson, Averell Harriman, Armand Hammer and Henry Kissinger of being KGB agents.

In 1986, I accompanied a group of Russian IPPNW doctors to California for a meeting with American physicians. In the middle of a get-together, we received a message from Armand Hammer who wanted to discuss the Chernobyl nuclear power plant disaster. A leading Soviet radiologist and I went to Los Angeles. We checked into a plush hotel, and drove around in a black stretch limo. The driver was a former FBI agent who expanded our rudimentary knowledge of insurance scams in the Bay Area - some were hilarious. Next morning we walked a few blocks to the Occidental Petroleum office at 10889 Wilshire Boulevard.

Dr. Robert Gale joined us; he achieved tremendous popularity for bone marrow transplants for the Chernobyl firefighters. We lunched on minute quantities of Norwegian salmon with saffron mayo, new potatoes, and chocolate pecan pie. The 1983 Chardonnay from the Robert Young Vineyard was a welcome addition.

Sitting below a Rembrandt painting and with dozens of Albrecht Durer prints lining the walls, Hammer made a generous offer of assistance in assessing the medical implications of Chernobyl. We promised to report to Moscow.

Unknown to Dr. Hammer, his offer produced consternation among the Soviet military. As my radiologist friend explained to me, Chernobyl presented the second unique opportunity, after Hiroshima and Nagasaki, to study short and long-term effects of massive release of radioactivity on the population and the environment - as close as could be to real nuclear war. This was of huge interest to military experts. In the atmosphere of mutual suspicion, the prospect of US scientists roaming the forests and fields of Belorussia and Ukraine taking air and soil samples for use in strategic planning was unnerving.

Hammer recalled our meeting in 1978. He was now working on an autobiography. Could I send him a copy of the amateur film I made in Crimea and any notes about the Brezhnev meeting? I made appropriate noises but was non-committal. Providing Dr. Hammer with my recollections proved a task no less easy than the US study of Chernobyl. As a civil servant, I had to obtain permission for transmitting to a foreigner any record pertaining to a former Soviet leader.

Back in Moscow, I cornered an old America hand, Deputy Foreign Minister Victor Komplektov, in the men's room. I knew the trick: interfering with the call of nature usually extracts a quick response from a superior. Victor scanned my memo, questioned the time I spent "on trivia," and gave permission to forward my recollections through our Embassy in Washington.

Hammer conveyed his thanks in a telex from the US Embassy in Moscow, and we met later that year at a Kremlin reception. His memoir and an autographed album, "The World of Armand Hammer," are a reminder of the admirable American quality of personal attentiveness. A friend cooled me down: "If there was a cat in the room, Hammer would have written it a thank-you letter as well." In his book, Hammer described the Brezhnev episode differently from what I remembered. The same year, the philanthropist donated

$100,000 to the Soviet Cultural Foundation, and presented the Tretyakov Gallery with a rare painting, "At the Village Fence," by Ivan Kulikov, an old master. He acquired it in the 1920s in Russia.

Our short visit to San Francisco held a sentimental reason. After spending the night at Dr. Phil Shapiro, an IPPNW activist's home three blocks from Divisadero Street, I walked to the intersection with Broadway. It was a warm Sunday morning and the street was deserted. I wanted to have a look at number 2563, an old mansion on the corner. The red brickwork was painted white. I entered the courtyard and rang the bell. The door opened a crack.

"Yes?"

I said I lived in the house in 1945. "Do you know this was the Soviet Consulate?" I asked.

"I don't." The man watched me through the crack.

"Could you tell me what's here now?"

"A rehabilitation clinic. Sorry, we're closed for today." He shut the door, but there was no sound of footsteps receding. I felt like an investigative reporter.

Walking down Divisadero I pondered the strange fate of the building. At the end of the World War II, it was a vortex sucking in America's nuclear secrets and transmitting them in five-numeral coded groups along the airwaves to the other side of the globe, to the earphones of stern young men and women in uniform. Klaus Fuchs, Ted Hall and others in Los Alamos had a powerful motive: removing the nuclear monopoly of one country. They believed that only a nuclear balance could prevent a new world war. It took another twenty-five years for nuclear parity between the US and the USSR. I wondered what the clinic management made of the strong room on the third floor with its one-inch steel door that opened only from the inside. My father, the Consul-General, once took me there. The code clerk said this was a place for misbehaving kids.

THE LEADERS: REAL AND TRANSFORMED

After 1974, Brezhnev and Nixon went their separate ways. They never wrote to each other again. They became strangers. Paradoxically, that year was Brezhnev's last chance to step down gracefully; he would have been remembered as a truly historic figure.

The political resurrection of the two men took a little over a decade. It was unpredicted. Nixon reemerged as a political guru. He had the resilience of a Russian "*Vanka-Vstanka*," a bottom-heavy wooden doll: hold it down, release it and it uprights itself. Brezhnev's satirical image loved by Russian stage impersonators gave way to nostalgia.

The two men were captivating individuals, but very dissimilar in intellect, negotiating skills, lifestyles and daily habits. Their backgrounds were small-town and humble; they came up the hard way. Their political careers followed a close course. Brezhnev became General Secretary in 1964. He was consolidating his power when Nixon won the 1968 election. The governance systems in which they operated determined some of their traits. Nixon was the Supremo. Brezhnev had to navigate within a collective leadership. Nixon was an astute PR man, paying attention to the sensitivities of Congress, the media and the American public. He evoked the difficulties he would face if suspected to be soft on the USSR: he had to "sell" the agreements. Brezhnev made fun of him for being afraid of the American press (for some reason he referred to the *New York Times*, rather than the *Washington Post*). He did not care as much about the mystique of his office; the Soviet system guaranteed it.

Nixon presented his burnished side to the Soviet comrades. At close range, the "sunny summit angle" appeared to be genuine. It was not a distortion; it was part of a composite picture, which, at the time, eluded me. I felt a grudging respect for his self-control, courtesy and more importantly, grasp of complicated issues. I never saw him angry. He projected a certain dignity, a measured mix of humility and resolve. Unlike Brezhnev, Nixon had mastered negotiating techniques, though he let Kissinger deal with technical details. Brezhnev, on the contrary, preferred a free-style negotiating format - with Kissinger, and gave it as much time as "Ghenry" could afford. His negotiating style was heavy on appeals to "morality" and "historical responsibility," as if semi-religious tenets motivate national policy. He often squandered time on table talk and on jokes (usually funny). The Soviet interpreter embroidered his speech, to make it appear forceful and orderly. He was best when he followed the negotiating brief to the letter.

Nixon had a secret for being effective with Brezhnev. He did not indulge in anti-Communist rhetoric or political wisecracks. He was a geopolitical strategist soaring high above ideology and dogma. He did not appreciate the Soviet system, but concealed it well. He placed America's security interests above a seductive urge to prod the USSR towards "greater freedom." Nixon did not try to score propaganda points, or lecture Soviet leaders on democracy, human rights and the market economy. Nixon never provoked Brezhnev. Ever patient, he did not press an issue if he sensed his comrade was annoyed or badly prepared. He was keenly aware of Brezhnev's emotions and deep-seated beliefs, and did not hesitate to show he respected them.

For his part, Brezhnev refrained from criticizing America's unbridled consumerism and inability to eradicate poverty at home. No phantom of Communism-preaching Khrushchev hovered over the negotiating table. If Brezhnev saw Nixon's opening to China as opportunistic, his readiness for arms reductions with the USSR was pragmatic. For him, Nixon's formal acknowledgement of peaceful coexistence and nuclear parity with the Soviet Union stemmed from realism. It took root in America's national interests, which, at the time, coincided with Soviet concerns. In June 1974, speaking to the Soviet leaders in St. Catherine Hall, Nixon said the US was not going to change the Soviet system, and the USSR was not going to change the American system.

Nixon made a distinction between words and actions. At the second Moscow summit, he showed Brezhnev how his mind worked. He recalled his debate with Khrushchev on the 1959 "Captive Nations Week" resolution of Congress. "It was just language," Nixon said, "it is not operative... It was theory, not fact." He smiled: "The Lithuanians I saw dancing last night did not seem to be captive." Without getting soft on Communism or getting chummy with his newly found comrades, the man had come of age. Never in his conversations with Brezhnev did Nixon and Kissinger evoke Hungary or Czechoslovakia. In effect, they accepted the right of the Soviet Army to defend geopolitical borders in Europe. (I have an idea how Nixon would have regarded NATO's eastward expansion in Europe or the crisis in Ukraine. Of course, post-Soviet Russia could not compare to the USSR of the 1970s, America's equal rival.)

Brezhnev knew he faced a politician with a record of obscurantist views and checkered political history. He never forgot Nixon's post-war crusade against Communist conspiracy and the Hollywood "Reds." This belonged to the past; he did not feel he was talking to a Cold Warrior of the 1950s, whom even Harry S. Truman detested. Joe McCarthy's "Scoundrel Time" was something for historians to ponder. Nixon's unsavory domestic deeds were irrelevant to détente. Brezhnev once told Kissinger that the Nixon he saw was not the Nixon of 1959, whom he heard during the "kitchen debate." He believed the President "was guided by noble intentions." I can imagine him apologetically telling his colleagues, "But he has changed, hasn't he?" He might have added - if he lived to read it - that Nixon changed so much, he thought Vice President Agnew had "a McCarthyite tinge."[65]

Strangely, in some ways Nixon's personality resembled Brezhnev's: both disliked arguing in public and having to listen to things unpleasant. Both were averse to overtly sting a foe, or appear irritated. Both valued flattery (Henry Kissinger was skillful in praise for both). Of the same generation, they believed in traditional values of friendship, family and love of country. They even dressed similarly, following a conservative code. Nixon strolled by the seaside in subtropical Crimea in a jacket and tie. Brezhnev wore a sport jacket and tie - this was as far as he could go.

Nixon assured his readers: "I developed with Brezhnev a closer personal relationship than any other pair of Soviet and American leaders has had since Stalin and Roosevelt."[66] This is debatable. True, Roosevelt did have a soft spot for "Uncle Joe," who, in turn, felt deep respect and compassion for FDR. But those were other times. Nixon could not have built a meaningful personal relationship with Brezhnev: they were too different. If Brezhnev was not, by circumstance rather than free elections, catapulted to the top, the most he could aspire to was regional Party Secretary (almost his own words). After resignation, Nixon toiled away, debated and gave political advice. After 1979, Brezhnev was in retirement. His idea of leisure was hunting and watching television, ice hockey and soccer matches and movies - an eclectic mélange of Soviet war dramas and Hollywood Westerns.

What was true - Nixon never referred to this publicly - was Brezhnev's touching concern for his comrade in the final weeks of Watergate, and his advice to hang on. It was very Russian. Dobrynin thought their confidential contacts on this tragic and highly personal issue were unique in the history of US-Soviet relations. In Oreanda, Brezhnev drew Nixon away from the aides, touched his elbow, and asked if he could help. Nixon shrugged: "Nobody can".

Despite his outspokenness about democracy and freedom, Nixon was drawn to authoritarian regimes, be it South Vietnam, Pakistan, Iran, South Africa, or the USSR. In fact, Nixon would have made a solid General Secretary with his tenacity, bent for secrecy and imperial style. His personality cult would have thrived in the Soviet Union, given the absence of parliamentary control, bureaucratic discipline and faith in the wisdom of the leader.

Nixon's resignation pushed the "personal relationship" ingredient back, for what it was worth. It was an artificial component of the US-Soviet engagement, which had a more solid foundation. Nixon's exit did not affect Brezhnev's standing in the Soviet leadership, because his appraisal of the domestic situation in the US was similar to his colleagues. They erred, by placing excessive hope on Nixon's determination to survive; they were taken in by his orchestrated façade.

The side Brezhnev demonstrated to Americans was his natural one. Nixon accepted him as a true-life figure; one could even detect a streak of envy because Brezhnev had a single personality, his own. He behaved naturally in public, in the office and at home. He could be angry, grave, sad, jovial or sentimental, but for brief periods. Among factors that contributed to Brezhnev's personality cult was his even temper, civility and an honest self-deprecating attitude. An aide told of Brezhnev's reaction to a draft speech he was to deliver at a Party Congress. Noticing quotations from Karl Marx in the text he told the speechwriter, "This won't do. Whoever believes that Uncle Leonid had read Marx?" Even his craving for presents, which many thought reprehensible, was regarded as "touchingly human" by Party sycophants. Brezhnev did not try hard to conceal his less agreeable qualities. All his sides were on exhibit.

While there are no known "Kremlin tapes" to expose political jealousies and scheming (which certainly existed), Brezhnev discouraged destructive infighting. He made an imprint on ways the Party Central Committee operated. He was a consensus builder. Party culture required the leader to be "simple" and "nice to ordinary folks." He had a natural acumen for unflustered charm – never a discouraging word. Before affixing his signature to a Politburo decision, he would pick up the phone and call a dozen regional party secretaries across the eleven time zones of his vast nation. "I thought I should consult you," was his usual opening to a startled but flattered official in Latvia, Tajikistan or Kamchatka. At times impulsive, Leonid Ilyich was circumspect in serious matters. Never reckless, he would postpone a decision before hearing the views of Politburo colleagues and agencies involved.

Brezhnev did not have to cajole others much: the huge Party and government apparatus followed the prevailing wind, and the wind always blew from the mountaintop. He managed to build an ingratiating and adaptive political coterie. Rather than bully and destroy the reputation of those who challenged his preeminence he maneuvered them into a quarantined niche, preferably early retirement.

This happened to Prime Minister Alexei Kosygin, with his bold vision of the country's future. If there was one monumental error of judgment that Brezhnev made it was to sideline the person who could have reformed the Soviet economy. Paradoxically, this lapse led to Brezhnev's own demise, because he was held responsible for economic stagnation. Kosygin could have been the Soviet equivalent of Deng Xiaoping, to lead the nation with the world's richest resources into a position unreachable by the United States. He would have made a better negotiating partner for Nixon, avoiding confusion and conversation detours, and using precious time wisely. He was always in command of issues, composed, rational and concrete - uncannily, a mirror image of Nixon.

What mattered for détente was Brezhnev's gift for choosing foreign policy aides. He lent them an attentive ear. If Nixon made his own judgments and final decisions, Brezhnev expected to be corrected by aides. They were smart, some brilliant; all were motivated by détente. They were no starry-eyed kids seduced by the West. They defended Russia's interests with vigor, and skillfully maneuvered around the demands of the military establishment. Advisers like Dobrynin, Alexandrov and Kornienko would have been priceless acquisitions for any country's national security apparatus. Foreign Minister Gromyko topped them all.

There was an aspect of the Nixon-Brezhnev relationship that both sides tried hard to conceal. In mid-1973, at the third summit, Nixon must have concluded that Brezhnev was unwell. In Russia, it was an open secret. His agonizingly long speeches, which he slowly read on Soviet State TV, his drawl, myopia and absent-mindedness were the focus of unkind jokes and impersonations that migrated from the streets to comedy acts. A fully equipped black ambulance - "the hearse", we called it - followed his motorcade everywhere. Some foreign leaders went to extremes to find out the truth: at Brezhnev's meeting with President Giscard d'Estaing in 1980 in Paris, the French collected hairs from his bathroom comb.

Nixon kept up appearances. For him, the leader of the Soviet Union was "an astute negotiating partner." Surely, he realized at some point that he was not negotiating with Brezhnev, who had become a front, but with the faceless Soviet political, military and industrial elite, which drafted the actual decisions. The important thing was for the world and the American public to see that the President engaged the leader of the other super power in a personal relationship crucial for peace. It made Nixon indispensable; it was now imperative for his political survival.

The Russian leadership had reasons to preserve the myth. It preferred a helpless Tsar at the head, a living icon. Brezhnev could not chair Politburo meetings for longer than an hour. After Nixon's resignation, he delegated national security issues to Gromyko, Ustinov and Andropov. Unlike Dorian Gray, who retained his youth while his portrait aged, Brezhnev's public portraits stayed young while he was aging before our eyes. The unfettered intake of sleeping pills rid him of critical judgment. Once he asked Dr. Chazov if he liked his new gold ring. Chazov said it looked awkward. Brezhnev was hurt: "My Politburo comrades assured me it was nice." At the end of his tenure, he returned a book on Leonardo da Vinci that Gromyko lent him. He said he stopped reading altogether; it was a strain.

Sadly, his plan of leaving a testimonial of the détente years fell through. He was too ill to embark on a memoir, despite eager ghostwriters.

He realized his state and suffered. He asked the Politburo to relieve him on health grounds, but colleagues implored him to stay: "The country needs stability; don't worry about work, we'll be there to help, just *zhivite…*" *Zhivite* in Russian means both "keep going" and "stay alive." The icon had no strength to argue. "Probably, they're right," Brezhnev thought. As the bureaucracy's creation, he believed that change would be fatal for the country.

The post-Nixon period was depressing: the dazzling horizons were contracting. With Nixon gone, Brezhnev was losing friends in the West. Georges Pompidou passed away the previous year, and Willy Brandt, architect of *Ostpolitik*, resigned in May after his aide Gunter Guillaume was unmasked as an East German spy. If he could help it, Brezhnev avoided personal encounters with those who took over in the White House. His brief meetings with Gerald Ford and Jimmy Carter were caricatures of his negotiations with Nixon and Kissinger.

By the time of Nixon's political re-emergence, Brezhnev was too feeble to care about his comrade. He could have read Nixon's books, since noteworthy foreign publications, even scathing ones, were translated for the eyes of the leadership. He felt no urge.

His family situation deteriorated; he was powerless to control his daughter's drinking problem. He found solace in the quiet of his Kremlin office, where nobody nagged him. He overstayed his summer vacation at Black Sea retreats, prolonging it to two months or more. "We're going crazy from inaction," a bodyguard told me in Crimea. "Every time we pack the bags for the return flight to Moscow, he postpones it."

The General Secretary snored softly in an easy chair by the pool in Oreanda, or floated in an oversized inflated tube in a plastic shower cap. He dozed in the warm clear water under the watchful gaze of KGB lifeguards, a few feet from the grotto where he tempted Nixon with his majestic design of a nuclear condominium. I doubt he cared much about who governed the country - probably his closest aides or friends in the Politburo. The weather was always excellent on the coast.

Leonid Brezhnev, the Benevolent Leader, passed away on November 10, 1982, at the age of 75. He remained at the pinnacle of power for eighteen years. I was among the first to learn the news, at a small meeting in preparation for a grand Soviet IPPNW conference. Chazov failed to show up - he usually chaired. A call came through on the *vertushka*, the Kremlin secure telephone. It was Chazov: "The conference is cancelled. Wind up all preparations. All delegates to return home." He did not elaborate. We were mystified. I walked to the Metro station past the Central Committee. I looked up at the fifth floor corner windows: the green curtains were drawn. The radio played Tchaikovsky's *Manfred Symphony*.

The announcement came the next day. Death struck the General Secretary in his sleep, shortly before 8 a.m. No doctor or nurse was present at the dacha that night. In late morning, Brezhnev was still in bed. A bodyguard tapped him on the shoulder. He attempted resuscitation, but it was too late.

The day of the mourning was mild and sunny. The body lay in state in the Trade Unions Hall of Columns. The police that guarded the route were courteous and relaxed. I saw few people shedding tears over Brezhnev. In 1924, in the coldest winter in Russia's history, Lenin's body lay in the same hall. Bonfires provided warmth to the mourners moving in an endless grieving human river.

Brezhnev was laid to rest with pomp at the foot of the Kremlin wall alongside the giants of the Russian Revolution. His end was strikingly similar to Stalin's lonely death of a stroke at his dacha: no doctor was present. I remember the cold March of 1953: with my school chums, I tried to reach the Hall of Columns. Thousands were doing the same, to catch a last glimpse of the wartime leader. We climbed over roofs and jumped down on wobbly sheds in narrow alleys. We never got closer than a mile to the building. Soldiers blocked our way; they told us to run home lest we were crushed in the stampede (many were).

On Brezhnev's 100th anniversary, I went to a photo exhibition by Vladimir Musaelyan, his likable personal photographer. There was Leonid Ilyich: the dashing wartime officer, the young Party organizer, the wise politician, the family man surrounded by grandchildren. Brezhnev epitomized the good and the bad in Russian history. Russians tend to forget the bad and remember the good. The intervention in Afghanistan accounted for less than two years of Brezhnev's life; he felt genuinely sorry for succumbing to pressure from the military. Many looked back on the Brezhnev era, "era of stagnation," as a time of safe streets, affordable housing, job security, and free healthcare and education. They were even willing to forget their impatience with the slowly rising living standards and limited personal freedom. Most of all they were nostalgic for the feeling of pride in their nation, the USSR, the equal of the United States, with a nuclear arsenal second to none, safe at last from any foreign attack. Brezhnev became a cult figure. In a 2013 opinion poll for "greatest Soviet leader," 56 percent granted him the lead. Stalin received 50 percent. Gorbachev and Yeltsin trailed far behind.[67]

Nixon's twilight years were different. Resigning a month after his last summit with Brezhnev, he dropped from the geopolitical game. For the comrades in Moscow, his return was a disappointment.

He reverted to his younger years, to dark thoughts about the USSR. In his *Memoirs*, he illustrated "Communist negotiating tactics" with instances from the 1972 summit. Discussing the placing of the second ABM system, Brezhnev unexpectedly referred to "1,200 kilometers from the national capital." The President reminded him that the sides had already agreed on 1,500 kilometers (in fact, they agreed on 1,300 kilometers).[68] Brezhnev suggested extending the interim agreement on offensive nuclear arms to ten years. Kissinger reminded him that the original Soviet proposal was eighteen months, and the sides had already agreed to five years. Brezhnev backed down. The explanation was simple: he forgot his brief. Our transcript of that session sensibly omitted the confusing exchange, lest the General Secretary looked a fool. The reason for the gaffs was bad preparation and faltering memory.

Fascinated by Russia's tumultuous history, Nixon must have had mixed feelings about the powerful tide that swept away the solid security structures he erected with Brezhnev. He lived to see the momentous changes, but he made a 180-degree political turn. *The Real War* and *Seize the Moment* might have been written in his HUAAC days. Were his warm encounters with Brezhnev a figment of imagination, did they ever take place? Deep at heart Nixon never broke free of his 1950s ideological cast. He assured biographer Monica Crowley that he fought the Soviets all his life.

His latent suspicions of Communism burgeoned. Despite his close relationship with FBI Director J. Edgar Hoover, Nixon privately felt, according to Bob Haldeman, that "the FBI was a failure; it hadn't found Communist backing for the antiwar organizations, which he was sure was there."[69] The exhortations hampered clear-headed analysis. He lauded the post-war Baltic "guerilla fighters" (actually remnants of local *Waffen-SS* units), and claimed that Brezhnev ordered "thousands of executions" in Moldavia and hatched "harebrained development schemes."[70] He skirted over the treaties with the Soviets and seemed to forsake his bold policy towards the USSR, which he used to call "historic." Astonishingly, he advised abrogation of the ABM treaty, the cornerstone of nuclear balance he was eager to maintain. He raved at George Bush and Bill Clinton, who failed to turn Russia into an ally.

The messianic truculence was at odds with the actual state of the Soviet Union: a steady slowing down of a militarized economy that had to support a subsidized welfare state.

Kissinger told us in Zavidovo, "All intelligence organizations make a similar mistake: they assume there is something rational behind the happenings in another country." Aldrich Ames, the most destructive Soviet mole in CIA history, provided an insider's account: "By the late '70s I had come to question the point, the value, of a great deal of what we were doing... Sources [in the Soviet Union] demonstrated a rather *ad hoc* defensive approach from Gromyko and Brezhnev... Not this secret master plan for world conquest that was so much at issue in the late '70s, when many people, including policymakers, took the view that the West was under a new coordinated aggressive assault. These materials just simply not only didn't support it, but tended to contradict it."[71] The cunning schemes of the Soviet rulers were not there. The Evil Empire was not intent on destroying the West; it never contemplated a preemptive strike. The nuclear deterrent was meant to discourage an attack, just as in the US. The contingency plans of the General Staff in Moscow and the Pentagon were similar, but in the final count, deterrence was based on bluff.

Besides, the world's second largest economy was supervised by a succession of ailing Party General Secretaries. They were too isolated to admit the need for change. No wonder the rot started at the top, in Brezhnev's family: his son-in-law, a top police official, landed in jail for corruption. As the leaders gradually lost their ideological fervor, the population was losing faith in a fossilized system of governance. A sizable part of the Soviet elite craved for Western consumer culture, to savor it today. Many of them viewed détente from this perspective. The people changed, but the leaders refused to, at their own peril.

Brezhnev lacked vision, but was circumspect in historical predictions. Nixon possessed vision, but committed mistakes. Reliance on intuition made Nixon's conclusions erratic: some were farsighted, others wide off the mark. He correctly evaluated Gorbachev as a "vacillator" and transitional figure (elected to the new post of "President" in 1990, he dumped his Party title, and survived for less than two years).

Nixon was certain the Communist world was not going to collapse "in some sudden cataclysm."[72] It did. He underestimated the turbulent political situation in Russia and made the wrong assessment of Yeltsin "the reformer." Strangely, he passed over the 78 per cent referendum vote in 1991 to retain the USSR, which Yeltsin ignored. Nixon's glaring mistake was that the United States could never regain military superiority over the USSR: this admission was basic for his acceptance of nuclear parity. By the end of the 20th century, America reigned supreme militarily. Sophisticated conventional weapons now buffered a new "gunboat diplomacy." The aging Russian nuclear arsenal was losing credibility.

In *Beyond Peace,* his final book, Nixon conceded that Brezhnev was right about China's future rise. When he entertained the Soviet leader in San Clemente, he gave China 25 years to become a significant military and economic power, but Brezhnev raised both hands. As Nixon wrote, "The translator finally interpreted his gesture: "Ten years." I recall the episode in Nixon's den and Brezhnev's outstretched hands, which I first took for an expression of disagreement.

Both leaders proved wrong: forty years on, China had far fewer ICBMs than the US or Russia. Probably the wise Oriental mind renounced the wild scramble for nuclear weapon superabundance, in the end an unusable, thus incomparably less effective tool than economic power.

Looking back to the first day of the first Nixon-Brezhnev summit in 1972, I thought it extraordinary that the time span usually envisioned by Brezhnev - "the next fifteen years" - was to be the highpoint of Mikhail Gorbachev and the downslide of the USSR into the biggest economic crash since the American Great Depression. It appeared Soviet strategic thinking did not extend beyond the 1980s. It assumed that history would advance in a straight line into infinity. Probably Brezhnev believed his engagement with Nixon would mark the "end of history." The catchy hypothesis proved as short-lived as the interval before new fundamentalist forces swept across the global landscape.

As the Soviet Union disintegrated, it shrank by a million square kilometers, back by almost three hundred years to the times of Peter the Great. Hitler's invading forces overran as much in 1941. Robert McNamara considered the loss of two thirds of economic capacity and half of the population as unacceptable in a nuclear war. In 1991, the USSR lost 40 per cent of its industry (Nixon was astounded when he learnt the figure) and almost a third of its population. Despite promises, NATO expanded close to Russian borders.

In the 1990s, Nixon made several private trips to Moscow to talk to the new Russian leaders. Incidentally, he noted the Russian translator "wasn't the best."[73] Of course, he had known several to compare with.

In 1991, he said he saw common values with the new Russia, which created "almost limitless" possibilities for cooperation with the US. Most Westerners made this blunder: assuming that Russia returned to a "normal state" after renouncing the "abnormal Soviet system." Americans value power, success and individualism. Russians respect power and made great sacrifices to attain it. As to success - there is a trait in the national character that places introspection, collectivism and compassion for the weak over individual accomplishment. The peculiar Russian brand of Communism was not an "unnatural" system (a double negative again!). It was no less normal than the Oriental version in China. A product of Western thinkers, it flourished on Russian patriotic tradition. Some speculate that this combination became a systemic weakness of the Soviet regime.

Nixon told George Bush that Yeltsin had "an indisputable claim to the support of the Russian people" and the "right chemistry" with them.[74] He thought American critics unjustly hounded Yeltsin. He was impressed with the latter's plan of swift and radical reform (despite the prospect of run-away inflation and widespread unemployment). He said Yeltsin "could discuss complex subjects without aides present or notes for reference." A peculiar observation: Yeltsin's sloppy homework and contempt of expert advice was notorious.

Years before, Nixon was taken in by the "earthiness" of Brezhnev. This time he admired "the animal magnetism" of Yeltsin, a career Party apparatchik (which speaks well of apparatchiks, I suppose). In 1991, Nixon claimed Yeltsin "took power through ballots, not bullets." In 1993, he hailed his "decisive action"[75] in assaulting a democratically elected parliament, where hundreds were killed by tank shelling and by Special Forces combing the offices. Most importantly for Nixon, Yeltsin was "pro-American." This rang the bells of Vietnam.

Bush was prudent: his opinion of both Yeltsin and Gorbachev was at the low end of the scale. The White House did not need unsolicited advice - this is why Nixon brooded in his private world. Like a caged animal, he was impatient and hungry for the kill. In March 1994, he travelled to Russia for the last time. Yeltsin snubbed him, ostensibly for meeting opposition leaders, including Communist Party Chairman Zyuganov. Nixon was hurt. He thought the Kremlin needed counsel on workings of State: he was incredulous when Andrei Kozyrev, the youngish Foreign Minister, asked for his advice on "formulating Russia's national interests." Nixon cautioned against "shock therapy" in Russia's economic transition. This was exactly what Yeltsin proceeded to do, with disastrous results for the economy and his political future.

Nixon had second thoughts about personal relationships. He suggested President Bush invested too much in personal diplomacy with Yeltsin and Gorbachev: "He believes that if you have a good personal relationship, it helps on substance. I believe that unless leaders' interests are compatible, a personal relationship doesn't mean anything."[76]

Yeltsin was fast losing credibility. In the fall of 1994, I was a delegate to the CSCE summit in Budapest. Boris Yeltsin delivered a speech and met several world leaders. The sustaining memory he left was a scene at a villa high up in Buda. In the middle of the night, he emerged unsteadily from his suite. He wore a loose white T-shirt and pajama pants. The night duty officer, a Russian Embassy diplomat, stood at attention. "Do you work here?" asked Yeltsin, "Could one get a beer at this hour?"

Nixon's transformations confounded many Russians who followed his career. It did seem twisted: from a HUAAC star, to torchbearer for détente, to born-again Communist baiter, an aging Hans Solo locked in mortal combat with the Evil Empire. His was an eclectic mixture of beliefs: from thoughts about "life with a purpose" to petty observations that "Moscow babes" did not wear pretty stockings. This may have reflected his dual personality: a geopolitical strategist and a spiteful schemer. His journey was circuitous and not without a touch of medieval tragedy: from Pat's "cloth coat" to the White House throne, only to be toppled by an ungrateful nation. In the end, he earned his place in history as the peacemaker, not the warrior - as he predicted.

Nixon the Human Being, as I called him in my Manhattan College lecture, died from a stroke on 22 April 1994. He was 81.

In the years that followed, outlandish theories spread about the main actors of that remarkable era. Many focus on the personality of Richard Nixon. Was he gay? Did he have connections to the Mafia? Did he beat his wife at times of personal crisis? Did he pop mood-altering pills?

Nixon's public bearing in the USSR was of a deeply conservative individual - he resembled a Communist Party official. Obviously, he was close to Pat. They held hands in the darkness of the Bolshoi Opera box and strolling along Moscow streets. Ivan the Terrible behaved dastardly towards his wives in the Kremlin dungeons, but Nixon? One could hardly imagine a frail Pat Nixon cringing under the blows of this reserved person.

As to drugs, I never noticed the symptoms, slurred speech and disorientation. Nixon was always alert and vigorous. I cannot pass judgment on reports that Dr. Walter Tkach (his name means "weaver" in Russian) condoned Nixon's supposed habit of taking personality altering medication. Tkach looked worried, but any leader's personal physician is under great strain. If his patient is addicted to tranquilizers, invariably the doctor fights a losing battle. Brezhnev's Chazov failed to screen sleeping aids secretly supplied by a sycophant, a sympathetic nurse and a bodyguard.

I asked a distinguished American doctor about his clinical view of Nixon. He was curt: "A psychopath." Nixon was not among his illustrious clients, so how could he tell? His policies, he said, his mental convolutions, it's in the White House tapes!

Nixon's drugs were politics: he never let off. Both he and Brezhnev became divorced from reality and lost the ability for objective judgment. In retirement, Nixon was isolated from insider sources of information. He relied on a smart Russian émigré and a 21-year old student of Russian politics (who did produce a remarkable account of Nixon's winter years). One knows the feeling: you retire; you continue to meet old colleagues and follow the political scene. Yet, once you stop reading diplomatic cables and intelligence reports, you are out of the loop. Many retired politicians are in constant quest for facts that corroborate strongly held beliefs. They preach and make predictions. Losing real power leads to losing responsibility for objective analysis. Nixon was a babe lost in the woods without a compass; he was marginalized and lost touch. His theories about Russia became biased, sometimes trivial. It was as painful reading his ravings as watching Brezhnev's mental slide.

My doctor friend dispensed with Kissinger, who, he said, embellished his "good" deeds, though compared to thugs running countries today he seems almost human… I disagreed: stretching the truth is diplomatic tactic that sometimes pays off. As to Nixon, I held a condescending view. Perhaps I fell under his spell: after all, he remembered my granddad dying from cold and hunger in 1942 in besieged Leningrad. Among a myriad of facts, this story was filed away in a corner of that strangely selective brain.

⤙

What was Nixon and Brezhnev's legacy?

Both rose to be the two most powerful men on Earth. They were successful in their adversarial engagement, with huge benefits for their stature. They shaped history in the style of their personalities, an enterprise they found engrossing because it worked. They edged their countries away from nuclear standoff and set limits to dangerous rivalry. It was an astonishing transformation of relations. Its impact was felt long after they left the scene.

Drawing counsel from two outstanding foreign policy advisers, Henry Kissinger and Andrei Gromyko, Nixon and Brezhnev played a catalytic role at the right moment - of nuclear parity - reached by two supreme powers. They saw an urgent need for relief in the suicidal race that threatened the world's survival. There was another reason. The USSR was approaching a point when it could not sustain an arms race; despite its economic power, the US faced a similar dilemma.

Nixon and Brezhnev breached the Cold War, for which both super powers carried the blame. One of its perverse consequences was the rise of a powerful class of bureaucrats, politicians, industrialists and scientists with a stake in international tension. Their lobbying contributed to massive mistakes made by both governments: the USSR thought it could surpass the US in military power; the US expected to stay in the lead indefinitely.

The two leaders opted for restraint and made the specter of nuclear war recede. This shift is not easy to measure. Even if it was by a millimeter, the contribution made by Nixon and Kissinger, and by Brezhnev, Kosygin and Gromyko, as well as by dozens of arms control aides on both sides of the divide, was immense. They launched a process that set rules for responsible super power behavior, by renouncing unilateral advantage and reducing the risk of accidental war. They managed to bring sanity to strategic doctrines by publicly admitting that nuclear weapons are unusable because they are tools of suicide. This amounted to a confession that MAD - mutual assured destruction - had been a bluff. These central achievements compensated the darker sides of Nixon and Brezhnev's legacy.

They also failed, unable to transcend nuclear weapons as the "ultimate" security guarantee. The existence of a deterrent force that cannot be activated is a contradiction that carries huge risks. As Ambassador Roland Timerbaev, one of the authors of the non-proliferation regime, used to tell me, the fact that nuclear weapons were not employed after Hiroshima and Nagasaki was due to caution, but also to luck. The US-Soviet assertion that resort to nuclear weapons is not a viable option did not stop some nuclear-weapon hopefuls. In fact, both super powers condoned them. In 1969, Nixon privately told Golda Meir he would tolerate Israeli nuclear weapons. In 1974, in a confidential message to Indira Gandhi, Brezhnev expressed "understanding" of the Indian nuclear test. Pakistan and North Korea followed.

Summit meetings are not particularly suited for serious negotiation. Nixon's three Russian summits stand out for intensity and substance. Actually, more than three, because Brezhnev and Gromyko's negotiations with Kissinger were on the same plane, with Nixon following them closely from thousands of miles away. The summits were a success because they led to tangible achievements, unlike the ephemeral "Spirit of Geneva" and "Spirit of Camp David" of the 1950s that raised hopes but fell short on substance.

Change came when both leaders perceived détente as strengthening, rather than weakening their countries' security. Both acted in the national interest. Both were in a unique position to bring the public along and handle the hawks at home. They discarded the myths of "Better dead than Red" and of "Communism, the Future of Humanity." Brezhnev and Gromyko long ceased to regard the Russian version of Marxism as a winning strategy. Nixon and Kissinger realized that combating an ideology that fires the enthusiasm of millions is futile. They saw late Soviet Communism as a transitory stage, while the Russian State would remain and fortify - hence their focus on inter-State engagement. Contrary to accepted wisdom, the Cold War was a fierce geopolitical competition between two great nation-States, rather than between opposing ideologies. The contest continued, taking dramatic turns in Europe - in Yugoslavia in the 1990s and more recently in Ukraine.

I would like to think Nixon was sorry to see his comrade's decline. But even if Brezhnev's health remained robust, it would have made no difference. Both nations were driven by powerful forces that transcended the helmsmen. True, détente proved brittle and short-lived, but the breakthrough the two men engineered made the 1970s a remarkable decade, probably never to be repeated. Nixon and Brezhnev left the world a safer place.

AFTER BREZHNEV

The years that followed Brezhnev's death in 1982 will be remembered for the televised Red Square funerals of aging leaders: Suslov, Ustinov, Andropov and Chernenko. A joker from the office suggested selling season tickets to watch the ceremonies. Kissinger thought that Nixon was lucky to negotiate with Politburo septuagenarians: their generation had been through the war, seen its ravages, and was committed to peace with America. If the West toppled the current Soviet system, the US might have faced a younger nationalist group. Henry said he was wary of "a Solzhenitsyn" coming to power.

In April 1985, the Party Central Committee elected Mikhail Sergeievitch Gorbachev as the new General Secretary.

At first, Gorbachev impressed us at the Foreign Ministry. He was young and open. He called for a bold revision of stale policy postures. He spoke without notes, though for increasingly long stretches. Not since Khrushchev we were deluged by such a bewildering torrent of ideas. *Uskorenie* (acceleration), *perestroika* (restructuring), *novoye mishlenie* (new thinking) and *glasnost* (openness): the catchwords were multiplying at astonishing pace. His speeches flowed effortlessly, switching from one visionary topic to another, from the Soviet Union's impending economic revival, to "restoring Leninist democracy in the Communist Party," to "ridding the world of nuclear weapons by the year 2000." Interagency task forces refined Gorbachev's ideas and translated them into messages to Western leaders and speeches at the United Nations. A growing body of MFA experts viewed his initiatives with skepticism.

Victor Sukhodrev could not avoid translating for Gorbachev, but before being manacled to his person forever, he maneuvered willing and able replacements into the top interpreting job. Igor Korchilov and Pavel Palazhchenko continued to serve the new leaders with distinction.

My association with Gorbachev was indirect. As head of the MFA environment section, I had my share of transforming his initiatives into manageable policy. It was no easy task, but there were occasional successes. One morning, an aide called, "We need to produce something for the General Secretary by tomorrow morning." Performing under severe time constraint sharpens the senses, though nervous breakdowns are not unheard of. The Minister approved our brainwave - an international environmental emergencies center. Gorbachev included it in his speech at the United Nations. Reaction was favorable. Several months later, a new unit was created in the UN Secretariat, a welcome development in any healthy bureaucracy.

Most new Administrations start with reform and personnel changes. Gromyko was shunted to the ceremonial post of Chairman of the Supreme Soviet. The new Foreign Minister's name, Eduard Amvrosiyevitch Shevardnadze, was a proofreader's nightmare. Staff greeted his appointment with dismay: the Georgian Communist Party leader was a *nomenclatura* apparatchik. At a Party Congress, he evoked Brezhnev twenty-two times in his speech, thus beating the runner-up, Geidar Aliev of Azerbaijan, by three counts. He never dealt with foreign policy and did not speak English. The ghost of Andrei Andreyevitch Gromyko was promptly exorcised from the MFA seventh floor. When an aide suggested that Gromyko lead a Soviet parliamentary delegation to Ethiopia, the Minister exploded: "I don't want to hear that name again!"

Shevardnadze admitted to ignorance of complicated issues and launched brainstorming sessions with issue experts. One was on chemical weapons. He wanted us to suggest *razvyazki* (unraveling) of obstacles to banning this particular weapon of mass destruction. He was under the impression that all difficulties were the work of Gromyko. This was partly true. When my turn came, I proposed we declassify statistics for the Soviet chemical arsenal. The absence of open data made negotiations on a total ban and destruction of stocks surreal; secretiveness provoked other countries to develop their own arsenals. Shevardnadze asked me about Soviet stockpiles. "Forty thousand tons," I replied. "The US has about thirty thousand." He looked astonished. "Something should be done about declassifying the figures," he said. It was odd he professed ignorance: his signature was on secret Politburo decisions on chemical weapons development.

Filing out of the room, we felt relief: verification of a disarmament measure was critical. We did not want a repetition of SALT and MBFR, when guesswork over contested numbers stalled negotiations for years. (The international chemical weapons convention entered into force in 1997. It boasts the most intrusive verification system of all arms control agreements. Today, almost all of American and Russian chemical stocks–have been destroyed.)

Shevardnadze's other actions were hard to explain by his supposedly liberal views. Kornienko and General Akhromeyev insisted on winding up the war in Afghanistan by setting an early date for Soviet troop withdrawal and persuading Kabul to share power with the mujahedeen. For three years, Shevardnadze resisted this proposal of the "conservative faction," as he called the two men. Kornienko resigned in protest over the Minister's serious errors of judgment regarding the war and his "dilettante attitude" to arms control.

Stranger still, Shevardnadze restructured the Foreign Ministry along ideological lines. All of Eastern Europe was lumped together, from East Germany to Albania, in an unwieldy "Department of Socialist Countries of Europe." It split established teams (the two Germanys always belonged to one department), wrought havoc with registries and institutional memory. Another monstrosity was the "Department of Socialist Countries of Asia."

Shevardnadze insisted that private letters addressed to the Ministry be sifted for precious gems to build a "progressive" Soviet foreign policy. I always thought that individuals who write to the MFA expecting action were out of their minds. Perhaps Shevardnadze was nostalgic about the perlustration of private correspondence, a function of the Georgian Interior Ministry he headed in Tbilisi.

A campaign "to weed out nepotism" was launched. Personnel drew a detailed chart of staff family relations crisscrossing the ten-thousand-strong apparatus. I was surprised to see my name on the offenders list: "1.7 per cent of nepotism," it said. The husband of my wife's sister, since divorced, was stationed in Burundi - the reason for the low rating. The campaign soon fizzled out. The extent of family connections was insignificant since the MFA was never noted for high salaries. In the meantime, the Minister quietly maneuvered his offspring into lucrative positions in the United Nations Secretariat.

By the moment Shevardnadze distinguished me in the crowd I was dealing with environmental issues. A bold (I thought) report I made to the MFA Collegium on Russia's tasks in promoting sustainable development pleased the Minister. Preparations for the 1992 "Earth Summit" in Rio de Janeiro were in full swing; "greening" Soviet foreign policy was fashionable. Always quick to grasp a winning strategy, Gorbachev gave environment his enthusiastic support.

The glow was short lived. One late Friday night, as I was leaving for home, the cream-colored scrambler phone rang. It was Shevardnadze's principal assistant, Igor Ivanov (later Foreign Minister). He said the boss received a letter from an eminent author who campaigned for cleaning up Lake Baikal. Could I have a look? The Minister wished to consult me. I went down three floors, turned the heavy bronze handle on the pine-paneled door and entered the familiar room. Shevardnadze was sitting at Gromyko's desk. He rose, extended a limp hand and beckoned to a chair. Red and blue folders, Politburo documents, telegrams and newspaper clippings cluttered the desk. Information overload, I thought, so unlike Gromyko's neat tabletop. Shevardnadze leaned back in his leather armchair; he looked tired and solemn. Gromyko never looked tired.

As I reviewed the writer's proposals (naïve and in parts counterproductive) I saw Shevardnadze's face taking on a red hew. With hardly concealed anger he said, "I was a refrigerator factory manager in Tbilisi, and I know a thing or two about the environment." He rose to show the meeting was over.

I had been in that room many times. Gromyko was annoyed when one proposed half-baked ideas; he expected factual reports and clear-cut views. But he always considered those he spoke to as colleagues. Despondent, I reported the incident to Deputy Minister Vladimir Petrovsky. He tried to sooth my nerves: "Just lie low, Andrey. It'll blow over. Too bad you didn't know." Apparently the eminent author was friend of Raisa Gorbachev's father, so he expected red carpet treatment at the MFA. I felt vindicated when attempts to follow-up the hare-brained ideas were buried under an avalanche of memos in reaction to some foreign crisis.

At the end of 1990, Shevardnadze abruptly resigned, alluding to a sinister plot against Gorbachev and *perestroika* (MFA wags renamed it *catastroika*). He left no fan club in Smolenskaya Square. He returned to Georgia, was elected President and started a virulent anti-Russian campaign. After steering his country into economic straits and antagonizing three autonomous regions into near defecting to Russia, he was ousted in December 2003 by a local brand of "Young Turks" led by Mikhail Saakashvili. He soon faded away.

Within two decades that followed détente, the household names of the 1970s became history. Several personages passed away still in their sixties: Bob Haldeman, John Ehrlichman and Ron Ziegler. Chuck Connors died at 71 of lung cancer on 10 November 1992, ten years to a day after Brezhnev. He had asked the State Department to be included in the US delegation to Brezhnev's funeral, but they turned him down. Bill Krimer, a fine State Department interpreter, died in 2001, at 86. The year 2008 saw the passing of NSC staffers for whom I felt deep professional respect, Bill Hyland and Peter Rodman. Helmut Sonnenfeldt died in 2012. It seemed like an ominous plague swept the slate clean.

General Vo Nguyen Giap, who battled the Nixon-Kissinger war strategy, the real victor on the ground in Vietnam, outlived them all: he died in 2013, aged 102.

At the time of writing, Henry Kissinger, the Terminator, as I called him in my lecture, was going strong, a *perpetuum mobile*. He has withstood criticism and accusations hurled at regular intervals, including for the military coup in Chile that toppled Salvador Allende. In a TV interview, he insisted the US was not trying to weaken Russia or encroach on its sphere of interest; NATO expansion to the East "was not threatening." Passing 90, he reminded me of Brezhnev - a bit overweight, slow in movement and speech. The impression is superficial: his mind is sharp. Though I suspect he is wary of Russia as ever, be it the Tsarist Empire, the USSR, or the Russian Federation, he remains a history-inspired pragmatist. He met Vladimir Putin, and advised direct talks with President Obama. He thought demonizing Putin was not a policy, rather an alibi for the absence of one. As the Ukraine crisis unfolded in 2014, Kissinger cautioned against ignoring the intertwined history, language and religion of Russia and Ukraine, with Kiev the cradle of the original Russian State.

The psychological trauma of a collapsing super power spurred on transitions on the Russian side of the divide. For many, détente was the high point of a lifetime career.

Alexei Kosygin passed away on 18 December 1980, inappropriately on the eve of Brezhnev's birthday. They postponed the official announcement for three days. Two months earlier, a terribly lonely man, Kosygin resigned under pressure from Brezhnev. They disconnected his secure Kremlin telephone line and struck him off the Politburo distribution list. He suffered a fatal heart attack soon after, at 76. The population genuinely missed him.

Two months previously, Pyotr Masherov died in a car crash in Belorussia: his limousine collided with a potato harvest truck that suddenly appeared from a side road. He was reading and did not buckle in. Rumors persisted that a political opponent had a hand in removing a potential General Secretary. He was 62. Kosygin and Masherov were the country's chance to embark on a new path.

Nikolai Podgorny's life ended in 1983 in obscurity, at age 79.

Ambassador Mikhail Smirnovsky, who reluctantly dispatched me from London to the first Nixon/Brezhnev summit conference, was 68 when he succumbed to cancer in 1989. That same year, General Antonov, who defended my trip to the United Sates, passed away. He was 67.

In July 1989, Andrei Gromyko died of a ruptured aneurism. At 80, he was one of the last Soviet leaders whose career began under Stalin. He remained Minister for twenty-eight years - a record - thanks to his diplomatic talent, but also prudence in navigating among the higher echelons. He used to tell us, "For a diplomat, it's better to remain silent on a hundred occasions than to say something silly once... Better ten years of negotiations than one day of war." He stressed two policy vectors crucial for world peace: progress in disarmament and improving relations with the US. He mused that he had two real enemies: time and ignorant officials whom chance raised to the top rungs.

I watched a muted ceremony in the Central Soviet Army Club. Gorbachev ruled that Gromyko did not qualify for a State funeral in Red Square. "A man with a heart of ice," was Gromyko's final judgment on the man he proposed for the top post in 1985. In the long line of mourners, I saw friends from the Foreign Ministry, Defense and other agencies, as well as ordinary Muscovites. The crowd was hushed and orderly. The Minister would have liked that.

Gromyko was one of the few Soviet leaders spared by historians. Henry Kissinger paid tribute on his centenary: "I think of him as an important colleague who defended the interests of his country with enormous skill, with enormous persistence. And he always understood that the peace of the world depends on recognizing that there are objectives beyond the simple assertion of national interest."[77]

Gromyko's son Anatoly showed me around his father's study once in their dacha in Vnukovo. It is small and sparse; there are rows and rows of books, mostly history and classical novels.

Alexandrov went on to serve, after Brezhnev's death, three successive Soviet leaders - Andropov, Chernenko and Gorbachev. He resigned when he could no longer stand the interminable monologues of his latest boss. He became a recluse of sorts, declassifying diplomatic papers in the Foreign Ministry archives. His book of recollections was unusually kind to Brezhnev. He died in 1993, aged 75.

In the spring of 2002, I called on Georgy Kornienko in his small apartment near Sokolniki Park. He was pensive about times past. His book, *The History of the Cold War: Testimony of a Participant,* told it all. He inscribed it for me in his calligraphic hand: "To remember our work together during times that were certainly not the worst." The inference to the times of Yeltsin was hardly veiled. Kornienko looked back on détente with a historian's aloofness, and told me a few stories. One concerned Ronald Reagan who assured Gorbachev the Cold War started when the Soviets refused to permit B-17 Flying Fortresses to land in Russian territory after bombing sorties over Germany. "I was a young aircraft technician in Poltava, Ukraine," smiled Kornienko. "I serviced American bombers which flew back to bomb Germany again." "Did you tell Reagan?" "No, I didn't want to embarrass him."

He reminisced about the foreign policy apparatus that Gromyko honed to a high degree of excellence. Throughout the 1970s, Soviet policy toward the US was remarkably free of Party control. The Foreign Ministry was both a provider of ideas and implementer. In most cases the Politburo rubber-stamped the MFA draft. If an initiative concerned an ideologically sensitive area - relations with Socialist countries is one example - it had to be cleared. In crisis cases, like Hungary in 1956, Czechoslovakia in 1968, and Afghanistan in 1979 (Kornienko authored a memo against sending troops), the Politburo or a smaller group within it overruled MFA experts. The results were dubious or disastrous. In the Presidential setup of recent years, the MFA acquired an ancillary role, and this affected staff morale. Strangely, Russia now resembled Nixon's style of government: ideas and decisions emanating from the Presidential Administration, a remake of the Central Committee, an inner circle, not always professional.

Kornienko's advice when battling fine points in summit declarations and communiqués was always heeded by Gromyko. His prodigious memory and tenacity exasperated Kissinger, whom he tried, not without success, to thwart. He told me that every time he saw Henry playing up to Brezhnev, including by suggesting empty formulations, he smiled knowingly. (These moments are described in the US transcripts as "Kornienko beams.") This unnerved Kissinger so much that he complained to Brezhnev that Kornienko was trying to distract him. He baited him: "If Kornienko agrees to anything it will be a historic event." Or: "Kornienko is trying to draft for both of us... He is joining our staff on the basis of equal torture for both sides."

I ventured there was some sense in Kissinger's approach: how far can one rely on political declarations? While we regarded these summit products as something akin to the Bible, or for that matter, *The Communist Manifesto*, Kissinger thought them nebulous and fleeting. In May 1973, he said that Brezhnev's pet project, "Principles of Relations," would remain an abstraction if not accompanied by concrete agreements. "UN Security Council resolution

242" [on the Middle East], he said, "is five years old, and still an abstraction." (It is over four decades old today and yet to be implemented.) Kissinger preferred realities on the ground, the armistice lines, and the hard balances of weapon systems. For this, he was willing to overlook lofty sounding text, so important to Russians for its political value. In late 1974 in Vladivostok, he was exasperated with slow progress on the joint Ford-Brezhnev statement; it was being ground to Saran-Wrap thinness by two hardliners, Kornienko and Sonnenfeldt. Kissinger entered the room, peered over his aide's shoulder, and muttered, "Hal, drop it." Gromyko would have squeezed his opponent dry.

Kornienko said, "We can't look at the past solely from the position of today. Kissinger fought like a tiger over issues he regarded as crucial for the United States at the time. Probably, they're not so important today." I knew what he meant: declarations and treaties continue to stand if supported by military and economic parity – no longer the case between Russia and the US. This was the reason for the abrogation or demise of agreements signed in the 1970s: the ABM treaty, the Helsinki Final Act, SALT-2…the list is long.

In 2005, Minister Lavrov, always considerate to old friends, led a small band of MFA colleagues to laud Kornienko on his eightieth birthday. He was ailing: impaired vision (macular destruction) made writing, his forte, a painful experience. He encouraged me to write this book and offered to review it. It was too late: the following year he passed away. The remembrance meal was an emotional farewell to the Soviet Foreign Service, exemplifying the bond that linked three generations. Kornienko belonged to the old guard, the finest. The torch was passed.

Anatoly Dobrynin, the grand maître of US-Soviet relations, was unwell for a long time. He lost an eye in a botched operation by the Kremlin doctors. His volume of recollections, *In Confidence*, was as engrossing as Kissinger's three-volume memoirs, even if they differed on some facts and perceptions. He passed away in April 2010, a few months after reaching 90. I have a lasting memory of Dobrynin: when Brezhnev's elocution passed the bounds of his brief, Anatoly would rise from his chair to whisper in the General Secretary's ear. Brezhnev reacted good-naturedly. As a disciplined pupil, he followed Gromyko's advice, but he welcomed a second opinion. He liked Anatoly and respected his common sense. Dobrynin once said his biggest enemies were "fools and demagogues on both sides of the Atlantic." Together with Kornienko and Gromyko, he was builder of the Russian State.

Few friends remain from the unforgettable days of détente. Victor Sukhodrev moved from his city apartment to a comfortable dacha in Nikolina Gora, a rustic settlement west of Moscow. He published a remarkable account of his experiences for Russian readers. In TV interviews, he commented on historical episodes, like Khrushchev's encounter with JFK and Brezhnev's final years. One night in a Manhattan bar, Victor told me about his father, a GRU (Military Intelligence) "illegal" who was exfiltrated in 1949 in a Soviet cargo ship from New York harbor to escape FBI arrest. A beautiful painting of birch trees hangs on the wall of Victor's dacha, done in the Atlanta Penitentiary by superspy Rudolph Abel before his exchange for U-2 pilot Gary Powers. "I did a small favor for him," Victor said, "brought some medicines from America."

Our friendship outlived our careers at the top. The years with Nixon and Brezhnev exerted a sentimental pull. "Do you realize," I told him recently, "you and I are the only living witnesses to some of their conversations." "You're right," he said. "The final secrets will be safe to the end." In May 2014, just days before I completed this book, Victor suffered a ruptured aneurysm. He was 81.

A crowd of friends and colleagues bid farewell to Victor. He was buried in a quiet country cemetery next to the graves of his mother and wife Inga. Sergei Lavrov sent his condolences (he was away on a visit to China). In my eulogy, I thanked Victor on behalf of all MFA interpreters, former and present, for setting the highest standards for "the man in the middle," the person who helps leaders communicate to build a saner world. "It is not possible to attain perfection," Victor used to say, "but try one must."

At the *pominki* I was approached by a gray-haired middle-aged man. He said he was the *Swan Lake* dancer whom Nixon pointed out to me in 1972. They had a great laugh in the troupe that night - Yuri was the only dancer whose name Nixon knew. It was now part of Bolshoi Ballet folklore.

Among the fallouts of détente were citizens' groups that went further than Nixon and Brezhnev - by advocating a nuclear-weapon-free world. The International Physicians for the Prevention of Nuclear War best explained the idea using medical statistics. They concluded that no health service, however sophisticated, would be able to save lives or even treat millions of victims of nuclear war. Two renowned cardiologists, Bernard Lown and Evgeni Chazov, who received the Nobel Peace Prize on behalf of IPPNW in 1985, made me look at the Nixon-Brezhnev achievements with greater deference.

Bernard diagnosed the aftermath of détente and the fall of the USSR with a surgeon's precision. The USSR presented itself as an advanced social system leading all nations to Soviet-type socialism, a land of milk and honey. It did not possess the means to achieve this, but the assertive stance provoked mistrust abroad. Brezhnev and his successors underestimated the power of American media to shape attitudes. Archaic Soviet propaganda - playing the braggart rather than the victim - was no match for the sustained effort to debilitate the USSR and convince its population of the viability of American-style capitalism in a traditional Russian setting. On 18 June 1973, as Nixon conferred with Brezhnev about equal security at the White House, Kissinger approved a memo from the "40 Committee" on a covert program against the Soviet Union and Eastern Europe using contacts and CIA-reprinted literature.[78]

For decades, both the US and the Soviet Union were tempted by Leon Trotsky's idea of "accelerating" political development, be it in Asia or Africa. The goals were different, but the methods to rev up the wheels of history were similar, and they did much damage. Present-day calls for revolutionary transition to Western-style democracy - from Iraq to Libya to Ukraine - are not unlike Trotsky's insistence on global "permanent revolution." Nixon and Brezhnev were successful because they transcended this kind of philosophy.

Bernard cautioned against despondency: the disappearance of one adversary in the duumvirate need not mean détente was in vain. He wrote to me, "The human condition is malleable and unpredictable, and ultimately people forge history. While in the case of the nuclear arms race, politicians could reverse the course of the Soviet-American confrontation, in environmental degradation there is no magic political switch. Profound economic

transformations are required that involve the basic structure of the existing social order and production and consumption patterns, through unprecedented
popular education and mobilization."

Could he personally bring about a change in thinking? He gazed at the
chestnut trees through his Boston house bay window and said, "Whatever I
could do, would suffice." Man needs illusions. The strength of illusion, mystery and idealism sustains us in childhood and drives us forward in later life.
In the summer of 2000 in Nairobi, at the Embassy send-off party, I ended
my thank-you speech with the words, "And now, filled with illusions, we're
heading home!" There was laughter: I was returning to a Russia very different
from the times of Brezhnev and Nixon.

EPILOGUE: MIGS IN A FLOWER FIELD

SHORTLY AFTER RETURNING FROM KENYA, I spoke to a group of young Russian diplomats training for a career at the United Nations. I told them several stories and warned against pitfalls of the profession. I advised them to keep a perspective of what happened in the past before trying to analyze the present. Richard Nixon's summits with his Soviet comrades might seem a footnote in history books, but to me they were a milestone to measure against the uncharted paths America and Russia were taking. Indeed, ancient history might serve as a tool for conducting foreign policy today.

The listeners asked pointed questions, but some names I mentioned drew blank stares. They belonged to a new generation that felt no need of schooling in the battles of the Cold War. They were certain no geopolitical confrontations were in the offing, except with a radical brand of Islam. They wanted to be good technicians, not historians. Perhaps they were right.

However, something bothered me. I remembered a young Canadian telling me he was impressed with a World War II photo of Soviet soldiers erecting a flag on a Pacific island. Was it a Japanese island, I asked. He was not sure. Iwo Jima? Yes, he said, that's it! Suddenly, I felt old.

It was a hot day in Moscow. My wife Marianna told me to take a stroll – she was preparing Sunday dinner. I took our little son George to the nearby Museum of Aviation and Space Exploration, in Red Army Street. We walked through the empty rooms and inspected aircraft models and space suits worn by the first cosmonauts. I had a strange feeling we were back in the USSR;

even the tickets were Soviet-issue, 20 kopecks each, now stamped "Three Rubles."

The only other visitors were two Americans, father and son - Phil, a high school student. Both turned out to be Soviet military aircraft buffs. They admired the scale replicas of MiG and Sukhoi fighter jets. I suggested crossing Leningradsky Prospekt to see the planes on exhibit in a disused airfield. They were astounded: "You mean real ones?"

As we approached the low wire fence, I saw the gate was on the far side of the field. The sun was high in a clear blue sky; it smelled of mown grass. Citing the new atmosphere of freedom in Russia, I suggested climbing the fence. The Americans liked the idea - we vaulted over. The next instant I realized our mistake. Two men were walking briskly in our direction. The tall one, with a bare torso, looked like a cross between Rambo and a Volga boatman. The other was in worn army fatigues; he was short and wiry and carried a walkie-talkie. We stopped and smiled. The men did not smile.

George hid behind my back.

"Why did you climb over the fence?" asked Rambo.

My story that we could not find the gate sounded hollow.

"Who are you?"

I explained that the boy and I were locals; the other two were guests.

He spoke into the walkie-talkie, "Four guys here. Two look like Russians, the other two are foreigners."

We waited. The Americans were subdued. They pictured night interrogations and stiff sentences in a Siberian labor camp. A slim chance of being exchanged for a Russian spy convicted in the United States.

The walkie-talkie barked back. The man in fatigues looked uncertain. He pointed to the camera Phil's father was carrying: "You want to take pictures? That'll be thirty rubles [about a dollar]. You also pay thirty rubles each for the tickets."

I translated.

He turned to me: "Twenty rubles for you and five for the kid."

"I am a senior citizen," I said.

"So be it, five rubles for you too." He did not ask for my ID.

Phil and his dad could not believe their good fortune. I realized they were the first Americans I translated for since Brezhnev's meeting with Jimmy Carter.

The attendants smiled broadly and pointed in the direction of the airplanes. They did not give us tickets.

Phil ran to a lone MiG-29. The aircraft was his love affair. He could not get his hands off the sleek powder blue body. He touched the backswept wings and the huge double engine exhausts. He climbed the ladder to peer inside the cockpit. His father took snapshots of the plane with the large Red Star on the stabilizers. In a quarter of an hour, Phil told me more about MiGs than I would have found about in a lifetime. His father was elated: "All this fantastic hardware just sitting here, in a field of daisies!" I told him this was the old Central Airport, where Winston Churchill, Harry Hopkins and Averell Harriman arrived on secret flights for wartime conferences with Stalin.

It was time for them to leave on another excursion. After extracting George from a giant Mi-26 helicopter, we turned to the gate. Phil ran back to the MiG-29 and patted the flaking paint: "Good bye, old friend."

We walked to Leningradsky Prospekt. Phil's father wanted to know what I thought of the changes in Russia. He was impressed with the colorful street ads, the elegant boutiques and traffic jams in Moscow's downtown area. I tried to explain about the crime rate, the decay of the school and health care systems, the uncertainty about the new man who had just replaced Yeltsin… I felt he regarded my concern with skepticism.

We directed them to Dynamo Stadium Metro Station, and wished them luck. They waved from across the wide avenue. I should have asked how they remembered Richard Nixon and his comrade, Leonid Ilyich Brezhnev.

INDEX

1   Peter Wright, *Spycatcher* (New York; Dell Publishing, 1987), p. 346.

2   *Soviet-American Relations: the Détente Years, 1969-1972* (Washington; US Government Printing Office, 2007) p. 909.

3   H.R. Haldeman, *The Ends of Power* (New York; Dell Publishing Co., 1978), p. 68; Richard Nixon, *RN: The Memoirs of Richard Nixon* (New York; Grosset and Dunlap, 1978), p. 870.

4   Gerard Smith, *Doubletalk: The Story of the First Strategic Arms Limitation Talks* (Garden City, New York; Doubleday and Company, Inc., 1980), p. 467.

5   *Newsweek*, 5 June 1972.

6   Richard Nixon, *RN: The Memoirs of Richard Nixon*, p. 619.

7   See *Sovetsko-Amerikanskiye otnosheniya 1969-1972: (Soviet-American Relations: the Détente Years* - in Russian; Moscow; Mezhdunarodnii Otnosheniya, 2007), Vol.1, Book 2, pp. 441-445.

8   See Gerard Smith, *Doubletalk*, pp. 407-408, 234, 414, 372.

9   *Foreign Relations of the United States, 1969-1976, Volume XV* (Washington; US Government Printing Office, 2011), pp. 630-631.

10 *Foreign Relations of the United States, 1969-1976, Volume XVI* (Washington; US Government Printing Office, 2012), pp. 632-636.

11 *Foreign Relations of the United States, 1969-1976, Volume XV*, pp. 114.

12 *Soviet-American Relations: the Détente Years, 1969-1972*, p. 991.

13 *Foreign Relations of the United States, 1969-1976, Volume XV*, pp. 947-949.

14 Richard Nixon, *RN: The Memoirs of Richard Nixon*, pp. 618-619.

15 *Foreign Relations of the United States, 1969-1976, Volume XV*, p. 1027.

16 See H.R. Haldeman, *The Ends of Power*, pp. 355, 358-359, 257-259.

17 H.R. Haldeman, *The Haldeman Diaries: Inside the Nixon White House* (New York; G.P. Putnam's Sons, 1994), p. 329.

18 John Ehrlichman, *Witness to Power: the Nixon Years* (New York; Simon and Schuster, 1982), p. 96.

19 David C. Martin, *Wilderness of Mirrors* (Guilford, Connecticut; Lyons Press, 2003), p. 70.

20 *Foreign Relations of the United States, 1969-1976, Volume XVI*, p. 701

21 *Foreign Relations of the United States, 1969-1976, Volume XV*, p. 634.

22 *Foreign Relations of the United States, 1969-1976, Volume XVI*, pp. 389-403.

23 Ibid., p. 396.

24 *Foreign Relations of the United States, 1969-1976, Volume XV*, p. 985.

25 National Archives and Records Administration (NARA), HAK Office Files, Box 32, country Files-USSR, page 061.

26 *Foreign Relations of the United States, 1969-1976, Volume XV*, p.189.

27 NARA, HAK Trip Files, Box 939, Brezhnev's US Visit, File 5, Doc. 003.

28 NARA, HAK Trip Files, Box 76, File 6.

29 NARA, HAK Trip Files, Box 939, Brezhnev's US Visit, File 022.

30 *Foreign Relations of the United States, 1969-1976, volume XVI*, p. 9.

31 *Foreign Relations of the United States, 1969-1976, Volume XV*, p. 88

32 Ibid., p. 292.

33 Ibid., p. 304.

34 *Foreign Relations of the United States, 1969-1976, Volume XVI*, p. 462.

35 William Burr, ed., *The Kissinger Transcripts* (New York; The New Press, 1999), pp. 142-143.

36 Ibid., p. 183.

37 http://www.sipri.org/yearbook/2013/files/SIPRIYB13Summary.pdf

38 H.R. Haldeman, *The Ends of Power*, pp. 129-130.

39 *Foreign Relations of the United States: 1969-1976; Volume XV*, pp. 16-17.

40 The *New York Times*, 26 August 2005.

41 A.F. Dobrynin, *Strogo doveritelno* (*Strictly Confidential* - in Russian, Moscow; Avtor, 1997), p. 214.

42 *Foreign Relations of the United States: 1969-1976; Volume XV*, p. 19.

43 *Foreign Relations of the United States, 1969-1976, Volume XVI*, p. 221.

44 Richard Nixon, *Leaders* (London; Sidgwick and Jackson, 1982), p. 78.

45 *Newsweek*, 1 June1975.

46 http://www.youtube.com/watch?v=MhqiBcShAKk

47 *Foreign Relations of the United States, 1969-1976, Volume XV*, p. 649.

48 Ibid., p. 668.

49 *Foreign Relations of the United States, 1969-1976, Volume XV*, p. 452.

50 Ibid., pp. 891-892.

51 John Chabot Smith, *Alger Hiss: the True Story* (New York; Holt, Rinehart and Winston, 1976), p. 432.

52 *Foreign Relations of the United States, 1969-1976, Volume XVI*, pp. 311-315.

53 Ibid., p. 317.

54 Ibid., pp. 608-609.

55 Henry Kissinger, *Years of Renewal* (New York; Simon and Schuster, 1999), p. 641.

56 *Foreign Relations of the United States, 1969-1976, Volume XVI,* p. 509.

57 Henry Kissinger, *Years of Renewal,* p. 658.

58 Henry Kissinger, *Years of Renewal,* p. 659.

59 Henry Kissinger, *Years of Renewal,* p. 658.

60 *Foreign Relations of the United States, 1969-1976, Volume XVI,* p. 460.

61 Ibid., p. 781.

62 Henry Kissinger, *Years of Renewal,* p. 865.

63 Seymour Hersh, *The Price of Power: Kissinger in the Nixon White House* (New York; Summit Books, 1983), p. 129, 617.

64 *MSNBC Report,* June 1, 2005.

65 John Ehrlichman, *Witness to Power,* p. 230.

66 Richard Nixon, *Leaders,* p. 211.

67 http://www.nakanune.ru/articles/1777

68 Richard Nixon, *RN: The Memoirs of Richard Nixon,* pp. 611-612.

69 The *New York Times,* November 6 1994, Section 7, p. 12.

70 Richard Nixon, *Seize the Moment* (New York; Simon and Schuster, 1992), p. 57.

71 http://www.gwu.edu/~nsarchiv/coldwar/interviews/episode-21/aldrich1.
html

72 Richard Nixon, *Leaders*, p. 214.

73 Monica Crowley, *Nixon in Winter* (New York; Random House, 1998),
p.119.

74 Mikhail Beschloss and Strobe Talbot, *At the Highest Levels* (Boston; Little,
Brown and Company, 1993), pp. 355, 360.

75 Monica Crowley, *Nixon in Winter*, p. 145.

76 Mikhail Beschloss and Strobe Talbot, *At the Highest Levels*, p. 166.

77 http://en.rian.ru/russia/20090714/155522589.html.

78 *Foreign Relations of the United States, 1969-1976, Volume XV*, pp. 462-466.